INTEGRATED

Secretarial Studies

Jubilee Edition

IROL WHITMORE BALSLEY

Head, Department of Office Administration
Louisiana Polytechnic Institute, Ruston

and

JERRY W. ROBINSON

Editor
South-Western Publishing Company

SOUTH-WESTERN PUBLISHING COMPANY

Cincinnati   Chicago   Dallas   Burlingame, Calif.   New Rochelle, N. Y.

K24—H366

Printed in U. S. A.

CONTENTS

◇ ◇ ◇ ◇ ◇ ◇ ◇ ◇ ◇ ◇ ◇ ◇ ◇ ◇ ◇ ◇ ◇ ◇ ◇ ◇

CONTENTS

PREFACE ◇

The secretarial curriculum of many schools permits only one year of advanced preparation beyond the first year of typewriting and shorthand. Secretarial duties encompass such a variety of activities, however, that the teacher is faced with the almost impossible task of providing instruction in these many activities in a one-year advanced course. There cannot be separate courses in transcription, advanced speed building, letter writing, filing procedures, calculating machines, duplicating processes, office behavior, and such secretarial duties as planning itineraries, handling mail, and preparing reports; yet, the teacher needs to provide the secretarial trainee with at least an introduction to these many facets of secretarial work. INTEGRATED SECRETARIAL STUDIES was designed specifically to meet this need.

The major emphasis in the first half of the book is on the development of high-level dictation skill. A complete review of theory principles of the Gregg system is included. Related business information is provided, however, in these lessons; for instance, types of business letters, work habits and attitudes, handling mail, telephone usage, and preparing itineraries.

Several new skill-building devices are used to stimulate students to improved performance. Some of these are Speed Acceleration Practices, Potential Rate Builders, Repetitive Phrase Builders, and Proportion Drills.

In the Theory Review exercises, outlines illustrating the principles being reviewed appear in color, thus focusing the attention of the students on them and enabling the teacher to drill intensively on those outlines. Likewise, automatic vocabulary preview is provided in the Practice Material for Building Fluency exercises by the use of color for troublesome outlines.

The key to every shorthand plate is given in the teacher's manual, marked in 20-word groups for dictation. The words that should be phrased are presented in italics, thus making drill on the phrases in any "take" an easy matter.

The shorthand plates for many exercises have the typing word count provided at the end of each line, facilitating the computation of transcription rate whenever the teacher desires.

In the skill-development lessons, the student proceeds from the simple to the complex; the dictation materials are designed to provide a review cycle of theory and rules of English usage.

New Material Dictation is provided in the teacher's manual so that there is no need to search for appropriate dictation material in other publications.

In Lessons 76-100 transcription is introduced. Beginning with straight-copy plate notes, the student progresses through easy stages to memorandums and letters, writing first from plates and then from notes taken from dictation.

The content of the 25 lessons in transcription is correlated with that of the first 25 lessons in the book so that, if desired, the teacher can teach transcription in the early part of the first semester's work, perhaps alternating speed-building sessions with transcription periods.

The major emphasis for the remaining lessons is on secretarial duties such as filing, duplicating processes, calculating machines, report preparation, and banking services. Skill development in typewriting and transcription continues to receive attention periodically, however.

Many illustrations are used throughout the textbook to facilitate understanding of office procedures and equipment.

A workbook is available for use with the materials in the second half of the textbook. In addition to selected letterheads and business forms, the workbook includes enrichment activities in English, arithmetic and related skills.

A complete testing program is provided in the teacher's manual for measuring the level of note-taking ability and transcribing efficiency. The problems of English usage are carefully controlled.

INTEGRATED SECRETARIAL STUDIES, then, is the first truly integrated course in secretarial practices and procedures for the second year of a two-year secretarial curriculum.

IROL WHITMORE BALSLEY   JERRY W. ROBINSON

a	by	gentlemen	it	opportunity	quantity	speak	this	why
about	can	glad	manufacture	order	question	state	those	will
acknowledge	character	gone	merchandise	ordinary	railroad	street	throughout	wish
advantage	circular	good	merchant	organize	recognize	subject	time	with
advertise	company	govern	morning	our	regard	success	under	won
after	correspond correspondence	great	Mr.	out	regular	such	upon	work
am	could	have	Mrs.	over	request	suggest	use	world
an	difficult	his	must	part	responsible	than	value	worth
and	during	hour	never	particular	satisfy satisfactory	thank	very	would
are	enclose	how	newspaper	present	send	that	was	year
at	envelope	I	next	probable	several	the	well	yesterday
be	ever every	idea	not	progress	shall	their	were	yet
between	experience	immediate	object	public	short	them	what	you your
big	for	importance important	of	publication publish	should	there	when	
business	from	in	one	purpose	situation	they	where	
but	general	is	opinion	put	soon	thing think	which	

-ville -burg	-ort	-ul
-ing	-ment	-therm term- term-
-ulation -ulate	-ly	sub-
-ship	-ful	re-
-rity	-cian -sion	-pur per-
-ily -ily	-tial -cial	mis-
-ings	-ble	in-
-ingly	-ily	im-
-ification		-tur fore- for-
-ward -hood	under-	ex-
-gram	trans-	en-
-cle -cal	super-	em-
-ture -ure	post-	-dis
-tual -ual	over-	di-
-ther	intr- inter- entr- enter-	de-
-ciency -tient	electric- electr-	con- com-
-tain	circum- self-	be-
-sumption -sume	un-	after-
-self -selves		al-

SIMPLE PHRASING: I cannot say, we are sure, that will not be, very important, we find, we know, we enclose, this was, at which time, for some time, I have not yet, very sorry, if you wish

ago: weeks ago, days ago, years ago, hours ago, long ago, months ago, minutes ago

been, able: had been, it has been, could have been, has been, could not have been, we would have been, has been able, in order to be able, should have been able, they have been able, they will be able, we have not been able, ought to be able

wasn't, is not, want: it wasn't, there wasn't, he wasn't, he is not, I wanted, you want, they want, he wants, who wants, do you want, if you want, we wanted

to (before downward stroke): to feel, to change, to speak, to participate, to supply, to join, to follow, to permit, to finish, to be sure, to say, to charge, to purchase

to (before forward or right s stroke): to inquire, to insure, to tell, to confirm, to convince, to those, to them, to cooperate, to give you, to send you

OMISSION OF WORDS: in the world, will you please, one of the most, on the market, one of the best, at a loss, none of them, men and women, for a long time, as a result, any of these, we are in a position, two or three, in addition to that, during the past year

SPECIAL FORMS, INTERSECTING PRINCIPLE: of course, I hope you can, we hope you can, as soon as possible, as soon as you can, to us, your order, to me, to make, to know, chamber of commerce, c.o.d., p.m., a.m., My dear Mrs., My dear Sir, Dear Miss, Very cordially yours, Very sincerely yours, Yours very truly, Very truly yours, Sincerely yours

MAILABLE-WORDS-A-MINUTE SCORING CHART
FOR 5-MINUTE TIMED WRITINGS

(Based on 26 seconds average time needed to make a correction without a carbon copy)

ERRORS

GWAM	1	2	3	4	5	6	7	8	9	10	11	12	13	14	15	16	17	18	19	20
75*	69*	64	60	56	52	49	47	44	42	40	38	37	35	34	33	31	30	29	28	27
74	68	63	59	55	52	49	46	44	42	40	38	36	35	33	32	31	30	29	28	27
73	67	62	58	54	51	48	45	43	41	39	37	36	34	33	32	31	30	29	28	27
72	66	61	57	53	50	47	45	43	40	39	37	35	34	33	31	30	29	28	27	26
71	65	61	56	53	50	47	44	42	40	38	36	35	33	32	31	30	29	28	27	26
70	64	60	56	52	49	46	44	41	39	38	36	34	33	32	30	29	28	27	26	26
69	64	59	55	51	48	45	43	41	39	37	35	34	32	31	30	29	28	27	26	25
68	63	58	54	50	47	45	42	40	38	36	35	33	32	31	30	28	27	26	26	25
67	62	57	53	50	47	44	42	40	38	36	34	33	32	30	29	28	27	26	25	25
66	61	56	52	49	46	43	41	39	37	35	34	32	31	30	29	28	27	26	25	24
65	60	55	52	48	45	43	40	38	37	35	33	32	31	29	28	28	26	25	25	24
64	59	55	51	48	45	42	40	38	36	34	33	31	30	29	28	27	26	25	24	23
63	58	54	50	47	44	41	39	37	35	34	32	31	30	28	27	26	25	25	24	23
62	57	53	49	46	43	41	39	37	35	33	32	30	29	28	27	26	25	24	23	23
61	56	52	48	45	43	40	38	36	34	33	31	30	29	28	27	26	25	24	23	22
60	55	51	48	45	42	40	37	35	34	32	31	29	28	27	26	25	24	23	23	22
59	54	50	47	44	41	39	37	35	33	32	30	29	28	27	26	25	24	23	22	22
58	53	49	46	43	40	38	36	34	33	31	30	28	27	26	25	24	23	23	22	21
57	52	49	45	42	40	38	35	34	32	31	29	28	27	26	25	24	23	22	22	21
56	52	48	44	42	39	37	35	33	31	30	29	27	26	25	24	23	23	22	21	20
55	51	47	44	41	38	36	34	32	31	29	28	27	26	25	24	23	22	21	21	20
54	50	46	43	40	38	36	34	32	30	29	28	26	25	24	23	23	22	21	20	20
53	49	45	42	39	37	35	33	31	30	28	27	26	25	24	23	22	21	21	20	19
52	48	44	41	39	36	34	32	31	29	28	27	25	24	24	23	22	21	20	20	19
51	47	43	40	38	36	34	32	30	29	27	26	25	24	23	22	21	21	20	19	19
50	46	43	40	37	35	33	31	30	28	27	26	25	24	23	22	21	20	20	19	18
49	45	42	39	36	34	32	30	29	28	26	25	24	23	22	21	21	20	19	19	18
48	44	41	38	36	33	32	30	28	27	26	25	24	23	22	21	20	19	19	18	18
47	43	40	37	35	33	31	29	28	26	25	24	23	22	21	20	20	19	18	18	17
46	42	39	37	34	32	30	29	27	26	25	24	23	22	21	20	19	19	18	17	17
45	41	38	36	33	31	30	28	27	25	24	23	22	21	20	20	19	18	18	17	16
44	40	38	35	33	31	29	27	26	25	24	23	22	21	20	19	18	18	17	17	16
43	40	37	34	32	30	28	27	25	24	23	22	21	20	19	19	18	17	17	16	16
42	39	36	33	31	29	28	26	25	24	23	22	21	20	19	18	18	17	16	16	15
41	38	35	33	30	29	27	26	24	23	22	21	20	19	19	18	17	17	16	15	15
40	37	34	32	30	28	26	25	24	22	21	20	20	19	18	17	17	16	16	15	15
39	36	33	31	29	27	26	24	23	22	21	20	19	18	18	17	16	16	15	15	14
38	35	32	30	28	27	25	24	22	21	20	19	19	18	17	17	16	15	15	14	14
37	34	32	29	27	26	24	23	22	21	20	19	18	17	17	16	16	15	14	14	14
36	33	31	29	27	25	24	22	21	20	19	18	18	17	16	16	15	15	14	14	13
35	32	30	28	26	24	23	22	21	20	19	18	17	16	16	15	15	14	14	13	13
34	31	29	27	25	24	22	21	20	19	18	17	17	16	15	15	14	14	13	13	12
33	30	28	26	25	23	22	21	20	19	18	17	16	16	15	14	14	13	13	12	12
32	29	27	25	24	22	21	20	19	18	17	16	16	15	14	14	13	13	12	12	12
31	29	26	25	23	22	20	19	18	17	17	16	15	15	14	13	13	13	12	12	11
30	28	26	24	22	21	20	19	18	17	16	15	15	14	14	13	13	12	12	11	11
29	27	25	23	22	20	19	18	17	16	16	15	14	14	13	13	12	12	11	11	11
28	26	24	22	21	20	18	17	17	16	15	14	14	13	13	13	12	11	11	11	10
27	25	23	21	20	19	18	17	16	15	14	14	13	13	12	12	11	11	11	10	10
26	24	22	21	19	18	17	16	15	15	14	13	13	12	12	11	11	11	10	10	10
25	23	21	20	19	17	16	16	15	14	13	13	12	12	11	11	10	10	10	9	9
24	22	20	19	18	17	16	15	14	13	13	12	12	11	11	10	10	10	9	9	9
23	21	20	18	17	16	15	14	14	13	12	12	11	11	10	10	10	9	9	9	8
22	20	19	17	16	15	14	14	13	12	12	11	11	10	10	10	9	9	9	8	8
21	19	18	17	16	15	14	13	12	12	11	11	10	10	9	9	9	8	8	8	8
20	18	17	16	15	14	13	12	12	11	11	10	10	9	9	9	8	8	8	8	7
19	17	16	15	14	13	12	12	11	11	10	10	9	9	9	8	8	8	7	7	7
18	17	15	14	13	13	12	11	11	10	10	9	9	8	8	8	8	7	7	7	7
17	16	14	13	13	12	11	11	10	10	9	9	8	8	8	7	7	7	7	6	6
16	15	14	13	12	11	11	10	9	9	9	8	8	8	7	7	7	7	6	6	6

* A student who types 75 gross words a minute with one error is typing 69 mailable words a minute.

The Secretary and Her Work

Lesson **1** ⬡◯⬡◯⬡◯⬡◯⬡◯⬡◯⬡◯⬡◯⬡◯⬡◯⬡◯

1A—The Nature of Secretarial Work

The work of a secretary varies according to the kind of product or service being offered by the firm by which she is employed, the size of the organization, the position of the secretary's employer in the organization, and her employer's manner or methods of work.

The secretary is the "contact" between her employer and his business associates, both inside and outside the firm. The contacts may be made through telephone calls, personal conferences, memorandums and letters, or telegrams. The secretary must be able to handle local and long-distance telephone calls, take dictation of various types of business correspondence and transcribe efficiently, handle details of arranging meetings or conferences, type and send telegrams, and file and find business papers quickly. She must be able to take directions and to follow them faithfully.

The secretary performs many duties that expedite the work of her employer. Such duties may be as simple as sharpening his pencils or dusting his desk; on the other hand, they may be as difficult as reporting a conference, searching out some data from source books, or composing letters for his signature. To be most effective, she must know efficient office techniques for planning her work, arranging working materials, and completing the various duties assigned to her. She needs to be able to use any office equipment, such as typewriters, duplicating machines, and calculating machines, that will make her work easier.

A secretarial position can be a stepping stone to a supervisory or an executive position. Businessmen are always looking for employees who are capable of holding more responsible positions. Secretaries are in an excellent position to demonstrate this ability. Many men and women now holding executive positions advanced to those positions through secretarial work.

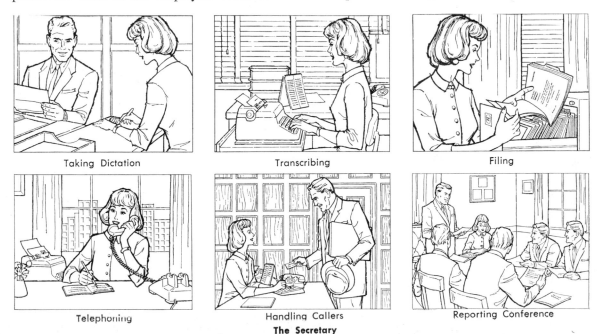

Taking Dictation   Transcribing   Filing

Telephoning   Handling Callers   Reporting Conference

The Secretary

MAILABLE-WORDS-A-MINUTE SCORING CHART
FOR 3-MINUTE TIMED WRITINGS

(Based on 26 seconds average time needed to make a correction without a carbon copy)

ERRORS

GWAM	1	2	3	4	5	6	7	8	9	10	11	12
75*	66*	58	52	48	44	40	37	35	33	31	29	27
74	65	57	52	47	43	40	37	34	32	30	29	27
73	64	57	51	46	42	39	36	34	32	30	28	27
72	63	56	50	46	42	39	36	33	31	29	28	26
71	62	55	50	45	41	38	35	33	31	29	27	26
70	61	54	49	44	41	38	35	32	30	29	27	26
69	60	54	48	44	40	37	34	32	30	28	27	25
68	59	53	47	43	39	36	34	32	30	28	26	25
67	59	52	47	42	39	36	33	31	29	27	26	25
66	58	51	46	42	38	35	33	31	29	27	25	24
65	57	50	45	41	38	35	32	30	28	27	25	24
64	56	50	45	41	37	34	32	30	28	26	25	23
63	55	49	44	40	37	34	31	29	27	26	24	23
62	54	48	43	39	36	33	31	29	27	25	24	23
61	53	47	43	39	35	33	30	28	27	25	24	22
60	52	47	42	38	35	32	30	28	26	25	23	22
59	52	46	41	37	34	32	29	27	26	24	23	22
58	51	45	40	37	34	31	29	27	25	24	22	21
57	50	44	40	36	33	31	28	26	25	23	22	21
56	49	43	39	35	33	30	28	26	24	23	22	20
55	48	43	38	35	32	29	27	26	24	23	21	20
54	47	42	38	34	31	29	27	25	23	22	21	20
53	46	41	37	34	31	28	26	25	23	22	20	19
52	45	40	36	33	30	28	26	24	23	21	20	19
51	45	40	36	32	30	27	25	24	22	21	20	19
50	44	39	35	32	29	27	25	23	22	20	19	18
49	43	38	34	31	28	26	24	23	21	20	19	18
48	42	37	33	30	28	26	24	22	21	20	19	18
47	41	36	33	30	27	25	23	22	20	19	18	17
46	40	36	32	29	27	25	23	21	20	19	18	17
45	39	35	31	29	26	24	22	21	20	18	17	16
44	38	34	31	28	26	24	22	20	19	18	17	16
43	38	33	30	27	25	23	21	20	19	18	17	16
42	37	33	29	27	24	23	21	19	18	17	16	15
41	36	32	29	26	24	22	20	19	18	17	16	15
40	35	31	28	25	23	21	20	19	17	16	15	15
39	34	30	27	25	23	21	19	18	17	16	15	14
38	33	29	27	24	22	20	19	18	17	16	15	14
37	32	29	26	23	21	20	18	17	16	15	14	14
36	31	28	25	23	21	19	18	17	16	15	14	13
35	31	27	24	22	20	19	17	16	15	14	14	13
34	30	26	24	22	20	18	17	16	15	14	13	12
33	29	26	23	21	19	18	16	15	14	14	13	12
32	28	25	22	20	19	17	16	15	14	13	12	12
31	27	24	22	20	18	17	15	14	13	13	12	11
30	26	23	21	19	17	16	15	14	13	12	12	11
29	25	23	20	18	17	16	14	13	13	12	11	11
28	24	22	20	18	16	15	14	13	12	11	11	10
27	24	21	19	17	16	14	13	13	12	11	10	10
26	23	20	18	16	15	14	13	12	11	11	10	10
25	22	19	17	16	15	13	12	12	11	10	10	9
24	21	19	17	15	14	13	12	11	10	10	9	9
23	20	18	16	15	13	12	11	11	10	9	9	8
22	19	17	15	14	13	12	11	10	10	9	9	8
21	18	16	15	13	12	11	10	10	9	9	8	8
20	17	16	14	13	12	11	10	9	9	8	8	7
19	17	15	13	12	11	10	9	9	8	8	7	7
18	16	14	13	11	10	10	9	8	8	7	7	7
17	15	13	12	11	10	9	8	8	7	7	7	6
16	14	12	11	10	9	9	8	7	7	7	6	6

* A student who types 75 gross words a minute with one error is typing 66 mailable words a minute.

Questions for Discussion

1. In what ways might secretarial work in one company differ from that in another because of each of the following factors:
   a. Kind of product or service being offered
   b. Size of the organization
   c. Position of the secretary's employer in the firm
   d. Her employer's manner or methods of work
2. In what ways may contacts be made with the employer through his secretary?
3. What does "expediting" the work of an employer mean?
4. What can a secretary do to show that she is capable of handling more difficult tasks?

Office Practice Problem

Ask one or more secretaries what duties they perform on the job. Prepare a written list of the duties they mention. Find out about such items as:

a. How much time they spend taking dictation and transcribing
b. How many telephone calls they usually handle a day
c. What office machines they use
d. What routine duties they perform
e. What they do in the way of "office housekeeping"
f. What they think you should learn in school in order to be a good secretary

---

1B—Building Speed in Taking Dictation

In this speed-building session and the one in Lesson 2, you will have an opportunity to write every brief form or a derivative of it at least once as you take dictation. All the brief forms are given on page vii of this book; they are presented in alphabetic order so that you can refer to them easily at any time.

You will remember that special shorthand forms are used for salutations and complimentary closes. In the dictation that you will take in this lesson and the next, you will have occasion to write each of the following special forms as well as the brief forms and some of their derivatives. Write each outline 3 times.

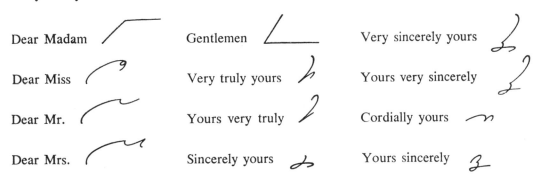

Dear Madam   Gentlemen   Very sincerely yours

Dear Miss   Very truly yours   Yours very sincerely

Dear Mr.   Yours very truly   Cordially yours

Dear Mrs.   Sincerely yours   Yours sincerely

Practice Material for Building Fluency

Directions. (1) Read the following letters. (2) Write 3 times each outline appearing in color, saying it to yourself as you write. (3) Write the entire copy through once. You will then find the letters easy to take from dictation. Follow the same procedure for similar exercises in later lessons.

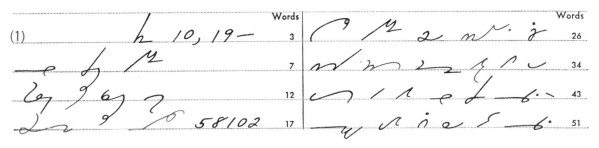

150B—Transcribing from Office-Style Dictation

Directions. Your teacher will dictate to you two letters and a memorandum in office-style dictation. For Letter 1, use mixed punctuation and modified block style with centered date and indented paragraphs. Transcribe on 7¼″ by 10½″ stationery. For Letter 2, use block letter style and open punctuation style. Transcribe on 8½″ by 11″ stationery. For the memorandum, use the arrangement shown on page 222. Copies go to: *Harold Bronson, Dwayne Wrigglesby, Paul Buttler,* and *Joe Briggs.*

150C—Supplementary Transcription

Miss Theresa Brooks, Secretary
Bingham Secretarial Club
Bingham High School
Los Angeles, California   90020

Mrs. Patricia A. Stoneleigh
Personnel Supervisor

(shorthand outlines, column 1)

58
67
76
83
92
98
107
115
128
136
142
155

S. K. Bradshaw 158
Vice-President 162
176

(2)   4, 19—   4
9
10   12
48515   17

27

(shorthand outlines, column 2)

37
49
55
62
69
76
83
88
93
99
109
117
125
133
137
144
150
15— 159

Wilbur Hall 162
175

Preview of New Dictation Material

Directions. Write each outline 3 times, saying it to yourself as you write. Then cover the shorthand outlines and see if you can write the shorthand outlines correctly from the printed words. Follow the same procedure for similar exercises in subsequent lessons. Some outlines other than brief forms and special forms that will occur in the new dictation material are given below.

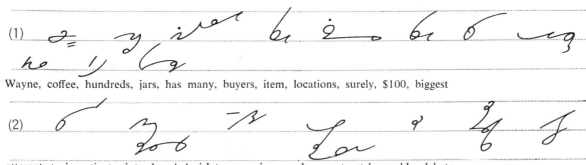

(1) *(shorthand outlines)*

Wayne, coffee, hundreds, jars, has many, buyers, item, locations, surely, $100, biggest

(2) *(shorthand outlines)*

attempt, to investigate, introduced, legislature, session, we have not yet been able, debate

Questions for Discussion

1. What opportunities exist for continuing your education in the locality where you hope to be employed?
2. What personality characteristics do you think most important in getting along with others in the office?
3. If you were an employer, what character traits would you value most highly in an employee?

Office Practice Problem

If your teacher were rating you on your performance in class according to the rating sheet shown in this lesson, how do you think you would be rated on the various points? Make a list of the items and the rating you think you would receive on each one.

What do you think would have caused her to give you such a rating? How could you earn a better rating?

Lesson 150 ○○○○○○○○○○○○○○○○○○○○○

150A—Vocabulary Preview

weeks ago, recommended, young, Barbara, Weston, employed, demonstrate, enthusiasm, contagious, congratulate, excellent, institution, vacancy, ability, unusual

Oxford, apparel, so much, appearance, attractive, personnel, ties, air-conditioned, comfortable, employees, shirts, beige, harmonizes, appropriate, subdued, restaurant, accessories, impede, walking, I hope that the, hesitate, jewelry, flashy, noisy, outfit, minimum

requests, applicants, legitimate, vacation, assignment, brochures, whether or not, unionized, seems to me, status, hesitant, curiosity, about this matter, deterred, weekly, availability

Lesson **2** ⬡ ◯ ⬡ ◯ ⬡ ◯ ⬡ ◯ ⬡ ◯ ⬡ ◯ ⬡ ◯ ⬡ ◯ ⬡ ◯ ⬡ ◯ ⬡

2A—Following Directions

Following directions carefully is one of the most important work habits you can acquire for secretarial work. To become adept at following directions, observe the following suggestions:

1. Don't trust your memory. Don't burden your mind with a lot of details; leave it free for more important work. *Write it down!*

2. Never approach your employer's desk without pencils or pen and notebook.

3. Give your undivided attention whenever instructions are being given—even if the work does seem simple. When you get back to your desk, you may find the job more difficult than it appeared when it was being assigned.

4. Record directions where you can find them easily. Don't jot them down on odd slips of paper or on the margins of papers on your desk. Your shorthand notebook is the safest place in which to record day-to-day instructions.

5. Make your notations of directions complete. You may not get to the task immediately and may forget an important detail later.

6. Read your directions carefully, not hastily. Many a stenographer has had directions accurately and completely written but has been careless in reading them.

7. If you work for more than one person, write the initials of each one immediately preceding the dictation he gives you.

8. Prepare a set of permanent instructions for certain reports or papers that are always to be done in the same way, unless, of course, your firm has a correspondence manual that gives complete directions for those reports and papers.

9. For periodic duties, keep a "follow-up" or "tickler" file with guides for the days and months. Type on file cards the duties to be performed on certain dates; place those cards under the proper date in the file; and then don't forget to check your file every day!

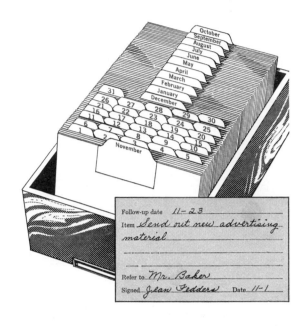

Card Tickler File

Questions for Discussion

1. Since your employer would usually be where you could get in touch with him if you forgot his directions, why is it important to write down detailed instructions?

2. Why is it not a good idea to approach your employer's desk without pencils or pen and notebook? After all, he may have summoned you just to hand you something to be filed or to tell you that he is going to some other office.

3. What is a "tickler" file and how is it used?

Office Practice Problem

Assume that your employer gave you a rough draft of a report, asking you to type it in final form. See how many points you can list about which you would need to have directions in order to prepare the final copy properly.

2B—Building Speed in Taking Dictation

In Lesson 1 you reviewed many brief forms and some special forms. All the brief forms and special forms that you did not write in taking dictation in Lesson 1 you will write in today's dictation; many of the ones that you did write you will write again.

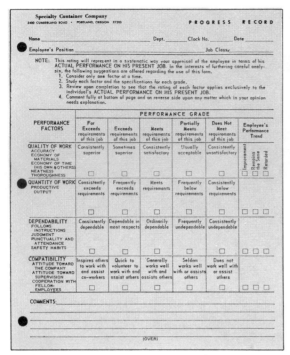

Employee Rating Sheet

He notes the expertness with which you perform assigned tasks, and he observes how well you get along with others in the office. In large firms each department head or supervisor is required to rate each employee under his direction two or three times a year. He may or may not discuss with you his rating of your performance. The rating sheet is filed in the Employment Department in your personal folder. When a vacancy occurs that you might possibly fill or when salaries are reviewed, the ratings in your folder will be studied in determining your eligibility. The rating sheet used by one firm is shown above. Notice the factors on which a supervisor rates his subordinates. Some of these factors were discussed in Lessons 1 to 5.

It is your responsibility to adjust to the job and the surroundings in which you work. You must be able to cooperate with your supervisor and your co-workers. To succeed, you must accept criticism in good spirit, avoid gossip, and observe the rules of office etiquette. Treat everything you do and handle as confidential; then you will never be responsible for a "leak" of vital information to the wrong person. Do not ask for special consideration or favors. You are hired as an adult who assumes responsibility; justify the confidence that was placed in you.

Opportunities for Improving on the Job. Several avenues are open to most employees for improving on the job. Some of these avenues are provided by the firm; some of them you "travel on your own."

Many companies have special classes conducted during working hours. These classes are open to employees who are interested in developing greater skill for their present position or to those who would like to meet the qualifications for a higher level position. Announcements are made through memos or bulletin board notices; and, if you are interested, you should discuss arrangements with your supervisor. These classes are referred to as "in-service training" programs.

Many business firms encourage their employees to take correspondence or night school courses. In fact, some pay the tuition for their employees when the courses taken will make the employees more valuable to the company.

You may wish to go to a local college or university to take courses that are not directly connected with your work. In that case, you should expect to pay your own expenses.

Through various civic, religious, social, or other organizations you may widen your understanding not only of the business world but of our entire society; and you will increase your circle of friends.

Practice Material for Building Fluency

Directions. Follow the same procedure you used for the similar exercise in Lesson 1.

Words

(1) [shorthand] *4, 19—* 3
[shorthand] 7
[shorthand] 11
[shorthand] *56301* 17

[shorthand] 24
[shorthand] 33
[shorthand] 40
[shorthand] 49
[shorthand] 59
[shorthand] 68
[shorthand] 75
[shorthand] 80
[shorthand] 88
[shorthand] 98
[shorthand] Karl Reese 105
Sales Manager 109
122

Words

(2) [shorthand] *10, 19—* 3
[shorthand] 6
[shorthand] 10
[shorthand] *66612* 14

[shorthand] 23
[shorthand] 31
[shorthand] 41
[shorthand] 49
[shorthand] 57
[shorthand] 64
[shorthand] 74
[shorthand] 81
[shorthand] 90
[shorthand] 99
Neil D. Pruett 103
114

Preview of New Dictation Material

Directions. Follow the same procedure you used for the similar exercise in Lesson 1.

(1) [shorthand]

Thomas, broadcasts, viewers, forecasts, coverage, refused, events, patrons

(2) [shorthand]

to handle, campaign, effectively, so long, glad to have, affords

(3) [shorthand]

Hamilton, surgical, dressings, instruments, Monument, zoning, difficulties, involved, could be done, disappointment

The following points are some that the interviewer will note as he talks with you about a position:

About your appearance and bearing—

How did she enter my office? Did she have good posture?

Did she look directly at me? Did she smile?

How did she sit in the chair—well back in it with her body erect and with her feet on the floor?

Was she chewing gum or mints?

Was her costume appropriate for our office?

Did she look neat and clean?

About your conversation—

Did she participate easily, or did I have to prompt her with continuous questioning?

Did her answers indicate that she had given some thought to her career?

Did she know anything about our firm?

Was her vocabulary adequate?

Did she have a pleasant voice?

Was she enthusiastic about working?

Could she give direct and complete answers to my questions?

Were her questions intelligent?

Did she try to bluff when she didn't know the answers to my questions?

Did her responses indicate that she could get along with others?

Did her comments indicate an understanding of business procedures and practices?

Postinterview Activity. After the interview, make pertinent notes about the conversation that you had with the interviewer. Did you offer to send additional information? Did he indicate a specific date on which he would be able to give you a definite answer about employment? What additional information did he give you about the company and its operations? What people did you meet, and what were their names and positions?

You may wish to write a follow-up letter within a few days, thanking the interviewer for the opportunity to talk with him, giving additional information if it seems warranted, and expressing your interest again in the opportunity to work for that firm.

When you have been offered a position, accept or reject promptly. If you do accept, write immediately to other firms to which you have made application, stating that you have accepted a position with another firm and ask that your application be placed in their inactive files.

When you accept a position, do so in good faith; that is, do not accept a position and then resign shortly afterward if you receive a better offer.

Questions for Discussion

1. How would your costume for an interview differ from your usual school costume? Why?

2. Discuss points of good grooming that should be observed by the applicant.

3. What preparation can an applicant make for an interview that would minimize nervousness?

Office Practice Problems

Come to class dressed as you would be for an interview. Discuss the points you had in mind as you selected the various parts of your costume. Demonstrate how you would do the following:

1. Announce yourself to the receptionist when you arrive for an interview.

2. Enter the office of the interviewer to be greeted by him.

3. Sit in the interview chair.

Lesson **149** ◇ ⬡ ◇ ⬡ ◇ ⬡ ◇ ⬡ ◇ ⬡ ◇ ⬡ ◇ ⬡ ◇ ⬡ ◇ ⬡ ◇

Earning Promotion in the Firm

Promotions usually come to employees who have demonstrated the ability to perform skillfully in their present positions and whose actions have indicated an ability to handle a position requiring greater skill or utilizing special talents. Excellence on the job is the first requisite to being considered for a promotion. The second is giving evidence of your ability to handle a more difficult assignment.

Daily Performance on the Job. As an employee, you should be aware of the fact that your supervisor is observing your performance on the job.

Lesson 3 ⬡⬡⬡⬡⬡⬡⬡⬡⬡⬡⬡⬡⬡⬡⬡⬡⬡

3A—What Impression Does Your Appearance Make?

You are a representative of the firm for which you work. Callers get their first impression of the company from your appearance, just as those who do their business by mail get their impressions from the letters you write.

It would not be good taste to send a letter typed in green ink on orange stationery. Neither is it good taste to wear frilly party dresses in the business office. Anyone receiving a smudged, poorly arranged letter would be likely to think of the sending company as being careless and unreliable. Anyone seeing a stenographer with a poorly fitted suit and unclean fingernails would have an equally bad opinion of the company.

As a secretary, you should ask yourself these questions:

1. Do others think of me as being dressed simply and in good taste? Party clothes at one extreme and saddle shoes and anklets at the other give equally bad impressions. Both are inappropriate for the business world.

2. Do I give the impression of being neat and clean? Are my fingernails well manicured? Are they too long? Is the polish too bright? Are my shoes shined? The hands of a secretary are seen at close range by her employer and often by other people—and so are her shoes.

Are there any unpleasant odors about me? Am I taking enough baths and using mouth washes and deodorants properly? "Even your best friend won't tell you" is an old saying, but it is a good one to remember. You really *can* lose friends—and even your job—if you offend frequently.

Are my clothes clean and pressed?

Do I change my make-up often enough to keep my face looking fresh and attractive?

Is my hair neatly combed and attractively styled?

3. Do I give the impression by my posture of being alert and competent? Am I standing erect or like a question mark? Am I sitting correctly or on the small of my back? Good posture is important not only for appearance but also for lessening fatigue as you work.

Questions for Discussion

1. Are the clothes you and your classmates wear to school suitable for the business office? Discuss in some detail.
2. Are the hair styles you and your friends wear suitable for the business office? Why or why not?
3. Make a list of specific accessories that would be suitable for office wear and a list of items that would not be suitable for office wear. For example, how would you list a bracelet that tinkled when you moved your arm? a ring with a large setting that slid between your fingers when you typed? button earrings?
4. What items should be kept in a small box or kit in your desk in order that you can take care of any emergency that might arise in connection with your personal appearance while you are at work?

Office Practice Problems

1. Select and bring to class newspaper and magazine advertisements of clothes that are advertised as being appropriate for the businessman and businesswoman. Attach to each advertisement a written list of good or bad points about the clothes.
2. Bring to class pictures of hair styles that you think would be satisfactory for office workers. Be prepared to explain orally why you approve of them.
3. List five or six points to check in determining whether you have good posture.

3B—Building Speed in Taking Dictation

In Lessons 1 and 2 you took dictation that required you to write all the brief forms and many of the special forms for salutations and complimentary closes. In Lessons 3 and 4 you will again take dictation that will include all the brief forms and many of those special forms.

Lesson 148 ○○○○○○○○○○○○○○○○○○

The Interview

The interview can be a pleasant experience for you and a successful one if you prepare for it carefully. The purpose of an interview is to enable an employer to observe your appearance, hear your voice and note your manner of speaking, and discuss in more detail your qualifications. Your written application left a favorable impression, so you are one step closer to a job offer. The interview helps you, too, to reach a decision as to whether you want to accept a position if one is offered. Preparation for the interview consists of two parts: (1) *preinterview collection of information* and (2) *preinterview personal preparation.* Each part is composed of many details.

Preinterview Collection of Information. Facts that you will want to assemble in preparation for an interview include at least the following:

About the firm—

Where is it located? How long will it take me to get there? How shall I plan to go?

What is the firm's official name?

What is the name and title of the person to whom I shall be talking?

What service or product is the firm engaged in providing?

What specific aspects of office work am I interested in doing?

About myself—

What are my qualifications for the job?

Why do I want to work for this firm?

Why have I chosen a career in this field?

Why do I want to be employed in this locality?

What are my interests outside my career? What are my hobbies?

What did I like most to study in school? What did I dislike?

What do other members of my family do?

What are my plans for the future? What do I plan to be doing five years from now?

Why am I going to work instead of pursuing a college education?

Preinterview Personal Preparation. In making personal preparation for the interview, you will want to give attention to at least the following:

About my costume—

Is it appropriate for the business office? Is the color in good taste? the style? Is it clean and pressed?

Are my accessories appropriate?

Are my shoes shined and of business style? Are they in good repair?

Am I prepared for both good and bad weather so I won't be caught at the last moment with unsuitable clothing?

About my appearance—

Is my body clean and fresh from a recent bath or shower?

Are my teeth clean? Have I eliminated the possibility of halitosis?

Are my hands clean? Are my nails filed to proper length? Are they clean? Is my polish of a subdued color and not chipped?

Is my hair combed and arranged attractively? Have I brushed off loose hair from my clothing?

Do I know how to stand and sit correctly?

Have I used only a lightly scented cologne? hair lotion? hand lotion?

Is my facial makeup attractive and appropriate for daytime and business situations? (*For men:* Am I closely shaven?)

About my readiness—

Do I have all necessary papers with me?

Do I have a handkerchief with me?

Do I have all supplies necessary in case I should be asked to take an employment test?

Have I reviewed the information supplied in my application?

Have I allowed sufficient time to get to my appointment on time?

Have I taken any gum or mints out of my mouth?

Am I planning to go to the interview alone?

Interview Participation. If you have made the necessary preinterview preparation, you should approach the actual interview with a feeling of pleasant anticipation. You know the firm has reacted favorably to your written application; you are well dressed and mentally alert for the interview itself.

(1)

[shorthand outlines] bass

74074

(2)

[shorthand outlines]

50401

[shorthand outlines]

Lucy K. Malone
Circulation Manager

168

Myra Carr
Personnel Manager

177

(1) *[shorthand outlines]*

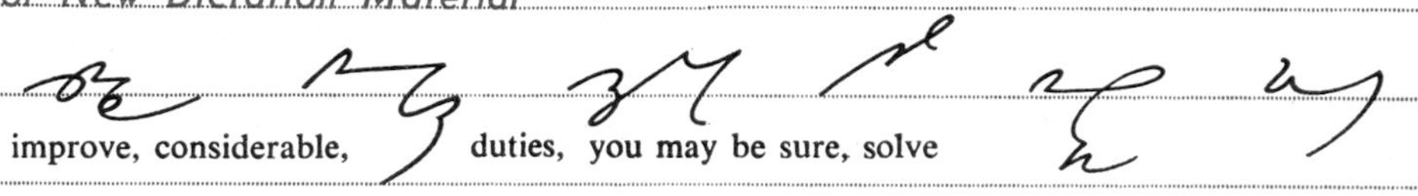

council, to improve, considerable, duties, you may be sure, solve

(2) *[shorthand outlines]*

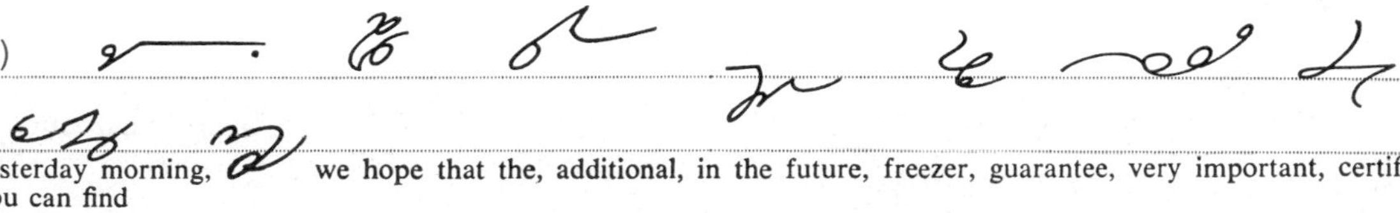

yesterday morning, we hope that the, additional, in the future, freezer, guarantee, very important, certificate, you can find

If you have no information to supply for a given question, do not leave the space blank. Insert an appropriate comment such as "None" or "Not Applicable" or use a dash. If a space is left blank, the reviewer does not know whether you overlooked the item or had nothing to state.

If you are uncertain whether you have room for the information you want to insert in a space, try it out on a blank sheet of paper first; then, if necessary, you can abbreviate or use a briefer explanation. Use the variable line spacer on ruled lines if lines do not conform to the vertical spacing on your machine.

You may be asked what salary you would expect. If you know what the company pays for that type of job, you can, of course, use that figure. If, however, you do not know what the customary compensation is and you hesitate to put down a definite amount, you may insert such a comment as "Open," "Your schedule," or "Your usual rate." Salaries vary considerably from city to city and from firm to firm. Some companies are in areas where the cost of living is high. Some firms pay lower salaries than others but give their employees better working conditions or hours or more fringe benefits (hospitalization, liberal vacations, etc.). Make a note of the information you fill in on a form; then, if you subsequently go for a personal interview, you can refresh your memory regarding the information that you had supplied. The interviewer may repeat some of the questions that were on the form, such as "Why do you want to work for our company?" or "Why did you prepare for secretarial work?" Your answers should be consistent with your application form.

If you do not receive a reply from a firm in ten days, you may write a follow-up letter. In this letter, you mention that you had applied for a position on a certain date, that you are very much interested in employment with that firm, and that you would be glad to furnish additional information if desired or come for an interview. Do not telephone; either write or go to the offices of the firm, whichever seems most appropriate.

If you have sent out several letters of application, you should, as soon as you have accepted a position, write a courteous letter to each of the other firms, withdrawing your application with the explanation that you have accepted employment elsewhere.

Reverse Side of Application Form

Questions for Discussion

1. Discuss the precautions you should take in filling in an application form.

2. Why should you keep a record of information that you filled in on an application form?

3. Why is a fairly brief letter of application accompanied with a data sheet preferable to a letter giving complete information?

4. Since a firm probably realizes that you are applying for jobs at other companies, why not save time and effort by duplicating your letter?

Office Practice Problems

1. Obtain an application blank from a business firm in your community or from the local post office and fill it in as though you were applying for a position (or use the form provided in the Workbook).

2. Write a letter answering one of the classified advertisements you obtained for Lesson 146.

3. Write a follow-up letter, assuming that you have applied for a stenographic position and have not had a reply to your original letter of application.

4A—Personality

"Personality" is what others think we are—the summation of the impressions others have of us. Many times we may not realize that our speech and actions have the effect on others that they really do have. It is a good idea now and then to ask ourselves, "What impression are we making?"

Speech. A well-modulated voice—neither too loud nor too soft—makes others think of us as poised, self-confident, tactful, and possessing good judgment. Correct use of grammar and a varied vocabulary will help leave the impression that we are capable, educated, and intelligent.

Choice of words designed to encourage friendly exchange of ideas rather than to force our way of thinking on others will pay handsome rewards in discussions. Compare the phrases in these two groups:

Group A—"You always . . ."
"No one in his right mind would . . ."
"Regardless of what you think . . ."
"I'm sick and tired of . . ."
"How stupid can you get?"

Group B—"You have a point there, but . . ."
"I can see your point of view, but . . ."
"Let's look at it from another angle for a moment . . ."
"Maybe I'm mistaken, but . . ."
"Could we attack the problem from this angle . . ."

Group A phrases tend to make those of the opposing point of view feel defensive and little inclined to consider other ideas; Group B phrases do not insult the intelligence of the opponents and indicate a serious weighing of all factors and appreciation of another point of view.

Actions. The smallest actions are sometimes the most revealing. Being punctual, being absent rarely, turning out neat transcripts—all reflect a sincere interest and pride in the job.

Keeping confidential information to oneself and not being critical of one's firm in the presence of outsiders will show that one is a loyal employee.

Letting gossip "die on the vine" when it reaches us and being courteous and friendly instead of domineering and demanding will mark us as persons of considerable tact.

Helping others without a big "to-do" is one of the easiest ways to cause others to regard us as cooperative; another way is to have a sympathetic attitude toward the ideas and problems of others. A willingness to give someone else the "benefit of the doubt" can contribute immeasurably to the harmony in an office.

The amount of initiative an employee has is revealed by the way he develops more efficient procedures in performing certain tasks.

Manners make lasting impressions. Are introductions made correctly? Are the words "Excuse me" and "Pardon me" quickly said when the occasion warrants? Is there polite attention when someone else is talking?

We should ask ourselves frequently: Do our speech and actions leave the impression we would have them leave?

Questions for Discussion

1. Businessmen who are looking for new employees may consult your teacher about your personality, character traits, and work habits as well as about your secretarial skills. What specific actions can you suggest that you might do or might not do in school that would leave your teacher with the impression that you have such important personality traits as tact, cooperativeness, initiative, dependability, and responsibility?

2. What points should be kept in mind in making introductions? Consult an etiquette book for correct procedures.

Office Practice Problem

One of the best ways to become aware of your personality problems is to evaluate yourself. On page 9 is a check list of the personal qualities a secretary should have. Make four copies of this list—typewritten if possible. Use one of them to score yourself as part of your preparation for this lesson. Keep the other three copies. You will have opportunities to rate yourself again later in the course. Check up on yourself frequently so that you will be able to give yourself a higher rating next time.

The Written Application

In Lesson 37, you studied some characteristics of effective application letters; and you were given some information about application forms. In this lesson you will give additional attention to the written application, since this is the means by which you usually attempt to get an interview and is, therefore, vitally important to you.

As an applicant, you need to be aware of the fact that you make an impression on the reviewer of your application in several ways: (1) by the stated qualifications, (2) by the manner in which you present those qualifications, and (3) by the appearance of the letter or form itself.

The Application Letter. Reviewing Lesson 37, you recall that a fairly brief letter of application accompanied by a personal data sheet is usually preferable to a letter incorporating all of the information within it. The reason is that more information can be given without fear of appearing boastful. In preparing the data sheet, first jot down all items you can think of that might be useful. Then group them under appropriate headings such as *Personal, Education, Employment History, Extracurricular Activities,* and *References.* Arrange the data attractively on the page. Use a good ribbon and type your letter on good bond paper that has at least 25% cotton content. Be sure the type is clean. Attach a photograph if one has been requested.

The application letter should be typewritten, not handwritten, since you are applying for office work and would be expected to use a typewriter skillfully. Make a file copy of your letter so that you have a record of what firms you have contacted, when you wrote, and what you said. Never duplicate a letter on a duplicating machine and send copies to a number of firms. You cannot convince a firm that you especially want to work for it if it is obvious that you are sending the same letter to several companies.

Be sure that the letter is attractively arranged and that there are no errors of any kind. Don't forget to sign the letter—and use black, blue, or blue-black ink for the signature.

The Application Form. Many firms ask you to fill in a printed application form, even though you may have sent in a written application that gave all the information requested on the form. In filling in such a form, follow directions precisely. Your ability to do so may be a factor in the firm's decision to hire you. Instructions on the form, for example, may direct you to fill in the blanks in your own handwriting; if so, do not type or print. Use ink, not pencil.

Read the entire form before filling in any part of it. Otherwise, you may write in information in one space only to discover that space is provided elsewhere on the form for it. Observe special instructions such as writing your last name first, using a check mark or "x" in certain places, or listing your work experience with latest employment first rather than in chronological order. Educational preparation is usually to be given in chronological order, but not always.

—By permission, Murphy Corporation

Application Form

Character-istic	The Unsatisfactory Secretary	The Average Secretary	The Top-Notch Secretary	My Score
Attitude	Not enthusiastic about the job Resents criticism Does minimum of work Not interested in improv-ing **1**	Enthusiastic about most of the job Usually accepts criticism well Sometimes does more than required Shows some interest in im-proving **2**	Enthusiastic about the entire job Always accepts criticism in good spirit Frequently does more than required Takes definite steps to im-prove **3**	
Efficiency	Does not organize work Does not follow directions Disorderly and untidy Cannot handle crises **1**	Organizes work quite well Usually follows directions Generally neat and orderly Meets crises fairly well **2**	Organizes work unusually well Follows directions exactly Uniformly neat and orderly Meets crises calmly **3**	
Judgment and Tact	Tactless Uses poor judgment Often at odds with co-workers **1**	Usually tactful Shows good judgment Usually on good terms with co-workers **2**	Always tactful Uses superior judgment Maintains excellent rela-tions with co-workers **3**	
Responsi-bility	Frequently tardy or absent Needs close supervision Does not complete tasks Unethical **1**	Infrequently tardy or absent Needs only limited supervision Ordinarily completes tasks **2** Ethical in most situations	Tardy or absent only for good reason Needs no supervision Always completes tasks **3** Highly ethical at all times	
Secretarial Skills and Knowledges	Types and transcribes poorly Unreliable in duties such as filing, duplicating, etc. Handles callers and calls ineptly Does not understand business procedures **1**	Types and transcribes with average skill Usually accurate in duties such as filing, duplicating, etc. Handles most callers and calls satisfactorily Has fair understanding of **2** business procedures	Types and transcribes with superior skill Efficient in duties such as fil-ing, duplicating, etc. Handles callers and calls with great skill Has keen understanding of **3** business procedures	
Behavior	Moody; erratic; selfish Does not know or abide by office customs and rules Overly friendly or not **1** friendly enough	Ordinarily pleasant and thoughtful of others Observes most office customs and rules Occasionally too friendly **2** or too reserved	Consistently good-natured and unselfish Fully aware and observant of office customs and rules Friendly to the right **3** degree	
Apparel Grooming Speech Posture	Wears soiled and wrinkled clothes Not neat and clean of person Dresses unsuitably Has poor command of English **1** Has poor posture	Wears clothes that are usually pressed and clean Acceptably neat and clean of person Dresses satisfactorily Speaks with acceptable English **2** Has fairly good posture	Always wears clean and well-pressed clothes Unfailingly neat and clean of person Dresses appropriately and attractively Speaks in clear, correct English **3** Has excellent posture	

TOTAL ——————

Self-Evaluation Chart

4B—Building Speed in Taking Dictation

All the brief forms that you did not write in Lesson 3, as well as many that you did write, are included in the familiar and new dictation material of this lesson.

designated address or called the number given for more details.

Employment Offices of Firms. An excellent source of information is, of course, the employment or personnel office of a firm in which you would like to be employed. You may write a letter of inquiry or you may inquire in person. Do not telephone. If you go in person, be prepared to fill in an application blank at that time, to take an employment test, or to have an interview with a company representative. Call at an appropriate time—not during a lunch hour, late in the afternoon, or on Saturday.

Temporary Help Companies. If you cannot find a full-time position immediately, you may wish to seek part-time or temporary work either by direct application to a firm or by seeking such work through a firm whose business is supplying temporary help to companies. Although this type of firm usually prefers experienced people on its rolls, if your preparation has been outstanding, you may be able to obtain temporary or part-time jobs through a contract with a firm such as Kelly Girl Service Inc., Manpower Inc., Western Girl, Inc., or Employers' Overload, Inc. When you are employed by this type of firm, you receive your pay from it—not from the company for which you actually do work.

Job Titles. Because there is little uniformity in job titles among business firms, you may not be able to make your inquiries by referring to specific job titles such as "Junior Stenographer" or "Clerk-Stenographer." You should be prepared to describe the kind of work you can do in specific terms such as "filing," "taking dictation," "being a receptionist," etc. Your interviewer can tell you what the job title is in his firm for that particular type of work and the nature of the responsibilities. In a large firm, the title "Secretary" is reserved for the highest level positions in the secretarial group; and a person with a high school education and little or no experience would not be qualified for it. In such a firm, positions for beginning workers have such titles as "Junior Clerk," "Typist A," or "Stenographer II."

In a recent office salary survey, the National Office Management Association used 23 job titles and descriptions in obtaining information from businesses. Some of these descriptions are shown at the top of the next column.

NOMA Job Titles and Descriptions *

SECRETARY A—Performs with skill and efficiency the complete secretarial job for a high-level executive or a person responsible for a major functional or geographic operation. Does work of a confidential nature and is able to relieve principal of designated administrative details as well as acting for him in matters not requiring his presence. Requires initiative, judgment, knowledge of company practices, policy, and organization. May direct the work of a small number of clerical or stenographic employees.

SECRETARY B—Performs with skill and efficiency the complete secretarial job for a divisional or department head, branch or area manager or other individuals with similar responsibilities. General requirements are the same as for "Secretary A" but limited to the area of responsibility of the principal.

STENOGRAPHER A—Records and transcribes dictation of more than average difficulty, rapidly and accurately, by use of shorthand and/or transcribing machine. May perform related clerical duties. Must have general knowledge of the firm's organization, products, terminology and procedures, and must use judgment in carrying out assignments with minimum supervision. May plan the setup for and type complicated tables, unusual reports or similar material. Should also be able to do volume typing with speed and accuracy.

STENOGRAPHER B—Records and transcribes dictation involving a normal range of business vocabulary in accordance with standard practices. May do related clerical work. May work in stenographic pool full or part time. On a temporary or occasional basis, could be given the "Typist B" assignment. All operations are generally closely supervised.

* *Office Salaries*, 16th Survey Summary, 1962 Guide to Salary Rates (National Office Management Association), page 3. *(Now known as Administrative Management Society)*

Questions for Discussion

1. Under what circumstances would you probably seek the help of a public employment agency? a private agency? classified advertisements?

2. What might be some questions you would ask yourself in deciding whether to apply for a position in a certain firm?

3. If you go to a firm's offices to inquire about a possible vacancy, why should you be prepared to take a test or have an interview?

Office Practice Problems

1. In the four job descriptions presented above, what are the important differences between (a) Stenographer A and Stenographer B, and (b) Secretary A and Secretary B?

2. List the items included in three classified advertisements in your newspaper. What other information would you like to have?

Practice Material for Building Fluency

Words		Words
$y^3, 19$— 3		67
of *pearce* 7		75
1396 11		82
31204 15		88
		95
23		103
32		108
38		116
45		122
51		130
61		Percy Tucker 133
		Sales Manager 136
		147

Preview of New Dictation Material

(1)

invested, has it been, real estate, apparent, projects, ahead, demand

(2)

we have had, I hope that the, entire, slow, this time

(3)

Owens, circumstances, permission, original, source, in this instance

(4)

has been made, evidence, court, devoted, witnesses, might have been, jury

(5)

Anderson, we are pleased, on that date, delegates, convention, loyalty

(6)

lost, happened, what else, mentioned, the only

Unit 1 · Lesson 4

Beginning Your Career and Advancing in It

Lesson **146** ⬡◯⬡◯⬡◯⬡◯⬡◯⬡◯⬡◯⬡◯⬡◯⬡◯⬡◯⬡◯⬡◯⬡

Seeking Employment

If you are planning to enter the business world as soon as you are graduated, you probably have already given considerable thought to the type of firm by which you would like to be employed and the type of work you would like to do. You may have decided that the most important consideration for you is the *kind of firm* with which you want to be associated; that is, whether it performs a service such as banking, insurance, or retail merchandising or whether it manufactures a particular product such as automobiles, television sets, or textiles. On the other hand, the kind of business activity may be unimportant to you; you may be most interested in obtaining a job in which you would perform a specific *type of work*, such as bookkeeping, stenography, or duplicating services.

Sometimes a "short-run" objective or consideration may be given precedence over a "long-run" goal in seeking employment. You should be careful to distinguish between these two in choosing your initial employment. Occasionally, a "short-run" objective has to be given priority over a "long-run" goal; for instance, you may have an obligation to take a job that enables you to live at home or that involves no transportation problem. If possible, however, the job that has the greatest "long-run" possibility (such as working in an area of your special interest or affording best opportunity for advancement), should be the one you give first consideration.

Sources of Information: School and Family. Regardless of the type of work sought, many sources of assistance in obtaining a position are available to you. Some of the best sources are the easiest for you to consult: your teachers, guidance counselor, or placement officer; your family, relatives, or friends. Businessmen may call your placement office to inquire whether there is a graduating senior who would be interested in and qualified for a vacancy that exists. A friend of yours may be an employee in a firm for which you would like to work and who may know of an opening for which you would be qualified. Discuss your hopes and plans with those who are most interested in your future and who are well acquainted with your qualifications; do not, however, expect them to find your job for you.

Employment Agencies—Public. Employment agencies may be helpful in your search for a position. Public employment agencies may be Federal, state, county, or city. The *United States Employment Service (USES)* is the largest such agency and has regional offices in many cities. This agency helps you find employment in either private business firms or in Government offices. If you would like a position with the Federal Government, go to an office of USES or to your local post office to obtain application forms for the type of position in which you are interested. Competitive examinations are given for certain positions; find out the date and place of the next examination. Such positions are called, "civil service" jobs, meaning that appointments and status are determined by examination or merit rather than by political patronage.

Individual states also have employment agencies with offices in the state capital and in various other cities. These agencies, like USES, have information concerning vacancies in both private and public offices. Some positions in state government offices are also "civil service" and require the passing of examinations. Public employment agencies provide their services without charge.

Employment Agencies—Private. Private employment agencies provide assistance in some cities; they, of course, charge for their services. They are particularly helpful if you are seeking employment in a town in which you are a stranger. If you seek the help of such an agency, be sure that it is a reputable one. Always read carefully any contract before you sign it. The fee charged is often the first week's salary or a certain percent of the first month's pay.

Classified Advertisements. Classified advertisements in newspapers can be helpful sources of information. Since such advertisements usually contain few facts, you may not be sure a position is one you would like until you have written to the

5A—Your Attitude Toward Your Job

After you leave school, you will probably spend a major part of your waking hours at work. It is important, therefore, that you have such an attitude toward your job that your life will be happy and rewarding.

Will your job be just something that you endure in order to get enough money "to do something you would like to do"? Or will it be an experience that you look forward to each day? It is well to remember that every job has its dull, routine aspects, its unpleasant moments, its trials and disappointments. But every job also has its pleasant aspects and its satisfying moments. By keeping a proper perspective toward the irritating as well as the satisfying experiences, you can get genuine enjoyment out of your life's work whether you are a file clerk, a bank president, or a homemaker.

When you take a job, go into it with the expectation of liking it, of deriving some real satisfaction from it. If you can do that, then difficulties will be challenges to be met with a determination to overcome them.

Genuine enthusiasm for one's work and for the particular task of the moment is contagious. Fellow workers gravitate toward the enthusiastic person; they shy away from the grumbler, the complainer, and the discontented. Your attitude will be reflected in your facial expression, your manner of speaking, and in the way you "tackle" your assignments.

Take pride in your work. If you are sincerely interested in your job, you will find yourself growing into a more and more valuable employee, and rewards will certainly follow in promotions in rank and salary.

Give a day's work for a day's pay. To do less is to be dishonest. Ask yourself occasionally, "If I were paid by my employer at the end of every hour, would I feel like accepting the money with no apologies for what I had accomplished during that hour?"

Questions for Discussion

1. From your experiences in typewriting and shorthand classes, what duties do you think you would enjoy most in the office?
2. What steps do you think you might take to keep at a minimum the feeling of irritation or unpleasantness in performing your tasks?

Office Practice Problem

Name four or five outstanding people you admire (either living or deceased). List the qualities that seem to have helped them in their work.

5B—Building Speed in Taking Dictation

Phrasing is an important factor in taking dictation rapidly because it enables you to keep to a minimum the number of times you lift the pen off the paper, thus saving valuable seconds. Also, a good phrase often has fewer strokes in it than would be required if each word in the phrase were written separately. For example, compare the strokes necessary to write the phrase *one of the best* with the strokes necessary to write each word of that phrase separately.

Compare: 〰 ✓ 🅑 and 〰 🅑 .

Phrasing also speeds transcribing because the thought can be grasped more quickly from one phrase outline than from the several outlines that would be written if the phrase were not used. Furthermore, a phrase outline can be out of proportion and still be easily recognized; whereas, if each word in the phrase were written separately and one or more of those outlines were out of proportion, considerable difficulty might be encountered in catching the thought.

On page ix of this book is a review of each phrasing principle you have learned. Each phrasing principle will be included in the dictation your teacher gives you in this lesson.

145A—Vocabulary Preview

[shorthand notation]

facilitate, preparation, Employee's, Weekly, Record, Payroll, converts, chart, useful, starting, quitting, reports, column, lunch

[shorthand notation]

account, daily, expenditures, classifications, accuracy, duplicate, retain, handwritten, signature, superior, attach, receipted, transportation, stubs, assembled, Cashier, unused, stamped, exceeded, originally, promptly

145B—Transcribing from Office-Style Dictation

Directions. Your teacher will dictate two memorandums to you in office-style dictation. Use the memorandum style shown on page 222.

145C—Supplementary Transcription

Directions. Use modified block style with indented paragraphs and centered date; use mixed punctuation style.

March 10, 19—

Mr. Harold Bryson
81 McDonald Drive
Houston, Texas   77002

[shorthand notation]

Crandall L. Blough
President

Practice Material for Building Fluency

NOTE: The proper pronunciation of *accessories* is ak-ses' o-ries.

[Shorthand outlines with word counts in two columns: 3, 7, 11, 17, 23, 31, 41, 47, 54, 63, 71, 79 on the left; 20, 99, 106, 114, 122, 130, 137, 149, 162, 171, 179, 186, 189, 202 on the right]

Leroy A. Roane 186
Sales Manager 189
202

Preview of New Dictation Material

(1) *[shorthand]*

one of the sportsmen, enthusiastic, during the past year, we have been able, demonstrated, effectively, we may be able, excited, Monday morning, if you want

(2) *[shorthand]*

in which you request, descriptions, qualifications, graduates, unable, incentive, to compensate

(3) *[shorthand]*

King, thorough, investigate, we do not find, duplicate, for your convenience

(4) *[shorthand]*

Hopkins, research, Chamber of Commerce, further, if you would like

(5) *[shorthand]*

we found, extended, deposit, will you please, send us, to comply, interruption, discontinued

In some cases all that is necessary prior to an activity is authorization to spend an approximate amount of money for a stated purpose. The individual uses his personal funds and then afterward submits a request for reimbursement.

In either situation, detailed records are kept of expense items. The secretary must obtain from her employer supporting documents such as hotel bills, ticket stubs, receipts, etc.

Income Tax Records. The preparation of the employer's business or personal state and/or Federal income tax returns will probably not be one of the responsibilities of the secretary. She may, however, have certain related duties that will facilitate the preparation of the returns by him or by his accountant. These duties may include:

1. Maintaining a calendar of due dates for reports and payment of taxes and preparing necessary reminders for her employer of these due dates sufficiently in advance to insure the meeting of deadlines.

2. Obtaining required forms for various tax reports. Extra copies are needed for rough drafts.

3. Maintaining a record of income and expenditures. This duty may involve making daily or weekly entries in a general record book or in a classified record book, depending on the number of items handled. The following list of possible items reveals the fact that such a responsibility might be quite time consuming:

Income Items	Expense Items
Wages or salaries	Dues
Rents	Casualty losses
Dividends	Depreciation
Royalties	Maintenance and repair
Interest	Wages or salaries
Tax refunds	Professional assistance
Insurance benefits	Contributions
Profit from business	Alimony
Bonuses	Certain taxes (such as
Annuities	gasoline, sales, etc.)
Prizes	Medical expenses
Awards	Business travel expenses
Honorariums	Losses from business

4. Filing *supporting papers.* These papers support the claims made on tax returns. They may be memos, receipts, canceled checks, income statements, etc.

5. Occasionally, but not usually, preparing rough drafts of tax returns.

6. Typing the final report form after the employer has prepared or approved the rough draft. All figures must be double-checked for accuracy. Before sealing the envelope containing the return,

Income Tax Record Book

the secretary should be sure all required signatures have been affixed and that all materials that should accompany the return have been attached.

7. Mailing the return. If the secretary is asked to see that the return is mailed, she should do the mailing personally—not release it to someone else for mailing. Obtaining a certificate of mailing is a wise precaution to take. The certificate with its canceled stamp should be filed with the file copy of the return along with a notation of the exact time and place of the mailing.

Cautions. Keep *all* papers. Failure to have proof of an exact amount of income or receipt for an expenditure can be costly.

Preserve all papers in a safe place, preferably in a locked, fireproof file or compartment.

Maintain records up to date so that no important detail will be forgotten.

Place in the tax files only material pertinent to tax records. Organize the materials within the file; keep each year's records and papers separate from those of other years.

Regard all tax information as confidential.

Questions for Discussion

1. What is the purpose of a petty cash fund? What precautions should be observed in handling it?

2. Why does a company require detailed reports of travel and/or entertainment expenditures?

3. Since a secretary probably will not be responsible for the actual preparation of the income tax return, why should she be informed about taxable income or deductible expenses?

Interoffice Memorandums
and Extraoffice Letters

Lesson **6** ⬡⬡⬡⬡⬡⬡⬡⬡⬡⬡⬡⬡⬡⬡⬡⬡⬡⬡⬡⬡

6A—Interoffice Memorandums

Correspondence within a firm is usually in the form of memorandums. These messages within the organization are called by various names, depending somewhat upon the purposes, such as "interior letters," "interoffice memorandums," "interdepartmental correspondence," "interorganizational correspondence," "interbranch correspondence," and "intracompany correspondence." We shall use the term "interoffice memorandums" to refer to all memos. In some types of businesses, more memorandums are written than outgoing (extraoffice) letters; for instance, in a manufacturing firm this might be the case.

The stationery used for memorandums is different from that used for extraoffice letters. The memorandum stationery is designed to save time in typing and handling. A special heading is usually used that includes such words as "To," "From," "Date," and "Subject," as shown in the illustration on page 14. If few memorandums are typed, the company may have its secretaries use plain paper rather than printed memorandum stationery. File copies are made of memorandums just as they are for letters.

There is a great deal of variation in the printed headings of memorandum stationery, as shown in the illustration on page 14.

The size of stationery most commonly used for memorandums is 8½ by 11 inches; however, many firms use other sizes, such as 8½ by 5½ and 8½ by 7¼. Some firms use more than one size of memo stationery. The quality of paper used for memorandums is usually not so good as that used for extraoffice letters since the correspondence remains within the firm. Sometimes colored paper rather than white is used for memos.

As a rule, no complimentary close appears on a memorandum; and the dictator's name is usually given in the "From" line and not repeated at the close of the memo. Some dictator's initial their memos; others do not.

Reference initials, enclosure notations, and carbon-copy notations are used just as they are on outgoing letters. Most commonly these notations are typed in the same position as on outgoing letters; however, they are sometimes placed elsewhere. Some firms, for instance, have the carbon-copy notation in the printed heading of the memorandum, as shown in the illustration on page 14.

While it is true that memos are usually typed on less expensive paper than extraoffice letters, you should remember that the memos you type are read by others in the firm. The within-the-company reputation of your office, of yourself as a secretary, and of your employer may depend largely upon the kind of correspondence you send to other members of the company. The respect of others in your firm is quite as essential to your success and happiness as that of outsiders.

Questions for Discussion

1. Look carefully at the illustration of various kinds of headings used for memorandum stationery. What lines do you think it would be advisable for every firm to have included in its heading, regardless of the type of business?
2. Why might it not be necessary for the dictator to sign his name or have it typed at the close of the memorandum?
3. Why do firms use memorandum stationery for correspondence within the offices of the firm instead of the regular company letterhead stationery?

Office Practice Problem

Study the printed memo headings given in the illustration. Count the number of carriage movements and tabulations the typist would have to make in using each style. Which style do you think is the most efficient?

PETTY CASH RECORD			
Date	Explanation	Received	Paid
19-- Mar. 3	Check #5	10 -	
3	Stamps		4 70
9	Telegram		1 10
16	Ink		1 50
29	Contribution for flowers for Mr. K.		75
31	Totals	10 -	8 05
31	Balance		1 95
		10 -	10 -
31	Balance	1 95	
31	Check #18	8 05	

Petty Cash Record

PETTY CASH REPORT
March 1 to 31, 19--

Balance on hand, March 1		$10.00
Expenditures:		
Stamps	$4.70	
Telegram	1.10	
Ink	1.50	
Flowers	.75	
Total expenditures		8.05
Balance on hand, March 31		$ 1.95

Petty Cash Report

Procedure for Replenishing the Fund. An amount approved by the proper administrative official is placed in the petty cash fund to "open" it. As expenditures are made from the funds, a record is kept of each payment. When the balance reaches a certain point, a request for additional funds to raise the amount on hand to the original sum is made out and sent, with proper signatures, to the office that handles this type of transaction. That office will examine the records, receipts, etc., approve them, and issue a check or currency to replenish the fund.

Caution. Never borrow from the petty cash fund for personal use, and do not permit others to do so. If an emergency makes borrowing a necessity, write a statement to put in the container giving the date, amount borrowed, and purpose. Have the person borrowing the amount sign the statement.

Expense Reports. Employees who travel or who must entertain persons as guests of the firm have to obtain money to pay these expenses. Payment may be made in advance in some cases; and, in others, reimbursement may be made after the trip or entertainment has been completed. The secretary usually has the responsibility of preparing the necessary forms for her employer. These

matters are handled in various ways by firms; therefore, only general suggestions can be given.

If a request is made for payment in advance, the requisition asks for such information as name of individual making request, purpose of expenditure, date needed, estimated amount needed, account number to which cost is to be charged, and signature of person authorized to approve items charged to that account. This request is processed by the appropriate offices and the necessary funds issued. When the trip or entertainment has been completed, a report of actual expenses incurred is prepared. If they exceed the estimate, a request for reimbursement is made; if they were less than anticipated, the balance is refunded by the em-

Requisition for Advance

Expense Report for Trip

Executive Offices		**STANDARD PUMPS, INCORPORATED**		*Interoffice Correspondence*
		476 Pacific Avenue ● Portland, Oregon 97210 ● 361-6311		

To:
From:
Date:

Subject:

Stimson Products Corporation

INTEROFFICE CORRESPONDENCE

490 MAIN BOULEVARD ● DENVER, COLORADO 80202 ● 623-6107

To: From: Date:

Subject: File:

Davis Equipment Company

INTEROFFICE COMMUNICATION

TO: SUBJECT:

FROM: COPIES TO:

DATE:

Printed Headings on Memorandum Stationery

6B—Building Speed in Taking Dictation

Brief-Form Practice

Directions. The following paragraph contains 45 brief forms and brief-form derivatives. If you can read it in 30 seconds, your reading rate will be 158 words a minute.

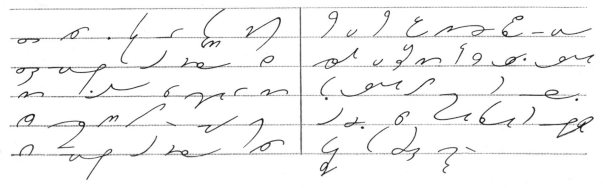

If payment is in currency and coin, the payroll clerk should determine the smallest number of currency and coin needed for each employee's pay; these items are then totaled to ascertain what denominations and their quantity need to be obtained from the bank. The money for each employee should be placed in a sealed envelope and on the outside a notation made of the employee's name, gross pay, deductions, and net pay.

A currency breakdown sheet facilitates these computations. If payment is by check, then the voucher half of the check shows gross pay, deductions, and net pay. The check should be placed in an envelope and sealed.

Salaries and wages are confidential information, and you should reveal nothing about them to others.

Preparation of Reports for State and Federal Governments. A W-2 Form must be prepared for each employee during January or upon termination of employment. One copy is retained by the company; one is sent to the Director of Internal Revenue; and two are given or sent to the employee, one to be retained and the other to be filed with the income tax return with the Director of Internal Revenue. Individual earnings records are kept for each employee to facilitate the completion of government reports.

Depending on the amount of FICA taxes withheld, payments are made at stated intervals by the firm to the authorized bank. An Employer's Quarterly Federal Tax Return is filed on or before April 30, July 31, October 31, and January 31.

W-2 Form

There is also an Annual Federal Tax Return of Employers to be filed, reporting payment of Federal unemployment taxes. Also, a summary form, W-3, is filed showing total income taxes withheld.

Cautions. Double-check all payroll reports. Keep all payroll records for at least four years; some firms keep them indefinitely.

If a woman marries, she should fill in and send to the Social Security Administration Form OAAN-7003 so that her name will be correct on her records. If a person wishes to find out how much has been contributed to his account, he can do so by filling in and sending to the Administration Form OAR-7004; a statement of earnings will be sent to him.

Questions for Discussion

1. What is the difference between a W-2 Form and a W-4 Form?
2. Discuss the two methods of paying employees their salaries or wages.
3. How is a social security number obtained?

Lesson **144** ○ ○ ○ ○ ○ ○ ○ ○ ○ ○ ○ ○ ○ ○ ○ ○ ○ ○ ○

The Petty Cash Fund, Expense Reports, and Income Tax Records

Petty Cash Fund. The purpose of a petty cash fund is to have money easily available for small purchases such as stamps, contributions for flowers, and miscellaneous office supplies. Such a fund saves clerical time and effort because it eliminates the paper work involved in making out requisitions, securing approvals, etc., for each item. The size of the fund depends upon what items may be purchased through it, how frequently such items are needed, and the frequency with which the fund may be replenished. The usual operating period is two weeks or a month. The amount may be some such sum as $10 or $25.

The money must be kept in a safe place under lock and key. The container should be unlocked only to handle a specific transaction and should be relocked immediately afterward.

Complete and accurate records must be kept of the payments made and replenishment of the fund. A receipt should be made for each expenditure, no matter how small. A petty cash record should be maintained, and each transaction should be recorded at the time it is made. Stamps, as well as money, are often kept in the petty cash container because they need to be protected from unauthorized use.

Practice Material for Building Fluency

NOTE: *Substance* means essential points.

Preview of New Dictation Material

NOTE: *Reappraised* means reexamined.

employee, effecting, facilities, Jasper, solicited, rewarded, acceptance, submit, ideas, nontechnical, reviewed, assist, stations, along the, system, out of these, attended, nonsupervisory, personnel, recommendations, committees, advisory, maintenance, Cheyenne, San Francisco, consists, president, summarized, bulletin, award, photographs, suggesters, during the year, reappraised, might be made, won't, let us have

A new employee may be hired by the hour, the week, or the month. If he is paid by the hour, his compensation is usually referred to as *wages*. If he is paid by the week or month, his compensation is usually referred to as his *salary*. In either case, a record is customarily kept of the hours actually worked. This record is kept either by having an employee *punch* a time clock or by having his hours recorded in a register.

The employee who is paid a salary may or may not be required to *punch* a time clock; however, records should be kept of hours worked because of their psychological effect in causing employees to be on time and to work the full number of hours for which they are paid. Such records may also be useful in proving conformity to Federal wages and hours legislation.

Prepayment Activities. The person responsible for handling the payroll prepares a payroll summary sheet for the pay period made up from individual employee's records. This task involves a complete statement of pertinent facts: hours worked, gross pay, deductions, and net pay. The number and size of deductions vary from employee to employee; they must be computed carefully. Deductions include such items as Federal withholding income tax, state withholding tax, hospital care insurance, group insurance premiums, U. S. Government bonds, medical care insurance, union dues, etc., as authorized by the employee.

For the hourly worker, the hours are totaled at the close of each pay period. His gross pay is determined by multiplying hours worked for the regular work week by the standard pay scale for that job. Overtime hours are usually paid for on the basis of time and a half; premium hours (holidays, Sundays, vacation periods, etc.) are usually paid for on the basis of double pay.

Preparation for Payment of Employee. Employees may be paid either in currency and coin or by check. The latter method is preferable because it is simpler, and there is less risk of mistakes or loss.

Time Card

Individual Earnings Record Form

Payroll Summary Record Form

Lesson **7** ⬡⬡⬡⬡⬡⬡⬡⬡⬡⬡⬡⬡⬡⬡⬡⬡⬡⬡⬡

7A—Sending Interoffice Memorandums

Interoffice memorandums may be sent to their addresses in several different ways. To offices within the same building, memos may be distributed by a messenger or mail clerk. Sometimes one copy of a memo is made and a routing slip attached, listing the names of the people who are to read it. The first person receiving the memo reads it, checks his name on the routing slip, and puts it in the outgoing mail to be picked up and distributed to the next person on the list. A routing slip is illustrated below.

Routing Slip

Sometimes a copy of the memo is made for each person concerned. When this procedure is followed, the list of names may be typed on the memo and a different name checked on each copy to guide the messenger in distributing the copies. See the illustration below.

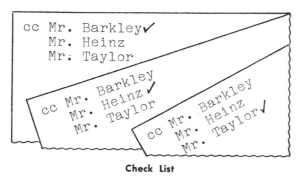

Check List

Quite frequently memos are placed in interoffice envelopes for distribution. Different sizes of envelopes are available. Some require folding the memo; others are large enough to permit leaving

the memo unfolded. Usually the interoffice envelope has ruled lines on it. The name of the person who is to receive the memo is written on the first unused line. The envelope is not sealed unless the matter in the memo is confidential. When the addressee receives the envelope, he draws a line through his name and saves the envelope to be used in sending a memo to someone else. Holes are sometimes spaced out down the middle of the envelope so that a person can detect quickly whether anything has been overlooked in emptying the envelope. Some styles of interoffice envelopes are shown below.

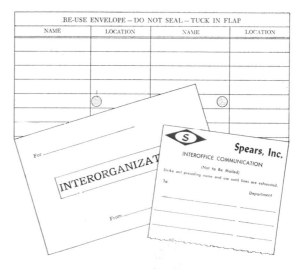

Interoffice Envelopes

If memos are distributed among offices in different buildings in the city, they may still be carried by a messenger or mail clerk just the same as for offices within a single building. When memos are sent to different buildings, however, the memos are usually placed in interoffice envelopes for protection. Sometimes interoffice memorandums (really inter*branch* or inter*divisional*) are sent between offices in different cities. In this situation, except for rush mailing, the memorandums in one branch that are being written to another branch are usually collected by the Mailing Department and put together in one envelope for dispatch once a day.

Determine the total amount of your outstanding checks. Subtract this total from the balance shown on the bank statement (plus late deposit, if any). The resulting figure should be the same as that shown by your checkbook. If it is not, check your additions and subtractions on your check stubs.

When you have made a satisfactory reconciliation, initial the statement and file it with the bank statement and canceled checks. Your employer may wish to see these before you file them.

Questions for Discussion

1. What are the distinguishing characteristics of the three types of endorsements?

2. What procedure should you follow in preparing funds for deposit?

3. Explain in detail how you would reconcile a bank statement.

```
BANK STATEMENT BALANCE
   (APRIL 30, 19--) . . . . . . . . . . $1,413.17

Less checks outstanding:
   No. 41 . . . . . . . . . $19.25
   No. 52 . . . . . . . . .  26.80
   No. 53 . . . . . . . . .  49.95          96.00

AVAILABLE BANK FUNDS . . . . . . . . . $1,317.17


CHECKBOOK BALANCE
   (APRIL 30, 19--) . . . . . . . . . . $1,336.78

Less:
   Service charge . . . . . $ 1.21
   Returned check . . . . .  18.40          19.61

CORRECT CHECKBOOK BALANCE . . . . . . $1,317.17
```

Bank Statement Reconciliation

Lesson 143 ⬡○⬡○⬡○⬡○⬡○⬡○⬡○⬡○⬡○⬡○⬡○⬡○

Handling Payroll Records

Setting Up Records for a New Employee. When a new employee reports for work, he must fill in immediately a W-4 Form, Employee's Withholding Exemption Certificate, which gives the employer the number of exemptions that are to be taken into consideration in maintaining the employee's payroll record. This form must be filed for safekeeping.

W-4 Form

Each employee must give his Social Security number. If the employee has not worked before and does not have a number, he must fill in an SS-5, Application for Social Security Account Number, to be sent to the Social Security Administration. The Administration will assign a number to the employee and send him a card consisting of two parts, both of which list his social security number. The employee separates the two parts,

keeping the upper part in his billfold and the other part where he can get it if he loses the upper part. When the employee receives his social security number, he gives the number to the person in charge of payroll, so that proper deductions may be made for FICA (Federal Insurance Contribution Act) taxes when his wages or salary is computed.

According to law, deductions for FICA are made from the employee's earnings each pay period. These deducted amounts are forwarded to the Federal Government along with an equal sum paid by the employer.

Social Security Card

Questions for Discussion

1. How may a memorandum be sent to several people within a building without making a copy for each person?
2. What is a disadvantage of using a routing slip or a check list rather than having a copy for each person who is to read the memo?
3. How do interoffice envelopes differ from envelopes used for extraoffice letters?

Office Practice Problems

1. Prepare a routing slip to be attached to a memo going to four members of your faculty. The order of names should be one that will provide for the most efficient movement from person to person.
2. Bring to class samples of interoffice stationery and/or envelopes. Be prepared to point out the different features of each.

7B—Building Speed in Taking Dictation

Phrase Builder

Directions. There are 10 phrases in the following paragraph. Write 3 times any word or phrase that you cannot write automatically, so that you can take the material rapidly from dictation.

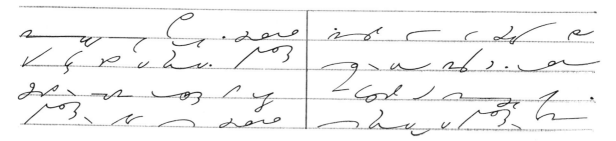

Practice Material for Building Fluency

(1)

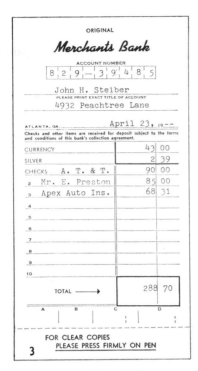

Deposit Slip

ORIGINAL

Merchants Bank

ACCOUNT NUMBER

8 2 9 — 3 9 4 8 5

John H. Steiber

PLEASE PRINT EXACT TITLE OF ACCOUNT

4932 Peachtree Lane

ATLANTA, GA. _____ April 23, 19--

Checks and other items are received for deposit subject to the terms and conditions of this bank's collection agreement.

CURRENCY	43	00
SILVER	2	39
CHECKS A. T. & T.	90	00
2 Mr. E. Preston	85	00
3 Apex Auto Ins.	68	31
4		
5		
6		
7		
8		
9		
10		
TOTAL ———→	288	70

A   B   C   D

FOR CLEAR COPIES

3 PLEASE PRESS FIRMLY ON PEN

Bank Statement

Statement of Account with   *Merchants Bank*

ATLANTA, GEORGIA 30304

829-39485

John H. Steiber
4932 Peachtree Lane
Atlanta, Georgia 30303

REPORT PROMPTLY ANY
CHANGE IN YOUR ADDRESS

CHECKS	CHECKS	DEPOSITS	NO. OF CHECKS	DATE	BALANCE
		BALANCE FORWARD →		Apr 1'--	1,300.00+
125.00-	7.16-		2	Apr 6'--	1,167.84*
21.65-	17.87-		4	Apr 9'--	1,128.32*
		184.75+		Apr12'--	1,313.07*
46.20-	18.40RT		5	Apr13'--	1,248.47*
		100.00+		Apr19'--	1,348.47*
		288.70+	7	Apr23'--	1,528.52*
75.00-	33.65-		9	Apr27'--	1,456.42*
66.80-	5.30-		11	Apr28'--	1,414.38*
8.85-	33.19-			Apr30'--	1,413.17*
	1.21SC				

CC—CERTIFIED CHECK   EC—ERROR CORRECTED   OD—OVERDRAWN
CM—CREDIT MEMO   LS—LIST OF CHECKS   RT—RETURNED ITEM
DM—DEBIT MEMO   NC—CHECK NOT COUNTED   SC—SERVICE CHARGE

THE LAST AMOUNT
IN THIS COLUMN
IS YOUR BALANCE

The reconcilement of this statement with your records is essential. Any error or exception should be reported immediately.

Making the Deposit. Place the funds to be deposited in a special envelope, purse, or bag, along with the two copies of the deposit slip (also the passbook if you have one). *Never* place the funds in your own personal purse with your money. Go directly to the bank; do not risk loss by making other stops en route.

Present your funds and copies of the deposit slip to the bank teller. He will sign or initial the duplicate copy. Retain it for your records.

Sometimes the teller gives you a receipt made on a teller's machine. If you have a passbook, he will enter the date and amount of the deposit in it and return the book to you.

If you deposit funds by mail, your bank will supply you with special deposit slips and envelopes. Never use a blank endorsement when banking by mail and do not enclose the passbook. Upon receipt of your deposit, the bank will detach the receipt stub from the deposit slip and return it to you.

Reconciling the Bank Statement. When you receive the bank statement showing deposits and withdrawals for the preceding month, *reconcile* the statement at once with your checkbook records. Any discrepancies must be reported to the bank within a specified number of days. A reconciliation of a bank statement appears on page 359.

Step 1. Compare the withdrawal items on the bank statement with the checks that were returned with it.

Step 2. Arrange the canceled checks according to check number; compare the amount of each one with that shown on its stub in your checkbook. If the amounts agree, place a check mark on the stub.

Step 3. Make a list of the checks that have not been returned; these are called *outstanding* checks. State the number of the check and the amount.

Step 4. In your checkbook, enter the amount of the service charge after making sure it is correct. Banks usually process a certain number of checks for a set minimum fee and then charge an additional fee for each transaction beyond that minimum. The bank gives a *credit* for maintaining a certain minimum balance; the charges for processing checks and deposits are deducted from the amount of this *credit*, and the remainder becomes your *service charge.*

Step 5. Compare the deposits shown on the statement with the deposits recorded in your checkbook.

Step 6. Prepare a reconciliation statement on which you list the bank statement balance. Add to it any late deposit that has not been entered on the statement.

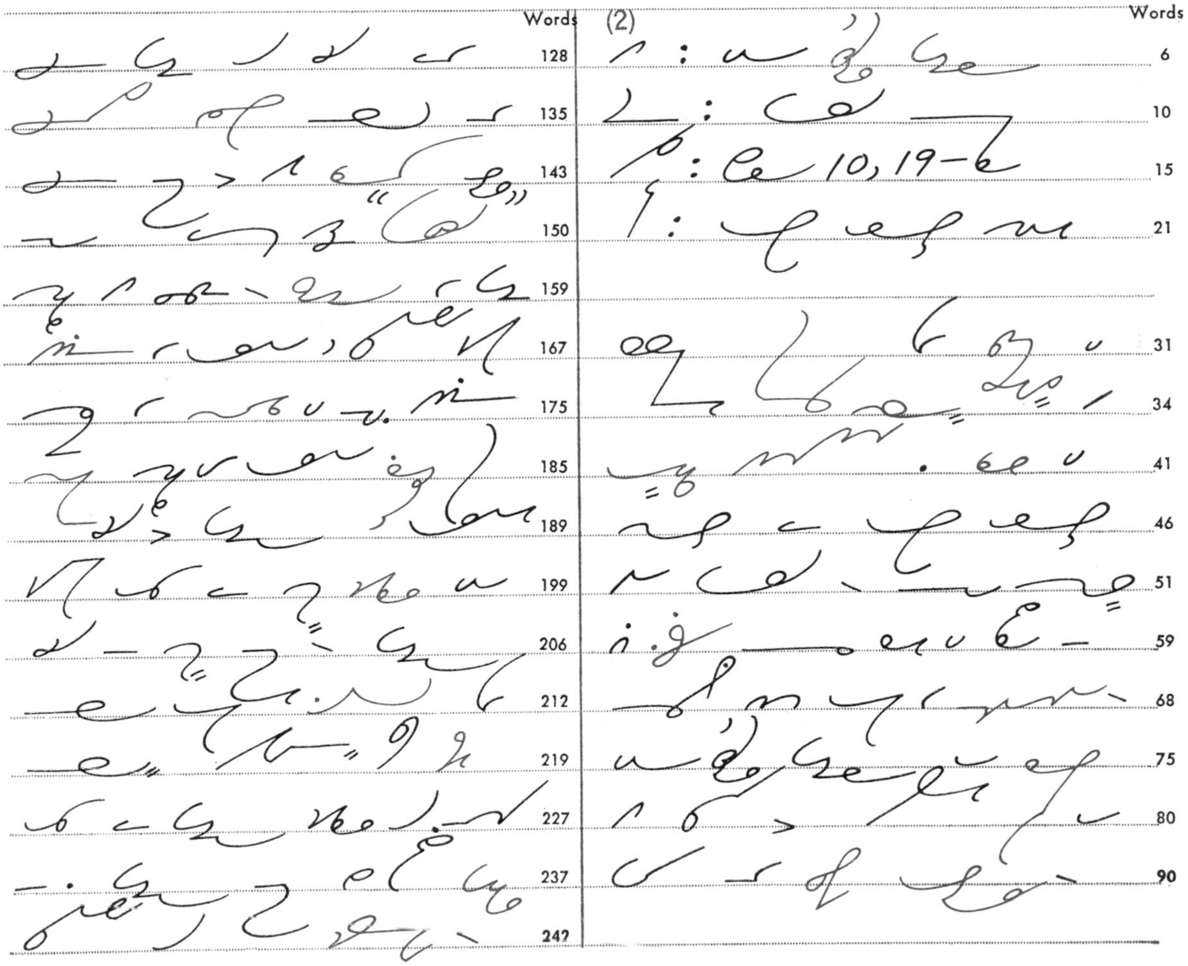

Words (column headings)

	Words
	128
	135
	143
	150
	159
	167
	175
	185
	189
	199
	206
	212
	219
	227
	237
	242

(2)

	Words
	6
	10
10, 19-6	15
	21
	31
	34
	41
	46
	51
	59
	68
	75
	80
	90

Preview of New Dictation Material

NOTE: *Demolition workers* are people who pull down (raze) damaged or old buildings.

(1)

Paterson, Sioux City, he was, you want, standard, 4 feet, you would like, to ship

(2)

civil, defense, Home Office, volunteers, activities, qualified, wardens, men and women, nurses, preferred, demolition, preferably, Hampton, within the, next few days, confer, to find, forward

Making Deposits; Reconciling Bank Statements

Making Deposits. Deposits may be made in person, by mail, by messenger, or by night depository. Regardless of the method, certain procedures should be followed in order to protect the funds and to facilitate the act of depositing.

Preparing Funds for Deposit. Coins, bills, checks, etc., should be prepared for deposit.

Step 1. Coins should be put in wrappers furnished by the bank. These wrappers hold the following amounts:

DENOMI-NATION	NUMBER OF COINS IN THE ROLL	TOTAL VALUE OF COINS IN ROLL
Pennies	50	$ .50
Nickels	40	2.00
Dimes	50	5.00
Quarters	40	10.00
Half Dollars	20	10.00

Write on each roll the amount and the depositor's name.

Step 2. Group together bills of the same denomination and arrange right side up with top edge at top. Large numbers of bills should be fastened together with a paper band (supplied by the bank) on which you write the amount and the depositor's name. Currency is wrapped in these quantities:

DENOMINATION	NUMBER OF BILLS	TOTAL VALUE OF BILLS
$ 1	50 or 100	$50 or $100
5	50	$ 250
10	50	500
20	25	500
50	20	1,000
100	25	2,500

Step 3. Arrange checks so that they are all right side up and with the top edge at the top. Endorse each one properly. There are three types of endorsement: *blank, restrictive,* and *full.* A *blank* endorsement gives the name of the payee only; it is the least desirable because, if the check is lost after endorsement, anyone can cash it. Use this type only when you are in the bank.

A *restrictive* endorsement includes a statement of the use to be made of the check and the signature of the endorser. This type is safer than the blank type. A firm may use a rubber stamp for this type on a check to be deposited; no manual endorsement is necessary.

A *full* endorsement includes the name of the person or firm to whom the check is to be transferred and the endorser's signature.

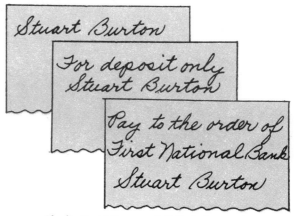

Blank, Restrictive, and Full Endorsements

Cautions. Before endorsing, examine each check to be sure the date is correctly and completely given, that the amount stated in figures agrees with the written amount, and that the check is signed.

If the name of the payee has been written incorrectly, write the name in that form in the endorsement and then immediately below it write the name as it should have appeared.

If a check bears a notation "Payment in full," be sure the check does cover the amount due before endorsing it.

Write an endorsement on the back of the check at the left end; always use ink.

Preparing the Deposit Slip. Obtain a pad of deposit slips from the bank. You may type or write in longhand on the slip; always make a carbon copy.

Fill in the account number and/or name of your employer, the address, and the date. List the total amount of currency and of silver on the lines provided. Checks must be itemized. Each check may be identified by (1) city and state of bank on which the check has been written, (2) by its ABA transit number, (3) by person or firm from which check was received, or (4) by name of bank if it is a local one. The ABA number (assigned by the American Bankers Association) helps the bank sort its checks for clearinghouse operations. The top number indicates city or state and specific bank; the lower number indicates the Federal Reserve District.

Traveler's checks, drafts, and money orders are itemized in a fashion similar to checks.

8A—Extraoffice Letters

"Extraoffice" letters, as contrasted with "inter-office" letters, are sent to persons outside the firm. These letters are ones that will be delivered by the United States Postal Service. They are typed on the printed letterheads of the firm.

Letterhead papers differ in size, weight, quality, finish, color, and grain. The most commonly used size of letterhead is 8½ by 11 inches, although many other sizes are used; and many firms use more than one size. Other commonly used sizes are 7¼ by 10½, 8½ by 7¼, 8 by 10½, and 8½ by 5½.

Most letterhead stationery is white, although some firms, such as novelty companies and flower shops, may use a colored paper.

Weights of paper commonly used for letterhead stationery are 16-pound, 20-pound, and 24-pound, with 20-pound being the most commonly used. "Twenty-pound" paper means that a manufacturer's ream of 500 17- by 22-inch sheets weighs 20 pounds. This paper cut in any size is referred to as 20-pound paper, and a package of it would be labeled "Substance 20" or "Sub. 20."

All paper has a right and a wrong side. The right side, the "writing" side, is called "felt"; and the wrong side is called "wire." A good quality stationery has a watermark on it that you can see by holding the sheet of paper toward the light. The side on which you can read the watermark is the right side for typing.

Paper made from wood pulp is called "sulphite"; paper made from cotton fibre is called "rag." The better the quality of paper the greater the rag content. Letterhead stationery is usually at least 25 percent rag.

The printed letterheads used by various firms differ considerably in depth. Some firms use a letterhead design only 1 inch in depth; other firms may use a design as deep as 3¾ inches. The depth of the design becomes a matter of importance to the secretary in transcribing letters because it affects the length of letter she can type on a sheet of letterhead stationery.

Printed Letterheads of Various Depths

Some business firms have guide marks printed on their stationery to indicate placement of various parts of the letter or where the letter is to be folded. Sometimes these guide marks are large enough to be plainly visible after the letter is typed; others are small and so lightly printed that they are not noticeable after the letter has been typed. Some samples of letterheads with guide marks printed on them are illustrated on page 20.

Step 5. Write in the amount in figures. The figures should be written clearly and should be placed close to the dollar sign. See the check on page 354. If the amount is less than $1, write it thus:

Pay to the order of *Junior Achievement* $ (52)
Only fifty-two cents ———————— ~~Dollars~~

Step 6. Write the amount in longhand or type it. Start at the extreme left on the "Dollars" line. Fill in any blank space on the line with a wavy or straight line drawn with your pen. If you are using a typewriter, make a line of hyphens.

Step 7. Sign the check if authorized to do so. If not, present it to your employer. If you have been authorized to sign checks, you will have filled in a signature card for the bank. Always use this exact form. If your employer has given you power of attorney to sign checks for him, you will have agreed upon some form such as

Betty Lane, Atty. or *Betty Lane*
Attorney

If the account name is not printed on the check, the signature may be something like this:

JOHN H. STEIBER

Betty Lane

Step 8. If your employer so directs, indicate the purpose of the check in the lower left-hand corner, such as "For dues 1966-68."

Cautions. Never erase anything on a check. If you make a mistake, write "Void" across the face of the check and on the check stub. Retain the voided check to place in order with canceled checks when reconciling your bank statement (if checks are prenumbered).

Never sign a check without filling in immediately the name of the payee. Avoid making a check payable to "Cash," since such a check can be cashed by anyone who has it in his possession.

Stopping Payment on a Check. Since the amount of a check is deducted from your employer's account when the check is returned to

SIGNATURE CARD

Date November 12, 19--   THE MERCHANTS BANK WILL
PLEASE RECOGNIZE IN PAYMENT OF FUNDS, OR THE TRANSACTION OF OTHER
BUSINESS ON THIS ACCOUNT, THE AUTHORIZED SIGNATURES BELOW.

Name of Firm
       CARLSON ADVERTISING, INC., Atlanta, Georgia 30304
By   *John H. Steiber*   Signature
By   *Stuart Burton*   Signature
By   *Betty Lane*   Signature
Phone 541-3758   1112 Brookhaven Drive   Address
Name to be filled in by Bank.   ADDRESS AS—

Signature Card

his bank, payment may be stopped if, for some reason after the check has been sent, your employer does not want it honored. To stop payment on a check, call the bank, give the name of the maker, the amount of the check, its date, and the name of the payee. Then send a letter at once confirming the call. If the check has not been received by the bank, payment will be refused when it arrives. This procedure is used if a check has been lost in the mail, incorrectly written, or an order for merchandise has been canceled.

Overdrafts. Overdrafts are embarrassing, and sometimes a charge is made for handling an overdraft. The secretary should double check entries on the check stubs to be sure that she has made no error in computations. If counter checks (blank checks made up in pad form without stubs, available on counters) are used, pertinent information should be entered immediately in the checkbook—date, amount, payee—or overdrafts are a possibility.

Checkwriting Machines; Ordering Checkbooks. If a considerable number of checks are written, your employer may have a checkwriting machine, which expedites the writing of checks and protects against alteration.

If the secretary writes checks, she must be sure to keep a supply of checkbooks on hand, being careful to order a new supply in plenty of time to avoid running out of blank checks.

Questions for Discussion

1. Compare the following: personal check, voucher check, certified check, cashier's check, bank draft, bank money order.

2. What precautions should be taken by the secretary in writing checks?

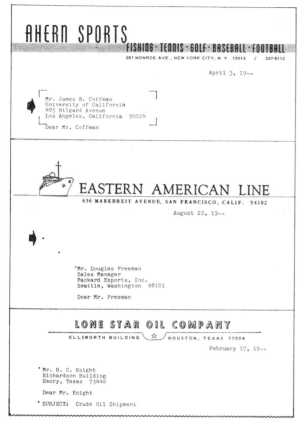
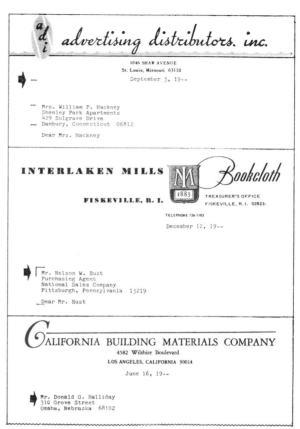

Printed Letterheads with Guide Marks

Questions for Discussion

1. In what ways do letterhead papers differ?
2. What is the most commonly used size of letterhead? What are some other commonly used sizes?
3. What is meant by "20-pound" paper?
4. Which side of paper is the "felt"? the "wire"?
5. What is the difference between "sulphite" paper and "rag" paper?

Office Practice Problem

Bring some letters to class that have been received in your home. Make a list of the following features of each letterhead:

a. The dimensions of the letterhead
b. The depth of the letterhead design
c. The kind of guide marks, if any
d. The watermark, if any
e. The weight of the paper, if you can tell what it is

8B—Building Speed in Taking Dictation

Potential Rate Builder

Directions. When your teacher dictates the sentence on page 21, write it in shorthand as many times as you can in 15 seconds. When your teacher calls "time," obtain your writing rate (words a minute) by multiplying the number of times you wrote the sentence by 13 (the number of words in the sentence) and then by 4. Follow the same procedure for similar exercises in later lessons.

Bank Draft

Bank Money Order

If your employer wants to send a check to a firm with which he has not established credit standing, he may send a *certified check*. To send a certified check, prepare a check as usual and present it to the cashier at the bank. He will check your employer's account to be sure that his funds are sufficient to "cover" the amount of the check. If they are, he stamps the face of the check "CERTIFIED" and signs his name under it. That amount of money is immediately deducted from your employer's account and put in a special account to await return of the check from the payee.

A *cashier's check* is another type of "guaranteed" check. To obtain one, give the bank a check or cash for the amount desired along with an application form you have filled in. The cashier then writes a check on the bank with your employer as payee. Your employer then endorses it and submits it in payment of his bill. Sometimes a small fee is charged for this service. A cashier's check can be purchased at a bank in which your employer does not have an account.

A *bank draft* is a form of check. It differs from the cashier's check in that a cashier's check is a check that a bank draws on its own funds; whereas, a bank draft is a check a bank draws on funds it has on deposit in another bank. You fill in a form similar to the one for a cashier's check and present it with the money to the bank. The bank writes a check on funds it has deposited in another bank. The bank draft is used by someone who does not have a checking account or who is sending money to another party who might not want to accept a personal check.

A *bank money order* is similar to a cashier's check. The amount of any one money order is limited. but any number of orders may be issued to the same person. Postal money orders and express money orders are similar.

Procedure for Writing Personal or Company Checks. Checks must be written carefully to prevent mistakes in your records or in those of the payee or the bank and to prevent checks from being cashed by unauthorized persons. Follow these steps:

Step 1. Fill in the stub. By so doing, you will always be able to account for every check and avoid overdrafts. Use ink or typewriter, never pencil.

Step 2. Number the check. Be sure it is identical with the number on its corresponding stub.

Step 3. Date the check. Use the current date, the same as on the stub. Avoid *postdating*, that is, using a date later than the current one. The payee may not note the date and cash the check before sufficient funds are on deposit to "cover" it.

Step 4. Write in the name of the payee. The payee is the person or company who is being paid. Be sure the name is spelled correctly; corroborate by correspondence, bills, or other reliable source. Do not use a courtesy title such as *Mr.* or *Dr.* before the name. If the payee is a married woman, use her legal name, that is, her given name, maiden name, and husband's surname. If her legal name is not known, then her married name preceded by *Mrs.* is used. If the payee is serving as an officer of a club or society, the check may be made payable to the organization or to the person followed by his title of office, as *James R. Udall, Treas.* In writing a firm's name, use the official name, not an abbreviation of it. For instance, do not write *Mac's* instead of *Mac's Service Station.*

Never sign a check until you fill in the name of the payee.

The rate you get indicates how fast you can write when you know the shorthand outlines for the words dictated so well that you can write them automatically. You can write shorthand just as fast as you can *think* it!

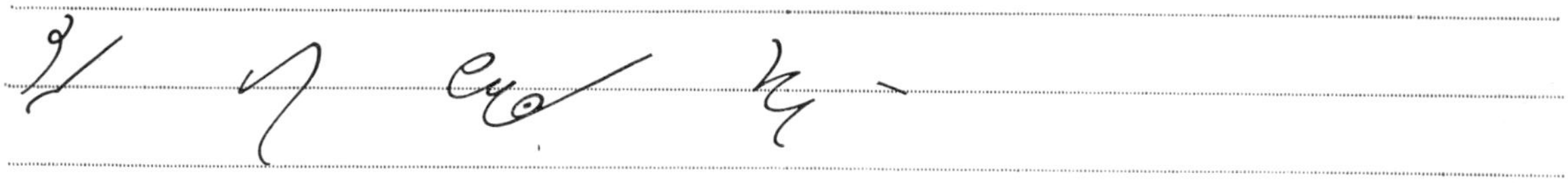

Practice Material for Building Fluency

NOTE: A *brochure* is a leaflet or pamphlet.

(1)

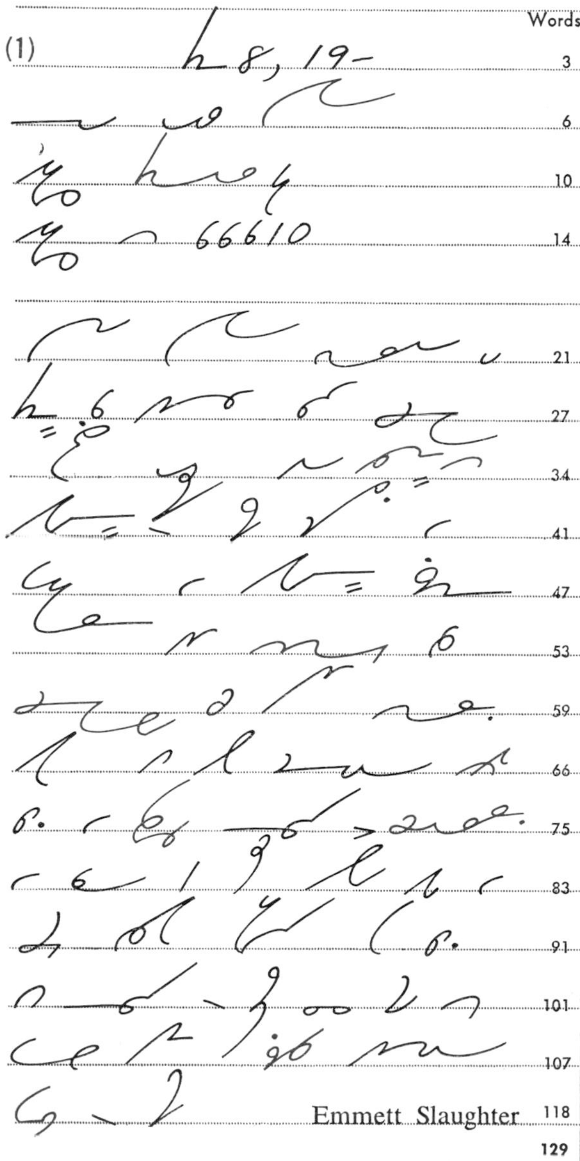
Words
3
6
10
14
21
27
34
41
47
53
59
66
75
83
91
101
107
118
129

Emmett Slaughter

(2)

Words
3
6
11
16
25
33
40
45
53
61
68
78
86
90
100
106
114
120
130
135
149

Julius McCarty

Financial Duties

Lesson **141** ⬡⬡⬡⬡⬡⬡⬡⬡⬡⬡⬡⬡⬡⬡⬡⬡⬡

Making Payments by Check or Draft

Verifying Bills. No bill should be paid by a secretary until it has been verified to make sure that it is correct. The computations should be proved on each bill. Prices and terms on an invoice should be substantiated. Toll charges on the telephone bill should be confirmed because sometimes a call is charged to the wrong telephone number. Credit-card statements should be examined carefully to be sure each item is valid. If no supporting papers are available for authenticating a bill, the secretary should ask her employer to authorize payment.

Types of Checks and Drafts. Checks or drafts are better for paying debts than currency and coins. They provide proof of payment, are less bulky to handle, and are safer. Of the several types of checks available, the most commonly used are personal, company, and voucher. *Personal checks* are usually bound together in a book of 25 for convenience in carrying. They may or may not be "personalized" by having the person's name printed on them. The stub provides space for keeping a detailed record of a check and for balancing the account after each payment or deposit.

Company checks are commonly bound together with two or three checks to the page. The stub portion is designed so that the balance of the account is brought up to date when all checks on a page have been used. These checkbooks are usually preprinted with the name of the company and also prenumbered; they should be kept in a safe place.

A *voucher check* is one that has written on the face of it or on a detachable stub such detailed information as number of invoice being paid, terms, date of order, etc. A salary check on which are listed deductions from gross pay such as withholding tax and social security is a voucher check. A secretary might not prepare voucher checks, but she might be called upon to deposit them. If she deposits them, she retains the "voucher" statement for her records.

Personal Check

Voucher Check

Certified Check

Cashier's Check

Preview of New Dictation Material

(1)

Christmas, Season, resolving, started, avoid, rush, unique, enables, down payment, of next year, you have made, fourth, in the event, one of our, Shopper, will be made, of all, equal, hope that this

(2)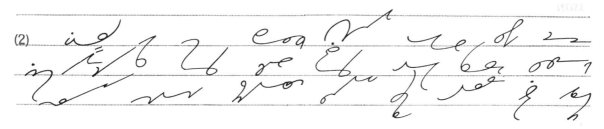

Holland, to be able, can be made, application, dividends, will you please, attached, someone, who can be, disinterested, witness, has been made, there will be, balance, accumulation, credited, contract, if you would like, withdraw, voucher, and return, it has been, to serve you

Lesson 9 ⬡⬡⬡⬡⬡⬡⬡⬡⬡⬡⬡⬡⬡⬡⬡⬡⬡⬡⬡

9A—Continuation Sheets and Envelopes

Continuation Sheets. "Continuation" sheets, used for second and succeeding pages of letters, should be of the same kind of paper stock as that used for the first page of letters. Most firms use plain paper for these sheets; some, however, have their name printed on stationery for second and succeeding pages, as shown in the illustration.

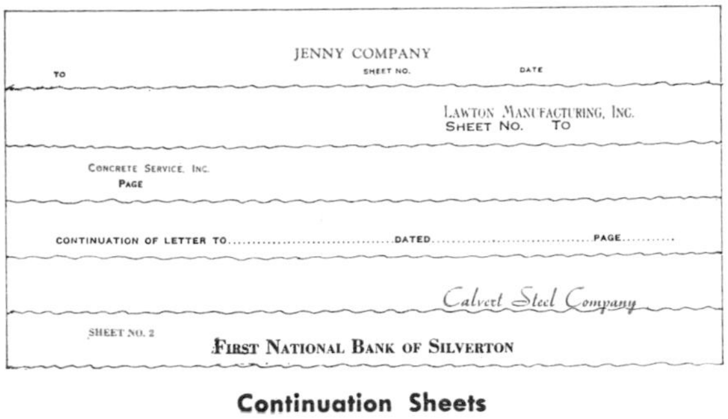

JENNY COMPANY

Continuation Sheets

Envelopes. The envelope should be of the same kind of paper as the letterhead. Different sizes of envelopes are used for the various sizes of letterhead stationery. The two most commonly used sizes are No. 6¾, which is 6½ by 3⅝ inches, and No. 10, which is 9½ by 4⅛ inches. The smaller size is usually used for letters of one page; the larger size, for letters of more than one page or for letters with enclosures. The secretary should be sure to use the correct size as given below.

LETTERHEADS		ENVELOPES	
SIZE	NAME	NUMBER	SIZE
8½ x 11	Business or Regular	⎰ 6¾ ⎱ 10	6½ x 3⅝ 9½ x 4⅛
7¼ x 10½	Executive or Professional	7¾	7½ x 3⅞
8½ x 5½	Half-Sheet	6¾	6½ x 3⅝
8 x 10½	Government	9	8⅞ x 3⅞

140A—Vocabulary Preview

awarded, exclusive, franchised, agency, office machines, Clayton, County, nationally, leadership, typewriters, calculators, showrooms, demonstrate, you might be, Bowen, serviceman, intensive, thoroughly, familiar, region, competent, furthermore, replace, temporarily, routines, interrupted, difficulties

140B—Transcribing from Office-Style Dictation

Directions. Your teacher will dictate a letter to you in office-style dictation. Use modified block style with blocked paragraphs and open punctuation. Center the date.

140C—Supplementary Transcription

Directions. Use the memorandum style illustrated on page 222.

To: Department Heads
From: B. K. Sellers, Head, Office
      Planning Staff
Date: May 15, 19—

Subject: Course in Operation of Electric
        Data-Processing Machines

Questions for Discussion

1. What are "continuation" sheets?
2. For what sizes of stationery is a No. 6¾ envelope used? No. 10? No. 7¾? No. 9?
3. What size of stationery is used by the Federal Government?

Office Practice Problem

Bring to class as many different sizes of letterheads and envelopes as you can. Measure the letterheads and envelopes; make a list of the sizes. If you can find continuation sheets with printed headings, bring them to class and list the items included on each continuation sheet.

9B—Building Speed in Taking Dictation

Proportion Drill

Directions. Writing shorthand outlines in correct proportion is essential to rapid and correct reading of notes. The following sentences contain several outlines that would be difficult to read if they were not written in correct proportion. As you write the sentences twice, strive for clear, correctly proportioned outlines. Follow the same procedure for similar exercises in later lessons.

Practice Material for Building Fluency

NOTE: *Attachés* is pronounced ăt-à-shāś and refers to persons who are members of the diplomatic staff of an ambassador or minister.

Keysort Data Punch

Key Punch

Tape-Punching Typewriter

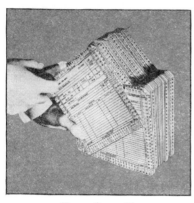

Keysorting with
Specially Designed Needle

Sorter

Tape-to-Card
Converter

Since information has been recorded in a uniform manner, the cards or tapes can be processed by various types of machines. For example, the cards can be sorted mechanically by a sorting machine. An electric brush "reads" the holes and the mechanism of the sorter distributes the cards into appropriate bins in the machine.

Punched cards or tapes can be "fed" into an accounting machine for the performance of a specified type of calculation. A control panel directs the machine to perform the calculation.

Other machines will make copies of punched cards so that more than one operation can be conducted simultaneously. Still other machines can be programmed to summarize the results of several computations. Information contained on the cards and tapes can be stored on drums for recall whenever needed.

The secretary will not have occasion to operate the machines used for an electric or electronic data-processing system; there will be operators employed for that purpose exclusively. She will, however, be handling reports containing material processed by such machines and needs to have some understanding of their functions.

Questions for Discussion

1. Explain the six operations involved in processing data. Illustrate.

2. Why do some firms not have electric or electronic computing machines?

Office Practice Problem

Survey firms in your community to determine which ones use electric data-processing or electronic computing machines and to determine how information on their source documents is prepared for automatic processing.

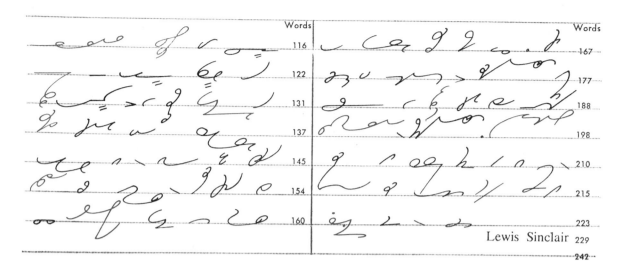

	Words		Words
	116		167
	122		177
	131		188
	137		198
	145		210
	154		215
	160		223
		Lewis Sinclair	229
			242

Preview of New Dictation Material

(1)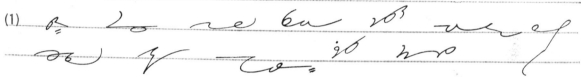

Young, foreman, cleared, payroll, status, no longer, eligible, canceled, at such a time, Employment, hesitate, suggest that

(2)

Rowland, Ward, Granite, Omaha Nebraska, 75 cents. points, in connection with this, washability, reusability, considerable, to do so, let us know

Lesson 10 ⬡⬡⬡⬡⬡⬡⬡⬡⬡⬡⬡⬡⬡⬡⬡⬡

10A—Characteristics of Good Business Correspondence

Each letter you write is a representative of your company. Your employer will be responsible for the actual content of the letter, but you will be responsible for its appearance. Sometimes you may be given the opportunity to write some letters yourself, and then you will be responsible for the content as well as the appearance. Here are some of the characteristics of good business correspondence:

Completeness. A letter should contain all the information necessary to give a complete response to the correspondence being answered. It is annoying to receive a letter that omits some of the information that had been requested; such a letter gives the impression that the company is careless and not dependable. Omission of information results in needless additional correspondence, which increases the cost of doing business. It has

names of all people who were dentists. On another occasion she might want to select cards having names of dentists who were also alumni of a college in the community, thus requiring sorting of the cards for that specific purpose.

A sales department might want to sort sales records according to geographical region or according to products sold.

Calculating. Some data must be processed to compute interest, discounts, taxes, shipping charges, etc. In Lesson 138, you learned about using desk models of adding and calculating machines for such purposes.

Summarizing. Sometimes a summary is needed of several types of calculations. For instance, payroll information may be summarized on an employee's monthly pay check to show gross earnings, deductions made for insurance and taxes, and net pay.

Recording. Recording manually is a time-consuming process; therefore, business uses mechanical devices when possible to prepare written records. Bookkeeping machines, for instance, are widely used to record decreases and increases in various types of accounts.

Communicating. Many devices are available for sending information from one point to another. Some use, for example, is made of telegraph and telephone for communicating more rapidly than by U. S. mail. When great quantities of information need to be sent, however, mechanical devices such as Teletype are employed because they may transmit information less expensively and more conveniently.

All six of these operations can be performed without any overall plan, but they will be performed more efficiently and at less cost if a uniform plan has been adopted by management.

Electric Data-Processing and Electronic Computing Systems. Large organizations having hundreds or thousands of items to process every day need a data-processing system that (a) minimizes rewriting of information that is to be handled by several different departments, (b) makes it possible for these departments to be performing their functions almost simultaneously, and (c) permits the storing of the information in such a way as to make possible the quick and easy recall of information needed for study or analysis by the executives in making decisions regarding the firm's activities.

For such large organizations, records must be kept in a uniform manner. Procedures must be standardized. When they are, electric data-processing machines or electronic computing machines can be employed to handle many of the activities of the firm.

For an electric data-processing system, information received on a source document is recorded on a card by punching holes in it according to a predetermined code. The punched card permits a great deal of information to be recorded in a minimum of space and makes it possible for the information on it to be processed automatically by machines. For an electronic data-processing system, information received is recorded on a tape according to a predetermined code. Special machines are used to prepare these cards or tapes. The key-punch machine is used for the punched card; the typewriter with a special attachment, for the punched tape.

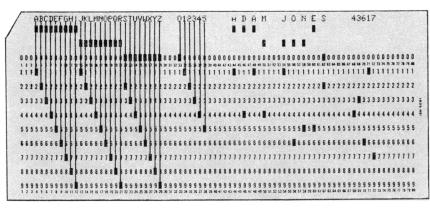

Punched Card

The foundation of the punched-card system lies in the representation of data by holes in a card. Each letter is identified by a punch in one of the three positions at the top of the card and a punch in one of the numbered columns. Each number is identified by a punch in its specific column only. As the cards are fed through machines, the position of the holes serves as a signal to electrically activate the equipment

—IBM Corporation

been estimated that a letter costs about $1.70 to write if you include the following elements in determining the cost: dictator's time, secretary's time to transcribe, mailing charges, filing costs, materials used, and fixed charges (such as lights, taxes, rent, etc.). You can see that unnecessary correspondence could become an important item in the expense of conducting a business.

Courteousness. A letter that says "No" should be as courteous as one that says "Yes." Courtesy implies respect for others; discourtesy implies a lack of respect. Choice of words is important in leaving the impression of courteousness. Do not write what you would not say in person.

Promptness. Every letter should be answered as promptly as possible. Some companies have a 48-hour rule—all letters received must be answered within 48 hours after they are received. If a complete answer cannot be given, a letter of explanation is written indicating when the necessary information will be sent. Promptness shows consideration for the other person.

Readability. A letter should be easy to read. If it is easy to read, it is clear and coherent; it is concise but not abrupt and cold.

Good choice of words and short sentences make a letter clear. Correct grammar is essential to easy reading. Misplaced modifiers, wrong number or tense in verbs, or incomplete sentences make comprehension of the message more difficult and may, in fact, so irritate the recipient that he will not react as desired. A conversational tone makes a letter more readable because, when you write as though you were talking to someone, you tend to use easily understood words and sentences. Stereotyped, or rubber-stamp, expressions hinder ease of reading. Here are some samples of expressions to avoid: *at an early date, enclosed herewith, enclosed please find, in the event that, thanking you in advance, beg to advise, esteemed favor, you claim, even date, permit us to state, at hand, we wish to advise.*

Friendliness. The opening and closing lines of a letter are perhaps the most important in the whole letter. The opening lines should catch the reader's interest and establish a friendly attitude;

the closing lines should reaffirm that friendliness. The opening lines establish a friendly, courteous tone, reveal the subject, and refer to the date of a preceding letter if there was one to enable the correspondent to refer easily to the file copy of that letter. The closing lines echo the friendly tone of the opening lines and summarize or pinpoint the main purpose of the letter—the action hoped for or the attitude being sought. Participial endings should be avoided (such as *trusting we will hear from you soon, looking forward to your next order,* or *assuring you in advance of our appreciation*) because they sound weak and stilted. Meaningless, stereotyped expressions seem to creep into opening and closing lines most easily; yet they are the most vital lines in the letter for creating a feeling of friendliness. The letter writer who can pretend that he is talking personally with the addressee is the one whose letters will have the YOU-attitude so important in establishing that feeling of friendliness.

Questions for Discussion

1. How can one be sure to answer a letter completely?
2. Why is courtesy so important?
3. What do you think of the 48-hour rule?
4. What would be better words to use than *at an early date? enclosed herewith? thanking you in advance? enclosed please find?*
5. How can the writer of a letter insure a tone of friendliness in it?

Office Practice Problems

Rewrite the following letters applying the principles you have studied in this lesson:

1. Gentlemen:

   As per your request I enclose herewith copy of the Daily Report under the above-mentioned policy. Trusting that same will be found in order, I am

   Yours very truly,

2. My dear Mr. Martin:

   Herewith I hand you a copy of the letter about which I phoned you at noon today. I am leaving you to reply to it as you see fit. Meanwhile I am recording in my records that the dinner will be held in your hotel on Thursday, May 30, at 6 p. m.

   Sincerely yours,

Business Machines as Aids (Concluded)

In Lessons 136-138, you learned that business forms and machines could expedite the handling of your duties. Forms and machines used by the secretary help her directly with her work; forms and machines used by other employees may be equally helpful to her, but indirectly. Whenever appropriate forms and machines are used in the firm, the time consumed in "paper work" is reduced. This paper work includes such activities as preparing orders, invoices, statements, memos; figuring costs, interest, discount, taxes; and preparing reports of profits, losses, and future plans. As long as business transactions have existed, there has been data processing; that is, handling business information in such a way as to complete a transaction satisfactorily.

Growth of Processing Data by Machine. Centuries ago data processing for business transactions was extremely simple and little "paper work" was necessary. The buyer and seller carried on their transactions orally; few, if any, records were kept. As industrial processes were mechanized and as transportation facilities improved, sellers had more goods to sell, could sell them to more buyers, and did not need to make personal contact with buyers. Buyers, in turn, were able to buy a greater variety of goods, to choose from the wares of more sellers, and to buy without personal contact. This situation increased the need for "paper work." This increase, naturally, spurred the development of machines to handle the routine aspects of operating a business so that the businessman could reduce his costs of operation and devote more time to improving or promoting his product or service.

Thus, data processing "by hand" began to be replaced by mechanical methods. Instead of writing orders manually, the businessman used the typewriter; instead of computing prices by pen or pencil, he used an adding machine; instead of having a clerk make handwritten copies of orders received, he utilized a duplicating machine. The mechanical devices for processing data increased tremendously the amount of work that could be handled in one day by one person.

As our society has become more industrialized, the need for more efficient means of processing data has continued. Hand-operated machines are gradually being replaced by electrically operated machines, and the machines' mechanisms have been improved so that more complex functions can be performed on the machines.

As a result of this expanding business activity and its faster pace, data-processing "systems" have been developed. A "system" is an overall plan for handling the information used by a firm in its activities, that is, for processing its data for maximum output at minimum cost. Probably no two business firms adopt identical systems, but they may have many procedures that can be handled similarly and by the same types of machines.

Operations Involved in Processing Business Data. The development of a "system" begins with a study of the "source documents" upon which the firm's operations are based. Examples of source documents are: a purchase order, an invoice, a statement, a credit memorandum, a deposit slip. Then a study is made of what is done with the information contained on that source document. The operations of what departments are involved? What items of information does each department need? How should the processing "flow" from one department to another?

Six basic operations are involved in processing data. The purpose (the end sought) of the processing determines which of the six operations will be conducted with any one set of data. The six operations are: classifying, sorting, calculating, summarizing, recording, and communicating.

Classifying. Listing petty cash expenditures under "Stamps," "Office Supplies," etc., is a simple example of classifying. Listing items for accounting purposes under such titles as "Accounts Receivable" and "Rent" is another example of classifying.

Sorting. The operation of "sorting" is the arranging of items to facilitate obtaining a specific type of information. For instance, a secretary might have a card file of 500 names of people. She might want to select cards on which were

Repetitive Phrase Builder

Directions. Phrasing not only increases the speed at which you can take dictation, but also makes transcription easier. This exercise will help you build speed in writing common phrases.

Write as far in the sentence as the first barricade; then go back to the beginning and write as far as the second; return to the first and write as far as the third; and then go back and write the entire sentence straight through. Follow the same procedure for similar exercises in later lessons.

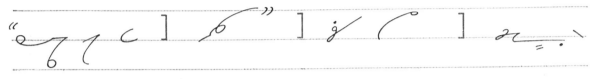

Practice Material for Building Fluency

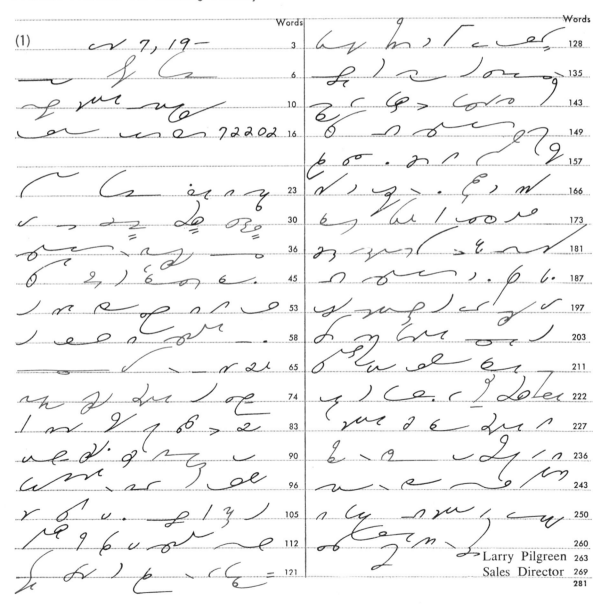

Larry Pilgreen 263
Sales Director 269
281

Power Utilized. Some machines are manually operated; that is, by hand; others are electrically operated. The main advantages of a manually operated machine are that it is less expensive and can be operated anywhere. The main advantages of the electrically operated machine are, of course, that it is speedier and less fatiguing for the operator. All the machines illustrated on page 348 could be either manual or electric.

Primary Use. Two major classifications of machines according to use are: *adding* and *calculating*. Accounting machines and data processing machines will be discussed in Lesson 139.

Adding machines are designed primarily to solve problems in addition; with many of them subtraction, multiplication, and even division can also be done but not easily. Calculating machines are designed primarily to perform multiplications and divisions, but they may also be used for addition and subtraction. They are better suited for general statistical work than adding machines. The advantage of the adding machine is that it is less expensive than the calculator and can be of the listing type, if desired. The advantage of the calculator is that it can handle more complicated computations than can the adding machine. Machines 1, 2, 3 are adding machines; machines 4, 5, 7 are calculators. Only No. 4 of the calculators can produce a printed record of items.

Common Secretarial Tasks Aided by Adding Machines and Calculators. Some of the secretarial duties for which a business machine may be used to advantage include:

1. Computing extensions and totals on purchase orders
2. Computing or verifying discounts on invoices
3. Computing payrolls—overtime, deductions, daily wages earned by employees on hourly pay
4. Preparing deposit slips for banking purposes
5. Totaling outstanding checks in reconciling checking account statements
6. Prorating expenses
7. Preparing travel expense reports
8. Verifying telephone and other bills
9. Checking totals in statistical reports
10. Preparing petty cash reports
11. Preparing purchase requisitions

Cautions in Using Business Machines. To make the most effective use of business machines, a secretary should observe the following precautions:

1. Keep handy the manual of directions that was provided with the machine. If you are a little uncertain about the correct procedure for a particular type of computation, consult the manual *before* attempting to make the computation. If you experiment, you may cause the machine to "jam" so that it cannot be used until a serviceman comes, resulting in delay of work as well as an expenditure of funds.

2. Be sure that the machine's "memory" is clear of all previous computations before beginning a new problem. Every machine has a bar or key that can be operated to test whether the last computation has been erased from the machine's memory; use it.

3. If the machine has a movable carriage, be sure that there are no obstructions for the carriage to hit as it moves. If the carriage is stopped before it can complete its normal movement, the machine's mechanism may be damaged and a serviceman will have to be called.

4. If you have a listing machine, be sure to keep rolls of tape and ribbons on hand sufficient to meet your needs. Having a machine idle because of carelessness in maintaining supplies is inexcusable.

5. Keep a record of each machine: when purchased, operational difficulties, schedule of service calls made, etc. This information will be helpful in making decisions regarding replacing a machine and in checking on whether a maintenance contract has been fulfilled.

Questions for Discussion

1. Distinguish between listing and nonlisting machines.

2. Compare the key-driven calculator with the rotary calculator in method of operation.

3. In what instances might a printed record of computations be desirable?

4. Differentiate between adding machines and calculators.

Office Practice Problems

1. Make a survey of business offices in your community to find out what classifications of machines are most commonly used.

2. Make a list of computations a secretary might make in handling financial responsibilities other than those listed in the discussion in this lesson.

(2)   *13, 19—*   3

6

619   10

44509   15

21

27

33

42

48

55

62

69

75

84

92

100

107

114

122

132

140

149

155

158

Adam Briggs   158

Advertising and Sales   162

Education Department   169

180

Preview of New Dictation Material

NOTE: *Stuffers* are small advertising leaflets.

(1)

Baggett, registered, Grimstead, bags, zipper, binders, tablets, miscellaneous, within the, reinstate, glad to receive

(2)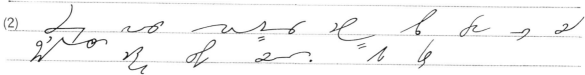

very much, you are now, Goldsmith, Staple, deeply, power, in us, we want, if you'd like, stuffers, attached, we are enclosing, to show, choices

(3)

Dailey, we have received, dye, transfer, in accordance with the, bulletin, quotation, replace

Business Machines as Aids

Business machines can be important aids to the secretary in handling her paper work if they are suited to the types of computations she must make and if she knows how to operate them correctly. Machines can be timesavers not only because computations can be made on them more rapidly than by hand, but because there is less likelihood of mistakes being made.

Before a machine is purchased, an analysis should be made of the kinds of computations that need to be made and the volume of each. Perhaps only columns of figures need to be added; on the other hand, multiplications involving percentages may be made frequently. Possibly a printed record of computations is necessary; then again, maybe not. Careful analysis prior to purchase will insure selection of the most useful machine at a minimum cost.

Classification of Business Machines. Business machines may be classified in several ways: (a) according to the form in which the result of the computation is presented; (b) according to the power utilized to operate the machine; (c) according to the primary use of the machine; and (d) according to the mechanism that records a number in the machine's "memory" or effects a computation.

Form in Which Result Is Presented. The terms "listing" and "nonlisting" indicate the form in which the result is presented to the operator. A *listing* machine is one that makes a printed record on a paper tape of the items that are placed in the machine's memory and of the results of computations.

Machines 1, 2, 3, and 4 are examples of listing machines. Machines 5 and 6 are examples of nonlisting ones.

A *nonlisting* machine is one that makes no printed record. The result of a computation is shown on a dial; this result is "erased" before another computation is made.

The advantage of a listing machine is that the printed record is available for future reference or computations or verifications. The advantage of the nonlisting machine is that, since the printing step is eliminated, the machine makes computations more rapidly.

—Monroe

1. Ten-Key Adding-Listing Machine

—Victor

2. Full-Keyboard Adding-Listing Machine

—Underwood-Olivetti

3. Automatic Multiplier

—Victor

4. Printing Calculator

—Burroughs

5. Key-Driven Calculator

—Monroe

6. Rotary Calculator

Building Speed in Taking Dictation

Lesson **11** ◇

11A—Brief-Form Practice

Directions. The following paragraph has 34 brief forms and brief-form derivatives. If you can read it in ½ minute, your reading rate will be 134 words a minute.

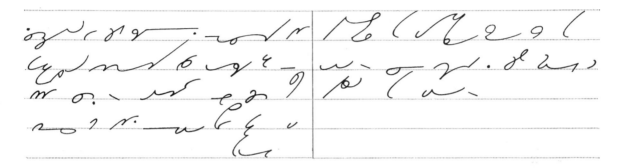

11B—Theory Review

Directions. The outlines in color indicate applications of the theory principles stated below. Write 3 times each outline that appears in red; then write the entire copy straight through once. Follow the same procedure for similar exercises in subsequent lessons.

The sound of *eu* is written 𝒪 ; the sound of *ow* is written 𝒪

The vowel sounds are omitted in the word endings *-ual* and *-tual*; the vowel sounds are also omitted in the endings *-ure* and *-ture*.

A *statement* rather than an invoice is sent for professional or business services. Statements are customarily issued once a month for services provided during the preceding month. Doctors and dentists, for example, send statements to their patients. Utility companies send statements for such services as telephone, electricity, water, and gas. Repair service companies send statements for maintenance or repair work.

A statement is also sent to the holder of a credit card. Multiple-purpose credit cards are now issued as well as single-purpose credit cards. It is possible to charge such expenses as lodging, food, entertainment, flowers, and travel, all with one credit card.

In some large cities a credit card may be obtained from a bank, permitting charges at several different stores in the city. The credit card holder receives one statement monthly from the bank on which is recorded all purchases from all the stores.

The charges on statements for business and professional services must be verified before being paid just as would be done before paying an invoice or statement for goods purchased from a business firm.

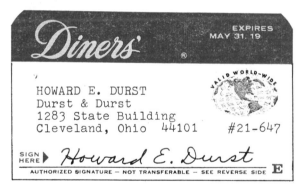

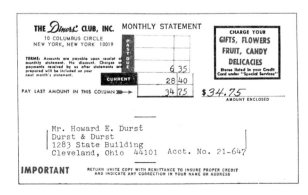

Credit Card and Monthly Statement

Cautions in Handling Invoices and Statements Received. Invoices and statements should be verified before they are paid or are approved for payment.

1. Be sure the order was completely and correctly filled. One or more items may have been backordered, or the price might have been computed incorrectly.

Be sure a statement correctly lists services provided. Sometimes charges are made to the wrong account.

2. Be sure no adjustments are pending.

3. Be sure the method of shipment for an order was correct. If a method other than that specified has been used, the shipping charges may be considerably more than they were supposed to be.

4. Be sure the terms are the same as originally agreed upon.

5. Be sure all special conditions have been met.

6. Do not pay any bill until authorized to do so by the proper person.

Questions for Discussion

1. Distinguish between a purchase requisition and a purchase order.

2. Distinguish between an invoice and a statement.

3. For what purpose is a credit memorandum used?

4. When the secretary receives an invoice or statement, what steps should she take in processing it?

Office Practice Problems

1. Compute the total price of each of the following items and also the grand total:

Quantity	Item	Unit Price
2	Salesmen's Desks	153.50
8	Posture Chairs	33.75
3	Filing Cases	60.00
16	Desk Sets	4.69
4	Chairs	18.05

2. If the merchandise in (1) is quoted prepaid and the terms are "2% 10 days/net 30 days," what would be the amount due if the bill is paid within 10 days?

11C—Punctuation Preview

Directions. In the dictation that your teacher will give you, you will find that the following punctuation rule needs to be applied. Study the rule and the example, then read the shorthand material, indicating where you would apply the rule. Follow the same procedure in similar exercises in subsequent lessons.

Rule 1: A dependent clause preceding an independent clause is set off by a comma.

Example: If you are considering the purchase of a new car, be sure to come in to see what we have to offer.

11D—Practice Material for Building Fluency

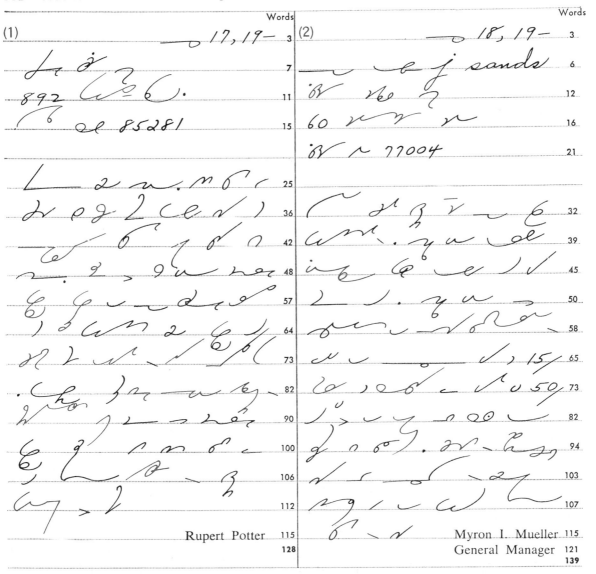

	Words
(1)	17, 19— 3
	7
892	11
	85281 15
	25
	36
	42
	48
	57
	64
	73
	82
	90
	100
	106
	112
Rupert Potter	115
	128

	Words
(2)	18, 19— 3
sands	6
	12
60	16
77004	21
	32
	39
	45
	50
	58
	15 65
	50 73
	82
	94
	103
	107
Myron I. Mueller	115
General Manager	121
	139

An *invoice* is a notification sent to the purchaser that the material ordered has been shipped. The information given on the invoice is similar to that given on the purchase order:

Name of customer
His address
Itemized list of goods
Unit price
Total price
Shipping charges

Invoice number
Order date
Date of invoice
Date of shipment
Tax

When the purchaser receives the shipment, he checks the merchandise against the invoice and his original order. If everything is in order, he sends payment to the shipper. If the purchaser does not pay the amount due within a certain length of time, the vendor will send him a statement. Sometimes a firm can save money by paying within a set time limit. For instance, the terms of payment may read "2% 10 days/net 30 days."

These terms mean that, if the purchaser pays the bill within 10 days from the receipt of the merchandise, he may deduct 2 percent of the amount due; if he does not, he is expected to pay the full amount within 30 days. The 2 percent is called a "discount."

A *credit memorandum* may be issued if an error in computation on the invoice or statement resulted in an overcharge or if unsatisfactory merchandise is returned. Such a memorandum includes the following:

Name of person or
firm receiving the
credit
His address
Items for which deduc-
tion is made
Number of items
Special directions

Date
Invoice number
Reason for credit
Unit price deducted
Total price deducted
Name of firm making ad-
justment

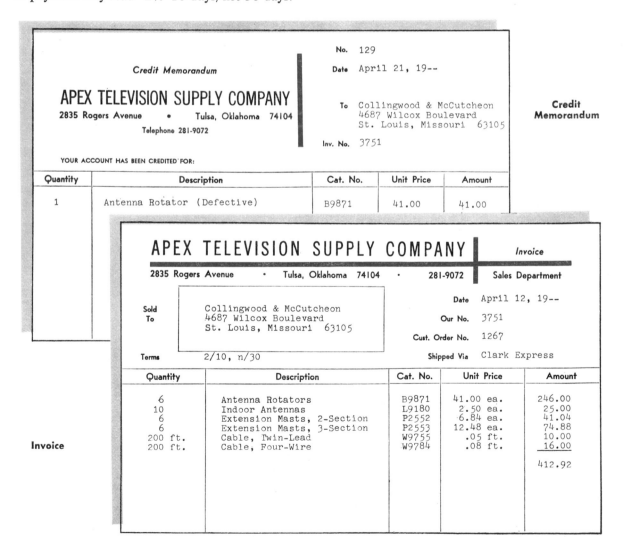

Credit Memorandum

APEX TELEVISION SUPPLY COMPANY

2835 Rogers Avenue • Tulsa, Oklahoma 74104

Telephone 281-9072

No. 129

Date April 21, 19--

To Collingwood & McCutcheon
4687 Wilcox Boulevard
St. Louis, Missouri 63105

Inv. No. 3751

Credit Memorandum

YOUR ACCOUNT HAS BEEN CREDITED FOR:

Quantity	Description	Cat. No.	Unit Price	Amount
1	Antenna Rotator (Defective)	B9871	41.00	41.00

APEX TELEVISION SUPPLY COMPANY   *Invoice*

2835 Rogers Avenue • Tulsa, Oklahoma 74104 • 281-9072   Sales Department

Sold To   Collingwood & McCutcheon
4687 Wilcox Boulevard
St. Louis, Missouri 63105

Date April 12, 19--

Our No. 3751

Cust. Order No. 1267

Terms 2/10, n/30

Shipped Via Clark Express

Invoice

Quantity	Description	Cat. No.	Unit Price	Amount
6	Antenna Rotators	B9871	41.00 ea.	246.00
10	Indoor Antennas	L9180	2.50 ea.	25.00
6	Extension Masts, 2-Section	P2552	6.84 ea.	41.04
6	Extension Masts, 3-Section	P2553	12.48 ea.	74.88
200 ft.	Cable, Twin-Lead	W9755	.05 ft.	10.00
200 ft.	Cable, Four-Wire	W9784	.08 ft.	16.00
				412.92

11E—Dictionary and Spelling Preview

Directions. Be sure you know the meaning and correct spelling of the following words; they will occur in the New Dictation Material. Consult a dictionary if necessary.

1. executive, procedure, evaluating, council, graduation, peculiar

2. rubberized, textiles

3. grateful

11F—Preview of New Dictation Material

(1) *[shorthand outlines]*

Browder, executive, council, uniform, procedure, exercises, lessen, confusion, exist, activities, outlined, advance, purely, is the time, peculiar, talents, administration, ounce, prevention, cure

(2) *[shorthand outlines]*

few days ago, one of the, rubberized, textiles, outlook, cotton, last year, it would be, to protect, delivery, right now

(3) *[shorthand outlines]*

this is, to tell, how much, few days ago, grateful, and hope, to have the, frequently

Lesson 12 ⬡⬡⬡⬡⬡⬡⬡⬡⬡⬡⬡⬡⬡⬡⬡⬡⬡⬡

12A—Phrase Builder

Directions. There are 10 phrases in the paragraph. Follow the same procedure you used for the similar exercise in Lesson 7.

[shorthand outlines]

Questions for Discussion

1. Why are business forms regarded as money-savers and timesavers?

2. In what ways do business forms differ?

3. Why should the person preparing a form be sure that the information given is 100 percent correct and complete?

4. Describe the typical purchase order, mentioning essential information needed for it.

Office Practice Problems

1. Assume that you wish to place an order for two dozen baseball uniforms from a Chicago firm. What specific information will you need to include in the order?

2. Obtain three copies of purchase order forms from two or three firms. Compare the items asked for on them. Is the terminology identical? Are the items arranged to make typing on the form as speedy as possible?

Lesson 137 ⬡⬡⬡⬡⬡⬡⬡⬡⬡⬡⬡⬡⬡⬡⬡⬡⬡

Business Forms as Aids (Concluded)

Activities for Which Forms Are Commonly Used. The purchase order described in Lesson 136 is not always prepared by the person who wants the merchandise. In large firms the person wanting the merchandise requests the purchasing department to obtain it for him. In such a case, he prepares a *purchase requisition*, stating the items desired and describing them, and sends it to the purchasing department. He may specify the vendor (company) from which he wishes the purchase made. A purchase requisition may contain the information at the right.

Name of person or department ordering
Names of items wanted
Number of items desired
Estimated unit price
Estimated total price
Authorization signature
Account number
Date
Characteristics of items such as color, size
Shipping preference
Preferred vendor

If a vendor is not specified, the purchasing department may send out a request for bids to several possible vendors. Companies wishing to obtain the sale will submit quotations. From the quotations, the best bid will be selected and a purchase order placed with that proper vendor.

PURCHASE REQUISITION

COLLINGWOOD & McCUTCHEON

SUGGESTED VENDOR:
Apex Television Supply Company
2835 Rogers Avenue
Tulsa, Oklahoma 74104

DATE
March 14, 19--
PURCHASE REQUISITION NUMBER
9463
DATE WANTED
April 20, 19--
DEPARTMENT
Television
ATTENTION OF
Roy J. Powers
REQUISITIONED BY
Fred R. Taylor
APPROVED BY
A. T. Fessel

TO THE PURCHASING AGENT: Please order the items listed below:

ITEM NO.	QUANTITY	CATALOG NUMBER	DESCRIPTION	UNIT OF PURCHASE	UNIT PRICE Dollars	Cts.	TOTAL Dollars	Cts.
1	6	B9871	Antenna Rotators	----	41	00	246	00
2	10	L9135	Indoor Antennas	carton	2	50	25	00
3	6	P2552	Extension Masts, 2-Section	----	6	84	41	04
4	6	P2553	Extension Masts, 3-Section	----	12	48	74	88
5	200 ft.	W9755	Cable, Twin-Lead	roll		05	10	00
6	200 ft.	W9784	Cable, Four-Wire	roll		08	16	00
				TOTAL			412	92

Purchase Requisition

Directions. Follow the same procedure you used for the Theory Review in Lesson 11.

The word endings *-tion, -sion, -shion,* and *-cian* are expressed by ∕ (sh).

The past tense is expressed by adding the stroke for the sound that is heard in the past tense.

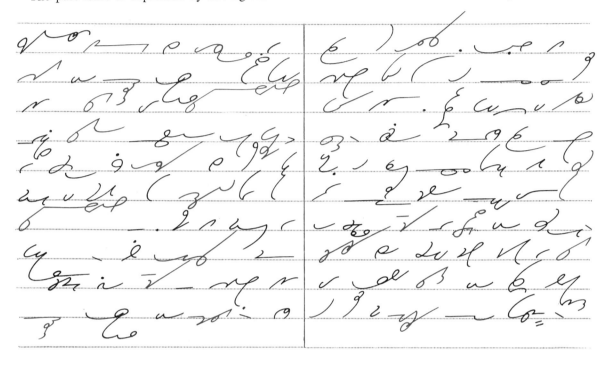

12C—Punctuation Preview

Directions. In punctuating the dictation your teacher will give you, you will need to apply the following rule. Follow the same procedure you used for the similar exercise in Lesson 11.

    Rule 2: Two independent clauses separated by a conjunction are set off from each other by a comma.

    Example: `We think we shall like our new location, and we hope that our customers`
                `will find it a convenient one.`

    NOTE: You will also need to apply Rule 1.

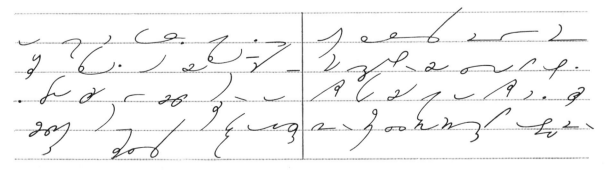

```
PURCHASE ORDER                    COLLINGWOOD & McCUTCHEON
4687 Wilcox Boulevard        •    St. Louis, Missouri  63105        •        564-2958
```

Ordered From	Apex Television Supply Company	No.	1267
	2835 Rogers Avenue	Date	March 15, 19--
	Tulsa, Oklahoma 74104	Ship Via	Clark Express
		Terms	2/10, n/30
Ordered By	Clyde S. Mills, Purchasing Agent	F.O.B.	

Quantity	Description	Cat. No.	Price	Amount
6	Antenna Rotators	B9871	41.00 ea.	246.00
10	Indoor Antennas	L9135	2.50 ea.	25.00
6	Extension Masts, 2-Section	P2552	6.84 ea.	41.04
6	Extension Masts, 3-Section	P2553	12.48 ea.	74.88
200 ft.	Cable, Twin-Lead	W9755	.05 ft.	10.00
200 ft.	Cable, Four-Wire	W9784	.08 ft.	16.00
				412.92

Cautions in Typing Forms. Business forms will not be timesavers or moneysavers if the person preparing them does not observe certain precautions.

1. Be sure to read all directions on a form before filling in any of the information requested on it. If the directions are not followed, the handling of the transaction may be slowed down, may be incorrect, or may be prevented entirely.

2. Be sure to give all information requested. If an item is omitted, time will be wasted with a follow-up procedure to obtain the missing data.

3. Be sure to make the required number of copies. If one copy is missing, the entire form will have to be retyped to supply it.

4. Be sure to route the copies correctly.

5. Be sure that no mistakes have been made. If a person's name is misspelled, that misspelling may cause errors in the records of five or six different departments. If you make an error in the catalog number of an item—even *one* digit, all the records in the firm receiving the form will have errors in them, the wrong merchandise will be sent, and your firm will have the inconvenience and expense of returning merchandise and correcting accounting records.

6. Be sure to verify information. If a copy from which you are typing is not clear, check the spelling or number *before* typing the form. If the form requires computations, check each one to be sure that it is correct.

7. Be sure to use the correct form. Each form has an identifying number in one of its corners. In business, forms are customarily referred to by this number rather than by the name of the form such as "Purchase Order."

8. When tearing copies off a pad of forms, tear the correct number all at once, thus retaining the top edges (or side edges) fastened together. By so doing, you will be sure that all the forms will be correctly aligned in the machine.

Activities for Which Forms Are Commonly Used. Certain business activities lend themselves to the use of forms. Whether a form is used or not, however, depends upon the frequency of recurrence of an activity within the firm, how many copies are required, and how well the data lend themselves to a "form" arrangement. The secretary should be familiar with typical forms.

A *purchase order* may be used to order merchandise or raw materials from a manufacturer, merchandise from a wholesale house, etc. Typically, the purchase order contains the following:

Name of purchaser	Date
His address	Order number
Name of supplier	Terms of purchase
His address	Shipping instructions
Names of items	Shipping weight
wanted	Number of each item
Characteristics of items	wanted
such as color, size	Tax
Unit price	Special instructions,
Total price	such as delivery date
Shipping charges	Signature of purchaser

12D—Practice Material for Building Fluency

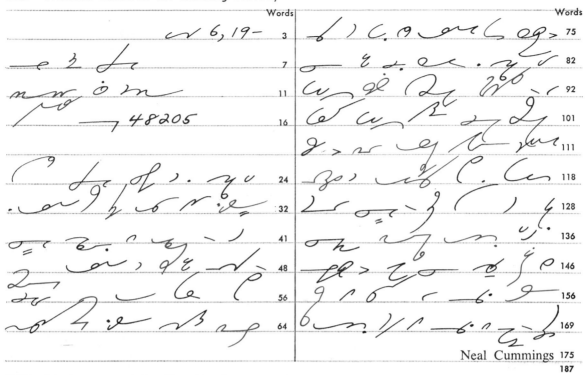

Neal Cummings 175
187

12E—Dictionary and Spelling Preview

Directions. Follow the same directions you used for the similar exercise in Lesson 11.

1. commendation, recommendation, strategic, requisition, enthusiastic
2. shady, leaflets
3. clinic, secretarial, concerning, confidential

12F—Preview of New Dictation Material

(1)

nonfiction, commendation, enthusiastic, humor, quotations, edition, strategic, injected, foundations, historical, documents, requisition

(2)

thank you for your letter, shady, areas, spots, leaflets, you desire, borders, various, flowers

(3)

Evansville Indiana, application, employment, clinic, secretarial, with us, ability, any information, you might be able, to give us, confidential, I wish, this means, in this matter

Secretarial Aids—Business Forms and Machines

Lesson **136** ◇

Business Forms as Aids

Reasons for Using Forms. Business forms expedite the handling of business transactions. They may be very simple, such as telephone call slips or telegrams; they may be complex, such as payroll summary records or tax records. As a secretary, you may use only a limited number of forms and ones of relative simplicity; but you should be familiar with all forms used that are related to the work you are doing. Business forms assist you in the efficient handling of your duties because:

1. They are timesavers for the *originator* of the form. Forms facilitate the giving of directions or listing of specifications because such information can be given under a few headings without the necessity of repeating the names of the categories.

They are also timesavers for the *receiver* of the form because of the columnar or tabular form. No unnecessary narrative copy must be read to obtain the key facts.

2. They increase the likelihood of complete and accurate information being given. Because a column or space has been provided for every item of essential information, there is less chance that an important detail will be omitted.

3. They provide uniformity of procedure for recurring transactions. The uniform arrangement of data on the form permits standard machine setup in typing a certain kind of form. This standard arrangement for data facilitates the setting up of a routine for processing the data by the receiver.

4. They are moneysavers. A maximum of information can be given in a minimum of space. A standard machine setup can be determined, thus saving time in typing the form. Precollated carbon sets and continuous forms further save the typist's time.

5. They facilitate analysis of the information for decision making because data regarding a single item can be selected quickly from each of many forms. For instance, if a company wishes to know for which sale items the most orders were received, this information can be obtained readily for study. Then decisions can be reached regarding, for example, continuance of sale or additional advertising.

Characteristics of Forms. Some business forms are made up in pad form with the top or left edges glued together. Such gluing makes it possible to detach the required number of copies from the pad, slipping in the necessary carbon sheets, and inserting the pack into the machine without disturbing the alignment of the lines on the various copies in the set. Sometimes the forms are printed in a continuous fanfold arrangement, either with one-time carbon inserts or with carbon sheets that can be moved independently of the forms and used for more than one set.

Forms are of varying sizes, depending on the use to which they are to be put, machines in which they are to be used, or the type of information to be recorded on them. The most commonly used sizes are 8½ by 5½ and 8½ by 11 inches.

If several copies of a form are to be prepared simultaneously, the destination of each copy may be indicated by color differentiation; that is, white may go to the sales department; blue, to the accounting department; pink, to the shipping department, etc.

If several copies of a form are to be prepared simultaneously but not all information is to be shown on all of them, carbonized blocks on the back of certain copies may be used to limit the printing of some items of information on selected copies.

Some forms are made from a specially treated paper that eliminates the need for carbon paper inserts.

Inexpensive sulphite paper is usually used for business forms.

Lesson 13 ⬡○⬡○⬡○⬡○⬡○⬡○⬡○⬡○⬡○⬡○⬡○⬡○⬡

13A—Potential Rate Builder

Directions. Write the following sentence in shorthand as many times as you can in 15 seconds. To obtain your rate, multiply the number of times you wrote the sentence by 16 (the number of words in the sentence) and then by 4 to get the number of words a minute you were writing. Follow the same procedure for similar exercises in subsequent lessons.

13B—Theory Review

A small hook is used to express the three vowel sounds ŏŏ, ŭ, and ōō. At the beginning of words, *w* is expressed by the *oo* hook; *sw*, by *soo*. At the beginning of words, the sound of *wh* is expressed by *h* and the *oo* hook.

The word beginning *be-* is expressed by *b*.

The word beginning *ah-* is expressed by two dots at the beginning of the word, one for *a* and one for *h*. The word beginning *aw-* is expressed by a dot and the *oo* hook.

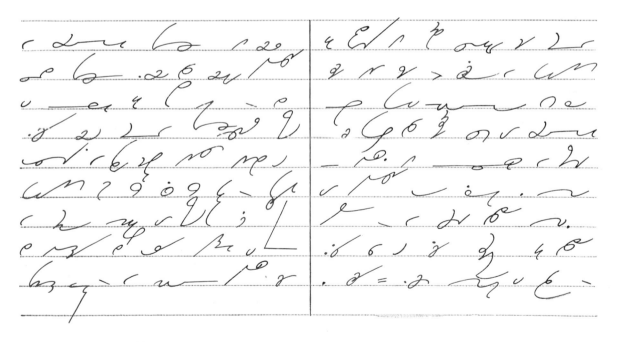

13C—Punctuation Preview

Rule 3: Two independent clauses not joined by a conjunction are separated by a semicolon.

Example: We have not dismissed any employee this year; we do not expect to dismiss anyone in the next year.

NOTE: You will need to apply Rules 1 and 2, as well as the one above.

135A—Vocabulary Preview

styli, medium, shading, wheel, we manufacture, that they will be, anticipate, to handle, booklets, assist, effective, instruments, very cordially yours

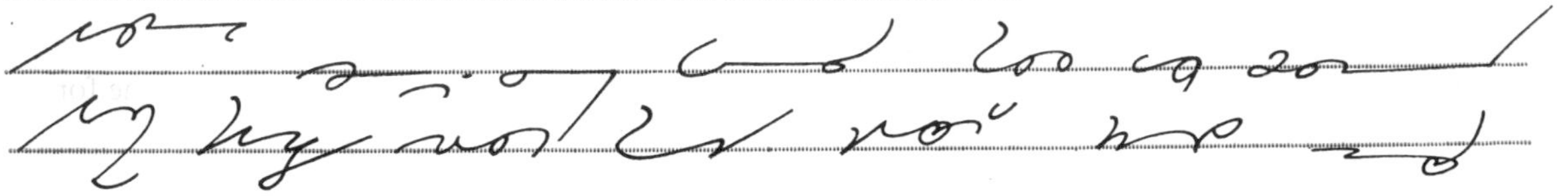

documents, chemical, image, permanent, frequently, occasion, we recommend, discover, photocopied, correction, fluid, strikeover, suggest that, in mind

135B—Transcribing from Office-Style Dictation

Directions. Your teacher will dictate a letter and a memorandum to you in office-style dictation. For the letter, use modified block style with indented paragraphs and date ending at the right margin; use mixed punctuation. For the memorandum, use the arrangement shown on page 222.

135C—Supplementary Transcription

Miss Grace Hester, Supervisor
Central Stenographic Pool
Browning-Hall Corporation
Miami, Florida   33110

Claude P. Lansdown

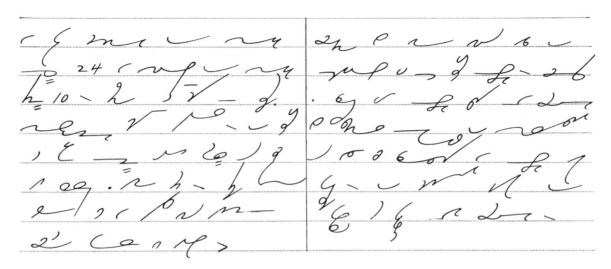

13D—Practice Material for Building Fluency

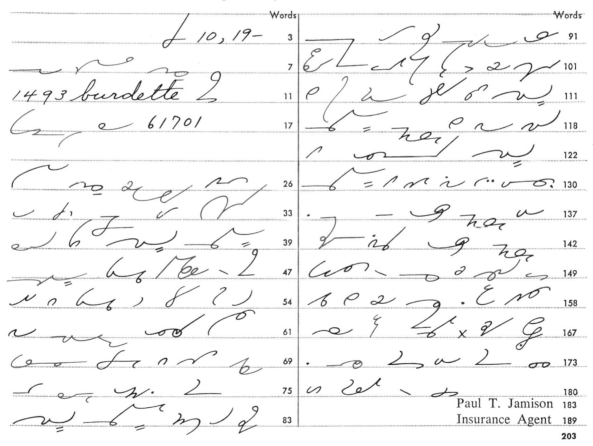

	Words
10, 19—	3
	7
1493 burdette	11
61701	17
	26
	33
	39
	47
	54
	61
	69
	75
	83

	Words
	91
	101
	111
	118
	122
	130
	137
	142
	149
	158
	167
	173
	180
Paul T. Jamison	183
Insurance Agent	189
	203

13E—Dictionary and Spelling Preview

1. Newark, collision, routing, diverted, uninjured, hospitalization

2. registered, attendance, spiral

3. varieties, attachments

Folding Collator

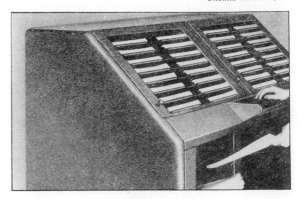

Semiautomatic Collator

Collating Duplicated Materials. Collating is the assembling of sheets and fastening them together in some manner such as stapling. Types of collators range from small stationary "bins" to folding type to automatic equipment. An office having a limited need for a collator will probably use a folding type similar to that shown above. A semiautomatic collator is shown above, right.

Rubber fingers can be used to assist the operator in separating sheets from each other, or some commercially prepared moistener can be applied to the fingers. Wetting the fingers with the tongue is to be avoided.

When collating, be careful to have all the sheets in proper sequence and facing in the same direction. Eliminate any blank sheets that sometimes slip through the duplicator as copies are run.

A staple remover is an inexpensive but handy tool for disassembling papers that have been incorrectly assembled.

Duplicating Requisition. If your firm has a duplicating department, you will probably send most, if not all, masters to that department for duplication. In doing so, you will need to send specific directions. Reproduction order forms are usually provided for you to fill in and attach to your materials. Fill in the order form completely and correctly because the operator who handles your order has only your written instructions to guide him.

DUPLICATING REQUISITION

JOB NO. 6903

PLEASE TYPE OR PRINT PLAINLY

PLEASE REFER TO THE ABOVE NUMBER FOR FOLLOW-UP

| SUBJECT | DATE REQUIRED | DATE THIS REQUEST |
| DEPARTMENT | | CHARGE ACCOUNT NUMBER |

PROCESS–CHECK WHICH ☐ PHOTOSTAT ☐ VERIFAX ☐ MIMEO ☐ DITTO ☐ OTHER (SEE BELOW FOR OFFSET)

| ENTER REQUIRED INFORMATION FOR ANY OF THE ABOVE PROCESSES | NO. SHEETS OF COPY | COPY SIZE | NO. NEGATIVES | NO. POSITIVES | REQUIRED SIZE | |

☐ OFFSET (COMPLETE REQUIRED INFORMATION BELOW) — LEAVE THIS SECTION BLANK

INTERNAL DUPLICATING				EXTERNAL DUPLICATING			
QUANTITY	STOCK–KIND OF PAPER	SIZE OF PAPER	COLOR OF PAPER	QUANTITY	STOCK–KIND OF PAPER	SIZE OF PAPER	COLOR OF PAPER
TOTAL NO. OF PAGES	NO. OF SINGLES	NO. OF BACKUPS	COLOR OF INK	TOTAL NO. OF PAGES	NO. OF SINGLES	NO. OF BACKUPS	COLOR OF INK
PUNCHING	YES ☐ NO ☐	HOW BOUND	ROUND CORNERS	PUNCHING	YES ☐ NO ☐	HOW BOUND	ROUND CORNERS
SPECIFY				SPECIFY			
COLLATE	YES ☐ NO ☐	STAPLE	YES ☐ NO ☐	COLLATE	YES ☐ NO ☐	STAPLE	YES ☐ NO ☐

NEGATIVES AND/OR PLATES ☐ DESTROY ☐ HOLD — RETURN ORIGINALS TO

| AMOUNT QUOTED | DATE QUOTATION | DELIVER TO | FLOOR | REQUISITION APPROVED BY | TITLE |

DO NOT WRITE BELOW THIS LINE

Office Practice Problem

Type the copy your teacher dictates to you in two 35-space columns with 3 spaces between them; justify the right margin of each column.

Duplicating Requisition

(1)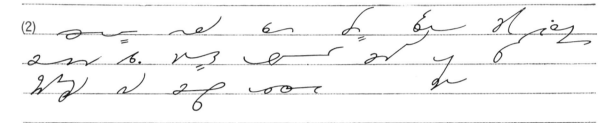

Durant, Newark, last night, oncoming, swung, outside, community, Tulane, swiftly, prevented, head-on. adults, injured, hospitalization, tourist, characteristic, diverted, erection, temporary, detour, routing, couple, uninjured, destination

(2)

Cameron, current, circular, Beck, spiral, we would be, hear from you, we looked, to seeing, St. Louis, last month, we couldn't, register, attendance, if you do not find, you want, we may be able, requirements

(3)

from your letter, we are not sure, cooler, for this reason, varieties, ice cream, cabinets, many other, water, attachments, review, in which you are, to quote

Lesson 14 ◯◇◯◇◯◇◯◇◯◇◯◇◯◇◯◇◯◇◯◇◯◇◯◇◯◇

14A—Proportion Drill

Directions. Follow the same procedure you used for the similar exercise in Lesson 9.

(1)

(2)

(3)

If you must rest your fingers on the master while erasing, place a clean sheet of paper between them and the typed copy.

Step 2. Type the correction with just enough pressure to make the typed letter or letters match the surrounding copy.

Caution. If it is necessary to reinsert a master into the machine to make a correction, make the erasure first. Cover the typed copy with a sheet of onionskin paper to prevent smearing. Insert into the machine. Align the copy; check the alignment by typing the correction on the onionskin. When the alignment is satisfactory, tear off the onionskin to a point below the correction area and type the correct letter or letters.

Drawings and Signatures. Signatures can be written on the master with a reproducing pencil or a pen containing a special ink. Drawings can be made with this ink also. A clean sheet of paper should be placed under the hand during signing or drawing.

Color Work. Colors other than black can be used for offset reproduction. Various colors of ink are available for use with an offset machine. If more than one color is used on one sheet of copy, a separate master has to be prepared for each color. Each master has typed on it only the material to be printed in a certain color.

Filing the Master. Paper masters from which the maximum number of copies has not been run can be filed for future use if the surface has been properly treated with a special fluid. When the master is run at a later time, this fluid is removed; then the master can be handled in the usual way. Metal plates are handled in a similar fashion. Care should be used in filing the masters or plates in order to be sure that the surfaces are not damaged.

Paper for Duplicated Copies

Sulphite paper (paper made from wood pulp) is usually used for the spirit and the stencil processes. Paper in which the grain runs the length of the paper is preferred over short-grain paper because it has a greater tendency to lie flat as it is fed through a machine.

The finish of copy paper for the spirit process should be smooth and glossy so that the fluid that dampens each sheet will evaporate rather than be absorbed. On the other hand, the finish of copy paper for the stencil process needs to be such that it will absorb the ink quickly in order to pre-

vent offset of ink from one sheet onto the back of the next sheet that comes through the machine. Many different kinds of paper can be used for the offset process, including letterhead stationery and spirit duplicator paper.

The most commonly used weights are 16-pound and 20-pound. When both sides of the paper are to be printed, a heavier weight may be needed.

Copy paper should be bought in wrapped reams; and a ream should not be opened until it is to be used. Exposure to light, dust, or moisture may result in feeding problems.

The label on the package usually indicates on which side of the paper the printing should be made for most satisfactory reproduction.

Skills Related to Duplicating Work

Justifying the Right Margin. Copy can be set up for any type of duplication so that the copy ends even with the right margin just as for the left margin. The procedure is as follows:

Step 1. Set up the copy within the line limitations decided upon for the job. Assume that the material is to be set up with a 40-space line. Type each line as close as possible to the 40th space, but do not type beyond it. Fill in the blank spaces at the end of each line with a diagonal as shown in this illustration:

```
    The All-Company Bowling Tournament///
    was held last night at the Star-Lite////
    Bowling Alleys in St. Louis.  Ten teams/
    participated in the event.  The winning/
    team was the Shipping Department; second
    place was captured by the Advertising///
    Department; and the Sales Department////
    placed third.
```

Step 2. The material is then marked for extra spaces within each line that had diagonals at the end:

```
    The All-Company Bowling Tournament///
    was held last night at the Star-Lite////
    Bowling Alleys in St. Louis.  Ten teams/
    participated in the event.  The winning/
    team was the Shipping Department; second
    place was captured by the Advertising///
    Department; and the Sales Department////
    placed third.
```

Step 3. The copy is then retyped with the extra spaces inserted at the predetermined points:

```
    The  All-Company  Bowling  Tournament
    was  held  last  night  at  the  Star-Lite
    Bowling  Alleys in St. Louis.   Ten teams
    participated  in  the  event.   The winning
    team was the Shipping Department; second
    place  was  captured  by  the  Advertising
    Department;  and  the  Sales  Department
    placed third.
```

Office Practice Problem

Type a paper master for the announcement that your teacher will dictate to you.

The shorthand strokes *n* and *d* are blended without an angle to express *nd*; also, *n* and *t* are blended to express *nt*.

The shorthand strokes *m* and *d* are blended to express *md*; *m* and *t* are blended to express *mt*.

Before a hook vowel, *y* is expressed by a small circle; *ye*, by a small loop; *ya*, by a large loop.

The word beginning *over-* is expressed by the *o* hook above the line.

14C—Punctuation Preview

Rule 4: A restrictive clause is not set off by commas because it is essential to the meaning of the sentence. A nonrestrictive clause is set off by commas because it is not essential to the meaning of the sentence.

Examples: The cheesecloth that I ordered has not been shipped.

Your letter of May 2, which reached me yesterday, contains many helpful ideas.

NOTE: You will need to apply Rules 1-3, as well as the one given above.

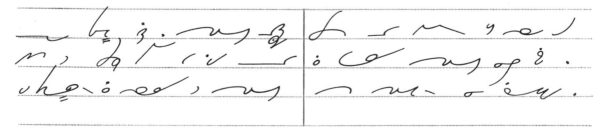

Color Work. Colors other than black can be used on stencil runs. If a duplicating department does a lot of color work, it will have several drums with a different color in each one. The drums are interchanged as needed. If more than one color is used on the same sheet, one color at a time is run with the other parts of the copy being masked. If a short run is required, an ink pad may be put over the protective cover and various inks spread on the pad with a brush before the stencil is laid on the pad.

Office Practice Problem

Type a stencil of the form letter your teacher will dictate to you. Sign the dictator's name on the stencil with a stylus. Run five good copies. Fill in these addresses: Mr. J. K. Bunt, 45 Lake Drive, Chicago, Illinois 60609; Mr. Lee Trace, 8 Elm Street, Chicago, Illinois 60610; Mrs. Jane Owen, Wrigley Place, Chicago, Illinois 60627; Mr. Ron Bond, 30 Twin Oaks, Chicago, Illinois 60613; Mr. Alex Fair, Wade Building, Chicago, Illinois 60607.

Address an envelope for each letter; fold and insert the letter.

Lesson 134 ⬡◯⬡◯⬡◯⬡◯⬡◯⬡◯⬡◯⬡◯⬡◯⬡

The Offset Process; Skills Related to Duplicating Work

The Offset Process

The preparation of a typewritten master for the offset process is as easy as for the stencil process. The running of copies is more complicated, however.

The Paper Master. The paper master (duplimat) has a special glazed surface. The guide marks on it are similar to those on a stencil except that the guide lines on a stencil enclose a space *less than* the dimensions of the copy paper, automatically providing for a margin of almost ¾" around the typed copy. On the paper master, the guide lines indicate the *perimeter* of the copy paper; and the typist must keep this in mind in setting margin stops or planning the layout.

Pretyping Activity. Clean the type thoroughly with a brush or liquid cleaner. Type must dry completely. Move the paper bail rollers outside the printing area because the rollers will pick up ink from typed copy and release it onto other parts of the master. Move the envelope holders away if they would touch the master. They, too, can cause marks that will print on the copies.

Place on the machine a special offset ribbon or a carbon paper ribbon. Set the touch control. Pressure should not be too heavy; if it is, letters will emboss (make indentions in the master). Then printing will be in outline form; for instance, a period will reproduce as a circle. Too heavy a touch also makes corrections more difficult.

Determine marginal and tabular settings. A nonreproducing pencil can be used to make light guide marks if needed.

Typing the Master. Insert the master into the machine. Do not touch the printing area with your fingers or any part of your hand. The oil in your skin will adhere to the surface, and the prints will show on finished copies or will blur the printing. Do not bend the master because a break or crack in the surface will reproduce as a line or smudge.

Use an even touch. Proofread the master before removing it from the typewriter. Place a sheet of onionskin over the typed master and clip it in place at the top. This protective covering will prevent smudging en route to the duplicating department. Do not put paper clips on the sides of the master because the slight "hump" caused by a clip may prevent the master from resting snugly on the drum, thus causing a smeared image.

Allow one-half hour to one hour between the typing and the running to permit the image to set firmly.

Correcting a Mistake. The sooner a mistake is corrected, the easier the correction job because the ink has not had time to soak in. Also you will avoid smudges that may be made by rolling the master backward and forward.

Step 1. Use a clean soft eraser that has no oil in it. Keep the eraser clean; you may need to clean it during an erasure as well as before and after. *All* ink must be taken off, but the glaze on the master must not be broken. A "ghost" of the error should remain; it will not reproduce. If the surface is "roughed up," a smudge will print at that point. Use *very* light strokes.

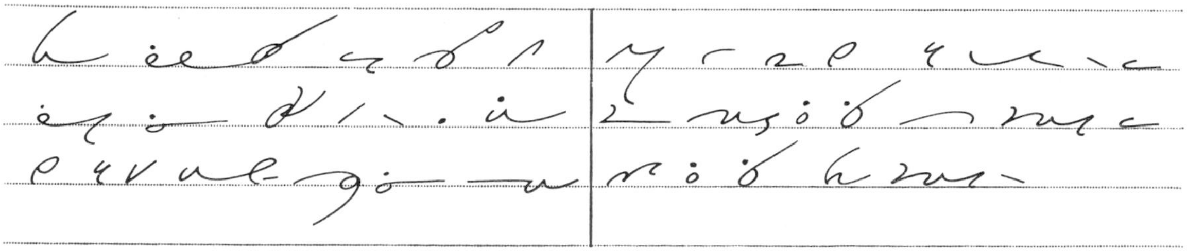

[Shorthand outlines — Gregg shorthand practice material]

14D—Practice Material for Building Fluency

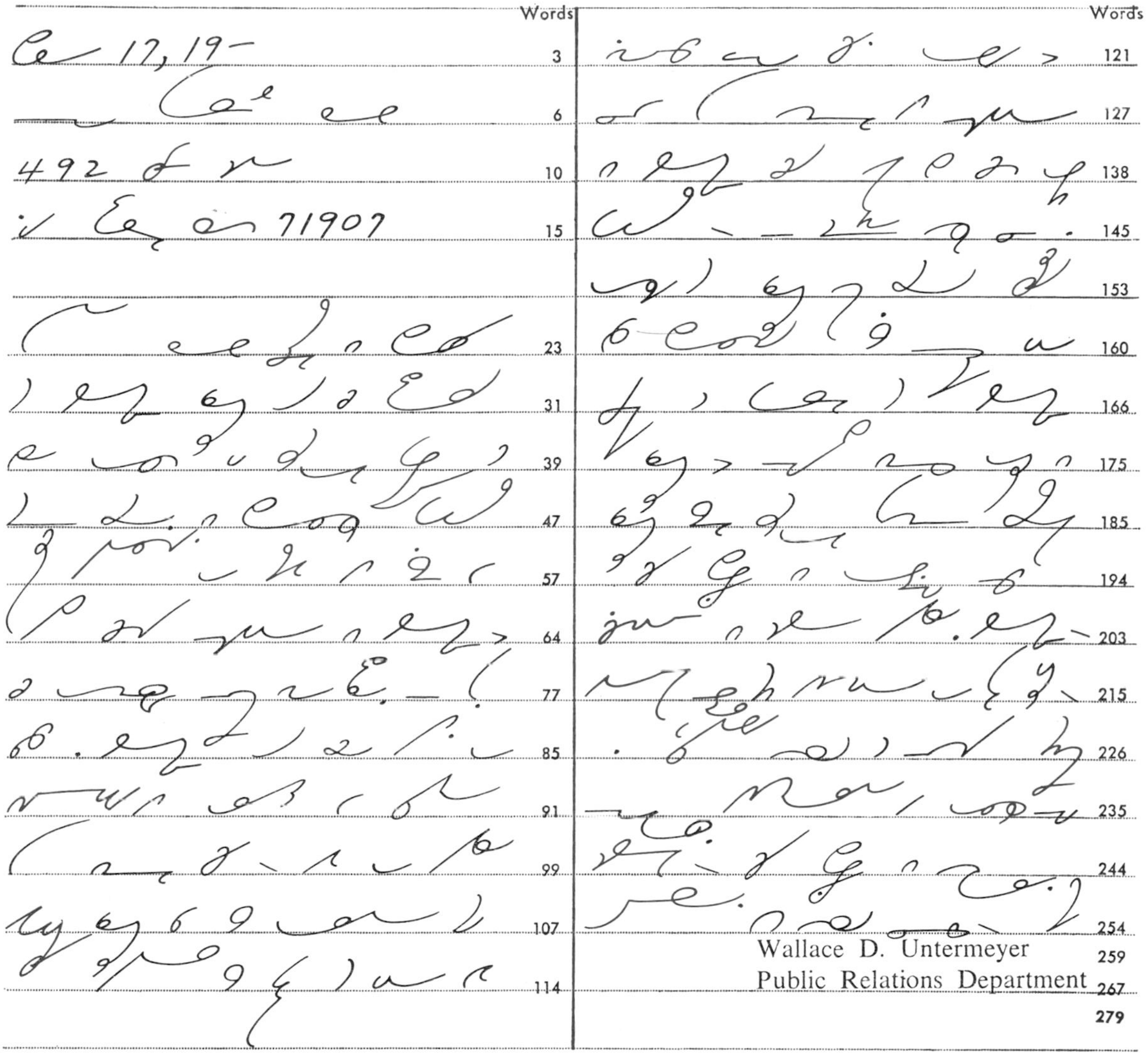

[Shorthand outlines with word counts in right margin]

	Words
	3
	6
492	10
71907	15
	23
	31
	39
	47
	57
	64
	77
	85
	91
	99
	107
	114

	Words
	121
	127
	138
	145
	153
	160
	166
	175
	185
	194
	203
	215
	226
	235
	244
	254
Wallace D. Untermeyer	259
Public Relations Department	267
	279

14E—Dictionary and Spelling Preview

1. slander, library, guarantee
2. calendars, dispose, discount
3. curriculum, bulletin

the machine. If you do not, ink will seep out of the drum onto the impression roller or other parts.

The copies reproduced should be permitted to rest in the receiving tray until the ink has dried in order to minimize smearing and offset. The type of ink used in the machine and the amount of copy on the sheets will determine how long the copies should rest before being handled.

If the stencil is not to be saved, fold it lengthwise twice with the inked side inside the fold, twist the stencil into a small ball, and wrap it in paper toweling before depositing it in the wastebasket.

Caution. Do not leave the drum exposed to the air. As soon as the stencil is removed, place another one on or replace the protective cover. After replacing the cover, feed through a few sheets of copy paper or rub over the cover with the hand to eliminate any air pockets that might cause the pad to dry out.

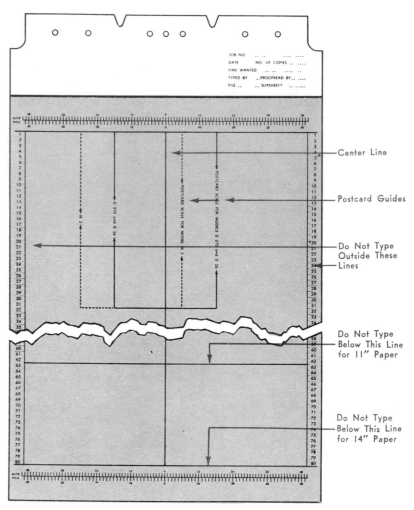

Guide Lines on the Stencil

Slip-Sheeting. If both sides of the copy paper are to be printed, it may be necessary to slip sheet each run so that there will be no offset on either side. Some machines have automatic slip-sheeting devices. On others, copies must be fed through the machine slowly enough for a slip sheet to be dropped on top of each copy as it comes through the machine into the receiving tray. The copy on one side must be permitted to dry thoroughly before the sheets are straightened and run through for printing on the reverse side.

Clean-Up. Be sure to place the protective cover on correctly. Wipe off the machine any excess ink that may be on it. Check to be sure the drum is in proper position and the brake on. Cover up the machine and remove any papers or materials from the work area if they do not belong there.

Filing the Stencil. If oil-based ink has been used, the stencil can be stored in a stencil file folder without removing the ink. Lay the stencil on one half of the folder with the inked side up. Lay the other half over the stencil, being sure that there are no wrinkles on the stencil. Record on the outside of the folder what is in it.

If a vertical stencil filing cabinet is used, remove the ink from the stencil by placing the stencil between two layers of newspapers, rubbing gently the top layer. Repeat the process between two more layers if necessary.

Drawings and Signatures. Use a writing plate between the stencil and backing sheet to give a firm writing surface when you sign a name on a stencil. Drawings can be made easily by using an illuminated drawing board. Various types of styli are available for handwriting and for drawing.

(1)

Yale, ashamed, to say, I haven't, to find, slander, I thought, library, yesterday morning, hunted, for some time, this morning, chairmen, named, reluctant, I shall make, to do so

(2)

Bent, secondhand, telephoned, dispose, to me, I remembered, to print, calendars, Alpine

(3)

many thanks, this information, curriculum, helpful, your name, bulletin, recommendations

Lesson 15 ⬡⬡⬡⬡⬡⬡⬡⬡⬡⬡⬡⬡⬡⬡⬡⬡⬡

15A—Repetitive Phrase Builder

Directions. Follow the same directions you used for the similar exercise in Lesson 10.

15B—Theory Review

The word ending *-ly* is expressed by a small circle. The word ending *-ily* is expressed by a narrow loop. The ending *-ually* is expressed by *l* and a small circle.

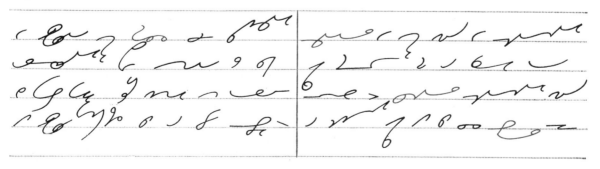

The Stencil Process

The stencil process is widely used; it is particularly suited to duplicating work in small businesses and in schools. In large firms, however, the offset process has become more prevalent.

A Stencil. A stencil consists of two basic parts: a stencil sheet and a backing sheet. The stencil sheet is affixed permanently to the top of the backing sheet. Various other kinds of sheets may be assembled with these two basic parts. *Cushion sheets*—tissue or coated—serve such purposes as (1) increasing the ease with which the stencil may be proofread; (2) bringing about variations in copy characteristics such as a fine-line copy vs. a medium-line copy; (3) facilitating handwriting or drawing. *Protective sheets* are sometimes inserted by the manufacturer on top and/or beneath the stencil sheet. *Typing films* are sometimes supplied with the stencils. Such a film usually comes attached to the front of the stencil sheet. Keys striking through this film make a broader impression than they would without it; thus copies will be blacker and broader-lined. The film also minimizes the possibility of letters like "o" being cut out by sharp keys. *Typing plates* are sometimes included in boxes of stencils. A typing plate can be inserted immediately in front of the backing sheet to give a harder surface.

Prestenciling Activity. Make a typed copy of the material exactly as it is to appear when reproduced. Then clean the type with a type brush and plastic cleaner or with a liquid cleaner. Set the ribbon indicator on "Stencil." This mechanism disengages the ribbon so that the keys strike directly against the stencil.

Check the touch control to see that it is set at a point that will insure the sharpest outlines without cutting out characters. Insert any special sheets needed between the stencil and the backing sheet and remove protective sheets.

Typing the Stencil. Insert the stencil into the machine, making sure that it is aligned properly.

Use a firm, staccato stroke. On some machines the punctuation keys must be struck more lightly than others, and certain letter keys such as "m" must be struck with more force.

Observe the markings on the stencil indicating the area within which you must type.

Proofread the stencil before removing it from the machine.

Correcting a Mistake. The basic steps in correcting an error on a stencil are as follows:

Step 1. Turn the stencil upward in the machine a line or two so that the error can be reached readily. If there is a film over the stencil, detach it and lay it over the hood of the machine.

Step 2. Use a glass burnisher or a paper clip to rub the surface of the error to "close" the fibers separated by the keystroke. Some cushion sheets make this step unnecessary.

Step 3. Open a bottle of correction fluid; dip the brush into the fluid, pressing it lightly against the neck of the bottle to release any excess fluid from the brush. Apply the fluid to the burnished area in one or two vertical strokes. Do not put a heavy layer of fluid on the error. Let it dry 30 seconds. Be sure to close the bottle as quickly as possible because the evaporation rate is high; and, when the fluid becomes thick, corrections are poor.

Step 4. Replace the film. Position the carriage properly. Strike the correct letter with a slightly lighter-than-normal touch.

Running Copies. Remove the cover from the machine. Remove the protective cover from the drum, laying it carefully, ink side up, on paper toweling or newspaper. Place the stencil on the ink pad. The exact manner in which it is fastened on depends on the type and brand of machine. On any type, however, the stencil sheet will be placed face down on the pad and the backing sheet torn off at the perforation. Care should be taken that the stencil sheet lays smoothly on the pad; wrinkles will reproduce on the copy sheets.

Release the brake. Place the copy paper on the feed table right side up as directed on the label of the package. Check to see that the paper guides are in correct position.

A few test sheets should be run through to be sure the ink is distributed evenly over the printing area. If not, ink may need to be added according to the directions of the manufacturer. If test copies show that copy is too high or too low, operate the adjusting mechanism that will alter the printing position. If the machine is equipped with a counter, set it at the proper number.

Always stop the drum at the point indicated on

15C—Punctuation Preview

Rule 5: Commas are used to set off words, phrases, or clauses used in a series.

Example: The St. Louis conference was attended by Mr. Andrews, Mr. Swenson, and Mr. Brown.

NOTE: The following material requires the application of Rules 1-4, as well as the rule above.

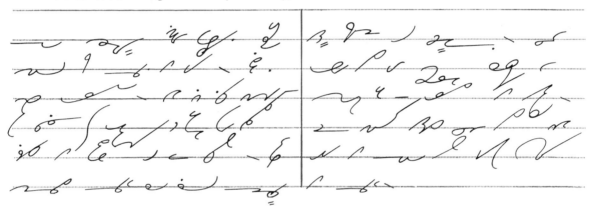

15D—Practice Material for Building Fluency

(1)	Words		Words
	3		66
	10		73
	15		81
	19		90
			97
	27		103
	35		112
	44		122
	49		129
	59	Wade H. Gunther	138
			154

a clean card between the sheet and the hood of the typewriter (or use a metal shield) to make a smooth surface. Using a pen knife or a single-edged razor blade, gently scrape off the carbon impression of the error. Make the strokes in one direction and do not scrape or cut the shiny surface of the master paper. Finish with a soft eraser or with a coating made with a white wax pencil. Remove the card or shield.

Step 2. Cut a small piece of carbon-coated paper from an unusable master sheet. This small piece of paper is inserted behind the area of the "erasure," with the coated side facing the back of the front sheet. This piece is inserted because the coating on the master unit is a "one-time" coating; it will not make a second impression as dark as the first one was. Position the copy for typing the correction.

Step 3. Type the correction, using the same firm stroking as for the rest of the copy. Remove the small piece of carbon-coated paper. The ribbon impression on the front side of the master set will appear as a strikeover, but on the negative side—the one that will be reproduced—only the correction will print.

Alternate methods of "erasing" the error can be used. They include: (a) covering up the error with correction tape; (b) covering up the error with a white wax pencil after taking off as much as possible with plastic cleaner; (c) cutting out the mistake (if nothing is to replace it); or (d) cutting out the mistake and then fastening over the hole a strip from another master on which has been typed the correct letter or letters. Scotch tape can be used to affix the strip properly.

Caution. Handle the carbon master with extreme care. Carbon coating on the fingers may be "transplanted" onto the negative side, causing smudges on the duplicated copies. Also avoid getting stains on typewriter keys, the frame of the machine, or your clothes. Keep a jar of specially prepared cleaning compound handy to assist you in removing stains when you wash your hands. Ordinary soap does not remove such stains easily.

Running Copies. Attach the master face down on the drum so that the carbon side faces outward. Be sure the master is clamped in straight; if it is not, it may wrinkle as the drum revolves, preventing complete reproduction.

After the master has been locked on the drum, set the pressure indicator properly and the counter for the number of copies needed. The speed at which the drum revolves affects the darkness of the imprint. If only a few copies are needed, darker copies can be made by revolving the drum slowly; if many copies are needed, revolve the drum rapidly.

Check the fluid in the machine to be sure that the correct amount is in the wick. Run a sheet or two of copy paper through before adding fluid. If the wick is overdampened, too much of the carbon coating will come off on the first copies; and you may not be able to get as many clear copies as you need. Position the guides for the copy paper so that the placement of the image on the paper will be exactly as desired.

Caution. If carbon stains appear on the drum or rollers, remove with a cloth moistened in the fluid.

Once you start to rotate the drum, make a complete revolution. If you hesitate at any point, more of the carbon coating will be taken off the master at one point than at another; and the image imprint will not be uniform in darkness.

Clean-Up. After the desired number of copies has been run, remove the master. If carbon smudges have been made on the drum or roller, remove them with a cloth dipped in the fluid. Replace the cover. Do not leave any materials in, on, or about the machine.

Filing the Master. If fewer copies have been run than could have been reproduced, the master may be filed for future use. A plain sheet of paper should be fastened to the reverse side to protect the carbon impression.

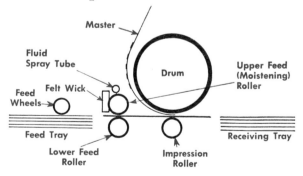

Fluid Duplicator Process

Office Practice Problem

Prepare a master for a memo that your teacher will dictate to you. Use the memo form shown on page 222.

(2)

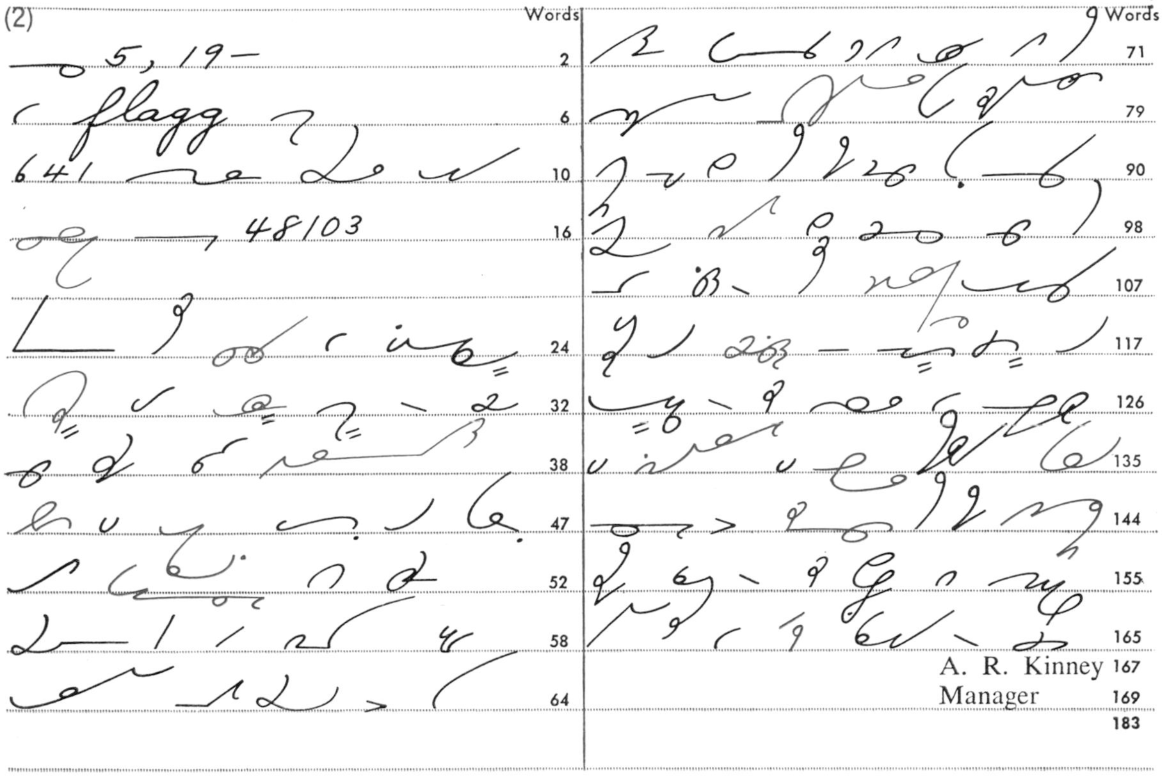
Words
5, 19–
flagg
641
48103
2
6
10
16
24
32
38
47
52
58
64
Words
71
79
90
98
107
117
126
135
144
155
165
A. R. Kinney 167
Manager 169
183

15E—Dictionary and Spelling Preview

1. habitually, tardiness, overall, thereafter
2. conscientiously, bureaus, rayon

15F—Preview of New Dictation Material

(1)

Benson, highly, gradually, eventually, assignments, habitually, thereafter, so long, tardiness, each time, we should like, honestly, you can give us

(2)

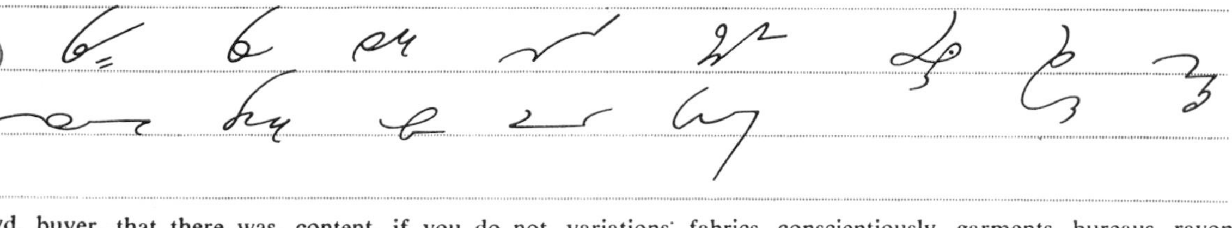

Boyd, buyer, that there was, content, if you do not, variations, fabrics, conscientiously, garments, bureaus, rayon, some of the, patronage

The Fluid Hectograph Process

The fluid hectograph process is simple and inexpensive. Special materials are needed to make the master copy, and a special kind of glossy paper is needed for the copy paper.

A Master Set. A master "set" consists of a sheet of specially coated white paper and a special carbon-coated sheet. For some machines these sheets can be purchased separately or in a "master unit set" in which the two sheets are fastened together at the top and have a perforation near the top edge for ease in separation prior to running copies. For some machines only a master unit set is available.

The sheets are put together so that the specially coated white paper is the one on which you type. The carbon-coated face of the other sheet comes into direct contact with the back of this front sheet. As you type, the carbon coating causes an image of what you type to be made in reverse on the back side of the front sheet.

For some machines, several colors of carbon paper are obtainable. Purple is most often used because it makes a more intense copy than other colors; however, black, red, and blue are also available.

In the commercially assembled master unit set, there is a loose protective tissue sheet between the two sheets of the unit to prevent the coating of the back sheet from rubbing off onto the reverse side of the front sheet and thus creating smudges. This protective tissue must be removed before you insert the set into the machine. The protective sheet is saved so that it can be reinserted after typing has been completed, to prevent smudges or unwanted marks from being inadvertently made on the master copy prior to reproduction.

Pretyping Activities. The typewriter keys must be cleaned thoroughly before a master is typed. Before the master set is inserted, set the touch control on the typewriter at the proper point. To determine this point, insert an unusable master set into the machine; type a line or two; then examine the reverse of the master sheet. The "take-off" is satisfactory if the characters are well defined and sharp. The "a's" and "s's" should not be filled in. Make a note of the proper position for the touch control indicator so that you will not have to make this test each time you type a master.

A hard-surfaced backing sheet may be placed behind the master set if the platen is so soft or worn that irregular impressions would be made.

Typing the Master. Use a sharp, firm stroking of the keys. Leave a minimum of one-fourth inch of space at the top and bottom for locking the master on the duplicating machine.

More than one color can be used on a master by inserting a piece of the desired color of hectograph carbon paper at the proper point between the two sheets of the master set.

Proofread the master before removing it from the machine.

Drawings and Signatures. These may be made on the master by placing the master set on a hard surface and doing the art work with a sharpened No. 3 pencil or a ball-point pen and exerting sufficient pressure to make a clear impression on the reverse side.

Correcting a Mistake. The following procedure is recommended for correcting an error:

Step 1. Roll the set upward far enough to allow the front sheet to be laid forward, making the mistake on the reverse side visible to you. Lay

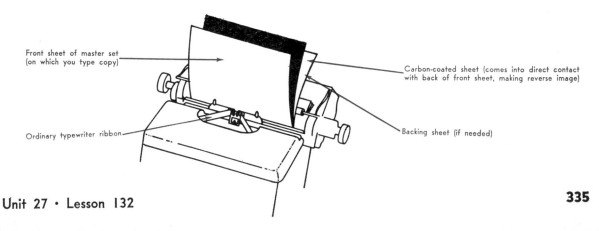

Front sheet of master set (on which you type copy)

Carbon-coated sheet (comes into direct contact with back of front sheet, making reverse image)

Ordinary typewriter ribbon

Backing sheet (if needed)

Taking Dictation and Transcribing

Lesson **16** ⬡⬡⬡⬡⬡⬡⬡⬡⬡⬡⬡⬡⬡⬡⬡⬡⬡⬡

16A—Handling the Notebook in Taking Dictation

Certain habits in handling the notebook will make you a more efficient secretary. Read the pointers given in the following paragraphs and apply them in your work.

1. In writing shorthand, you will find that a pen is preferable to a pencil. Pen-and-ink notes are easier to read, quicker to transcribe. Use a pen to write your notes. Take along with you well-sharpened pencils to use in case your pen runs out of ink.

2. Date the first page of each day's notes with the day, month, and year. Some stenographers place this information in the lower left-hand corner of the page for ease in locating a certain day's dictation. Others who may frequently begin a day's dictation on a partially filled page place the date at the beginning of the notes for that day.

3. Always leave a few lines blank at the beginning of each memo or letter for special instructions you may be given regarding number of copies to be made, order of transcription, special mailing directions, and so forth.

4. Write in longhand the names of individuals or firms if they are unfamiliar to you. The spellings of proper names vary so much that writing them in longhand is the only sure way of transcribing them accurately.

5. If the number of copies to be made is different from the usual requirement, make a notation about the number above the shorthand notes for the memo or letter. It is discouraging and time-wasting to complete a transcript only to discover that several additional copies should have been made.

6. The ideal practice is for the stenographer to insert punctuation and paragraph marks as she takes dictation. Doing this speeds up the transcription and makes it more nearly accurate. Whenever time permits, therefore, insert punctuation and paragraph marks in the notes that you write for transcription.

7. If you take dictation from more than one person, put the initials of each beside or under the date where his dictation begins in your notebook.

8. Place a rubber band or paper clip at the point in your notebook where the transcription should begin. A "finder" of this kind will help you start your work quickly.

9. Make some sort of distinguishing mark at the end of the notes for each memo or letter so that you can judge quickly the length of each transcript.

Study the illustration below, which pictures many of the suggestions just given.

Identify dictator and date first page of each day's dictation.

Write unfamiliar names in longhand.

Leave space for special instructions.

Extra carbon-copy requirements should be noted at beginning.

When time permits during dictation, insert punctuation marks.

Identify end of letter so length can be judged quickly.

Handling the Notebook in Taking Dictation

Color work is more difficult to do with the stencil than with the hectograph because the color is obtained through using various inks at the time of duplicating, whereas the color work for the hectograph process is done while preparing the master.

Common brand names of stencil machines are: Rex Rotary, A. B. Dick Mimeograph, and Gestetner.

Offset Process. This process has increased greatly in popularity in the last decade. With it more attractive copies can be made than with the hectograph or stencil processes, but it is more expensive. Many different kinds of paper can be used for copies; the product resembles printed copy; and more copies can be produced from a master. The equipment is more expensive than for the hectograph or stencil processes. Since greater skill is needed to operate the machine, the process is most often used in firms having enough duplicating work to justify not only the purchase of the equipment, but also to make practical the hiring of at least one full-time employee to operate the machine.

Many types of reproduction can be handled by the offset process, including, for instance, photographs. Color work is handled through using various inks at the time of duplicating, as is true of the stencil process. If metal plates are used, an unlimited number of copies can be made. Copies are permanent.

A stenographer or secretary will rarely be called upon to run the offset machine, but she will need to be able to prepare the masters or plates. The number of copies and the kind of copy to be run determine the type of master to be prepared: (1) short-, medium-, or long-run paper master, (2) plastic-coated master, or (3) metal plate. Increasing use is being made of this process for the printing of books and manuals, as well as form letters and business forms.

Common brand names are Multilith and A. B. Dick Offset.

Multigraph. Multigraph printing requires the setting of type by hand or machine and is, therefore, relatively expensive. The process is used for such items as form letters, card forms, and covers for manuals. Many variations are possible in type styles and in kinds of copy paper used. There is virtually no limit to the number of copies that can be made.

Automatic Typewriting Process. This process permits rapid reproduction of individually typed letters. The automatic typewriter types letters by "reading" a prepared stencil or tape. This method is popular for direct-mail advertising. The equipment is expensive and is used by firms having a large volume of identical messages to produce.

Company brand names include Burrough's Flexowriter and IBM's Magnetic Tape Selectric Typewriter.

Copying Processes. A number of copying processes are on the market. In each process a "picture" is taken of an original document. Special copy paper is required. In some cases, the copy produced is inferior to that which would be produced by a duplicating process.

Copying machines differ in the process used for reproducing, in the colors they will reproduce, in the size of original copy they can handle, and in the type of material of which they can make copies. Some machines permit copying from a book; others, from a single sheet of paper only. Some reproduce only black ink; others, several colors. Some make copies by a heat process; others, by a chemical solution.

Copying machines are relatively simple to operate; explicit directions accompany each machine. Some brand names of copying machines are: Ozalid, Thermo-Fax, Verifax, Photocopier, and Xerox.

Addressing Process. Through the use of a special machine, thousands of advertising leaflets, bulletins, newspapers, or envelopes can be addressed. Each address is placed on a metal or stencil plate and filed. A system of tabbing or notching enables the machine to "select" from the files plates having addresses in certain categories. Two brand names of addressing machines are: Addressograph and Elliott Addressing Machines.

Questions for Discussion
1. Discuss some of the factors that need to be considered in selecting a reproducing process.
2. Which process do you think would be best for:
   a. notice of a ball game for bulletin boards;
   b. a monthly newspaper to be distributed to 200 students;
   c. a letter from the Red Cross soliciting funds?

Office Practice Problems
1. Bring some duplicated materials to class and identify the processes used. Compare the quality of reproduction.
2. Find out from your local office supply store the cost of masters and copy paper for two processes.

Questions for Discussion

1. Why would pen-and-ink notes be easier to read than ones taken with a pencil?
2. If you take dictation from more than one person, what precautions should you take in handling your notebook?
3. Give some common names that are spelled more than one way.
4. Why should you mark the end of each letter or memo?
5. Why should notations be made of extra carbon copies or special mailing notations?

Office Practice Problems

1. Compose a letter to be signed by your employer, John Hardy, writing it in shorthand in your notebook. Assume that you are answering a letter from Mr. Sam Penney, 198 First Street, New York, New York 10010, in which he asked Mr. Hardy what qualities he thought were most important for a secretary to possess. The letter is to be sent airmail.

2. Compose a letter to be signed by your employer, John Hardy, writing it in shorthand in your notebook. Assume that you are answering a letter from Mrs. Sarah Brian, 2981 Clover Road, Cambridge, Massachusetts 01922, in which she asked Mr. Hardy what characteristics in an incoming letter made the most favorable impression on him.

After writing the notes, check to see if you have observed the pointers given at the beginning of this lesson.

16B—Building Speed in Taking Dictation

Brief-Form Practice

Directions. The following paragraph has 41 different brief forms and brief-form derivatives. If you can read it in 30 seconds, your reading rate is 122 words a minute.

Punctuation Preview

Rule 6: A comma (or commas) should be used to set off parenthetical expressions if a definite pause is indicated.

Example: We think, however, that you should have a talk with him.

NOTE: You will need to apply Rule 1, as well as the one given above.

Duplicating and Copying Processes

Lesson **131** ◯ ⬡ ◯ ⬡ ◯ ⬡ ◯ ⬡ ◯ ⬡ ◯ ⬡ ◯ ⬡ ◯ ⬡ ◯ ⬡ ◯ ⬡ ◯

Selecting the Appropriate Process

Modern business activity requires an almost incredible number of extra copies of papers—letters, memos, reports, brochures, bulletins, notices, manuals, names and addresses, and so forth. Many different kinds of processes are on the market to produce these extra copies. The secretary must be able to select the most appropriate one from those that are available to her.

The term "duplicating process" is sometimes distinguished from the term "copying process" by restricting the term "duplicating" to a process that involves the preparation of some type of master copy from which additional copies are made and the term "copying" to a process that involves no preparation of a master copy but in which a "picture" is taken of an original document. "Copying processes" cost more per copy and are, therefore, restricted to jobs requiring a limited number of copies—from 1 to 10, usually.

Several processes will be available in the firm in which you work, either in a duplicating department or in individual offices. Whatever the situation, you will have the problem of choosing the best method from those available. Some of the questions you must answer in making your selection of a process are:

1. What is the nature of the material to be copied or duplicated? Is it handwritten, typewritten, or drawn? Is it in color? Does it include photographs, tables, drawings, etc.? Is the content confidential?

2. What is the size of the original source? What is to be the size of the reproduction?

3. On what type of paper is the reproduction to be made? What weight of paper is desired? Are both sides of the paper to be used?

4. What quality of reproduction is desired? How are copies to be used: Are they work sheets, temporary records, permanent records?

5. How urgent is the job? Must copies be available in 30 minutes, a week, or a month?

6. How many copies are needed in total? Are additional copies likely to be needed later?

7. What expense limitations must be observed?

8. Is an operator with the necessary skill available to run the machine involved in the process?

If your firm has a duplicating department, you probably can get help from its manual or directly from its personnel.

Some of the most commonly used reproducing processes are discussed in this unit.

Fluid Hectograph Process. This process is known by several names, for example, fluid hectograph, direct, spirit, and chemical. It is an inexpensive method, used when a small number of copies is to be made and when the printing on the individual copies does not have to be identical in sharpness of impression. The process is usually used for 10 to 150 copies, although as many as 350 may be obtainable, especially if preprinted or commercially prepared masters are used.

The masters are easy to prepare; they can be typed or handwritten. Color work is simple and inexpensive. The skill needed to operate the machine is easy to acquire. Hectograph copies fade when exposed to light, so they are not good for permanent records. Special paper is needed for masters and copy paper.

Common brand names of fluid process machines are: Ditto Direct, A. B. Dick Azograph, and Rex-O-Graph.

Gelatin Hectograph Process. This process is also known as "indirect." It produces the same type of copies as the fluid hectograph process, but masters are prepared and run differently. The gelatin process produces fewer copies per master than does the fluid process. A common brand name is Ditto.

Stencil Process. The stencil process is popularly known as "mimeograph," once the brand name of one firm's product. By this process, copies can be made that are identical in sharpness of impression; and many more copies can be run from a stencil than can be run from the hectograph master. Up to 10,000 copies can be made from a long-run stencil. Short- and medium-run stencils are available for shorter runs. Preprinted or commercially prepared stencils will run more copies than those prepared in the office. The process is more expensive than the hectograph. Copies are permanent; special copy paper should be used.

[Shorthand outlines with word counts: 3, 6, 10, 16, 26, 33, 41, 48, 55, 63 on left column; 72, 80, 90, 96, 101, 106, 113, 120, 130, 138, 141, 147, 160 on right column]

92 *33308*

Foster O. Rich 141
Vice-President 147
160

Dictionary and Spelling Preview

1. humorous, unanimous, enthusiasm, partiality

2. review, unique, professors, reputable, evaluation

3. forepart, ascertain

Preview of New Dictation Material

(1) [shorthand outlines]

humorous, consecutive, universal, stoutly, continuation, unanimous, Youth, dampen, utilization, Van Buren, undoubtedly, dispute, defend

(2) [shorthand outlines]

review, factual, among the, reputable, institutions, consumption, usefulness, Houston, we are sending you

(3) [shorthand outlines]

explanatory, forepart, discount, forward, ascertain, various, to check, since the

Building Skill in Transcribing

Transcribing from Shorthand Notes

1. Write in shorthand Memo (1) given below.

2. Transcribe the memo from your notes as a 5-minute writing. Determine your *mwam*. If you complete the memo before time is called, repeat it from the beginning.

3. Transcribe Memo (2) as a 5-minute writing. Determine your *mwam* and compare it with your *mwam* on Memo (1).

(1)

		Words
TO:	Alan P. Fredericks, General Sales	8
	Manager	9
FROM:	Richard D. Edwards, Eastern	16
	Sales Manager	19
DATE:	April 15, 19—	24
SUBJECT:	Quarterly Sales Report, Eastern	32
	Region	33

Attached is our quarterly sales 40
report covering gross sales for the months of 49
January, February, and [1] March. 55

It is significant, we think, that all 63
the salesmen except one showed a sales in- 71
crease of at least 5 percent [2] over the same 80
period last year. I am sure the slight reduc- 89
tion in sales for Mr. Jennings' territory [3] is a 99
reflection of the general business conditions 108
in his area. You will recall that for a number [4] 117
of months his territory was part of an eco- 126
nomically depressed area. Only recently [5] have 135
there been signs that business is beginning to 145
recover. It is the hope of both Mr. Jennings 154
and me that [6] this recovery will be reflected as 163
increased sales in the next quarterly report. 173

You will be pleased, too, to [7] note 179
that sales returns have been reduced by a 188
substantial percentage over the first three 197
months of last year. Part of [8] this is due, we 206
believe, to the improvement you made re- 214
cently in the assembly of new items. 221

We shall all [9] welcome your reac- 228
tions to this report and your suggestions for 237
improving our sales performance. (211) 244

Attachment 246

(2)

Transcribing from Dictation

Your teacher will dictate an interoffice memo and minutes of a meeting to you for transcription.

Lesson **17** ⬡⬡⬡⬡⬡⬡⬡⬡⬡⬡⬡⬡⬡⬡⬡⬡⬡⬡⬡

17A—Office-Style Dictation

Much of the dictation you take in the classroom is given at an even rate because that helps you to increase your speed in recalling shorthand outlines. At an appropriate time, your teacher will begin to give you "office-style" dictation, so that you will be prepared to take notes of dictation that is given in the business office.

All dictators have an idea of what they want to say in a letter when they start dictating, but most of them have not thought through the exact wording they want to use; therefore, their rate of dictation is uneven. Sometimes a dictator will desire to rephrase something he has already dictated. At other times he may wish to insert an additional sentence or paragraph after he has completed dictating the letter or memo. There may be times when he decides to delete certain words, phrases, or sentences for which you have already written the shorthand. You, the secretary, must be able to indicate those changes in such a way that you can transcribe your notes accurately.

There are two basic methods of indicating changes in dictation. The one most commonly used is the "cross-out" method. In this method the secretary crosses out with a single stroke of her pen the notes that are to be changed and inserts

the correct words. This method is desirable when the dictator dictates well within the shorthand writing speed of the secretary and when the dictator is likely to be interrupted so that reading back of notes is necessary.

The "continuous-writing" method is one in which the secretary does no crossing out. She indicates that a change is being made by a series of vertical strokes at the beginning and end of the change and then within those strokes writes down everything the dictator says—directions for change as well as the actual wording to be changed. This latter method is useful when the dictator talks rapidly and when there is little occasion for reading back after interruptions. There should be no resentment on your part when the dictator wishes to change what he has already dictated. Your job is to handle expertly the dictation given you, regardless of the fact that the dictation method may seem inefficient to you.

Later you will learn how to handle more complicated changes in dictation.

These two methods of taking office-style dictation are illustrated on this page and on page 45. Study them carefully.

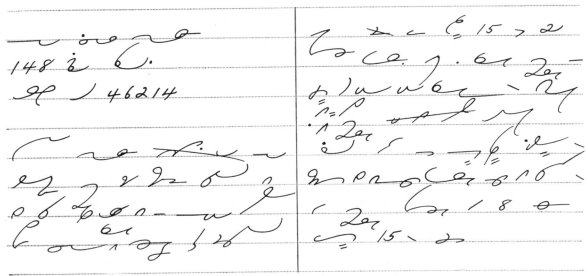

Cross-Out Method

Unit 4 · Lesson 17

44

page number of the corrections. It is best for all corrections to be initialed by the secretary and the presiding officer to indicate who authorized the changes.

9. Place the minutes in the minutes book. Keep the book in the place designated by the company.

10. Prepare a card index of subjects for each set of minutes and arrange the index cards in alphabetic order by subject titles. The subjects chosen for indexing purposes should be major motions made and passed or rejected and major proposals made and approved or rejected. The captions in the margins of the minutes book are an efficient guide to the preparation of the index cards.

Questions for Discussion and Office Practice Problems

1. What types of organizations hold meetings important enough to require the keeping of permanent records of the meetings?

2. What is the name given to the official written record of a meeting?

3. Who ordinarily records the minutes of a meeting and prepares a typewritten transcript of them?

4. What pattern or arrangement do minutes ordinarily follow?

5. List the types of information usually included in the minutes of a meeting.

6. Why is the secretary usually given a copy of each report made at a meeting?

7. Why should a secretary prepare a rough draft to submit to her employer before preparing the final draft of the minutes of a meeting?

8. Why should the secretary follow a definite procedure in making corrections in the minutes of a previous meeting?

9. After the minutes have been typed and properly signed by the secretary and the required

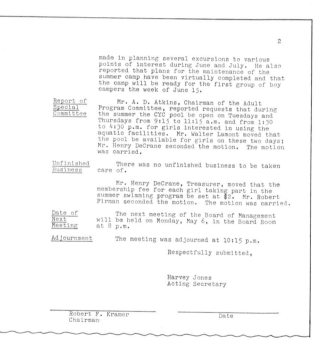

Portions of Minutes of a Meeting

officers of the organization, what does the secretary do with the minutes?

10. Your teacher will dictate to you the minutes of the Board of Management meeting, portions of the minutes of which are illustrated on this page. Transcribe the minutes of this meeting in the form used in the illustration. Prepare 3 carbon copies for distribution to the members of the Board.

Continuous-Writing Method

Questions for Discussion

1. How does dictation in the office differ from much of your classroom dictation? Why?
2. What are the two basic methods of indicating changes in dictation? Under what circumstances could each be used satisfactorily?

Office Practice Problem

See if you can read the following notes that were taken from office-style dictation. If your teacher so directs, transcribe the letter.

Preparing Minutes of Meetings

Meetings are one of the important activities of businesses, service organizations, social organizations, church groups, and many others. Accurate records must be kept of the proposals offered, the decisions made, the actions taken at such meetings, as well as of other pertinent details. The official record of a meeting is known as the *minutes*.

Many times the secretary of a business executive is expected to attend a meeting and to assume the responsibility of recording the minutes and of preparing a typewritten transcript of them.

Minutes need not be arranged in any special pattern, but they ordinarily follow the outline of the order of business that is recommended by the organization bylaws or that is established by the agenda prepared by the meeting chairman. However, the minutes of a single organization are always prepared in the same general form.

Content of Minutes of Meetings. The minutes of a meeting usually include:

1. The name of the organization; the time, the date, and the place of the meeting; and the type of meeting held—regular or special.

2. The names of the presiding officer and the secretary and the result of the roll call. (In a small meeting the names of all those present are listed; in a large meeting the number of persons present is sufficient.)

3. A statement regarding the reading of the minutes of the previous meeting, the approval of the minutes as read, or the approval of the minutes with suggested corrections.

4. Reports of officers and the chairmen of various committees. (A copy of each report is usually given to the secretary so that she can file it with the minutes.)

5. A summary of action taken on unfinished business from the previous meeting.

6. A summary of action taken on new business brought up for consideration.

7. The announcement of the date of the next meeting.

8. The time of adjournment.

9. The signature of the secretary who prepared and typed the minutes.

The summaries listed in Items 5 and 6 are of the proposals made and actions taken. They should include the name of the person making a proposal or a motion, the name of the person seconding the motion, and the result of the action.

Suggestions for Preparing the Minutes. Transcribe your notes in correct form as soon as possible after the meeting while the details of the meeting are still fresh in your mind. If you were not present at a meeting and your employer dictates the minutes to you, get all the pertinent information from him at the time of the dictation so that you will not overlook anything. Submit your rough draft to your employer for approval before preparing the final draft.

The following guides will be of help to you.

1. Center and type in all capitals the heading of the minutes, that is, the name of the organization calling the meeting.

2. Single- or double-space the minutes according to the style established by the organization for the minutes of previous meetings. If the minutes are to be inserted into a loose-leaf binder, allow a margin of 1½ inches at the left and a margin of 1 inch at the right.

3. Type subject captions for the various sections of the minutes.

4. Type the minutes on only one side of the sheet.

5. Check to be sure that you have included all the essential information.

6. Number the pages so that no one can remove a page for any reason without having the removal noticed.

7. When the minutes are in final form, send them to the secretary of the organization or the presiding officer, or both, for signatures. At the end of the minutes type lines on which the signatures and the date may be written.

8. If at a meeting it is necessary to make any corrections in the minutes of a previous meeting, the secretary may draw a line through the incorrect words and insert the corrections above them. If more than a few words are affected, the secretary may draw a line through the sentences or paragraphs affected and type the corrections on a new page. In this case she should indicate on the original page the

Phrase Builder

There are 10 phrases in the following sentence.

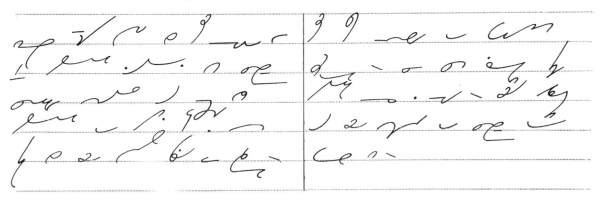

Punctuation Preview

Rule 7: Use a semicolon between coordinate clauses that are joined by a conjunction when these clauses contain commas.

Example: When you are in doubt about the spelling of a word, look it up in the dictionary; and never take a chance on guessing correctly.

NOTE: You will need to apply Rules 1, 2, and 6, as well as the one presented here.

Practice Material for Building Fluency

(1)

	Words		Words
	3		42
	7		49
	11		59
	17		70
			81
	24		91
	30		100
	36		109

Table 2

Los Angeles Firms Making Studies of Letter Costs

Number of Letters Written Per Month	Number of Firms	Firms Reporting Cost Studies	
		Number	Percent
1-99	13	0	0.0
100-499	41	1	.9
500-999	16	0	.0
1000-4999	20	1	.9
5000 and over	11	3	2.8
No data on number of letters	8	0	.0
Total	109	5	4.6

The activity of the different firms classified by the number of letters written per month may be illustrated by showing what the firms in each group have done in relation to that group. For example, in the group of firms writing 1 to 99 letters monthly, 100 percent had not made a letter cost study; while of those writing 5,000 letters or more, 27 percent had made such studies.

Graph 1 clearly shows that large firms are not seriously considering correspondence costs. Smaller firms, where less specialization is generally practiced, appear to have less need for such studies. The fact that none of the firms which write from 500 to 999 letters monthly had analyzed letter costs through a formal study indicates an apparent lack of interest in possible savings.

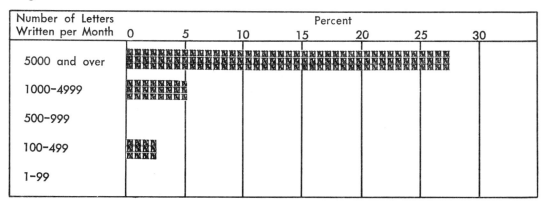

Graph 1. Relationship of Number of Letters Written per Month to Incidence of Letter-Cost Studies

Spot Checking Correspondence. One method by which correspondence can be controlled is to examine samples of outgoing letters. This is sometimes called "spot checking." It is not usually feasible for managers or correspondence specialists to examine every letter mailed; thus, the letters prepared by each writer may be sampled periodically.

The literature on correspondence control contains frequent reference to the use of specialists and consultants but refers much less frequently to "spot checking." One writer does, however, speak of ". . . reviewing carbons once a month and rating each correspondent." [2]

[2] Richard H. Morris, "Poor Letters Are a Luxury," *Management Review,* XLII (March, 1954), 165.

Words

(shorthand outlines) 116

(shorthand outlines) 122

(shorthand outlines) 132

(shorthand outlines) 141

(shorthand outlines) 150

(shorthand outlines) 159

Edward S. Silverstein 167
General Manager 171
184

(2)

(shorthand) 2, 19 _(shorthand)_ 2

(shorthand outlines) 6

2046 _(shorthand outlines)_ 11

(shorthand) 39209 16

Words

(shorthand outlines) 23

(shorthand outlines) 29

(shorthand outlines) 35

(shorthand outlines) 43

(shorthand outlines) 51

(shorthand outlines) 62

(shorthand outlines) 70

(shorthand outlines) 75

(shorthand outlines) 81

(shorthand outlines) 91

A. W. Pollock 94
Treasurer 98
112

Dictionary and Spelling Preview

1. auditions, sizable, cancellations, accommodations, participate

2. ammunition, avocation, exclusively, expedition

3. onionskin

Preview of New Dictation Material

(1) _(shorthand outlines)_

I wish, specific, musical, accommodations, you might like, to participate, competition, must be made, duplication, installation, festival, piano, participants

(2) _(shorthand outlines)_

ammunition, perfection, expedition, Mission, demonstrations, target, we have had, avocation, as you might, marvelous, exclusively

(3) _(shorthand outlines)_

generally, onionskin, to such, concerned, forward, likewise

Table 1*

Letter Cost Chart of the Average-
Length Dictated Business Letter

DICTATOR'S TIME:

    based on an average salary of $168 a week;
a 40-hour week; and an average of eight
minutes for each letter written . . . . 56¢

STENOGRAPHIC COST:

    based on an average salary of $70 a week;
a 40-hour week; and an average of 24 letters
a day, including time taking dictation . . . . 58¢

NONPRODUCTIVE TIME:

    time lost by dictator and stenographer
because of waiting, illness, and other causes . . . . 04.62¢

FIXED CHARGES:

    depreciation, supervision, rent, light, interest,
taxes, insurance, and similar overhead . . . . 18.48¢

MATERIALS:

    letterheads, envelopes, carbon papers, typewriter
ribbons, pencils, and other supplies . . . . 06.75¢

FILING COSTS:

    clerical time, costs of filing supplies . . . . 01.67¢

MAILING COSTS:

    postage, gathering, sealing, stamping, and
delivering to the post office . . . . 04.48¢**

                                TOTAL COST . . . . $ 1.50

* Aurner, op. cit., p. 24.
** As of January, 1963, mailing costs are a minimum of 5.48 cents.

What are businesses in the Los Angeles area doing in the way of studying letter costs? Table 2 indicates that of the 109 companies responding, 4.6 percent made some type of letter cost study while 95.4 percent have not made such a study. The number of companies that made a study of letter costs was so small that no trend could be determined when firms were classified by the number of letters written each month. Of the five letter cost studies made, three were in firms writing 5,000 letters or more each month. Thus, it appears that greater activity in correspondence results in greater concern for controlling letter costs.

Lesson **18** ⬡⬡⬡⬡⬡⬡⬡⬡⬡⬡⬡⬡⬡⬡⬡

18A—Interruptions and Pauses in the Dictation

Some dictators are interrupted frequently as they dictate by people coming to the office or by telephone calls. What should you do at such a time?

If the interruption appears to be a routine one of short duration, your employer will probably want you to remain where you are. If so, keep your eyes on your notebook and use the time to correct any poorly written outlines or to insert punctuation marks in your notes. Do not watch your employer or the visitor if there is one.

If the call seems to be of some length or of a confidential nature, your employer may indicate by a word, gesture, or nod of the head that he wants you to return to your desk.

If an office visitor asks a question to which you know the answer, do not volunteer the information. If your employer wants you to participate in the discussion, he will ask you to do so.

When the interruption is over, you will need to read back to the dictator the last paragraph or sentence to help him recall what he was saying.

Many times a dictator has not thought out exactly what he wants to say in a letter. He will dictate at varying speeds as he thinks through just what he wants to say. When a dictator pauses, you, the secretary, should not look up inquiringly,

tap your pencil or your foot, or give any other indication of annoyance or boredom. Neither should you give any indication of annoyance if he does considerable rephrasing so that you are required to make numerous changes in your notes. It is your job to serve your employer to the best of your ability and not to be critical of his dictation habits. Many times you will be grateful for the pauses or interruptions because they give you an opportunity to "catch up" when the dictation has been too fast for you to take easily.

Questions for Discussion

1. What should you do when the dictator is interrupted by a telephone call?
2. What should you do when a visitor comes to the dictator's desk?
3. What should you do when the dictator is groping for the right word or phrase?

Office Practice Problem

Changes in dictation were made in the following notes by using the continuous-writing method. See if you can read the letter in its correct form. If your teacher so directs, transcribe the letter.

Unit 4 · Lesson 18

48

Arranging and Typing a Business Report

In Unit 25 you reviewed the principles of and the procedures for arranging and typing manuscripts of various papers and for centering typewritten material on various sizes of stationery. In the last two lessons you learned how to organize reports through careful planning and outlining procedures, how to collect report information and to prepare related bibliography and note cards, and how to prepare effective tables and graphs.

In this lesson, therefore, you are given the opportunity to apply what you have learned. A section of a business report appears below and on the following pages. The report includes two types of tables, a bar graph, and footnotes. Before you begin to arrange and type this report section in correct manuscript form, you will want to review the information and the guides presented in Lessons 121, 122, 126, and 127.

Office Practice Problem

Type in correct manuscript form the following section of a business report adapted from Erwin M. Keithley's *A Manual of Style*. The report is to be bound at the left. Double-space the data of Table 2 (page 329). Use your typewriter to prepare the segments of Graph 1 (page 329). Underline italicized words.

center over the line of writing

SECTION 2 II

ANALYSIS OF CORRESPONDENCE INSTRUCTION
AND CONTROL PRACTICES

← *Triple-space*

In order to focus attention on correspondence instruction and control practices questions were ~~asked~~ *directed* as follows: (1) To what extent has business studied letter costs and developed controls? (2) Which *types of* instructional programs are being used? (3) What use is made of correspondence specialists?

← *Triple-space*

Letter Costs and Controls

Since the ~~study~~ was made of firms represented in the *Local* Cost Accountant's Association, it ~~is~~ *might be* assumed that controls of *the costs and* letter production ~~are~~ *would be* of real concern. The data following, however, *do not verify* ~~don't justify~~ this assumption.

Studies of Letter Costs. The firms represented in this study have done *very* little to determine letter costs. One can find a wide range of *letter* costs reported in the literature. For example, a study was made by the Mutual *Life* Insurance company which found that the *average* cost of a letter was between $1.00 and $1.25. Table 1 shows a more recent estimate of the cost of the average-length dictated business letter.

---

1 Erwin R. Steinberg, "Thinking Through a Letter-Writing Program," *Management Review*, XLIV (September, 1955), p. 614.

4

Potential Rate Builder

There are 17 words in the following sentence.

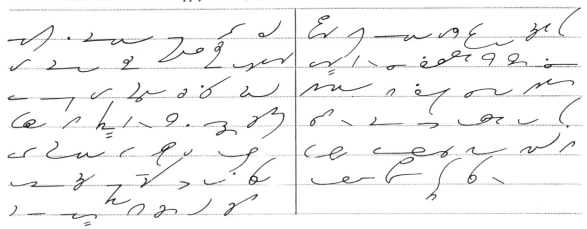

Punctuation Preview

Rule 8: (a) To set off an introductory adverbial phrase containing a verb, use a comma.

Example: In order to meet the deadline, we shall have to work late tonight.

Rule 8: (b) Use a comma to set off an introductory phrase that does not contain a verb if a pause would be made at that point in reading or if a comma is essential for emphasis or clearness.

Example: As a result, the shipment was delayed a week.

NOTE: You will need to apply Rules 1, 2, 3, 6, and 7, as well as the rules given above.

Practice Material for Building Fluency

Words

4, 19 — 2

6

89 9

37204 15

25

34

Words

43

51

59

68

78

87

98

Kinds of Graphs. A graph is a statistical picture. Well-designed graphs often present business data more vividly than tables, and they may also make possible a more clear-cut comparison of data. In most cases, however, graphs are limited to the presentation and comparison of fewer factors than are possible in comprehensive tables.

Graphs are of six general types: *simple bar* (horizontal or vertical), *segmented bar, line, parallel bar, surface,* and *pie* or *circle* graphs. Of these six types, the line, the horizontal bar, the vertical bar, and the pie graph are most frequently used. The basic structure of each of these types is illustrated at the right.

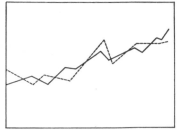

Line Graph

Guides to Graph Preparation. The following suggestions will guide you in preparing well-designed, meaningful graphs:

1. Use bar graphs instead of line or surface graphs where possible.

2. Label each bar or segment with figures and identifications (words or symbols).

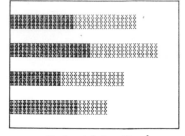

Horizontal Bar Graph

3. Vertical and horizontal graphs are equally effective so long as there is room to label the segments horizontally. Appropriate labeling in many cases makes horizontally arranged bars essential.

4. A pie graph and a bar graph may be used equally effectively for presenting percentage breakdowns or comparisons, but the bar graph is easier to design.

5. Use a graph heading or title that clearly identifies the content of the graph.

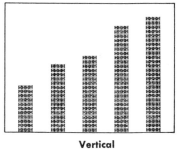

Vertical Bar Graph

6. To aid the reader in comparing the factors and the degree of difference among them, short vertical and horizontal guide lines should be provided. These guide lines should be carefully labeled.

7. Solid segments can be made on the typewriter by striking several letters over one another; for example, *m, n, w,* and *v*:

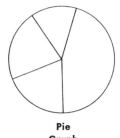

Pie Graph

8. Light segments can be made on the typewriter by striking the *m* or the *x*:

Questions for Discussion and Office Practice Problems

1. Why are primary, rather than secondary, sources most often used in preparing business reports?

2. Why is it desirable to prepare a bibliography card for each reference used in the preparation of a report?

3. What four elements should a note card include?

4. Obtain a copy of a summary table and one of a comparison table. Analyze the tables carefully and be prepared to describe them in class and to discuss their effectiveness.

5. Make a typewritten copy of each of the tables selected for Problem 4. Place each one on a separate sheet of paper.

6. Obtain from newspapers or magazines a copy of each of the four types of graphs illustrated above. Analyze each one carefully and be prepared to discuss in class how effectively it presents its data and what, if anything, might be done to improve it.

7. Prepare a copy of each of the graphs selected for Problem 6, making whatever improvements you think are desirable.

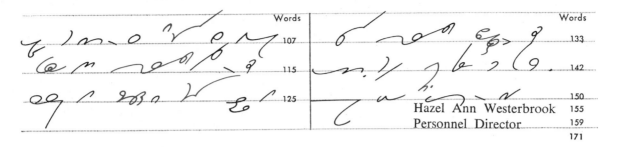

Words

107

115

125

Words

133

142

150

Hazel Ann Westerbrook 155
Personnel Director 159

171

Dictionary and Spelling Preview

1. radiator, efficient, either, servicemen, windshield

2. unexcelled, bristles, medium, angled

3. hazard, latch

Preview of New Dictation Material

(1)

windshield, servicemen, wiped, soiled, radiator, waste, watch, wax, they don't

(2)

toothbrushes, adults, unexcelled, younger, angled, bristles, druggist, medium, soft, consult, Warren, who want

(3)

performed, as a rule, destroyed, smouldering, overlooked, windows, ruined, debris, janitors, electrical, hazard, to be sure

Lesson 19 ⬡○⬡○⬡○⬡○⬡○⬡○⬡○⬡○⬡○⬡○⬡○⬡

19A—Handling the Notebook in Transcription

Just as there are certain work habits that will help you take dictation efficiently, so there are certain work habits that will help you transcribe your notes efficiently. Read the following suggestions carefully and put them into practice.

1. Check through the dictation given for any rush items that should take precedence over others.

2. Check the beginning of your notes for each letter or memo before you begin transcribing it to see whether extra carbon copies are to be made or

The new employees and their weekly earnings are as follows: Addison, John, $62.50; Carroll, Virginia, $70; Fitzgerald, James, $100; Harris, Loren, $83.50; Jackson, Eula Mae, $67.50; and Kline, Shirley, $55.

Comparison Tables. Comparison tables are arranged so that the data in them can be easily analyzed and compared. In the following table, for example, the stenographers in a stenographic pool are compared in terms of the average number of letters they transcribe per day and in terms of the total transcribed for the week. Note that the data are arranged from high to low according to the number of letters transcribed rather than by alphabetic order of the stenographers' names.

TRANSCRIPTION PERFORMANCE OF STENOGRAPHERS

(Mailable Letters Transcribed)

Stenographer	Weekly Total	Daily Average
Wright, Lori	200	40
Gregory, Betty Jane	185	37
Morrison, Norma	175	35
Bradley, Janice	150	30
Prentiss, Mildred	130	26
Rehme, Dolores	110	22
Collins, Frances	100	20
Pool Average	150	30

Note how easy it is to determine from this table the best transcriber and the poorest, the average number of letters transcribed each day by each stenographer, the daily average for the entire pool, the total letters transcribed by each stenographer each week, and the weekly average for the entire pool.

Major Parts of a Table. A properly prepared table has four major parts:

1. Title: Tells briefly what the table contains.

2. Main Body: Consists of vertical columns and horizontal rows of data. The left-hand column is known as the *stub*, and the items in the stub explain the material in the horizontal rows. The other columns are known as *data columns*. *Captions* head the stub and data columns.

3. Footnotes: Consist of explanatory notes and exceptions. They are placed at the foot of the table and should be lettered or identified clearly with special symbols.

4. Source: Indicates the publication from which the data came if a secondary, rather than a primary, source was used.

Guides to Preparing Tables. The following guides will be helpful to you in constructing tables:

1. Since the eyes tend naturally to read down a column of figures rather than across a row, place the items to be compared in the same column rather than in the same row. (See the illustrative table on page 324.) If, however, the items are to be compared in more than one way, arrange the data for both vertical and horizontal comparison. (See the illustrative table at the left on this page.)

2. Unless a table is an integral part of the body of the report, is introduced by a statement that indicates the content of the columns, is only a few lines long, and includes only two or three columns, begin the table with a descriptive heading and head each stub and data column with a descriptive caption. The headings and captions should be short and neatly centered over the copy they head.

3. If a table is used as a separate exhibit or if it requires a full page, center it vertically. (Follow the vertical centering steps on page 310.) Leave a triple space between the table heading and the column captions, a double space between the column captions and the first row of data. When a secondary heading follows the main heading, leave a double space between the two, and leave a triple space between the secondary heading and the column captions.

4. Whether a table appears as a part of the body of the report or is prepared as a separate exhibit, center it horizontally. (Follow the horizontal centering steps on page 310.) Centering a row of data is the same as centering a line of continuous type except that the blank spaces between columns replace the actual typewritten strokes in the line of continuous type.

5. Leaders may be used to connect the items in the stub to the appropriate sets of data in the first data column for easy matching. Likewise, vertical rules may be used to guide the eye down the columns for easy comparison.

6. Align words at the left, but align numbers at the right. Keep decimal points in alignment.

7. Place the dollar sign in an amount column before the first dollar amount and before the total, positioned in each instance one space to the left of the longest dollar amount in the column.

whether there are special mailing instructions to be followed.

3. If you have information to obtain or facts to check before completing the transcription of a letter, do that before you start to transcribe. The information may mean changing the content of the letter or setup of the typescript.

4. Note the amount of notes you have so that you can judge the length of the letter for good placement. Remember that such lines as subject and attention, quoted matter, and tabulations have the effect of increasing the length of the letter, so that a longer writing line or a reduction in space between certain opening and closing lines is required.

5. Read in thought phrases so that you do not have to read your notes more than once. By so doing, you read just far enough ahead of your typing to get the thought. This procedure keeps you from misreading an outline that may have been incorrectly written or may be somewhat out of proportion.

6. When you complete the transcribing of a letter or memo, strike a vertical line through the notes to indicate that it is finished.

7. If you are interrupted by a telephone call or someone coming by your desk, quickly make a check at the point where you are in your notes so that you will not lose time finding your place when you resume transcription. A red pencil will make a check mark that is easy to find.

8. Type the envelope for a letter before going to the next letter. Attach any enclosures securely.

9. The envelope should be placed at the top of the letter, face up, with the flap hooked over the letter. This arrangement enables the dictator to glance quickly at both the address on the envelope and in the inside address.

10. Finished letters should be placed face down on your desk or in a tray in a desk drawer so that no one passing your desk will be tempted to read the correspondence.

11. In some offices the secretary retains the file copies until the letter has been mailed, and then files them. In some offices the file copies are placed in the outgoing mailbox, and the mail messenger picks them up and takes them to the Filing Department.

12. Filled notebooks should be disposed of according to the firm's practices. Some firms have notebooks dated and filed for a specified length of time. Other firms permit the secretary to destroy a filled notebook immediately.

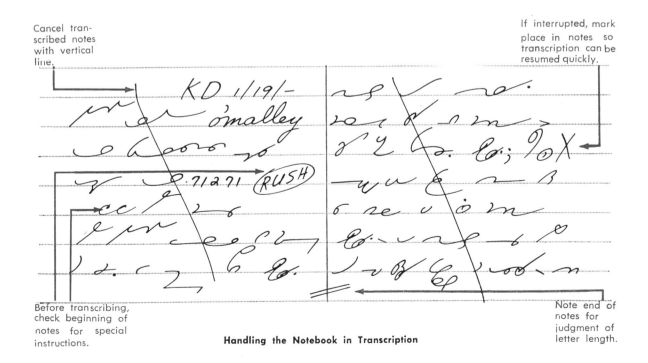

Cancel transcribed notes with vertical line.

If interrupted, mark place in notes so transcription can be resumed quickly.

Before transcribing, check beginning of notes for special instructions.

Note end of notes for judgment of letter length.

Handling the Notebook in Transcription

Preparing Note Cards. Note cards represent to the report narrative what bibliography cards represent to the footnotes and bibliography of the report—convenient sources of reference.

In recording reference notes, it is best to use cards (5″ by 3″ or larger) because they make it easy to sort the notes into a logical sequence according to the report outline. Use only one side of a card and limit the information on each card to a single specific topic.

Each note card should contain the following information:

1. The *topic* of the recorded information placed in the upper left-hand corner of the card.
2. The *source* of the information indicated by the same number as that assigned to the bibliography card, placed in the upper right-hand corner.
3. The source *page number* on which the information is found, following the source number.
4. The *information* written either as a direct quotation (exactly as given in the original source) or as a summary statement or as a paraphrase of the original statement.

Bibliography Card

Note Card

Preparing Tables and Graphs

Short tables and simple graphs are being used more and more to support statements made in the narrative body of business reports. This is true because tests of report comprehension have shown that:

1. Text (narrative) accompanied with a well-designed graph does the best job of delivering the message.
2. Text accompanied with a short, well-prepared table does the next best job of delivering the message.
3. A well-designed graph alone is better than text alone.
4. A short, well-prepared table alone is better than text alone.
5. Text alone, even when it includes supporting or explanatory statistical data, does not deliver the message effectively.

The best guarantee of getting the message across is to present the information in two forms: *text with graphs* or *text with tables*.

Kinds of Tables. In general, there are two types of tables the secretary is asked to prepare. They are *summary tables* and *comparison tables*.

Summary Tables. Summary tables merely provide a vivid, easy-to-grasp form for listing data to portray conditions and relationships. For example, a summary table may be used to list the names of salesmen in one column and their annual dollar sales volume in another or the names of employees in one column and their weekly earnings in another. If the items in one of the columns are arranged alphabetically or by some other sequential method, desired information can be found easily and quickly. Note the greater ease with which information can be found in the following table than in the paragraph which appears at the top of page 325.

The new employees and their weekly earnings are as follows:

Addison, John	$ 62.50
Carroll, Virginia.	70.00
Fitzgerald, James.	100.00
Harris, Loren	83.50
Jackson, Eula Mae	67.50
Kline, Shirley	55.00

Questions for Discussion

1. Why should you read your notes in thought phrases?
2. What should be the order of your activities in getting ready to transcribe the notes you have written?
3. How should the typed letter be presented to the dictator?
4. What should be done with filled notebooks?
5. What should you do with each letter or memo as you complete it?

Office Practice Problem

The following letter was taken from office-style dictation. The secretary used a combination of cross-out and continuous-writing methods. See if you can read the notes correctly. If your teacher directs, transcribe the letter.

[shorthand notes] 87105

19B—Building Speed in Taking Dictation

Proportion Drill

(1) *[shorthand notes]*
(2) *[shorthand notes]*
(3) *[shorthand notes]*

Punctuation Preview

Rule 9: Use a comma to set off an introductory phrase beginning with a participle (verbal adjective). No comma should follow an introductory phrase beginning with a gerund (verbal noun).

Examples: Thinking the peak load had been reached, we planned to begin reducing our work force.

Thinking the peak load had been reached was a mistake.

NOTE: This exercise requires the application of Rules 1-4, as well as Rules 6-9.

Collecting Report Information

Two general types of sources are available to report writers for collecting report information: primary sources and secondary sources. Some reports rely upon primary sources exclusively; others call upon secondary sources; while still others use both.

Primary Sources. Many business reports written today use primary source material as their basis. Among the most common of these sources are the records kept by the businesses themselves—records of production costs, unit and dollar sales volume, sales expense, employee performance, cost and performance of office machines and other equipment, and other records. With the vast amount of record keeping required in modern business, many report writers follow the dictum: "Don't go to the store until you have looked in the pantry; you may already have a wealth of facts in your own records."

Other primary sources include time-and-motion studies, experimental studies, observations, questionnaire surveys, and interviews. Before embarking upon one of these methods to gather data, however, the report writer should check to see if such studies have been made by others and if the findings are applicable to his report. In other words, "Don't grow it yourself if you can get it better and easier from someone else."

Secondary Sources. Secondary sources of report information include such materials as encyclopedias, dictionaries, atlases, directories, textbooks, journals, magazines, newspapers, bulletins, and other reports. Thus, they represent the work of other researchers and writers. Even though many reports are based essentially upon primary source data, secondary sources provide rich background material, related statistics, and valuable facts. Indeed, frequent reading of materials such as these often points up the need to analyze business operations and procedures and to report findings.

Many businesses subscribe to information services that can be used as secondary sources of report information. Among the most popular of these bulletins are *Business Inventory—Commodity Price Forecast, Business Management—Sales and Wage Forecasts, Daily Report to Executives, Dartnell News Letter, The Kiplinger Washington Letter,* and *Report on the Business Outlook.*

In addition, many businessmen subscribe to such business-related periodicals as *Administrative Management-Office Executive, Business Week, Dun's Review and Modern Industry, Fortune, Monthly Labor Review, Nation's Business,* and *The Wall Street Journal.*

Guides to these and other publications include *Ayer's Directory of Newspapers and Periodicals, Business Periodicals Index, Reader's Guide to Periodical Literature, The Monthly Catalog of U. S. Government Publications,* and *The Vertical File Service Catalog* (a guide to pamphlets and leaflets).

Other less frequently published source materials that contain a wealth of information related to business operations are *Census Reports, The Economic Almanac, Information Please Almanac, The Statesman's Yearbook, The Statistical Abstract of the United States,* and *World Almanac.*

Many of these publications will not be available in the office in which you may work as a secretary. The most important ones, however, may be found in the local public library. The secretary who wants to be informed about business and who wants to be a capable office assistant will take the time at least to scan the information bulletins and periodicals her employer reads and to check the local library to see what other sources of business information are available there. It is not enough that she read magazines such as *Today's Secretary* and *The Secretary* to keep current on happenings and trends in secretarial work; she should also be alert to what is happening in the business world generally.

Preparing Bibliography Cards. Before making notes from a secondary source, such as one of those given above, prepare a bibliography card for the publication. The bibliography card (usually 5″ by 3″) should include: the library call number, if it is a library publication; the author's name; the title of the publication (and the article title if it is in a magazine); the name and location of the publisher; and the date of the publication. Carefully prepared index cards are a real aid in preparing footnotes and bibliographies.

As each bibliography card is prepared, number it in the upper right-hand corner. That number is used to identify all notes that are taken from the publication that is assigned that number. Numbering the cards consecutively saves a great deal of time in identifying the sources later when preparing note cards and typing the footnotes.

Practice Material for Building Fluency

Words
3
11
16
27
34
40
47
54
60
69
77
83
92
100
107
117

Words
125
133
143
152
157
166
175
182
191
198
205
213
220
229
238
242

Developing the Body of the Report. If the report outline is to serve well the purpose for which it was prepared, it should guide the writing of the body of the report. In fact, if the guiding outline was well planned in the beginning and modified as changes in structure seemed desirable, the writing of the body of the report can be thought of as merely the expansion and development of each of the topics and subtopics in the outline.

Characteristics of Effective Reports. To be effective, a report must meet the following test of desirable characteristics:

1. The report is *complete:* (a) it answers all the questions with which the study was concerned; (b) it presents all the facts that are pertinent; (c) it draws conclusions and makes recommendations based on those facts.
2. The report is *correct:* (a) it has been checked and rechecked so that all data used are accurate; (b) it is correct in form, in arrangement, and in grammatical structure.
3. The report is *clear:* (a) it includes a predominance of familiar words and appropriately short sentences; (b) it presents only one central idea in each sentence; (c) it is written to the reader in his language, not to the writer in his.
4. The report is *concise:* (a) it plunges right into the subject to be covered by a topic heading; (b) it says enough, but just enough; (c) it avoids needless "filler" words and irrelevant material.
5. The report is *concrete:* (a) it presents crisp details rather than vague generalities; (b) it uses strong, picture-making words to make facts vivid.
6. The report is *interesting:* (a) it has variety in sentence length and structure; (b) it uses a variety of methods in developing paragraphs —narration, description, analysis, comparison, argumentation, and presentation of details and examples; (c) it uses transitional words carefully to connect parts of sentences, to relate sentences to each other, and to relate one paragraph to another.

Rewriting and Revising. It has often been said that "effective reports are not written, they are rewritten." Certainly no report should be considered finished unless it has been rewritten and revised until the writer can make no further improvement in it. Any effort less than this guarantees nothing more than a mediocre report.

1. What are the four parts of introductory material of a formal report and why are they not prepared until the body of the report has been completed?
2. Why is it important to define the problem carefully and to state precisely the purpose of the report before taking any other step?
3. Give at least three reasons for preparing a guiding outline before beginning the research for report information and writing the report.
4. Why is it sometimes necessary to modify the guiding outline after work on the report has begun?

Office Practice Problem

One of the best ways to learn to write material that has the characteristics that effective reports must have is to rewrite ineffective material prepared by others. The following paragraphs are examples of poor writing that appeared in a report from a department head to his employees.

(1) Prepare a topic and subtopic outline for a revision of the paragraphs.
(2) Rewrite the paragraphs, incorporating as many of the characteristics listed at the left as you can. By appealing to their sense of fair play, try to enlist the cooperation of the employees.

Listed below are a few situations in which we believe employees are taking advantage of priviledges set up for there benefit. It is these kind of abuses that we trust you will help us stop.

1. Some employees are abusing the coffee break. They leave their work stations early and return to them late--as much as 5 minutes in each direction, 20 minutes in all. And this twice a day. Everyone knows you are entitled to two 15-minute coffee breaks a day, station to station --no more and no less.

2. Many of you abuse the personal telephone call privilege--both out and in. You place and recieve personal calls too often and you talk too long. Sometimes our wires get all tied up with these personal conversations and we can't place or receive legitimit business calls.

3. Too many of you show to many red marks on your time cards. You check in late in the morning and after lunch, and you check out early at noon and at night. Working hours are from 8:15 a.m. in the morning until 12:15 and from 1 p.m. until 5. Please observe.

indignant, ventilating, vandalism, loosened, emergency, further

Preview of New Dictation Material

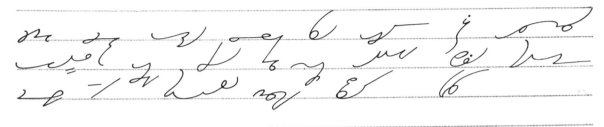

citizens, seems to be, loosened, emergency, band, resentment, hopeful, indignant, Laundry, refinished, jammed, curfew, endorsed, apprehend, vandalism, smashed, entered, volunteered, unaccompanied, expanded, by that time

Lesson **20** ⬡⬡⬡⬡⬡⬡⬡⬡⬡⬡⬡⬡⬡⬡⬡⬡⬡⬡

20A—Use of the Dictionary

A dictionary is an indispensable aid to the secretary. She should have one that is reliable and up to date.

Many kinds of information a secretary needs can be found in the dictionary, so she needs to be thoroughly familiar with all its parts. An unabridged dictionary will, of course, have much information not given in an abridged one. Here are a few pointers to follow in using the dictionary.

1. Words are marked into syllables. When an accent mark appears, no syllable mark is used; the accent mark serves both to indicate emphasis in pronunciation and a syllable.

2. A hyphen is a heavier, bigger mark than a syllable mark. Be sure you can distinguish between them.

3. In using an unabridged dictionary, be very careful in turning the pages. Corners are easily torn or pages folded because the paper is extremely thin. An unabridged dictionary should always be left open and not closed after each use, as such opening and closing will cause the binding to wear out and increase the danger of pages becoming torn or wrinkled.

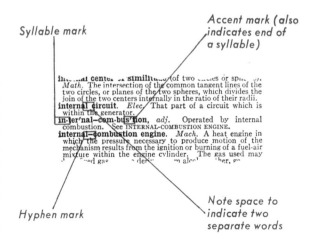

In *Webster's Third New International Dictionary* accent marks are indicated with the pronunciation of the word.

Dictionary excerpts by permission. From *Webster's New International Dictionary*, Second Edition, copyright 1959 by G. & C. Merriam Co., Publishers of the Merriam-Webster Dictionaries.

(2) Body Material. The body material, or *textual content*, expands each of the headings and subheadings listed in the table of contents. This division of the report not only constitutes the bulk of the entire report but also is the most difficult to organize and prepare.

(3) Supplementary Material. The supplementary material includes *appendix* items (tables and exhibits that might clog the main body of the report and make it more difficult to study) and a *bibliography*, or reference list, that lists alphabetically all sources of information upon which the report is based.

Summary

Organizing the Body of the Report. As mentioned earlier, of all the parts of the report, the body material is the most difficult to organize and prepare. This is true because report writers generally do not think through the report problem carefully enough before they begin their work and because too often they do not prepare a topic outline to guide them in accumulating data in a systematic manner and in preparing the narrative copy for the body of the report. Perhaps one of the greatest services you can render the report writer is to prepare a tentative guiding outline for his consideration and revision or to encourage him to prepare one.

An outline is a short summary, often in the form of headings and subheadings, presenting the most important features or elements of a subject to be studied or written about. The real value of an outline rests upon three essential qualities: (1) its conciseness, (2) its simplicity, and (3) its usability. A good outline seldom carries its subdivisions of the main topics farther than two or three subtopics. It is complete enough to be a handy guide, yet brief enough to be easily remembered and readily understood.

In the illustration of *outline form* given at the left below, note the orderly arrangement of major topics, followed in turn by first-, second-, and third-order subtopics. In addition, notice that there is never a single numbered or lettered item under any order of heading; that is, there is never a *I* (or *1*) without a *II* (or *2*) or an *A* (or *a*) without a *B* (or *b*). In other words, if subtopic A, for example, cannot be divided into at least two smaller subtopics, it is best not to subdivide it at all and to include the entire content of subtopic A under the subtopic A heading.

Now, study the outline for a report given immediately below. This outline was written by an office manager to guide the preparation of a report on office machines, comparing their cost and usefulness in a specific company. The final report was used as a guide to the purchase of new equipment, to the better utilization of existing equipment, and to the trade-in of older equipment that was not being efficiently used.

Outline Form

Outline for a Report

4. A word not given in the regular alphabetic listing may be found (a) at the bottom of the page in the footnotes; (b) under its prefix or suffix if one is part of the word, or (c) under the New Words (Addenda) section at the front of the dictionary. In the Third Edition no words are listed in footnotes, in an addenda, or under a prefix or suffix.

(a)

in'ter·na'tion·al-mind'ed, adj. See -MINDED.
in'ternd'. Interned. Ref. Sp.
in'ter·ne'cin. Internecine.
in'terne·ship, n. = INTERNSHIP.
in'ter·neu·ron'ic, adj. See IN-TER- c.
in'ter·ni'dal (-nī'dăl; -d'l), adj. Zool. See INTER- d.   [TER- c.]
in'ter·nod'u·lar, adj. See IN-
in'ter·nonce, n. [F.] An in-ternuncio Obs.

‖in'ter nos' (ĭn'tĕr nōs'). [L.] Between ourselves; entre nous.
in'ter·nunce, n. [F. internonce.] An internuncio. Obs.
in'ter·nun'ci·a·ry (ĭn'tĕr·nŭn'-shĭ·ĕr'ĭ; -ĕr·ĭ), adj. = INTERNUN-CIAL, 1.   [-SHIP.]
in'ter·nun'ci·o·ship', n. See
in'ter·nun'ci·us (ĭn'tĕr·nŭn'shĭ-ŭs), n.; pl. -CII (-ī). [ML.] = INTERNUNCIO, 1.   [TER- d.]
in'ter·of'fice (66), adj. See IN-

... or ... ... orm. ... ure.
commonly heightens the implied contrast with what is ac-quired or artificial, and frequently denotes, esp. in the case of qualities, that which is inborn or inherent; as, "a wretch whose natural gifts were poor to those of mine" (Shak.); "If ... sweetest Shakespeare, Fancy's child, warble his

rät'), n. [G.] Austria & Swit-zerland. See LEGISLATURE, Table.
na'tion·hood, n. See -HOOD.
na'tion·less, adj. See -LESS.
na'tion·wide', adj. See -WIDE.
na'tiv. Native. Ref. Sp.

h in G. ich, ach (109); boɴ; yet; zh = z in azure.
ʟ., preceding the Vocabulary.

(b)

-stem

rived from it with some formative suffix. Thus the root duc serves as the stem of Latin dux (ducs), ducis, leader, and is developed with suffixes into ducere, to lead, ductor, leader, ductus, act of leading, ductilis, ductile. b Obs. An origi-nal word, serving as a basis for the formation of derivative words by the addition of suffixes, etc.
12. Skiing. Act or instance of stemming.
☞ COMBINATIONS and PHRASES:

stem-bearing, adj.	stem-cutting, adj.	stem sapper
stem borer	stem end	stem sawfly
stem cutting	stem father	stem work

— from stem to stern. Figuratively, throughout;
...

(c)

so... ...ism*, ... Someth..., as an ac...ity or principle, that is characteristic of the U.S.S.R.
$o'vi·et'ize*, v. t. 1. To bring into accord with the U.S.S.R., esp. as to its political and economic policies. 2. To make (a work of art) expound or further the ideology of the Supreme Soviet.
space*, n. Popularly, the region beyond the earth's atmos-phere, especially that between and beyond the planets and stars; — used also attributively to indicate concern with, or adaptation for traveling in, that region; as, space flight; space station; space suit.
$pace'ship' (spās'shĭp'), n. A vehicle for interplanetary travel outside the earth's atmosphere.
spall*, v. i. Physics. Of a surface, target, nucleus, etc. to...

5. Be sure to read the information given about a word because sometimes words spelled similarly have different meanings.

flo...es'cence (flo·rĕs'ĕns; -ŭs), n. [L. ...rescens, p...s. part. of florescere to begin to blossom, incho. fr. florere to blossom. See FLOURISH.] State of being in bloom; blos-soming; anthesis; also, period of blooming or, figuratively, flourishing. — flo·res'cent (-ĕnt; -'nt), adj.
flor·es'cence (flor·ĕs'ĕns; -ŭs; 181), n. [L. flos, floris, flower + E. essence.] Pharm. A pure essence of the odor-ifer... principl... of flowers.

1. ...atter ... ...e fluo... ...radia... ...erally ... longer wave length than that of the absorbed radiation. If waves of the same wave length as that of the absorbed radi-ation are included in the fluorescent light they are called resonance radiation. See RAMAN EFFECT.
2. The radiation due to fluorescence. Cf. STOKES' LAW.
flu·o·res'cent (-ĕnt; -'nt), adj. Having, due to, or showing, fluorescence.
f... ...ent ... Phy... ...screen ...card...

6. The spelling of the names of many cities is given in the Pronouncing Gazetteer. Quite a number of cities have the same pronunciation but different spellings. In the Third Edition there is no pronouncing gazetteer.

... araoh by t... Hebrews.
Pitman (pĭt'măn) borough, SW New Jersey, S of Camden; pop. 7000.
Pittsburg (pĭts'bûrg) 1 city, W California, near mouth of Sacramento. 2 city, SE Kansas; pop. 19,300.
Pittsburgh (pĭts'bûrg) city, SW Pennsylvania, at confluence of Alleghen... hela rivers; pop. 676,800.
Pittsburg Landing, hamlet, SW Tennessee, on Tennessee river; scen... ... battle ... ...loh, ... 1862

7. Be sure to check the part of speech given for a word because sometimes a noun form is syllabi-cated differently from a verb form, etc.

... Stitched out; projected; also, abandoned. Obs. — pro-ject'ed·ly (-jĕk'tĕd·lĭ; -tĭd·lĭ; 119), adv.
pro·ject' (pro·jĕkt') v.; PRO·JECT'ED; PRO·JECT'ING. [L. projectus, past part. of proicere, projicere, fr. pro forward + jacere to throw; cf. F. projeter. See JET, v.]
Transitive: 1. To throw or cast forward, as bodies, sub-stances, heat; to beat forth.
Befor... feet herself ... did project ... S... ...

P... ...tion) into ...e crucible ...d thereu... ...uce pre... ...substance.
proj'ect (prŏj'ĕkt; -ĭkt; 277), n. [L. projectum, neut. past part.; cf. F. projet, fr. the v. See PROJECT, v.; cf. PROJET.]
1. A plan or design. Specif.: a Obs. A draft or tabular outline; a pattern. b A plan as devised or proposed; a scheme; a proposal; as, to present his project to the com-mittee; a head full of projects. c A planned undertaking; s... ...def... ...formul... ...iece of ... ...rch.

..., an un... ...ed eso...al gland, ... usually ...de-veloped proboscis. It includes the groups Rachiglossa and Toxoglossa.
sten'o·graph (stĕn'ō·grȧf; 83), v. t.; -GRAPHED (-grȧft); -GRAPH'ING. To write or report in stenographic char-acters; also, to work as a stenographer.
sten'o·graph (-grȧf), n. 1. A production of stenography. 2. Any of various keyboard instruments for writing by some method of stenography.
ste·nog'ra·pher (stě·nŏg'rȧ·fẽr), n. One who is skilled in taking dictation in shorthand and transcribing dictated ma-terial, usually on a typewriter.
sten'o·graph'ic (stĕn'ō·grăf'ĭk), adj. Also sten'o·graph'-i·cal (-ĭ·kȧl). [Cf. F. sténographique.] Of, pertaining to, or using, stenography. — sten'o·graph'i·cal·ly, adv.
ste·nog'ra·phist (stě·nŏg'rȧ·fĭst), n. A stenographer.
ste·nog'ra·phy (stě·nŏg'rȧ·fĭ), n. [steno- + -graphy; cf. F. sténographie, G. stenographie.] 1. That art of writing in shorthand, by using abbreviations or characters for whole words; shorthand, esp. written from dictation or oral di... ...al... ...ly, th... ... of sh... ...not...

8. Explanations such as that given under the word "well" are helpful in determining whether or not to hyphenate a word.

... conce... ...oistu... ...verin... ...s ya... the like.
Ant. — Poorly, unsatisfactorily, badly, faultily, imper-fectly, inadequately.
— as well. In addition; also; too. — as well as. a In as good, satisfactory, etc., a manner as; as, he did it as well as he could. b To the same extent or degree; as much as. c Not only ... but also. d And not only; and in addi-tion; as, oysters as well as other delicacies. — well then. A transitional phrase of little meaning used in continuing a discourse or argument or in drawing or implying some deduction from previous statements, arguments, etc.
☞ In the COMBINATIONS listed below, well is combined with: (1) an adjective, as in well-able; (2) a participle, as in well-abounding, well-acted; (3) a word or suffix con-sisting of a noun + -ed, as in well-ancestored; (4) another adverb, as in well-beseemingly. All such expressions are hyphened when used as attributive adjectives (a well-acted play, a well-ancestored man). When used predi-catively they are, however, treated as separate words (the play was well acted), except for combinations of the third type (the man is well-ancestored), and a few others that have from long usage become hyphened (well-read) or, rarely, solid words (wellborn). Many combinations of well that have developed special meanings or that other-wise stand in need of definition are separately entered in the Vocabulary as well as many combinations that usually or always appear as hyphened or solid words.

well-able	well-agreeing	well-assimilated
well-abolished	well-aimed	well-assisted
well-abounding	well-alleged	well-associated
...head	...ell-...	...arte...

Preparing Business Reports

Lesson **126** ◇○⬡○◇○⬡○◇○⬡○◇○⬡○◇○⬡○◇○⬡○◇○⬡○◇○⬡○◇○⬡○◇

Business reports may be as brief and simple as a half-page memorandum in which an executive reports a decision reached in a conference called to discuss a change in departmental policy or procedure. On the other hand, they may be as comprehensive and complex as a 30-page report summarizing the activities and accomplishments of the entire operation of a business for a year or more, including carefully prepared tables and graphs that present an easy-to-grasp picture of company operations and results. In either case, or in any other reporting situation, you will likely be asked to assist in gathering the data, in summarizing the data, in preparing tables and graphs, and in preparing the final typescript of the report for distribution or duplication. Thus, it is highly important that you be familiar with the steps in report preparation, that you know the structural parts of reports, and that you be able to assist your employer with the preparation of them.

Organizing Reports

Steps in Report Preparation. Everyone who is faced with a report-writing assignment should follow five steps preliminary to the writing of the final report. He should:

1. Define the problem and state precisely on what he is to report.
2. Determine a method of finding the information he needs to write a complete report.
3. Locate and record in a systematic manner the information he needs.
4. Organize the information and report the findings in approved form.
5. Draw conclusions by analyzing the findings, and state those conclusions clearly.

Regardless of the length or formality of the report and regardless of the type of report (whether it be a report of progress, a periodic report of some business activity, a statistical report, or a report on recommendations), the report writer takes the foregoing steps, if only mentally. The longer and more formal the report, the more essential it becomes that he prepare a written plan of procedure.

Structural Parts of Formal Reports. Although reports differ somewhat in structure and in the number of parts included, depending upon their length and degree of formality, a study of the structural parts of a formal report will equip you to assist in the preparation of any type of report assigned to you.

Formal reports are composed of seven structural parts organized into three main divisions: (1) *introductory material,* (2) *body material,* and (3) *supplementary material.*

(1) Introductory Material. The introductory material of a report includes, in the order given, a *title page* which indicates the title of the report, to whom the report is addressed, by whom it was prepared, and the date of completion; a *transmittal letter* addressed to the intended recipients of the report, stating the purpose of the report and giving a brief description of the problem; a *table of contents* which lists the headings and subheadings used in the report, together with the page number on which each appears; and a *summary,* containing the core information in capsule form. All these introductory parts are written after the body of the report has been completed.

Title Page

Transmittal Letter

Table of Contents

Questions for Discussion

1. How can you distinguish a syllable mark from a hyphen?
2. If a word is not given in the regular alphabetical listing, where else in the dictionary might you be able to find it?
3. Give some pointers about proper handling of the dictionary.
4. Does an accent mark indicate a syllable or is it only for pronunciation?

Office Practice Problem

List the correct spelling of each of the italicized words and tell where you verified it:

a. *fluorescent* lighting or *florescent* lighting
b. *inter-office* memorandum or *interoffice* memorandum
c. *Cincinatti*, Ohio, or *Cincinnati*, Ohio
d. *ghost town* or *ghost-town*
e. *ready-cooked* meat or *ready cooked* meat

20B—Building Speed in Taking Dictation

Repetitive Phrase Builder

Punctuation Preview

Rule 10: Use a comma to separate two consecutive parallel adjectives modifying a single noun. If the adjectives are not parallel, no comma is used. Ordinarily, parallel adjectives can be identified by the fact that they might be connected with *and*.

Example: Experienced, pleasant salespeople will serve you at our store.

NOTE: The following copy requires the application of Rules 1-10.

Building Skill in Transcribing

Transcribing from Shorthand Notes

1. Write in shorthand Letter (1) given below.
2. Transcribe the letter from your notes as a 5-minute writing. Use block style with open punctuation. Determine your *mwam*. If you complete the letter before time is called, repeat it from the beginning.
3. Transcribe Letter (2) as a 5-minute writing in the same style. Determine your *mwam* and compare it with your *mwam* on Letter (1).

(1)

	Words
February 13, 19—	4
Mr. Donald A. Gordon	8
Lone Star Plastics, Inc.	13
1320 Sam Houston Boulevard	18
Wichita Falls, Texas 76301	24
Dear Mr. Gordon	27

	Words
Here are the suggestions you requested for	36
the improvement of your machine dictation	44
techniques.[1] These suggestions are equally	53
helpful for machine and person-to-person	61
dictation.	63
1. Make written notes[2] to help you organ-	71
ize the dictation and make a mental out-	79
line of the content and structure of each	88
letter[3] before you begin to dictate it.	96
2. Speak in a normal conversational tone	104
and at a normal speed. (Hold[4] the micro-	111
phone within two or three inches of your	119
mouth as you dictate.)	125
3. Speak clearly and distinctly. (Pronounce[5]	134
unusual names with special care or spell	142
them.)	144
4. Use voice inflections to give meaning to	152
your dictation and[6] to suggest punc-	160
tuation.	162
Try to remember when you dictate that you	170
are talking to a person, not to a[7] machine.	179
Capturing this feeling, you will dictate more	188
helpfully and effectively. (167)	194
Sincerely yours	197
	218

(2)

Words

	Words
February 18, 19—	4
Mr. John B. Gerhardt	8
Voco-Records, Incorporated	13
729 North Michigan Avenue	18
Chicago, Illinois 60603	23

	35
	43
	48
	53
	61
	67
	74
	80
	84
	90
	97
	102
	109
	116
	122
	128
	134
	142
	148
	155
	160
	180

Transcribing from Dictation

Your teacher will dictate a two-page letter and an interoffice memo to you for transcription. Prepare the letter for the signature of Ronald G. Ellis, Attorney-at-Law.

Practice Material for Building Fluency

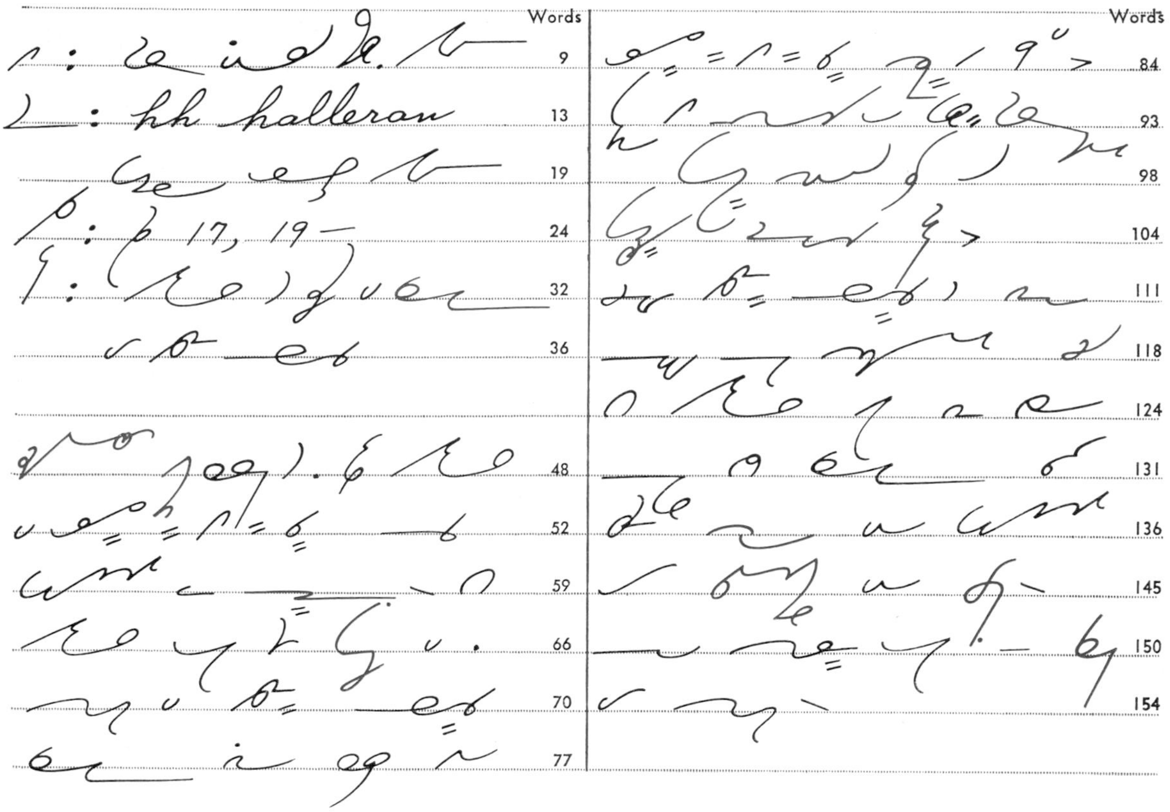

Dictionary and Spelling Preview

1. pioneers, utensils, decided, exhibits, permanent, semiannually, occasionally
2. pharmacy, pharmacists, physician, registered, prescription, privilege

Preview of New Dictation Material

(1)

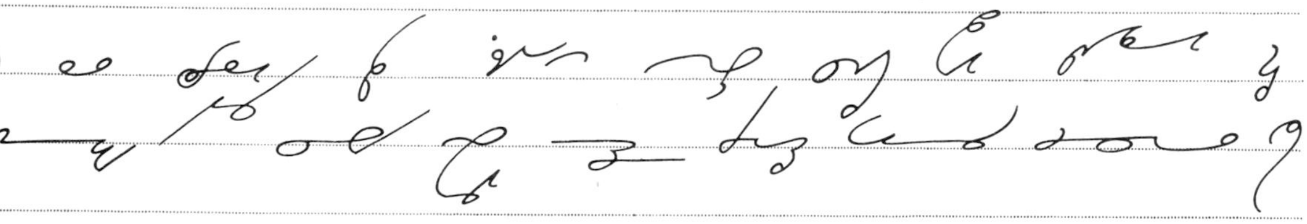

early, pioneers, busily, historical, garages, actively, exhibits, utensils, socially, one of the most, donated, amazed, cabinets, museum, generously, prominent, semiannually, they have been

(2)

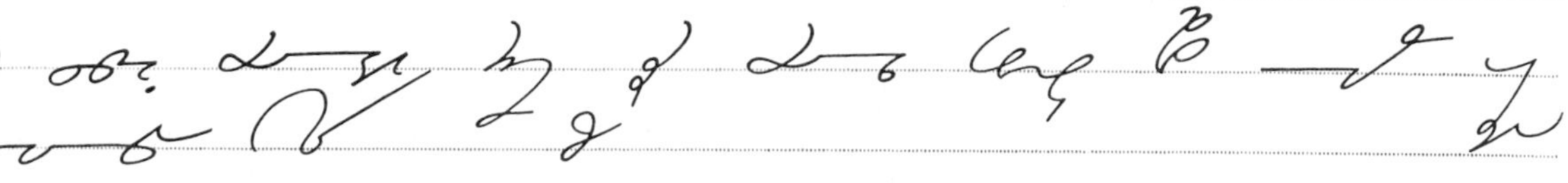

announcing, pharmacists, for your convenience, physician, pharmacy, prescription, we hope that, modern, registered, no matter, devoted, asset

Some Guides to Efficient Machine Transcription. Machine transcription can be an enjoyable, efficient method of converting dictated material into neat, error-free transcripts if the following suggestions of experienced transcribers are followed:

1. When first asked to operate a transcribing machine, request a live demonstration of the machine and an operator's manual from the local office of the machine company. Each type of equipment has its special operating procedures, and no one set of instructions works equally well for all types.

2. Adjust the controls of the machine to suit your particular needs: the speed control, until the voice is clear (neither too fast nor too slow); the volume control, to suit your own listening preference; and the tone control, for pleasant listening.

3. Use the indicator slip which accompanies each recording as a guide to letter placement and as a key to corrections in the dictation. Listen to the corrections and special instructions *before* you begin to type from the recording.

4. Spot check all belts or discs and indicator slips to locate telegrams and other rush items which should be transcribed immediately.

5. Edit the dictation before you begin to transcribe, particularly when you first begin using transcribing equipment. Check the spelling of unfamiliar words and names, questions of grammar and word usage, prices or quantities that must be verified, and facts to be rechecked.

6. Start transcribing slowly: start the machine; listen to a few words at a time; stop the machine; transcribe those words; start the machine again and repeat the process. As your proficiency increases, you will be able to transcribe more or less continuously.

7. Even though most transcribing machines have a repeat key the use of which permits you to repeat the last few words of the dictation, develop the power to carry dictation in your mind for more continuous transcription.

8. Learn to read a phrase or two ahead of your fingers as you type. Develop the habit of keeping the typewriter carriage moving, starting and stopping the dictation accordingly.

9. Avoid errors in dividing words at line endings: one- and two-letter syllables at the beginning and at the end of words, dividing words at more than two consecutive line endings, and dividing the last word of a paragraph.

10. Proofread each transcribed item twice: once as you transcribe it, again after the transcript is completed.

11. Check off each item as it is transcribed by making an appropriate mark on the indicator slip at the proper point. In this way you will be sure to transcribe every item on a record even though some of the items may be transcribed out of dictated sequence because of priority or urgency.

12. Return to the executive's desk partially used recordings with the transcribed portions clearly indicated; otherwise, you may repeat an item when that record is returned to you with the previously unused space filled.

Questions for Discussion

1. Give two or three advantages of machine dictation-transcription over shorthand dictation-transcription and indicate why you consider them advantages.

2. Give two or three advantages of shorthand dictation-transcription over machine dictation-transcription and indicate why you consider them advantages.

3. In what circumstances is machine dictation most likely to be used?

4. Some writers have suggested that the machine transcriber first make a rough draft of each transcript, then prepare a final copy from the rough draft. Why is this an inefficient procedure?

5. An indicator slip provides two lines for inserting transcription guides: The line marked "C" is for indicating corrections; the line marked "L" is for indicating the beginning and ending of each message. Why is it important for the transcriber to check these lines carefully before beginning to transcribe?

6. Why is it considered good practice to edit the dictation before beginning to transcribe?

Building Speed in Taking Dictation

Lesson **21** ⬡⬡⬡⬡⬡⬡⬡⬡⬡⬡⬡⬡⬡⬡⬡⬡⬡⬡⬡⬡⬡

21A—Brief-Form Practice

Directions. The following paragraph has 31 brief forms and brief-form derivatives. If you can read it in 30 seconds, your reading rate will be 128 words a minute.

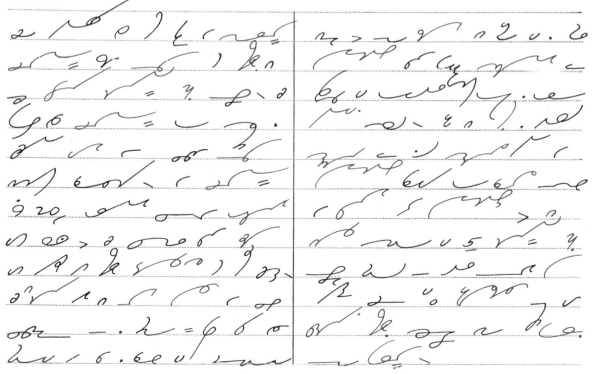

21B—Theory Review

The sound of *den* is written by blending *d* and *n*: . The same blend is used for the sounds *ten* and *tain*.

The sound of *dem* is written by blending *d* and *m*: . The same blend is used for *tem*, *tom*, and *tim*.

The ending *-ing* is expressed by a dot at the end of the word.

Machine Transcription

Even though you will probably be employed as a shorthand writer and transcriber, you may from time to time be asked to transcribe dictation that has been recorded on a machine. Some executives use voice-recording machines to handle after-hours dictation; some use portable machines to record letters and reports while they are away from the office on business trips; still others prefer to handle most, if not all, their dictation in this manner. It is important, therefore, that you be acquainted with the operating principles of voice recording and transcribing machines and that you follow efficient procedures in using them.

Operating Principles of Voice Recording Machines. Although there are six types of voice recording machines—*wax disc, plastic belt, magnetic belt, magnetic disc, magnetic paper,* and *tape*—the basic operating principles of all recording machines are quite similar.

The recording machine consists of: (1) a recording microphone to receive and transmit the voice; (2) a motorized turntable or rotating cylinder or spool; (3) a recording receptacle (disc or belt) on which to record the message; (4) a needle to transfer and imprint the sound into the receptacle; (5) a button to start and stop the turntable motor; (6) a volume control; (7) an indicator-slip mechanism (on some machines) to mark the beginning and the end of a message and to indicate points of correction; and (8) a playback device so that the dictator can listen to what he has recorded.

Operating Principles of Transcribing Machines. A transcribing machine has the same basic operating parts as a dictating machine with the exception that the microphone of the dictating equipment is replaced by a listening mechanism (the earphone) on the transcribing machine. So similar are the two machines, in fact, that for some models, you can buy a combination dictating-transcribing unit.

Transcribing machines usually are equipped with speed, volume, and tone controls. Generally, too, they have either a thumb or foot control to start and stop the turntable to control the amount of dictation received at one time.

In addition, the indicator slip or "log" sheet made on the dictating machine fits the companion transcribing machine and serves to help the transcriber estimate letter length, and in the case of the indicator slip, indicates points of correction in the dictation.

Voice Recording-Transcribing Equipment Illustrated. The following illustrations will acquaint you with frequently used types of voice recording and transcribing equipment.

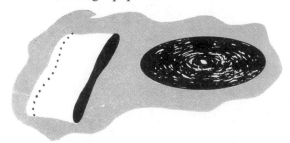

Recorder Belt   Recorder Disc

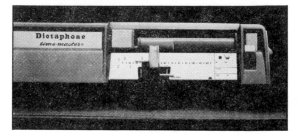

Indicator Slip

Belt Transcriber

Disc Transcriber

21C—Punctuation Preview

Rule 11: A clause of reason introduced by *for* or *as* and a clause of concession introduced by *though* or *although* is separated from the main clause by a comma.

Examples: We do not plan additional construction at this point, for there is not enough money available to complete it.

We are not expecting new equipment to be purchased, although we do need it badly.

NOTE: Rules 1 and 6 are applied in this material, as well as Rule 11.

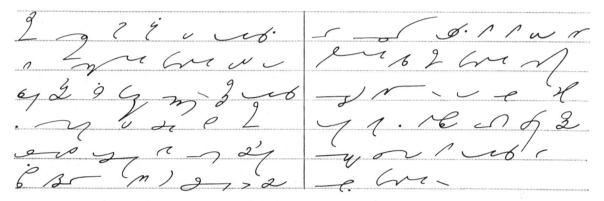

21D—Practice Material for Building Fluency

	Words
	6
	7
	13
	16
	21
	29
	30
	36

	Words
	44
	53
	58
	66
	72
	78
	89
	97
	104

21E—Dictionary and Spelling Preview

1. Captain, impacted, hesitant

2. infestation, weevils, ascertained, adjoining

3. convenience, lubrication, petroleum, accessories, cordial

3. Rule three sheets of typewriting paper to approximate ruled legal paper. Type the following *partnership agreement* with two carbon copies. Use the current year when the year has been left blank.

PARTNERSHIP AGREEMENT

THIS AGREEMENT, made in the City of Greensboro, State of North Carolina, on the 21st day of April, 19—, between GEORGE H. RANDOLPH and JAMES B. WATSON, both of Greensboro, North Carolina,

WHEREIN IT IS MUTUALLY AGREED, AS FOLLOWS:

1. That the parties hereto shall, as partners, engage in and conduct the business of buying, selling, and dealing in furniture, at wholesale and retail.

2. That the name of the partnership shall be Ranson Furniture Company.

3. That the term of the partnership shall begin on May 1, 19—, and shall end on April 30, 1985.

4. (a) That the capital of the partnership shall be the sum of Forty Thousand Dollars ($40,000); and each party shall contribute thereto, contemporaneously with the execution of this agreement, the sum of Twenty Thousand Dollars ($20,000) in cash.

(b) That any addition to capital shall be in proportion to the amounts originally contributed by each partner.

(c) That neither party's contribution of the capital of the partnership shall bear interest in his favor.

5. (a) That neither party shall, without the written consent of the other, advance any moneys to the partnership, in excess of the amount of his aforesaid contribution to the capital thereof; but any advance that shall be made by either party, with the written consent of the other, shall bear interest at the rate of six percent (6%) per annum.

(b) That if either party shall, with the consent of the other, become indebted to the partnership, such indebtedness shall bear interest at the rate of six percent (6%) per annum.

6. That each party shall devote all his time and attention to the business of the partnership, and shall not, during the term of his partnership, either directly or indirectly, engage in any other business.

7. That each party shall be entitled to draw One Hundred Fifty Dollars ($150) a week from the funds of the partnership.

8. (a) That, at the end of each calendar year, a full and accurate inventory shall be prepared; and the assets, liabilities, and income, both gross and net, shall be ascertained; and the net profits, or net loss, of the partnership, shall be fixed and determined.

(b) That the net profits, or net loss, shall be divided equally between the parties hereto, and the accounts of each shall be credited, or debited, as the case may be, with his proportionate share thereof.

(c) That at the end of each calendar year, when the profits, if any, have been credited to each partner's account, it shall be determined by mutual agreement of the partners what, if any, portion of the profits shall be reinvested in the business.

IN WITNESS WHEREOF, the said parties have hereunto set their hands the day and year first above written.

_____

_____

Signed and delivered
in the presence of

_____

4. Type the proper endorsement on a legal back for each of the first two copies of the partnership agreement you typed in Problem 3. Bind and fold the agreements for filing. Assume you are secretary to *Lars H. Crandall, Attorney-at-Law, 405 Glenn Building, Greensboro, North Carolina 27408.*

21F—Preview of New Dictation Material

(1)

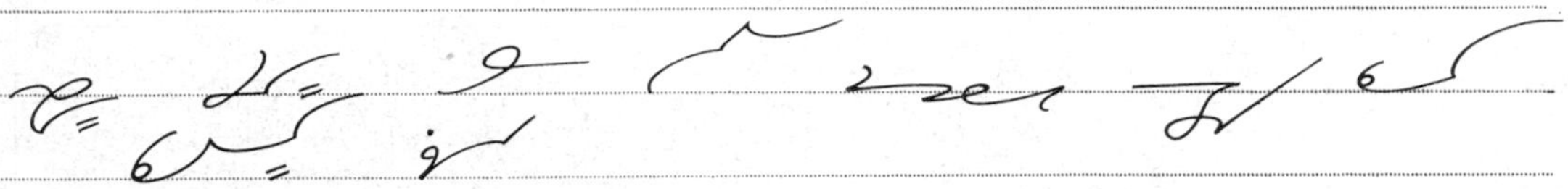

Captain, Fenton, and I am, dental, someone else, impacted, seldom, Pendleton, hesitant

(2)

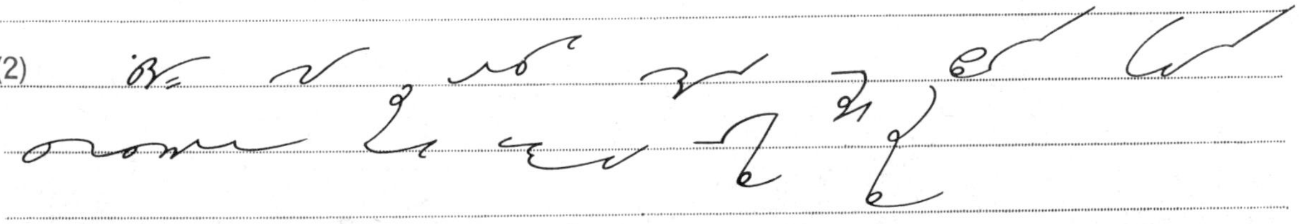

Houston, cotton, threatens, constant, infestation, ascertained, broadened, agricultural, weevils, onslaught, endanger, vigil

(3)

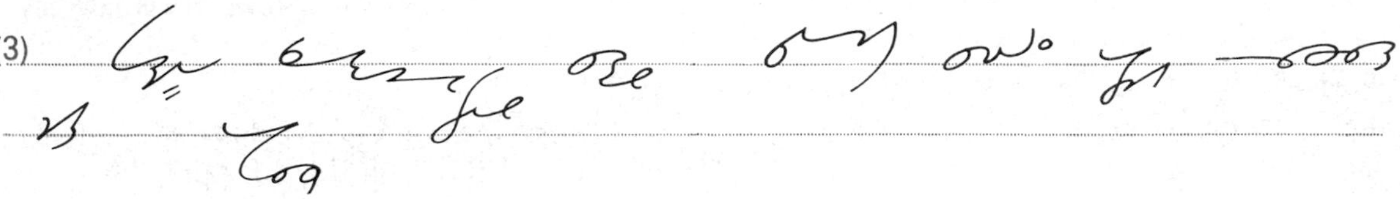

Brewster, salesrooms, accessories, attractive, accordingly, reputation, mechanics, stations, lubrication, batteries

Lesson **22**

22A—Phrase Builder

There are 9 phrases in the following paragraph.

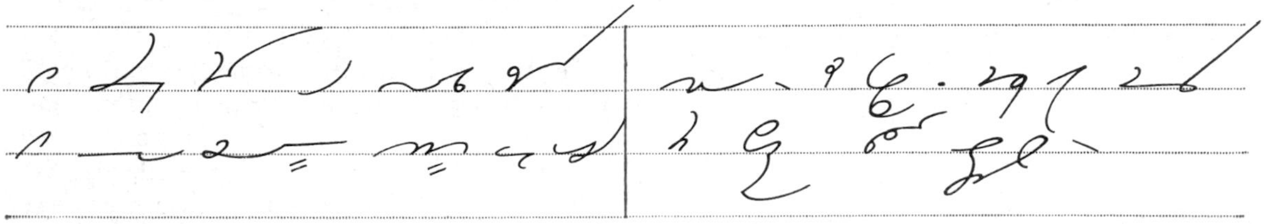

22B—Theory Review

The word beginnings *dis-* and *des-* are written *ds*: .

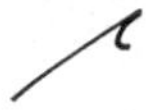

The short sound of *u* is omitted before *n, m,* or a straight downstroke.

Type L.S. for seal

This will and testament is subscribed by me on this ~~twentieth~~ *20th* day of April, 19--, at Portland, Oreg~~on~~ *on.*

(L.S.)

The foregoing instrument, consisting of ~~one~~ *two* page*s*, was subscribed on the date which it bears, by the testator, DONALD R. WELLS, and at the time of subscribing was declared by him to be his Last Will and Testament; and we, at the testator*s* request and in his presence and in the presence of each other, have signed such instrument as witnesses.

_____ residing at _____

_____

_____ residing at _____

_____

---

2. Rule two sheets of typewriting paper to approximate ruled legal paper. Type the *power of attorney* given below. Type the *acknowledgment* or *notary statement* in the form shown in the illustration. Prepare one carbon copy.

```
Signed and acknowledged
in the presence of us

_____

_____

State of Illinois)
                 : ss.
County of Cook   )

     I, WALLACE M. FREEMAN, notary public, do hereby cer-
tify that LOLA M. FAIRCHILD, personally known to me to be the
same person whose name is subscribed to the foregoing instru-
ment, appeared before me this day in person and acknowledged
that she signed, sealed, and delivered the said instrument as
her free and voluntary act, for the uses and purposes therein
set forth.

     Given under my hand and official seal, this 18th day
of April, 19--.

                         _____
                              Notary Public
```

Typewritten Form of Acknowledgment

POWER OF ATTORNEY

KNOW ALL MEN BY THESE PRESENTS: That I, LOLA M. FAIRCHILD, of the City of Chicago, County of Cook, State of Illinois, by these presents do make, constitute, and appoint ARNOLD J. FRISBEE, of the City of Chicago, County of Cook, State of Illinois, my true and lawful attorney, for me and in my name, place, and stead to negotiate for the purchase of the property situated at the corner of 87th Street and Morgan Avenue, Chicago, Illinois, known as the Foster Park property; giving and granting unto the said attorney full power and authority to do and perform all and every act and thing whatsoever, requisite and necessary to be done in negotiating for this property; and I hereby ratify and confirm all that my said agent or attorney will lawfully do, or cause to be done, in connection with this purchase.

IN WITNESS WHEREOF, I have hereunto set my hand and seal this 18th day of April, 19—.

_____(L.S.)

Signed and acknowledged
in the presence of us

_____

_____

State of Illinois)
                  : ss.
County of Cook   )

I, WALLACE M. FREEMAN, notary public, do hereby certify that LOLA M. FAIRCHILD, personally known to me to be the same person whose name is subscribed to the foregoing instrument, appeared before me this day in person and acknowledged that she signed, sealed, and delivered the said instrument as her free and voluntary act, for the uses and purposes therein set forth.

Given under my hand and official seal, this 18th day of April, 19—.

_____
Notary Public

22C—Punctuation Preview

Rule 12: A comma (or commas) is used to set off words in apposition.

Example: Mr. Peterson, your representative, called yesterday.

NOTE: Rules 1, 2, 6, 7, and 11 need to be applied in this exercise, as well as Rule 12.

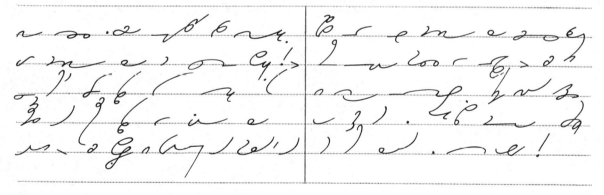

22D—Practice Material for Building Fluency

	Words		Words
5, 19–	3		24
	7		34
3/20 haddad	10		40
07213	16		47

Office Practice Problems

1. Rule two sheets of typewriting paper to approximate ruled legal paper. Type the rough draft of a *will* shown below and at the top of page 315. Prepare one carbon copy. Neat erasures and corrections are permitted in legal documents except for figures, names, places, and dates.

Approximate 2" top margin for all pages

Center heading between ruled lines

10-space paragraph indention; double spacing; copy typed within marginal rules; testator's name in all caps

Introductory words in a paragraph usually typed in all caps; the words Last Will and Testament *typed with initial caps*

Single-space or double-space for acceptable paging

Approximate 1" bottom margin; if more than 1 page, page numbers centered ½" from bottom edge

Center on one line

THE LAST WILL AND TESTAMENT
OF DONALD R. WELLS ← Triple space

I, Donald R. Wells, a resident of the City of Portland, State of Oregon, declare this to be my last Will and Testament, and revoke all former Wills and Codicils.

First: I direct that all my just debts and funeral expenses be paid, and satisfied as soon as conveniently may be after my decease.

SECOND: I declare that I am married, and my wife's name is CLARISSA STONE WELLS; I have three children now living, ANDREW STONE WELLS, ANNA LOUISE WELLS, and TIMOTHY LEE WELLS.

THIRD: I give, devise and bequeath all property, real and personal, and wherever situated, to be divided into equal portions, one fourth to my wife, CLARISSA STONE WELLS, one fourth to my son ANDREW, one fourth to my daughter Anna, and one fourth to my son TIMOTHY. In the event my wife does not survive me, then her portion is to be divided equally among my three children.

Fourth: I appoint as Executrix of my will my wife, CLARISSA STONE WELLS, to serve without bond. In the event she is unable or unwilling to serve, or to complete such service as executrix, then it is my wish that DR. MAURICE A. STEVENS, a long-time friend of mine, shall be appointed as Executor.

FIFTH: If any provision of this will or of any codicil should be invalid, it is my intention that all the remaining provisions thereof shall continue to be fully effective.

	Words			Words
	55			160
	61			165
	70			172
	77			181
	87			190
	95			199
	102			204
	109			212
	116			220
	122			227
	128			235
	135			241
	143			250
	150		Byron A. Philbrick	256
				269

22E—Dictionary and Spelling Preview

1. experiencing, disappear, description   **2.** disagreement, discretion, concert

3. eighth, pertinent, effect

22F—Preview of New Dictation Material

(1)

discomfort, discontinue, accompanying, literature, distinctive, ordinary, disappear

(2)

disband, disputes, forced, disinterest, outsiders, as it is, composition, discord, distinguished, concert

(3)

undoubtedly, traffic, dividends, administration, attached, standpoint, chief, pertinent, we feel, less than, Plattsburg, stimulating, challenging

Legal Typing

Printed Legal Forms. Printed legal forms are available for many legal documents such as affidavits, leases, and wills. When printed forms are used, the secretary types the appropriate information in the blank spaces provided on the forms.

Typewritten Legal Papers. When printed legal forms are not available, legal documents are typed on legal paper 8½ by 13 or 14 inches with left and right ruled margins. When using ruled legal paper, type within the vertical rules, leaving 2 or more spaces between the ruled lines and the typing. Leave a 2-inch top margin on all pages.

If you are using plain paper instead of ruled legal paper, set the margin stops for a 1½-inch left margin and a ½-inch right margin.

Indent paragraphs 10 spaces. Double-space the copy, with the exception of land descriptions and quoted matter. These parts should be single-spaced and indented 10 spaces from both margins.

Page Numbers. The first page of a legal paper is usually not numbered, but subsequent pages are numbered between the marginal rulings a half inch (3 blank lines) from the bottom of the page. Type a hyphen before and another after the page number.

Signature Lines. The maker or makers of a legal document sign at the right of the page.

Witnesses, if any, sign at the left. In typing signature lines, leave two or three blank lines between them for the signatures.

You should always have at least two lines of typing on the page that contains the signature of the maker and the witnesses.

Legal Backs and Endorsements. Legal documents are usually bound in a cover that is slightly heavier and larger than the sheets on which the documents are typed. These covers are called "legal backs."

In some law firms, a description of the legal paper called the "endorsement" is typed on the outside cover as illustrated below, or the backing sheet may have a printed endorsement (usually including the name of the document and the name and address of the law firm). The completed document and the backing sheet are then folded in a special way for convenient storage in a safe deposit box, or for filing in special filing containers. In modern legal practice, legal documents usually are stapled to a backing sheet and filed without folding and without an endorsement on the backing sheet.

Portions of the first and second pages of a correctly typed legal document, the folding procedure for the endorsement, and the binding procedure for unfolded documents are shown below.

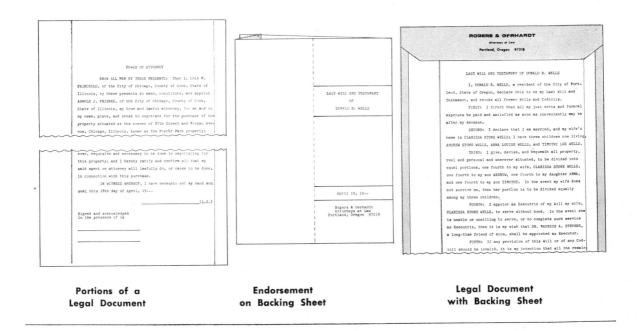

| **Portions of a** | **Endorsement** | **Legal Document** |
| **Legal Document** | **on Backing Sheet** | **with Backing Sheet** |

23A—Potential Rate Builder

There are 18 words in the following sentence.

[shorthand outlines]

23B—Theory Review

The word beginning *mis-* is expressed by *ms:* _____

Some long words can be abbreviated by dropping the endings. Some of these words fall into family groups such as *-titude*.

[shorthand outlines]

23C—Punctuation Preview

Rule 13: Commas are used to set off words of direct address.

Example: We have heard, Mrs. Gaines, that you are a talented painter.

NOTE: Rules 1-3, 6-8, 11 and 12 need to be applied in this exercise, as well as Rule 13.

Office Practice Problems

1. Insert into your typewriter a postal card or a piece of paper cut to postal card size (with the short side against the paper guide). Center each line of the following announcement on the card horizontally and the entire announcement in exact vertical center. Use double spacing.

THE BUSINESS CLUB

will meet on Friday, May 20

to hear an address

"Automation's Challenge"

given by

Mr. Harold R. Watson

Room 315 at 3:30 p.m.

2. Repeat Problem 1, but this time insert the card with the long side against the paper guide and place the announcement in reading position.

3. Insert a half sheet of typewriting paper into your typewriter (with the long side against the paper guide). Type the following letter in modified block style with blocked paragraphs. Use mixed punctuation. Type the date centered on Line 7.

April 18, 19— Mr. Edward J. Laurie   11274 Manhattan Avenue   White Plains, New York 10603

Dear Ed   Seeing your name on the program for the annual convention of the Automation Association was a welcome surprise. I am sure your address will fill the members with enthusiasm and satisfaction.

Because it has been so long since our paths have crossed, I am particularly eager to visit with you personally. You will be busy, I know; but since "everything that lives must eat," won't you join me for breakfast on Thursday morning, April 28, at 7:30.

I shall arrive at the convention hotel on Wednesday around 8:30 p.m. Why don't you telephone me between 8:30 and 9 so that we can confirm our plans.

Cordially yours   John A. Wellington ld

4. Insert into your typewriter a two-carbon pack of executive-size paper (7¼″ by 10½″). Type the following letter in modified block style with indented paragraphs. Used mixed punctuation. Type the date at the right on Line 10.

April 18, 19— Dr. Evan K. Richards, Chairman Department of Business Education   The American University   4821 University Boulevard Kansas City, Missouri   64112

Dear Dr. Richards It will be a real pleasure for me to address your fine group of business teacher trainees on May 15 at your regular monthly luncheon. Since you leave the choice of a topic to me, may I suggest that we use the title

SUFFER THE NEW ONES

for the printed program. The talk will be devoted to the problems of adjustment faced by the beginning office worker and what teachers can do to prepare students to solve those problems.

If you have any particular points of guidance you wish me to emphasize, I shall be glad to work them into my remarks.

As soon as your program is published, will you please send me a copy so that I'll know the exact time and location of the meeting.

Sincerely yours Rogers B. Wyatt Personnel Director mw

5. Type the letter of Problem 4 again, this time on government-size paper (8″ by 10½″). Prepare three carbon copies. Use block style, open punctuation. Type the date on Line 14.

6. Your teacher will dictate two letters to you. Transcribe the first on a half sheet (5½″ by 8½″), the second on executive-size paper (7¼″ by 10½″). Prepare a file copy for each letter. Use modified block style with blocked paragraphs; mixed punctuation; date flush right.

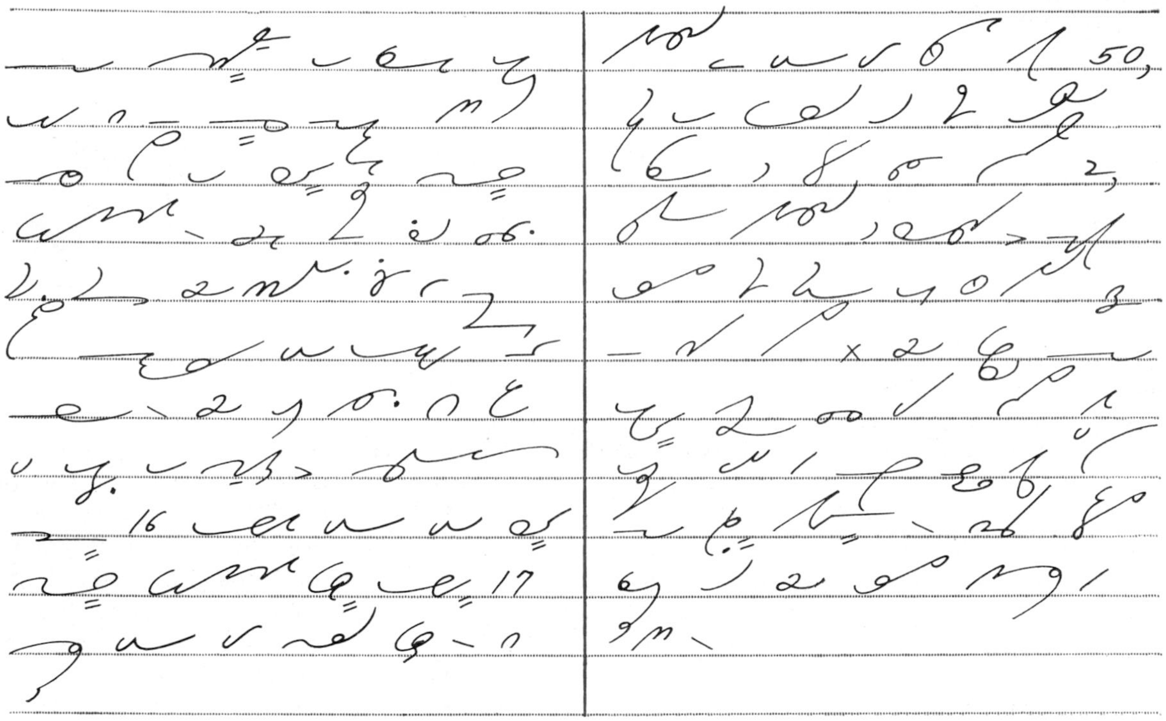

23D—Practice Material for Building Fluency

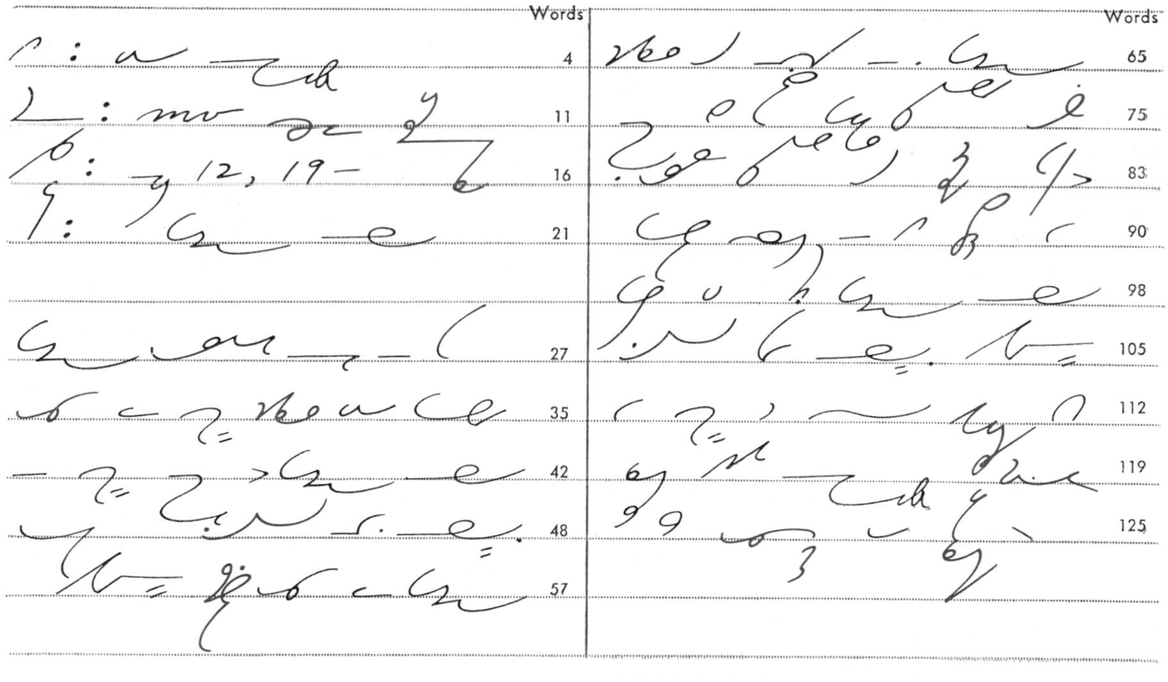
Words
4
11
16
21
27
35
42
48
57
Words
65
75
83
90
98
105
112
119
125

23E—Dictionary and Spelling Preview

1. mischief, sinister, viaduct, vindicated

2. financial, bankruptcy

3. professional, symphony, sponsor, musicians, substantial

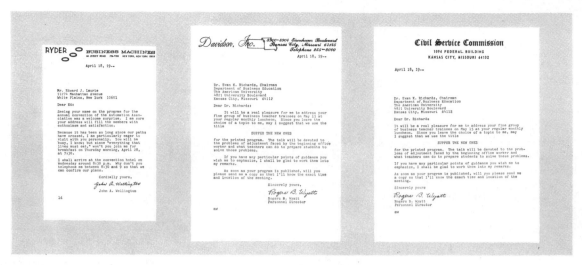

Typing Letters on Off-Size Stationery. Many offices use letterheads of a size other than the standard 8½″ by 11″ and 8½″ by 5½″. Such letterheads are often known as "off-size" stationery and include the following popular sizes: half-size (5½″ by 8½″), executive-size (7¼″ by 10½″), and government-size (8″ by 10½″). Each of these sizes is illustrated above.

The major problem you will encounter in using off-size stationery is determining the margins to be used and the number of spaces to be left between the date and the letter address. The smaller the letterhead and the longer the letter, the narrower the margins and the fewer blank lines left between the date and the address. For *half sheets*, margins range between ¾ of an inch and 1 inch and the date-to-address space varies from 3 to 6 blank line spaces; for *executive sheets*, the margins range between 1 and 1½ inches and the space between date and address varies from 3 to 7 blank line spaces; and for *government sheets*, the margins range between 1 and 2 inches and the space between date and address varies from 3 to 8 blank line spaces.

A letter having an unusually long address, an attention line, a subject line, or a special feature such as enumerated items or a table requires more space than one without such features. In planning the placement of such a letter, therefore, you may need to use a longer writing line, adjust the vertical placement, or both, to compensate for these items.

The general placement guide given above is nothing more than a temporary aid to the effective placement of the letter problems in this lesson. You should not continue to use it as a crutch after you learn from experience to estimate accurately the placement of letters.

Another problem you may face in using off-size stationery is that of centering special lines or tables in the body of the letter. When this problem arises, it is first necessary for you to determine the horizontal center of the off-size letterhead. As for any off-size sheet, this is done by reading on the platen scale the figures at the left and right edges of the paper, adding them, and dividing by 2. Once you determine the center of the letterhead, you proceed to center the copy by backspacing from the center point.

Typing Messages on Postal Cards. Standard postal cards are 5½ inches wide by 3¼ inches deep. They provide space for 20 typewritten lines of copy. Cards are frequently used for very brief, more or less routine messages and for informal invitations and announcements.

Generally, it is best to begin typing no nearer the top than the third line space and to end the typing on or before the third line from the bottom. The left and right margins may vary in width, depending upon the length and arrangement of the message, but you should always try to have side margins of at least half an inch.

```
Omaha, Nebraska  68103, September 23, 19--

Gentlemen

We acknowledge receipt of your Purchase Order
No. 579234.  Shipment will be made immediately
by National Trucks to St. Louis and Western
Shipping to Wichita.

Very truly yours

WHITING PRODUCTS, INC.
```

Correctly Typed Postal Card

23F—Preview of New Dictation Material

(1) *[shorthand outlines]*

unfortunately, viaduct, sinister, misinformation, clearance, mishap, vindicate

(2) *[shorthand outlines]*

McGregor, misgivings, mistakenly, avoid, by the time, bankruptcy

(3) *[shorthand outlines]*

cultural, symphony, musicians, enthusiastically, concentrated, years ago, actively, orchestra, handful, creditable, contributor, has made, support, musical, exceptionally, Maxwell, who are now, past year

Lesson **24** ⬡⬡⬡⬡⬡⬡⬡⬡⬡⬡⬡⬡⬡⬡⬡⬡⬡⬡⬡

24A—Proportion Drill

(1) *[shorthand outlines]*

(2) *[shorthand outlines]*

(3) *[shorthand outlines]*

24B—Theory Review

The sound of *oi* is expressed by *[shorthand symbol]* .

[shorthand outlines]

Typing on Off-Size Stationery

Centering on Off-Size Paper. As a secretary, you will be called upon from time to time to prepare copy on paper of a size other than the 8½″ by 11″ and 8½″ by 5½″ paper to which you are accustomed. Centering on paper, regardless of its size, is easy if you know how to find both the horizontal and vertical center of the sheet.

Determining the Horizontal Center of Any Sheet. To determine the horizontal center of any sheet of paper: (1) insert the sheet with the left edge against the paper guide; (2) read on the platen scale the figures at the left and right edges of the sheet; (3) add these figures; (4) divide the total by 2. The resulting figure is the horizontal center of the sheet.

Determining the Vertical Center of Any Sheet. To determine the vertical center of any sheet of paper: (1) insert the sheet with the top edge aligned with the alignment scale; (2) set the line-space regulator for single spacing; (3) space with the carriage return lever or key until you reach the last line space on the sheet, counting the spaces as you go, the last number you count being the total number of lines available for typing; (4) divide this number by 2 to determine the vertical center of the sheet. (Another method is to measure the length of the sheet in inches, multiply by 6—the number of typewriter spaces in a vertical inch—and divide the resulting number by 2.)

Centering Copy Horizontally. Horizontal centering may involve either of two situations: (1) a series of lines each of which is to be centered, as in an announcement; (2) a body of copy the longest line of which is used as the basis for centering, as in an outline.

When you must center each of a series of lines horizontally: (1) determine the horizontal center of the sheet; (2) clear all tabulator stops, then set a new stop at the center of the sheet; (3) from this point, backspace once for each two strokes in the first line to be centered, disregarding any odd stroke; (4) begin typing the line at the point at which the backspacing ends. Repeat this procedure for each line to be centered.

> Centering on Off-Size Paper
> Determining the Horizontal Center of Any Sheet
> Determining the Vertical Center of Any Sheet
> Centering Copy Horizontally
> Centering Copy Vertically

When you must center a body of copy using the longest line as a basis: (1) determine the horizontal center of the sheet; (2) determine, by inspection or counting, the longest line in the copy to be centered; (3) backspace from center once for each two strokes in that line; (4) set the left margin stop at the point at which the backspacing ends and move the right margin to the end of the scale; (5) begin all lines at the left margin, aligning whatever numbers may appear in listed items.

> LETTERS ON OFF-SIZE STATIONERY
>
> I.   LETTERS ON HALF-SIZE STATIONERY (5½" by 8½")
>
>   A. Margins
>   B. Space Between Date and Letter Address
>
> II. LETTERS ON EXECUTIVE-SIZE STATIONERY (7¼" by 10½")
>
>   A. Margins
>   B. Space Between Date and Letter Address
>
> III. LETTERS ON GOVERNMENT-SIZE STATIONERY (8" by 10½")
>
>   A. Margins
>   B. Space Between Date and Letter Address

Centering Copy Vertically. Either of two methods may be used to center copy vertically.

Mathematical Method. To center vertically by the mathematical method: (1) determine the number of line spaces available on the sheet for typing; (2) determine the number of line spaces required for the copy to be typed, counting not only the lines of copy but also the number of blank lines to be left between them; (3) subtract the number of lines required for typing from the number of lines available; (4) divide the resulting figure by 2 to find out how many spaces are to be left in the top and bottom margins. If you want to place the copy in *reading position* instead of *exact center position*, subtract 3 from the number you determined in Step 4 and use the resulting number for the top margin.

Backspace-from-Center Method. To center vertically by the backspace-from-center method: (1) determine the vertical center of the sheet; (2) from the center point, turn the platen toward you once for each two line spaces in the copy to be centered; (3) type the first line of the copy on the line space at which the backspacing ends. If you want to place the copy in *reading position*, simply turn the platen toward you three more times before you begin typing.

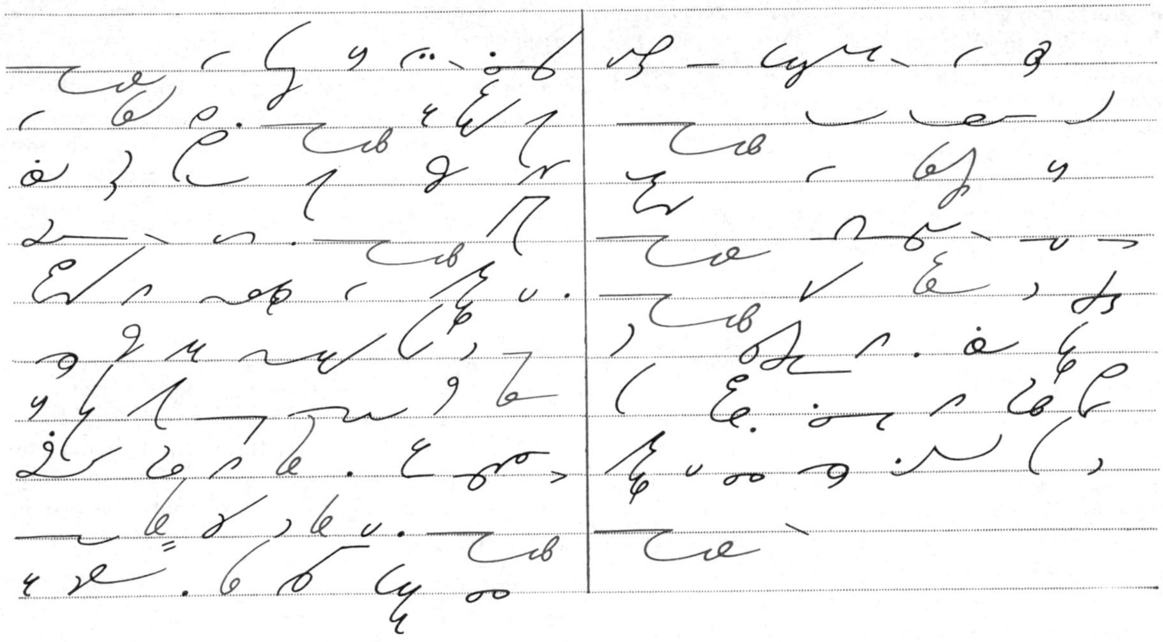

(shorthand outlines)

24C—Punctuation Preview

Rule 14: A comma is used to indicate the omission of words necessary for the completeness of a sentence.

Example: Forty boys reported for basketball; only ten, for track.

NOTE: Rules 1-4, 6-9, and 11-13 need to be applied in the following material, as well as Rule 14.

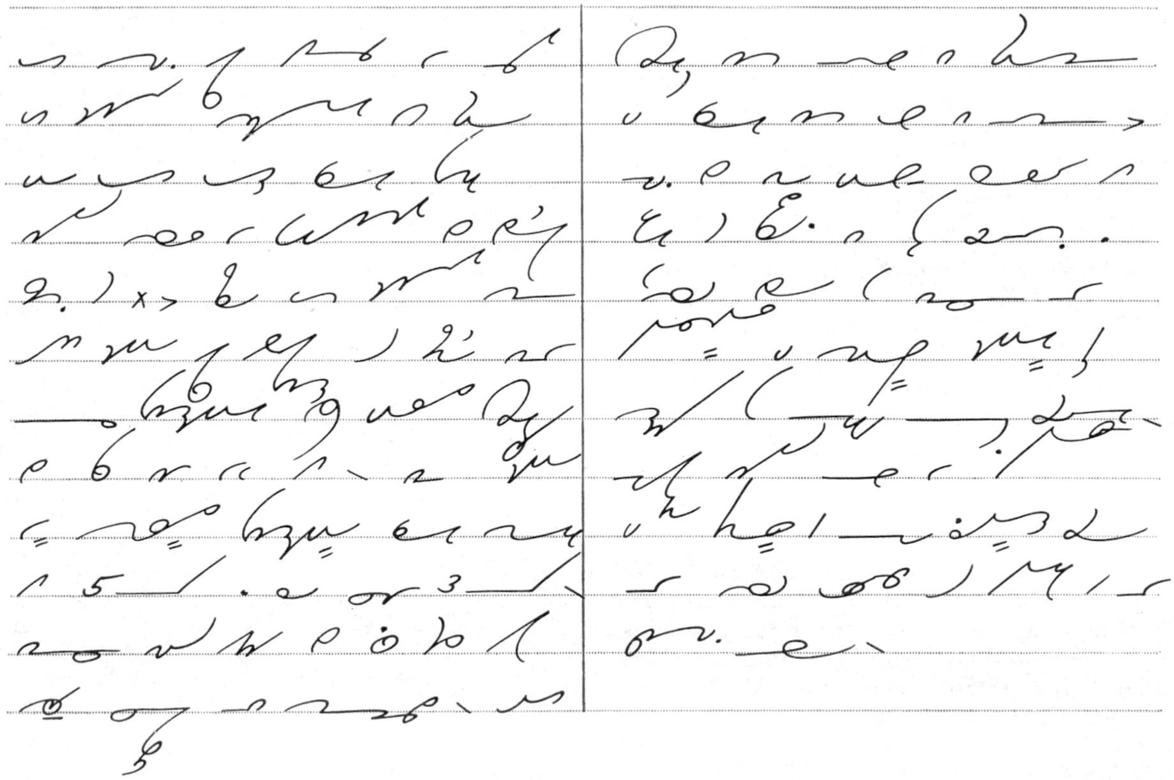

(shorthand outlines)

The forward-looking secretary is always on the alert for short cuts and time savers that will improve her efficiency. These improved procedures she organizes into a handbook, placing each one under its proper classification: typewriting, dictation, transcription, filing, mail handling, telephoning, and so forth. The following paragraphs will give you some ideas for compiling such a handbook of your own. It is essential to remember, though, that the compilation of a handbook of short cuts has value only when you make the short cuts a part of your daily work habits.

Filing Time Savers

Stapling Papers to Be Filed.[2] The usual procedure for stapling papers together is to place the staple in the upper left-hand corner so the reader can flip through them easily. This method of stapling, however, often causes papers to get mixed up in file folders. Some employers, therefore, have papers stapled in the upper right-hand corner so that the closed corner is in the upper left-hand corner of the file folder when filed. The reader can still flip through the pages easily, and you will have more orderly files.

Filing Folded Materials. Oftentimes it is necessary to file charts, reports, and accounting papers that are too large to fit into a regular file folder without first folding them. If folded in the usual way, with the written material on the inside, the folded pieces require valuable time to unfold and inspect in the finding process. These papers will immediately reveal their identity if folded with the written material on the outside.

Removing Folders from a File Drawer. Lifting a folder by its tab often causes the folder contents to shift and spill and eventually causes the tab to break and tear, necessitating the substitution of a new folder. Time, trouble, and expense can be reduced if a folder is lifted by the untabbed portion of its upper edge. If a folder is unusually full, it is even better to lift it by its bottom edge.

Dictation and Transcription Time Savers

Typing Subscripts and Superior Figures.[3] To type a subscript in a chemical formula, as in H_2O, or a superior figure for a footnote, use the ratchet release lever or "automatic line finder." The ratchet release lever, like the variable line spacer, permits you to revolve the platen to any point to type subscripts and superior figures and symbols. But, unlike the

variable line spacer, the ratchet release lever, when re-engaged, returns the platen to the original writing line.

Inserting Multiple-Carbon Packs. Multiple-carbon packs often slip and smudge when inserted into the typewriter. To overcome this difficulty, use one of the following procedures:[4]

1. Slip the top of the assembled carbon pack under the flap of a large business envelope and use the envelope to guide the pack into the machine.

2. Assemble first the original and copy sheets only; insert the sheets into the typewriter just far enough for the platen to hold them in place; then insert the carbon sheets one by one (carbonized side *toward* you), finally turning the entire pack forward to typing position.

Locating Paragraphs in Shorthand Notes. One of the "pet peeves" of employers is the need to wait while the secretary searches for a paragraph sign to read back "what I said in the second paragraph." An easy way to avoid this problem is to start each new paragraph of shorthand notes on a new line in the notebook, indenting if that will be helpful. It is easy then to spot the beginning of a new paragraph. Little, if any, time is lost in skipping to the new line, and very little space is wasted at the line endings.

Using the Notebook Efficiently.[5] Date each day's dictation above the first letter or memo, indicating by initials whose dictation it is if you take dictation from more than one person. It is also a good idea to date each page of notes in the lower left-hand corner. Then, if you are later asked to check notes taken earlier, you have a quick reference guide.

Keep a rubber band around that portion of the notebook containing notes that have already been transcribed. Thus, when a quick call to dictation comes, you can quickly and easily flip the notebook open to the first unused page.

---

[2] *Office Short Cuts and Time Savers* (Englewood Cliffs, New Jersey: Prentice-Hall, Inc., 1961), p. 7.
[3] D. D. Lessenberry, T. James Crawford, and Lawrence W. Erickson, *20th Century Typewriting* (8th ed.; Cincinnati: South-Western Publishing Company, 1962), p. 87.
[4] *Tough Typing Assignments Made Easy* (Englewood Cliffs, New Jersey: Prentice-Hall, Inc., 1962), p. 9.
[5] Wallace B. Bowman and Mary Ellen Oliverio, *Shorthand Dictation Studies* (3d ed.; Cincinnati: South-Western Publishing Company, 1961), p. 28.

24D—Practice Material for Building Fluency

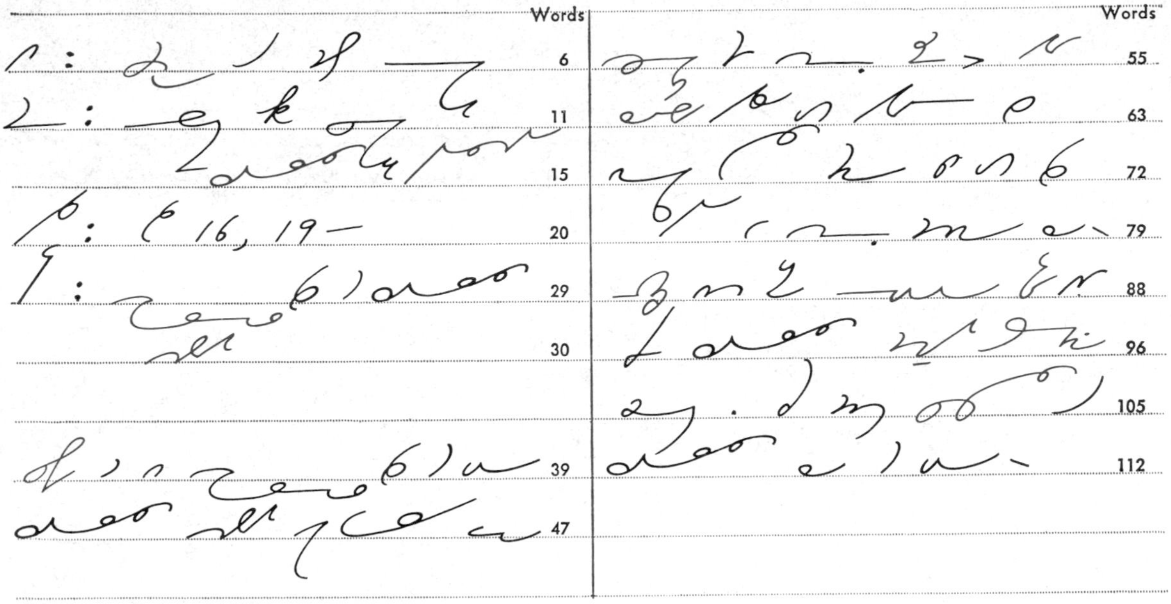
Words
6
11
15
20
29
30
39
47
Words
55
63
72
79
88
96
105
112

24E—Dictionary and Spelling Preview

1. aluminum, lengths, fragile
2. abatement, loitering, eliminated
3. levies, loyalty, pledge, assistant

24F—Preview of New Dictation Material

(1) 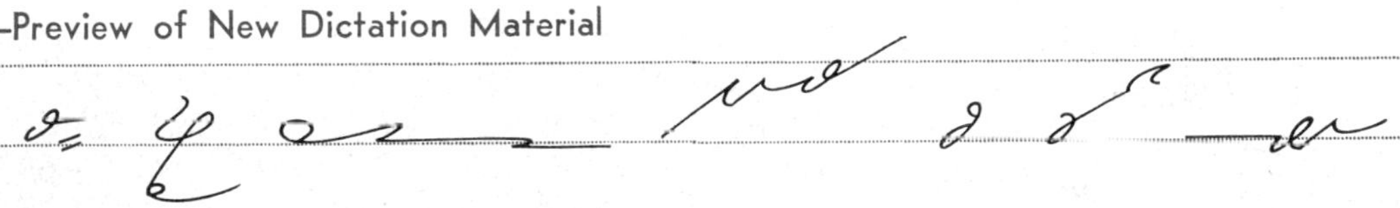

Owen, fragile, aluminum, destroyed, easily, widths, moisture

(2) 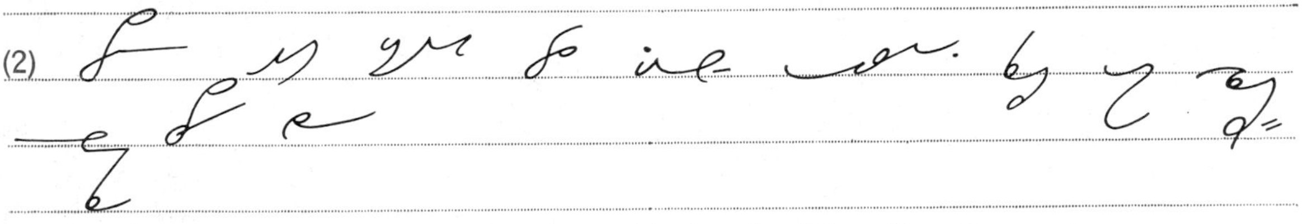

abatement, thoughtful, offenders, particularly, hallways, loitering, cheerfully, rubber, Conservation, messenger, abide, they will

(3) 

Treasurer, assistant, highest, for the past year, Democratic, formerly, unexpired, capacities, liberty, for one year, loyalty, Bookkeeper

1. Type the following manuscript (in duplicate) for left binding. Underline italicized words. (See key to rough-draft symbols, page 248.)

2. When you have completed typing the body of the report, prepare a bibliography page, a contents page, and a title page.

look with disfavor upon workers who waste time and supplies, so do they also

center over the line of writing SOME SECRETARIAL TIME SAVERS

speed and accuracy in

¶ Although skill in typing, writing shorthand, and in transcribing short-
hand *notes are* is essential in getting *skills for obtaining* a job, other factors are more ~~important~~ *vital* to

your sucess in ~~receiving~~ *earning* salary increases and promotions to positions of

greater responsibility. Of these other factors efficiency of work habits

is ~~one~~ of ~~the most important.~~ *high significance, just as* Employers favorably notice ~~workers~~ *employees* who

constantly seek a better way of performing more or less routine activi-

ties. According to Beamer, Hanna, and Popham:[1]

¶ To work efficiently is to work with a minimum of motion, effort,
time, and fatigue. It is seeing where motion, effort, time, fatigue, or
any combination of them can be reduced, and proceeding accordingly.

¶ Some of the questions you should ~~constantly~~ *continually* ask yourself ~~in acquir-
ing the efficiency habit are these:~~ *as you approach each of your assigned tasks:*

1. Where shall I place each of my working materials to reduce
   the motion, effort, time, and fatigue of completing this job?

2. How and in what order shall I ~~do~~ *perform* each of the steps in this
   procedure to reduce motion, effort, time, and fatigue?
3. What can I do to eliminate repetitive work? *add space*

Since efficiency, like personality, is essentially self-acquired, here are

---

[1] Esther Kihn Beamer, J. Marshall Hanna, and Estelle L. Popham,
Effective Secretarial Practices (3d ed.; Cincinnati: South-western
Publishing Company, 1962), p. 38.

1

Continued

Lesson 25 ⬡⬡⬡⬡⬡⬡⬡⬡⬡⬡⬡⬡⬡⬡⬡⬡⬡⬡⬡⬡⬡

25A—Repetitive Phrase Builder

25B—Theory Review

The word beginning *de-* is expressed by *d* except before *k* or *g*.

The word beginning *circum-* is expressed by the left *s* above the line.

25C—Punctuation Preview

Rule 15: Use a semicolon between clauses of a compound sentence that are joined by a conjunctive adverb, such as *so, therefore, hence, however, otherwise, yet, still,* and *furthermore.*

Example: The meeting had to be postponed indefinitely; however, we are not abandoning plans to hold it later in the year.

NOTE: In the following material, Rules 1-14 need to be applied, as well as Rule 15.

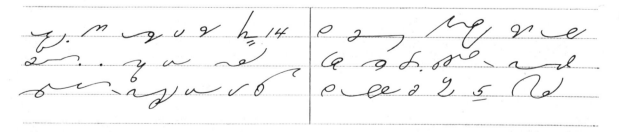

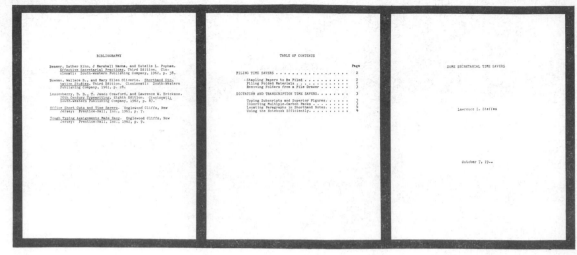

Bibliography   **Contents**   **Title Page**

Bibliography. A *bibliography* (sometimes called a *reference list*) is an alphabetic list of publications or information sources used as references in compiling the report. Generally a bibliography contains all sources cited in the footnotes, and it may also contain additional references that are not specifically cited within the body of the report.

Start the first line of each bibliographical entry at the left margin; indent each subsequent line 5 spaces. Single-space the lines of a single entry, but double-space between entries.

Table of Contents. A *table of contents* of a report is a list of the major divisions and subdivisions, with corresponding page numbers, to show at a glance not only the nature of the content, but also how the report is organized. A contents page is not normally prepared for a report of only a few pages having just a few headings because it is an easy matter to leaf through the report and note the content and organization from the headings themselves. On the other hand, a contents page is highly desirable for a long report that contains many headings.

Because it is necessary to include an appropriate page number for each heading that appears in a table of contents, the contents page can be prepared only after the body of the report, any appendix material, and the bibliography have been typed in final form.

Leaders (alternated periods and spaces) guide the eye from the headings to the corresponding page numbers. To align leaders vertically, note first whether the first leader period in the first line is typed on an odd or an even space. If on an odd space, begin subsequent lines of leaders on odd-numbered spaces; if even, begin on even-numbered spaces.

Title Page. The *title page* of a report contains the title of the report, the name of the author or his department or his company, and the date of the report. Short, informal reports usually do not require the preparation of a title page; whereas, long, formal reports do.

There is no single format or arrangement that must be followed in typing a title page. Rather, any one of a number of arrangements may be used. The important point to remember is that the title page must include necessary information in an easy-to-read, pleasant-to-look-at format.

Line-by-Line Page Gauge. A *line-by-line page gauge* is a valuable guide in typing manuscripts: in positioning page numbers, in establishing top and bottom margins, and in placing footnotes correctly. With the first number typed in the first line space below the top edge of the sheet, a glance at the page gauge will tell you where to type the page number and where to begin the first line of the body of the report. The numbers beginning with 1 in the last line space at the bottom of the sheet will tell you at a glance how many lines are left on the page for typing.

A page gauge like the one illustrated at the right is best prepared on onionskin paper so that it can be inserted between the top sheet and the first carbon sheet in a carbon pack with the numbered edge extended at the right.

[Shorthand practice material — Gregg shorthand outlines]

25D—Practice Material for Building Fluency

(1)

	Words
shorthand outlines	3
shorthand outlines	7
shorthand outlines	12
shorthand outlines 8, 19	16
shorthand outlines	22
shorthand outlines	25

	Words
shorthand outlines	94
shorthand outlines	101
shorthand outlines	108
shorthand outlines	114
shorthand outlines	122
shorthand outlines	131

	Words
shorthand outlines	34
shorthand outlines	40
shorthand outlines	48
shorthand outlines	55
shorthand outlines 208-B	60
208-C *shorthand outlines*	65
shorthand outlines	72
shorthand outlines	79
shorthand outlines	86

(2)

	Words
shorthand outlines 6, 19	3
shorthand outlines	8
shorthand outlines 32	11
shorthand outlines + 08610	16
shorthand outlines	25
shorthand outlines	30
shorthand outlines	35
shorthand outlines	43

Secretarial Typing and Machine Transcription

Lesson **121** ⬡ ⬡ ⬡ ⬡ ⬡ ⬡ ⬡ ⬡ ⬡ ⬡ ⬡ ⬡ ⬡ ⬡ ⬡ ⬡ ⬡

Typing Manuscripts

As a secretary, you will often be required to type manuscripts (sometimes with footnotes; sometimes without) of business reports, sales handbook materials, office manual inserts, and the like. Sometimes these materials will be dictated to you; more often, however, they will be "roughed out" by your employer by hand or on the typewriter with handwritten corrections. Often, too, such materials will consist of hand revisions of typed pages that for one reason or another need revision or correction.

Whatever the reason and whatever the kind of copy, though, you must be able to prepare correctly arranged and typed manuscripts for your employer's approval. It is the purpose of this lesson to reacquaint you with the basic information and procedures needed to do this work well.

Margins and Spacing. In typing manuscripts, leave top, bottom, and side margins of approximately 1 inch on all pages with these exceptions: Leave a 2-inch top margin on the first page, a 1½-inch left margin on all pages if the manuscript is to be bound at the left, and a 1½-inch top margin on all pages except the first if the manuscript is to be bound at the top.

Unless otherwise directed, type manuscripts and reports with double spacing on standard 8½- by 11-inch typewriting paper, indenting the first line of each paragraph either 5 or 10 spaces. Single-space quoted material of 4 or more lines and enumerated items, indenting them 5 spaces from left and right margins.

Headings and Subdivisions. Type the main heading of a manuscript or report in all capitals; center it over the line of writing used in the body of the report; and follow it by a triple space.

Type side headings (preceded by a triple space, followed by a double space) in capital and lowercase letters, underlined, even with the left margin.

Indent and type paragraph headings (usually with important words capitalized) with underlining on the first line beginning the paragraph.

Pages 1 and 2 of a Manuscript

Page Numbers. Center and type the first page number (Arabic 1) a half inch from the bottom of the page. If the manuscript or report is to be bound at the left, type other page numbers in the upper right corner of the page even with the right margin and a half inch from the top of the page. If the manuscript is to be bound at the top, however, center them a half inch from the bottom of the page. Leave a triple space below page numbers in the upper right corner of pages, a double space above those at the bottom.

Footnotes. Use an underline approximately 1½ inches in length to separate the last line of the body of the manuscript from the footnotes. Leave a single space above this underline and a double space below it.

Indent the first line of each footnote to the paragraph point (5 or 10 spaces). Single-space the lines of a single footnote, but double-space between footnotes.

Type a superior figure a half space above the line of writing (both in the body of the manuscript and in the footnote itself) to identify the footnote. You may number footnotes consecutively throughout the manuscript, or you may number them anew on each page. Consecutive numbering is often used for short reports; whereas, numbering anew on each page is more often used for longer reports. The latter method makes it possible to add or delete a footnote reference without renumbering all subsequent notes.

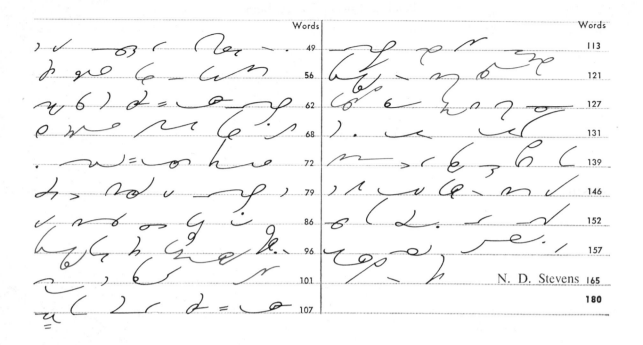

	Words		Words
	49		113
	56		121
	62		127
	68		131
	72		139
	79		146
	86		152
	96		157
	101	N. D. Stevens	165
	107		**180**

25E—Dictionary and Spelling Preview

1. De Luxe, atmosphere, decide

2. depot, descend, convenient

3. independent, intention, assurance, solemn, definite

25F—Preview of New Dictation Material

(1)

De Luxe, tasteful, Cafe, atmosphere, delicious, decorations

(2)

Dickinson, departure, modern, designed, baggage, confusion, depot, easier, we decided

(3)

Trout, independent, effective, absolute, no longer, we are now, assurance, obviously, you may be sure, prevailing, depleted, as long, we want

Building Skill in Transcribing

Transcribing from Shorthand Notes

1. Write in shorthand Letter (1) given below.

2. Transcribe the letter from your notes as a 5-minute writing. Use block style with open punctuation. Determine your *mwam*. If you complete the letter before time is called, repeat it from the beginning.

3. Transcribe Letter (2) as a 5-minute writing in the same style. Determine your *mwam* and compare it with your *mwam* on Letter (1).

(1)

	Words
January 17, 19—	3

Mr. A. J. Cochran, Office Manager	10
Littleton and Forbes, Inc.	16
444 Commercial Square	20
Springfield, Massachusetts 01102	27

Dear Mr. Cochran	30

Several days ago we sent you a brochure	38
showing the comparative cost of sending [1]	46
direct-mail pieces according to the old postal	56
rates and the recently effected ones. With	64
the volume of [2] direct-mail advertising you	74
do, the increased mailing cost is considerable.	83

As graphically illustrated [3] in the brochure,	91
the increased rates can be significantly offset	101
by the use of our new Mail-Lite papers. [4]	109
Several grades are available—from the	117
Memo-Lite grade for interbranch correspond-	126
ence to the Air-Lite [5] grade for first-class mail-	135
ings to customers. Although light in weight,	144
these papers have more than adequate opac-	153
ity [6] and a crispness comparable to that of	161
heavier-weight bond.	166

It would be well worth your while to discuss	175
these cost [7]-saving papers with our local repre-	184
sentative, Mr. Clauson. He will be glad to	193
arrange an appointment [8] if you'll simply	201
check and return the addressed, postage-paid	210
card. (181)	211

Sincerely yours	214
	240

(2)

	Words
January 18, 19—	
Postmaster	6
Post Office Department	10
215 West Main Street	14
Dubuque, Iowa 52001	19

	29
	36
	45
	53
	61
	68
	75
	83
	94
	101
	108
	116
	124
	132
	140
	149
	158
	167
	175
	185
	200
	215

Transcribing from Dictation

Your teacher will dictate a telegram, a letter, and an interoffice memo to you for transcription. Prepare the telegram and the letter for the signature of Luther T. Ryan, Head, Shipping Department.

Kinds of Business Letters

Lesson **26** ⬡○⬡○⬡○⬡○⬡○⬡○⬡○⬡○⬡○⬡○⬡○⬡

26A—Letters of Inquiry or Request

Many, many thousands of letters of inquiry or request are written every year. Inquiries may be made about any one of a multitude of subjects: whether a company manufactures a particular type of product, where a certain bit of information may be obtained, who should be consulted about a problem, etc. Requests, too, may concern a wide variety of subjects, such as requests for advice, service, information, recommendation, action of some kind, and so on.

Most inquiries and requests are brief; their messages can be expressed in a few words or sentences. Although brief, such letters should never be regarded as unimportant and, consequently, be carelessly written.

Here are some characteristics you will find in well-written inquiries and requests:

1. The inquiry or request is definitely, completely, and clearly stated. If a request is made, the reason for it is given.

2. Courteous wording is used. A demanding tone creates resentment. If you are in a position to demand, it is necessary only to ask; if you are not in a position to demand, demanding will probably bring forth a refusal.

3. Stereotyped phrases are avoided. Probably in no type of business letter is it easier to use worn-out phrases such as "thanking you in advance," "assuring you of my appreciation, I remain," "please advise," or "valued favor."

4. If there are several parts to the inquiry or request, tabulating of the items insures a complete reply.

5. Appreciation is expressed, but not by saying "thanking you in advance," or some similar phrase.

6. The appearance of the letter is good. In many cases someone is being asked to use his time and knowledge without any compensation. The least the writer can do is present his inquiry or request in as attractive a form as possible. If he hasn't the few minutes needed to present his inquiry or request in good form, he can't expect someone else to spend *his* time answering.

Inquiries or requests are frequently called "routine" letters, and, being thus labeled, are often regarded as unimportant. No letter is unimportant; if it were, it wouldn't be written. Any inquiry or request is important to the person who writes it; if it looks or sounds unimportant, the response to it may be inadequately or carelessly written—or not written at all.

Dear Mr. Jones:

I understand that you are now the agent in this area for the United Duplicator. The machine that we have is ten years old, and we are considering the purchase of a new model.

We should like to have the following information about the United Duplicator:

1. Overall dimensions of the machine
2. Initial cost
3. Supplies needed
4. Service contract provided
5. Types of duplicating jobs that can be handled

We should, of course, like to have a demonstration of the machine before making a decision. When could this be arranged?

Sincerely yours,

Letter of Inquiry

Dear Mrs. Hardy:

We have some important information for you in connection with your land holdings at Lakeview Park. It is urgent that you get in touch with us immediately.

Please telephone or write us within the next day or two, telling us when it would be convenient for you to come to our office. If you cannot come to our office, let us know when we may call at your home.

Yours very truly,

Letter of Request

Questions for Discussion

1. What are stereotyped phrases? Name some that should be avoided.
2. Why is the appearance of a letter of inquiry or request important?
3. Name some kinds of inquiries or requests that might be made.
4. Why should a reason for a request be given?

TelAutograph

Teletypewriter

The TelAutograph. The *TelAutograph* will electrically transmit and receive handwritten messages. As a message is written with a metal stylus on a metal plate on the sending unit, the pen of the receiving unit instantly records that message on a roll of paper. The TelAutograph is used for high-speed written communication over short distances, as between the warehouse and the main office, between local branches of the same store, and between the teller in a bank and an account clerk on another floor.

The Teletypewriter. The *teletypewriter* operates on the same principle as a telephone except that the typewritten word, rather than the spoken word, is transmitted. As the message is typewritten on the typewriter keyboard of the teletypewriter, it is instantaneously reproduced stroke by stroke on the receiving unit in another office or on several units simultaneously in several offices (depending upon the type of service). Teletypewriters are often used when speed is an important factor and when a written record of the message is desired. Airlines, oil companies, and many governmental departments are among the users of teletypewriter service.

Two types of teletypewriter service are available —teletypewriter exchange service and teletypewriter private line service. *Teletypewriter exchange service (TWX)* operates through a central telephone office. Each subscriber to this service has an assigned number and is provided a directory of all subscribers in the United States and can have message service with each of them. Rates for TWX messages (based on time and distance) are considerably lower than rates for comparable station-to-station long-distance telephone calls.

Teletypewriter private line service (PWPL) or *leased-wire service* is a direct service between offices connected by direct wires. PWPL service is used by many companies for interoffice com-

munication between their branch offices and plants throughout the country.

To send a message using TWX service, you must first signal the operator in the central office and type the exchange and the number you wish to reach. When the connection has been made and the called unit is ready to receive, you can type the message.

To send a message using PWPL service, you merely signal the branch or office you want to reach; then, as soon as that office is ready to receive, you can type the message.

Questions for Discussion

1. Why might a company specify payment by postal or express money order rather than by check?
2. What are the steps in purchasing a postal money order?
3. When you buy a postal money order, why is it important to fill in immediately the name of the person who is to be paid?
4. Under what circumstances might a person or a business firm send a telegraphic money order?
5. Is it possible to file a telegraphic money order by telephone and have it charged to your regular telephone bill? Check with your local telegraph office.
6. What advantages are there in using an "intercom" system for interoffice voice communication instead of the telephone?
7. What advantage does a TelAutograph have over regular interoffice memorandums or duplicate copies of business papers?
8. What is the difference between TWX service and PWPL service?
9. Since teletypewriter service and telephone service are both provided by the telephone company, why would a company use the teletypewriter instead of long-distance telephone?

Office Practice Problems

Criticize the following letters. Rewrite them so that they are in better form.

1. Gentlemen:

Last year we furnished you black lab aprons. We want you to know that we appreciate your valued orders and hope you will be in the market at an early date.

We await your favorable reply.

Respectfully,

2. Gentlemen:

We are very glad to advise that we are again having our showing of toy and holiday goods at the Conrad Hotel in Sioux City, Iowa.

We are looking forward to seeing you on one of the following dates: July 27th thru August 2nd.

In order that we can arrange to work with you when you come in, we would appreciate your using the enclosed card to advise what time and date would be most convenient for you.

Thanking you for your early reply, we are,

Very truly yours,

26B—Building Speed in Taking Dictation

Brief-Form Practice

Directions. The following paragraph has 24 brief forms and brief-form derivatives. If you can read the paragraph in 20 seconds, you will be reading at the rate of 123 words a minute.

Writing of Numbers

Rule 16: Definite numbers over ten are written in figures; ten, and under, in words. Approximate numbers are written out as a general rule when they can be expressed in one or two words.

Certain numbers are written in figures whether they are definite or not, whether they are ten and above or ten and below. Some of these numbers are: percentages, amounts of money, and dimensions.

Example: We bought two desks for $200 each, which was 15% more than we had paid for similar desks last year; furthermore, they were 5 inches narrower.

NOTE: Amounts of money less than $1 are written in figures followed by the word "cents."

Special Communication Services

Postal and Express Money Orders. *Postal* and *express money orders* are used to transfer money from one person or business to another. A postal money order may be purchased at all post offices, branches, and stations in the United States and its territories. An express money order may be purchased at any American Express or Railway Express Agency office. Fees for postal money orders and American Express money orders are the same. A properly completed postal money order is illustrated below.

Postal Money Order

To purchase a postal money order:

1. Tell the window clerk the amount desired and pay that amount plus the required fee.
2. After receiving the money order, write on the face of the order the name of the person or firm to be paid and the name and address of the person or firm making the payment.
3. Detach and keep the purchaser's receipt.

It is important to fill in the money order immediately because a lost money order can be filled in and cashed by anyone. Keep the receipt because no money order can be traced without it.

Telegraphic Money Orders. A *telegraphic money order* is one of the safest, speediest ways to transfer money from one person or company to another. The amount to be transferred is given to the telegraph office clerk together with the name and address of the recipient and any accompanying message. Upon payment of the necessary fee, the clerk will give you a receipt for the amount of money to be dispatched and have the message sent.

When the message is received in the destination office, the recipient is notified and may collect the money upon proper identification of himself. A properly typed telegraphic money order is illustrated at the top of the next column.

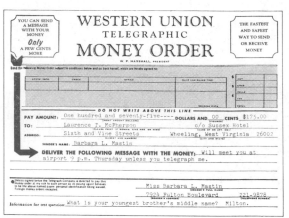

Telegraphic Money Order

Instantaneous Interoffice Communication Systems. Three often-used interoffice communication methods, in addition to the telephone and the written interoffice memorandum, are the *intercom* (for voice transmission), the *TelAutograph*, and the *teletypewriter*. Each makes possible the instantaneous transfer or exchange of information between offices.

Voice Transmission. A number of interoffice communicating devices for two-way voice transmission are available, among them the Dictograph, the Executone, the Teletalk, and the Bel-fone. In general, their operating principles are the same. Using one of these devices, an executive can talk with his secretary (or with some other employee) from his private office merely by depressing the talk button on his "intercom" set and speaking into the mouthpiece. The secretary, likewise, can talk with him from similar equipment on her desk. A variety of sets are available, from the one-button set to sets with many lines to individual offices.

—Dictograph Products, Inc.

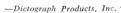

Dictograph

Practice Material for Building Fluency

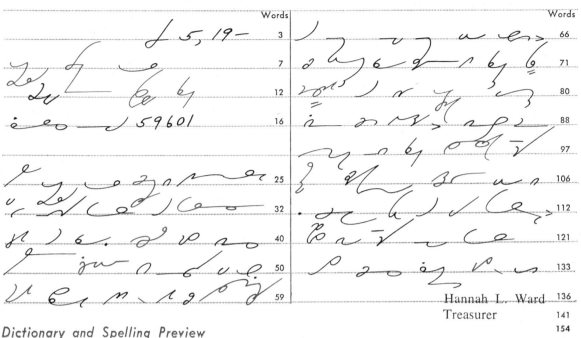

Words: 3, 7, 12, 16, 25, 32, 40, 50, 59

Words: 66, 71, 80, 88, 97, 106, 112, 121, 133

Hannah L. Ward 136
Treasurer 141
154

Dictionary and Spelling Preview

1. reflector, mogul, wrought, antique

2. serviceman, indisposed

3. encroaching, hazardous

4. premium, remittance

Preview of New Dictation Material

(1)

student, sketch, antique, socket, reflector, we can make, parchment, whether or not, approximately, mogul, decorated, in the market

(2)

indisposed, minimum, we want, so that, somewhat, you can have, inspection

(3)

superintendent, Winkle, hazardous, in order that the, Chamberlin, New Mexico, identify, hesitated, Beckwith, encroaching, Kingston, Southern

(4)

Winslow, thank you for this, renewal, coverage, if you / desire, et cetera, expiring, premium

2. An item not easily broken is best packed in a box or carton just large enough to accommodate it, or the extra space should be stuffed with paper or other packing material to keep the contents from moving within the container during transit.
3. An item that is fragile or easily breakable should be packed in a larger container, carefully wrapped and completely surrounded by shock-absorbent paper or other packing material, and further protected with a double layer of corrugated cardboard. In addition, such a package should be prominently labeled FRAGILE or BREAKABLE.

To collect the insurance on packages that are damaged in shipment, you must take the damaged package to the shipping agency. Unless it can be shown that the package was carefully packed, wrapped, and marked, there may be some difficulty in collecting the insurance.

Marking Goods for Shipment. Regardless of the method of shipment, it is essential to the prompt movement and delivery of the shipment that the goods be marked correctly. Careful labeling of less-than-carload (L.C.L.) shipments is particularly important because they may be handled and transferred many times.

The following guides if carefully followed should insure the proper delivery by the carriers:

1. Marking should be made by typewriter, brush, stencil, crayon, or rubber stamp. If hand lettering is used, the style should be clear and neat. Labels or paper tags should be prepared on the typewriter and fastened securely to the packages. Metal tags should be fastened by wire.
2. The consignee's (addressee's) name and address and the bill of lading destination should be shown.
3. The name and address of the shipper should be preceded by the word *From*.
4. When the goods are consigned to a place not located on the line of the carrier, the package should be marked with the name of the station where the consignee will accept the goods.
5. If the shipment is to be made by order bill of lading, the words *To Order* should be shown on each package.
6. Packages containing articles easily broken should be marked *Fragile* or *Handle with Care*. Packages containing perishable commodities should be marked *Perishable*.

Questions for Discussion and Office Practice Problems

1. What factors determine the rates charged for express and freight shipments?
2. Which of the three air services (air express, air freight, air parcel post) would be cheapest for a shipment weighing 40 pounds?
3. What advantages does motor freight have over railway freight?
4. What factors should be considered in deciding whether to send a shipment by one of the express services or by one of the freight services?
5. Why is the cost of a carload shipment proportionately lower for the same distance than a less-than-carload shipment?
6. Who is a consignor? a consignee? a carrier?
7. Which type of bill of lading would you use if you were shipping merchandise directly to a customer on open account?
8. Why should a bill of lading be prepared in triplicate?
9. What is the difference between a C.O.D. shipment and a collect shipment?
10. If a shipment from New York to Denver is sent f.o.b. Denver, who pays the shipping charges from New York to Denver?
11. Under what conditions might bus express be used more advantageously than R E A Express, air express, or freight?
12. Under what conditions might the address of the addressee and the name of the destination point shown on a bill of lading differ?
13. In labeling a package, why should you precede the name of the shipper by the word *From*?
14. What do the words *To Order* on a package mean?
15. In a brief typewritten paragraph, indicate what is meant by:

   a. railway express   **d.** railway freight
   b. air express   **e.** air freight
   c. bus express   **f.** water freight

16. Make a typewritten list of the following shipping terms, leaving five blank lines between words. Using the dictionary as a reference, type opposite each word a definition of that word.

   a. avoirdupois   **d.** hundredweight
   b. cartage   **e.** sight draft
   c. hogshead   **f.** waybill

27A—Favorable and Unfavorable Responses to Inquiries and Requests

Letters of inquiry or request that can be handled favorably are rather easy to answer. When the requested information can be given, the main points to be remembered in the response are:

1. Give complete and accurate information. Try to put yourself in the position of the inquirer, thinking through his problem as he has presented it. By so doing, you may be spared the necessity of answering a second letter asking for additional, more specific information.

2. When giving information that is not original with you, indicate the source of it. Do not take credit for someone else's work.

3. Answer promptly. The information may be urgently needed.

4. If you or your firm has been complimented, be appreciative of it.

Letters of inquiry or request that cannot be handled favorably are somewhat more difficult to answer. A curt, blunt refusal is not only discourteous but may actually harm the person or firm that writes it. When a refusal must be made, some important points to observe are:

1. Start the letter on a friendly note. Don't begin immediately with "No." Express an understanding of the inquirer's problem and a wish that you could be helpful. If any information at all can be given, give that much right away.

Explain carefully why the information requested cannot be given. Sometimes knowing why a refusal must be made takes the "sting" out of it for the recipient.

2. If you know somewhere else the information or help might be obtained, suggest that source.

3. Close on a friendly note, perhaps expressing the hope that the inquirer can get help elsewhere or that you might be able to help on some other problem at a later time.

4. Answer promptly. If you cannot help, you have an obligation to let the writer know immediately so that he can look elsewhere for assistance.

It is well to remember that a routine request or inquiry is frequently the beginning of a long and profitable business relationship if it is handled promptly, sincerely, and in a friendly fashion. Never underestimate the potentialities of such a letter when you answer it.

Dear Mr. Jones:

We have received your inquiry about the October (PURCHASING GUIDE) issue of the INFORMER.

Mailing of the PURCHASING GUIDE has not yet been completed, although it is possible that your copy has reached you already. If it has not, it should arrive within a short time.

Sincerely yours,

Response to Inquiry

Dear Professor Penney:

We shall be most happy to provide you with all the information and materials that we have available. In order to be sure you get everything you need and that all of your questions are answered, we are sending these materials to you through our Branch Office in Jackson, Mississippi.

A representative will get in touch with you within a few days. You can be sure that he is ready and eager to help you in any way possible.

Yours very truly,

Favorable Response to Request

Dear Mr. Clarion:

We are pleased that you are interested in a Hoosier transistor radio, for we know that you will get a great deal of pleasure from it. Since we are a wholesale jobber, we cannot, we regret, handle your inquiry of November 10 directly.

Our retail outlet in your city is Timson Radio and TV Shop, 42 Federal Building. The owner, Mr. Paul Donner, will be glad to serve you.

We hope that you will have many hours of enjoyment from the Hoosier transistor radio of your choice.

Cordially yours,

Unfavorable Response to Inquiry

Questions for Discussion

1. What points should be remembered in responding to inquiries or requests when favorable action can be taken?
2. What points should be remembered in responding to inquiries or requests when unfavorable action must be taken?
3. Why is it important to answer all letters promptly?

Motor Freight. *Motor freight* refers to shipments, either local or long distance, that are transported by truck. Trucking companies provide a variety of transfer plans: from daily pickup of packages for local delivery, to truckload and less-than-truckload pickup and delivery for long-distance hauls, to specialized trucks that carry single commodities such as gasoline, new cars, and building materials in truckload quantities. In addition, they work with railway companies to make shipments partially by truck and partially by railway for quicker, more economical service.

Speed of delivery is extremely important to many manufacturers and merchants, particularly to those who deal in perishable or seasonal commodities. Trucking companies are usually able to provide direct manufacturer-to-merchant and rush delivery service.

Air Freight. *Air freight* service is operated by the airlines directly rather than through a division of R E A Express. Air freight is often used for heavier shipments while air express is used for lighter ones. Generally, shipments weighing less than 25 pounds can be sent more cheaply by air express, while shipments weighing 25 pounds or more can be sent more cheaply by air freight. Air freight should be used only for long-distance deliveries and if time is an extremely important factor. The airlines provide pickup and delivery service for air freight.

Water Freight. *Water freight* refers to shipments transported on barges, boats, and freighters. Such shipments are carried both on inland waterways and on the seas and oceans. Shipping on inland waterways is much slower than transportation by truck or railway. For this reason water transportation is used chiefly for bulky, heavy merchandise for which speed of delivery is not so important as low freight rates. Information on services provided and rates charged can be obtained from the shipping companies.

Bill of Lading. A *bill of lading* is a receipt for goods to be shipped and a contract to deliver them. For every freight shipment a bill of lading must be prepared in triplicate. The original copy is mailed to the addressee (consignee) who is to receive the goods or to his bank or agent; the second copy (the shipping order) is given to the carrier; the third copy (the memorandum) is kept by the shipper (consignor). Two types of bills of lading are in common use: *straight bill of lading*

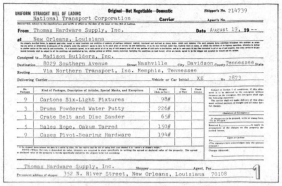

Correctly Prepared Bill of Lading

when a shipment is made on open account or is sent C.O.D. directly to the addressee; *order bill of lading* when a shipment is deferred until the consignee pays the sight draft attached to the bill of lading that is sent to his bank or agent.

C.O.D., Collect, and F.O.B. The abbreviation C.O.D. means *collect on delivery* or *cash on delivery*. When a shipment is made C.O.D., the carrier collects the required payment before he gives the addressee possession of the shipment.

The term *collect* does not mean the same as C.O.D. When a shipment is made *collect*, the carrier collects for the transportation charges only; whereas, when a shipment is sent C.O.D., the carrier collects for the cost of the commodity only or for the cost of the commodity and the transportation.

The shipping charges may be prepaid by the shipper; they may be prepaid by the shipper and included in the bill for the shipment; or they may be collected by the carrier on *collect* shipments.

The abbreviation F.O.B. (or *f.o.b.*) means *free on board*. It is used with an address to indicate the point to which the freight is paid by the shipper. If a shipment from Chicago to Detroit is made f.o.b. Detroit, the shipper pays the freight from Chicago to Detroit. If the shipment is made f.o.b. Chicago, however, the shipper delivers it to the freight depot in Chicago and the addressee pays the transportation charges from Chicago to Detroit.

Preparing Packages for Shipment. Regardless of how a parcel is to be shipped—parcel post, express, or freight—it must be carefully packaged, sealed or securely tied, and properly marked to insure delivery in good condition. Here are some guides for preparing packages for shipment:

1. Any item of merchandise, whether large or small, should be boxed or protected by cardboard instead of merely wrapped with paper.

Office Practice Problems

Criticize the following letters. Revise them so that they follow good practices in letter writing.

1. Dear Miss Merrill:

We are in receipt of your card requesting the address and phone number of Mr. Swank and in reply beg to advise that we do not have Mr. Swank's address as he has not been associated with us for some time.

Sorry that we are unable to give you this information, we are

Very truly yours,

2. Gentlemen:

We are herewith enclosing circular illustrating and describing the portable radios we have on hand and can furnish at this time, together with price list.

We have these in stock and can make immediate shipment.

Thanking you for your inquiry, and assuring you we are looking forward to the privilege and pleasure of serving you, we are

Sincerely yours,

27B—Building Speed in Taking Dictation

Phrase Builder

There are 10 phrases in the following paragraph.

Punctuation Preview

Rule 17: Hyphen an adjective composed of two or more words if used before a noun. Do not hyphen these words if they follow the noun they modify (except an adjective composed of an adjective and a noun to which *-ed* has been added, as *ill-mannered*). Do not hyphen compound adjectives containing an adverb ending in *-ly*. Do not hyphen proper nouns used as adjectives. Hyphen an adjective composed of a number and another word to form a unit modifier.

Example: The world-wide campaign aroused considerable interest in Latin American countries, since the first prize, an attractively built home for a 70-foot lot, was up to date and suited for that climate.

NOTE: You will need to apply Rule 16, as well as Rule 17, in the following material.

Shipping Services

Every business makes shipments of various kinds by means other than the postal services described in Lesson 117. These methods of shipment include airways, railways, trucks, busses, and ships. The secretary should know the kinds of services that are available, the advantages of each, and the sources to consult for current information.

Railway Express. *Railway express* is provided by R E A Express. Speed is an important feature of this service; there is practically no limitation on the size, weight, or character of packages thus shipped; and each shipment is given the required care and protection. C.O.D. service is available.

In most cities R E A Express provides pickup and delivery service at no extra cost. The expressman makes out a receipt for the pickup at the point of origin and a delivery receipt at the destination point as proof of dates of shipping and delivery. Express shipments travel in fast-moving passenger trains and special R E A Express trains.

Railway express charges include free insurance up to $50 on shipments weighing 100 pounds or less. For heavier shipments and for higher valuations, additional insurance is available for an additional fee. The cost of shipping depends upon the weight of the shipment, the distance it is to be transported, and the kind of item being shipped. All items are classified in an index according to the classes of rates by which they can be shipped: first class, second class, and third class. Shipping distances from each area are divided into 82 different zones for "rate scales." Since the minimum express rate is $2.90, very lightweight items can be sent cheaper by first-class mail.

The R E A Express office will, upon request, furnish the secretary with a copy of the classification index of items and the local rate scales.

Air Express. *Air express* is handled by the Air Express Division of R E A Express. Shipments to communities not served by airlines are transmitted partly by air and partly by railway or truck. Among the advantages of air express are speed, relatively low cost, liberal insurance coverage, pickup and delivery service at no extra cost within prescribed distance limits, and free radio and wire facilities for expediting shipments and pickups and for tracing shipments. Although there are special rates for certain types of items, rates are generally based on the weight of the shipment and the distance it is to be transported.

The secretary should compare carefully the rates for air parcel post, air express, and air freight because considerable savings may be effected by using the least expensive service. Local post office and express company personnel will be glad to give information about their services. In addition, *Leonard's Guide* and the *Official Air Express Guide* might be of help.

Bus Express. *Bus express*, offered by most bus lines throughout the country, provides speedy package delivery to smaller towns where there are no airports and often no railways. Round-the-clock service is offered, including Sundays and holidays. Many points receive same-day service; many receive service within a few hours, faster than air service. Door-to-bus pickup and delivery service is available at extra cost. Packages are insurable up to $50. There is a weight limit of 100 pounds and a size limit of 24″ by 24″ by 45″.

Freight Services. *Freight* is usually thought of as shipments sent by any method other than mail or express. Because freight service is most often used to transport heavy, bulky goods in large quantities, the secretary is less likely to be concerned with freight shipments than with express shipments. Nevertheless, she should be familiar with the most commonly used freight services.

Railway Freight. *Railway freight* is used for shipping bulky articles and commodities when speed of delivery is not vitally important. Shipping by railway freight is less expensive than shipping by truck or any other ground method.

Ordinarily when goods are shipped by railway freight, they must be delivered by the shipper to the local freight office and picked up by the addressee at the point of destination. But some railway companies provide store-door delivery.

Shipments may be made in carload lots or in less-than-carload lots, the first being transported at the lower rate. Freight-forwarding companies are sometimes used to assemble less-than-carload shipments of several shippers to take advantage of carload rates. In addition to these two variations in rates, there are two other rate distinctions: class rates which are based on the class of the commodity and the distance the shipment is to be transported, and commodity rates which are based on the volume of the shipments. Commodity rates are usually lower than class rates.

Practice Material for Building Fluency

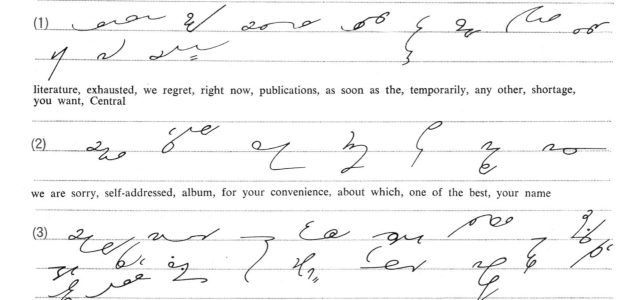

Words column (left):

26, 19— 3
ross 6
110 9
29401 16
26
23 21 37
45

Words column (right):

53
59
65
74
83
91
100
Hamilton Burger 104
Secretary 106
118

Dictionary and Spelling Preview

1. temporarily, exhausted, preferred

3. dictionary, descriptions, anticipation, stipulation

Preview of New Dictation Material

(1)

literature, exhausted, we regret, right now, publications, as soon as the, temporarily, any other, shortage, you want, Central

(2)

we are sorry, self-addressed, album, for your convenience, about which, one of the best, your name

(3)

we are pleased, walnut, movable, supplier, casters, dictionary, in a position, we have not had, insists, bindings, hearing from you, Stipulation, postmarked, unabridged, datings, anticipation, and return

an insurance fee. The postal clerk makes out a receipt for the parcel, stamps the package INSURED, and gives you the receipt. If the parcel is damaged or lost, the post office will, upon presentation of the receipt and the sales slip to establish the cost of the item, reimburse you for the cost of the item.

C.O.D. Service. Merchandise may be sent to a purchaser C.O.D. (collect on delivery) by agreement with the purchaser and the seller. To obtain C.O.D. service, the seller must pay a fee in addition to the regular postage. The maximum collectible on one parcel is $200; for registered C.O.D. mail, $1,000. The fee charged depends upon the amount to be collected, the weight of the parcel, and the distance to the purchaser's post office.

Postage. *Postage stamps* are available in sheet, coil, or booklet form. Sheets or coils of 100 stamps are frequently used for business purposes. A strip of stamps from either a sheet or coil can be quickly affixed to several envelopes. Simply arrange 6 to 8 envelopes one on top of another with just the upper right portion of each exposed. Moisten the strip of stamps with a damp sponge and affix one after the other.

Precanceled stamps and precanceled stamped envelopes (often used for direct-mail advertising campaigns) may be obtained by special permit from the post office. They save canceling time at the post office at the time of mailing.

Stamped envelopes and cards in various sizes, kinds, and denominations may be purchased at the post office in quantity lots or individually. When ordered in quantity, the post office will imprint the sender's return address for a nominal amount. First-class postal cards are available in single or double (business-reply) form. Airmail postal cards are available only in single form. Unserviceable or spoiled stamped envelopes and cards may be exchanged for stamps, stamped envelopes, or postal cards if they have not been canceled.

One of the most efficient means of affixing postage is provided by the *postage meter machine.* The postage meter prints on each piece of mail the postmark and the proper amount of postage. Thus, the mail need not be postmarked or canceled when it is delivered to the post office. The postage meter machine is bought outright, but the postage is purchased periodically by having the post office set and lock the meter for a specific amount of postage upon payment of the required fee.

The amount of postage for each envelope or card is set by a dial. After the piece is inserted

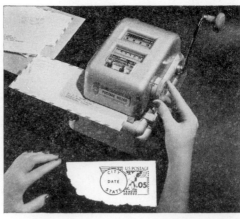

Postage Meter

into the machine and the handle is pulled, the postage is printed on the envelope or card. For parcel post and bulky mail, postage is printed on gummed tape and manually pasted on the package.

Questions for Discussion and Office Practice Problems

1. What kinds of mail must be sent first class?
2. What kinds of mail may be sent third class? fourth class?
3. How are rates determined for fourth-class mail?
4. What is the difference between insured and registered mail?
5. What is a postage meter machine and what are its advantages?
6. When is payment made for postage used in a postage meter machine?
7. Why is mail divided into several classes with different rates for each?
8. What is the difference between special delivery and special handling services?
9. What should you do with spoiled prestamped envelopes and postal cards that you had bought from the post office?
10. How should you determine and affix the postage on a parcel post package with a first-class letter enclosed?
11. For each item listed below, indicate the class of postal service that should be used, the kinds of fees that must be paid in addition to postage, and special notations that should appear on the parcel.
    a. A 6-ounce parcel sent airmail, special delivery.
    b. A check for $50 sent to a city 250 miles away.
    c. An income tax report sent certified mail.
    d. A 560-page textbook weighing 3 pounds to a city 890 miles away.
    e. A 5-pound parcel of merchandise measuring 14″ x 10″ x 3″, insured.

Lesson **28** ⬡⬡⬡⬡⬡⬡⬡⬡⬡⬡⬡⬡⬡⬡⬡⬡⬡

28A—Letters of Order and Acknowledgment

The person who writes an order letter is responsible to a great extent for the amount of correspondence necessary to complete the transaction and, of course, the speed with which his order is filled. If his letter gives all essential information, the correspondence will be kept at a minimum; and the order will be filled correctly. Here are some points that should be included in every order letter:

1. Give the name and address of the person sending the order. Indicate plainly whether the merchandise is to be sent to that person or to someone else. If the merchandise is to be sent to someone else, the name and address should be clearly indicated. If at all possible, the name of the person writing the order should be typewritten; so many signatures are illegible.

2. Make a complete statement of the goods or services wanted. The description should be specific and detailed. Many orders require the following information about the merchandise: quantity, size, color, name of goods, style, price, shipping weight. When services are requested, care should be taken to give all needed information such as the exact nature and extent of service required, when it is desired, where it is to be performed, etc.

3. Explain how and when the merchandise ordered is to be sent. Sometimes shipment should be made by freight; other times, by express, bus, truck, or boat. Occasionally only part of the order is to be sent immediately; sometimes all of it is to be delayed until a specified date.

4. Specify how payment is being made or will be made. The kind of remittance and the terms should be clearly indicated.

Some firms have printed order blanks. If you use these, be sure to fill in all necessary data for each item ordered. If you do not have a printed order blank, set up the specifications in a tabulated form.

A letter of acknowledgment is a business courtesy. When a sender of an order receives such a letter, he knows his order has been received and is being handled immediately. Some firms use printed acknowledgment cards to save time.

A letter of acknowledgment should express appreciation of the order, identify the order being handled, and explain any delays, substitutions, or cancellations that may be necessary.

Dear Mr. Blanford:

Will you please send me by express on the usual terms the following material as described in your catalog on page 57:

```
1 dozen No. 843 Expert penholders
½ dozen No. 843C Fine Writer pen points
½ dozen blotters
4 dozen No. 900 Business Writing practice
        sheets
```

Will you also please send me one of your Ornamental Penmanship pamphlets. Some of our students have expressed an interest in ornamental penmanship.

Sincerely yours,

Order in Letter Form

Dear Mr. Smith:

In response to your request of February 5, we are pleased to enter your reservation as follows:

```
      Name:  Dr. Carver Smith
   Arrival:  February 24, 19--
Type of Room:  Single
```

Should it become necessary for you to cancel this reservation, we shall appreciate your notifying us as soon as possible.

Unless you inform us of a later arrival time, we do not hold reservations after 7 p.m. on the date of arrival.

All reservations are made subject to strikes, failure of guests to vacate, or causes or conditions beyond our control.

We look forward with pleasure to having you as our guest here at the Strickland Hotel and assure you that every effort will be made to make your visit pleasant and comfortable.

Sincerely yours,

Letter of Acknowledgment

Library Materials. The *library materials* rate (formerly called the "library book" rate) applies to materials sent to or from libraries, schools, and certain nonprofit organizations. These materials most often include books, periodicals, theses, music, sound recordings, films, and microfilms. The package may be sealed or unsealed and must be marked LIBRARY MATERIALS. The rate is the same to all zones.

Air Parcel Post. Air parcel post may be used for parcels weighing from 8 ounces to 70 pounds. Generally, it is less expensive to send packages weighing 7 pounds or less by air parcel post than by air express or air freight. Letters may be enclosed in air parcel post packages at no extra cost.

(5) Airmail. Airmail is carried by air and the speediest connecting ground carriers. In addition, it is given the quickest handling in dispatch and delivery, except for special delivery for which a special-delivery fee must be paid. A standard rate per ounce applies to all airmail letters and packages not exceeding 8 ounces in weight regardless of the distance. A lower rate is charged for air postal cards and postcards. For parcels weighing more than 8 ounces, air parcel post, air express, or air freight is used. Airmail parcels may be sealed or unsealed.

To be able to use airmail services most advantageously, the secretary should obtain from the local postmaster or superintendent of mail airmail dispatch schedules. These show when airmail is dispatched from the post office to the airport to make certain flights to specific cities. Mail must usually be in the post office thirty minutes prior to the time airmail is scheduled to leave for the airport.

(6) Mixed Classes of Mail. Sometimes it may be desirable to send two pieces of mail of different classes together as a single mailing to insure arrival at the same time. A first-class letter may be attached to the address side of a larger envelope or parcel of mail of another class or it may be enclosed in the larger envelope or parcel. In either case, postage must be paid on the two parts at their respective rates. When a first-class letter is *attached*, the correct postage is affixed to each part separately. When a first-class letter is *enclosed*, postage is determined for each piece separately but is affixed together on the outside of the parcel, and the parcel is marked FIRST-CLASS MAIL ENCLOSED below the postage and above the

address. A properly marked parcel-post package containing first-class mail is illustrated below.

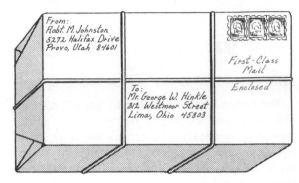

Mixed-class mail is handled and transported by the post office as mail of the class in which the bulky portion falls—not as first-class mail.

Other Classes of Mail. So limited in use that they do not warrant special description here are official mail (franked and penalty), free mail, mail for the blind, and international mail. These classes of mail are covered in detail in the *Postal Manual.*

Special Mail Services. In addition to the special mail services for first-class mail described on pages 134 and 135, the Post Office Department provides special services for other classes of mail. The most frequently used ones are described below.

Special Delivery. Special delivery mail is handled at the destination post office with the same promptness given to first-class mail. In addition, it is given immediate delivery (within prescribed hours and distances) from the post office to the addressee. Special delivery, for an additional fee, is available for all classes of mail. The fees vary according to the weight of the parcel. In addition to the regular postage, the parcel must bear the special delivery postage and must be marked SPECIAL DELIVERY.

Special Handling. Fourth-class (parcel post) parcels may be sent with *special handling* service upon the payment of an additional fee (less than special delivery), depending on the weight. The parcel must be marked SPECIAL HANDLING. Special handling provides the speediest handling and ground transportation, but it does not give special delivery service at the destination post office.

Insurance. You may obtain insurance up to $200 on a piece of third- or fourth-class mail and on airmail containing third- or fourth-class matter by taking the parcel to the post office and paying

```
BLAKE DISTRIBUTORS
3516 Broadway
New York, N. Y. 10012
                              Date_____

Thank you for your order #_____ which was
received today.

  ☐ We shall start processing immediately.
  ☐ Please allow _____ days for delivery.
  ☐ You neglected to include _____
  _____

                        Very truly yours,

                        E. C. BLASINGAME
```

Printed Acknowledgment Card

Questions for Discussion

1. What points should be covered in an order letter?
2. Select an item of clothing; list every point that would need to be mentioned in order to be sure of having an order for it filled correctly.
3. Why is a letter of acknowledgment usually written? What are some points that may be covered in such a letter?

Office Practice Problems

Criticize the letters below. Rewrite them so that they conform to good business writing practice. Supply any missing information that should be included.

1. Dear Sir:

   Referring to your order of August 30, we regret to advise that 2 pcs Dark Grey is all sold out and we will not have again this season; however, we can supply light grey cloth. If you can use please advise.

   Thanking you for this order and continued favors.

                        Very truly yours,

2. Gentlemen:

   Please send me 1 dozen cotton short-sleeved sport shirts medium size.

                        Yours truly,

28B—Building Speed in Taking Dictation

Potential Rate Builder

There are 12 words in the following sentence.

Punctuation Preview

Rule 18: Titles of books, booklets, newspapers, and magazines are either underlined or written in solid capitals. Quotation marks are used to enclose titles of articles in magazines, headlines of stories in newspapers, titles of chapters in books, titles of essays, lectures, and papers. Capitalize the first word and all important words in titles.

Example: The New York Times had a good discussion of Raymond Bowers' new book, ONLY TROUBLE AHEAD--especially of the chapter entitled "The New Military Strategy." This book was presented in abridged form in The Reader's Digest.

NOTE: You will notice that the solid caps method has been used for the book title, and the underline method has been used for the newspaper and magazine titles. Either method of writing is correct for either kind of title. However, within one sentence the thought may be a little clearer if the writer uses one form for books and the other form for magazine titles. It would be entirely correct, of course, to use the same form for both.

A number at the beginning of a sentence is written out.

In the following material, you will have to apply Rules 16 and 17, as well as the rule given above.

Postal Services

The Postal Manual. The *Postal Manual* of the United States Post Office Department contains regulations and procedures regarding postal services. It explains the services that are offered and prescribes the rates, fees, and conditions under which they are available. A secretary is not expected to memorize all the services of the Post Office Department and the prescribed rates, but she is expected to know where and how to find them. The *Postal Manual* is her best source of this information. As a secretary, you will therefore want to have your own copy for reference. You can obtain one for a nominal amount from the Superintendent of Documents, Washington, D. C. 20025. New pages, as well as revisions of old ones, will be sent to you as additions and changes are made.

Classes of Domestic Mail. *Domestic mail* includes all mail transmitted within, between, and among the United States and its territories and possessions, Navy (FPO) and Army-Air Force (APO) post offices; and mail for delivery to the United Nations in New York City.

Domestic mail is divided into six basic categories, as described below. Knowing what types of mail are included in each of these categories will enable you as a secretary to select more intelligently the service best suited for the transmittal of all kinds of outgoing mail.

(1) First-Class Mail. First-class mail, given the speediest ground transportation service, includes: letters in any form (typewritten, handwritten, carbon-copy, or photocopy); typewritten or handwritten reports and documents; matter partly in typewritten or handwritten form, such as checks, bills, and punched cards; business-reply cards and envelopes; postcards and Government postal cards; and all matter sealed against inspection that does not bear a special *class* notation. In order to be mailable, a piece of mail must be at least 3 inches wide and 4¼ inches long.

(2) Second-Class Mail. Second-class mail, which is sent at a lower rate than third- and fourth-class mail, includes printed newspapers and periodicals. The basic second-class rate applies to each two ounces or fraction of an ounce. Publishers and news agencies are granted second-class rates if they file the proper forms, pay the required fees, and otherwise comply with the regulations. Such mail must carry a notice of second-class entry.

(3) Third-Class Mail. Third-class mail is mail matter that cannot be classified as first- or second-class mail and that weighs up to 16 ounces. The same matter in parcels of 16 ounces and over is considered fourth-class mail. Third-class mail includes: circulars, advertisements, and other printed matter; books and catalogs having 24 or more pages; hotel keys and identification devices mailed unenclosed; unsealed greeting cards without written messages.

All sealed pieces mailed at the third-class rate must be marked: THIRD CLASS. This notation may be printed anywhere on the envelope (front or back) except in the permit imprint or meter stamp. Unsealed third-class mail does not require an endorsement.

(4) Fourth-Class Mail (Parcel Post). Fourth-class mail (parcel post) includes merchandise, books, printed matter, and all other mailable material not in the first, second, or third class that weighs 16 ounces or over.

Parcel-post rates are determined by the weight of the parcels and the distances the parcels are to be transported or by the zones of delivery. Every local post office charts the country into eight zones, and the postage is the same for a given weight for all points within one zone.

The Post Office Department has established both weight and size limitations for fourth-class parcels according to delivery zones. These limitations, which are specified in the *Postal Manual*, determine whether a parcel is mailable; therefore, you should use the *Postal Manual* as a current source of reference.

Both third- and fourth-class parcels may be sealed or unsealed. A sealed parcel is automatically treated as parcel post unless it is conspicuously marked FIRST CLASS or THIRD CLASS, regardless of what rate of postage has been paid.

Special low rates can be applied to certain kinds of packaged mail as described below.

Educational Materials. Formerly called "book rate," the *educational materials* rate applies to books, manuscripts, music, tests, films, and related materials that are marked EDUCATIONAL MATERIALS. The parcels may be sealed or unsealed. The rate is the same for all postal zones.

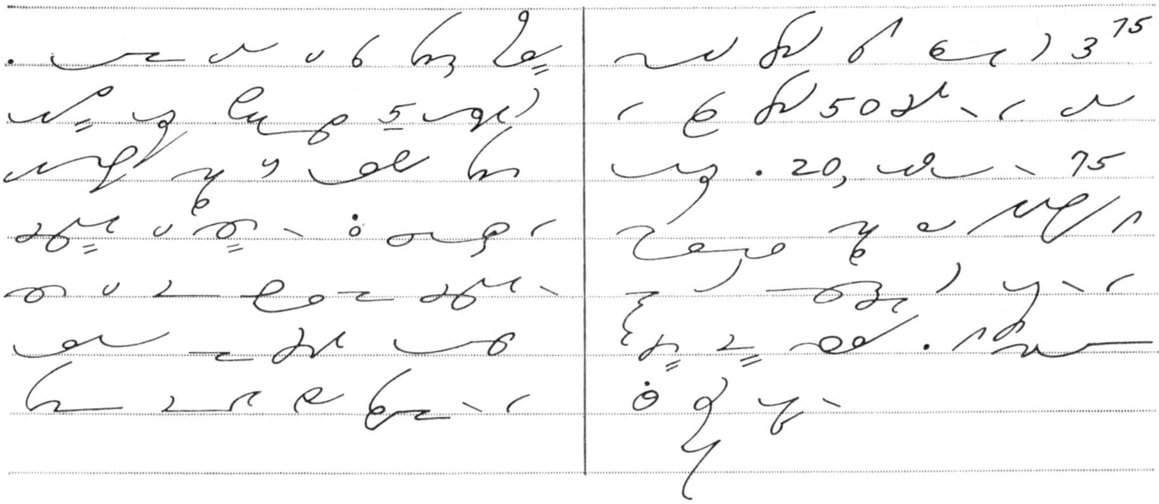

[Shorthand notes]

Practice Material for Building Fluency

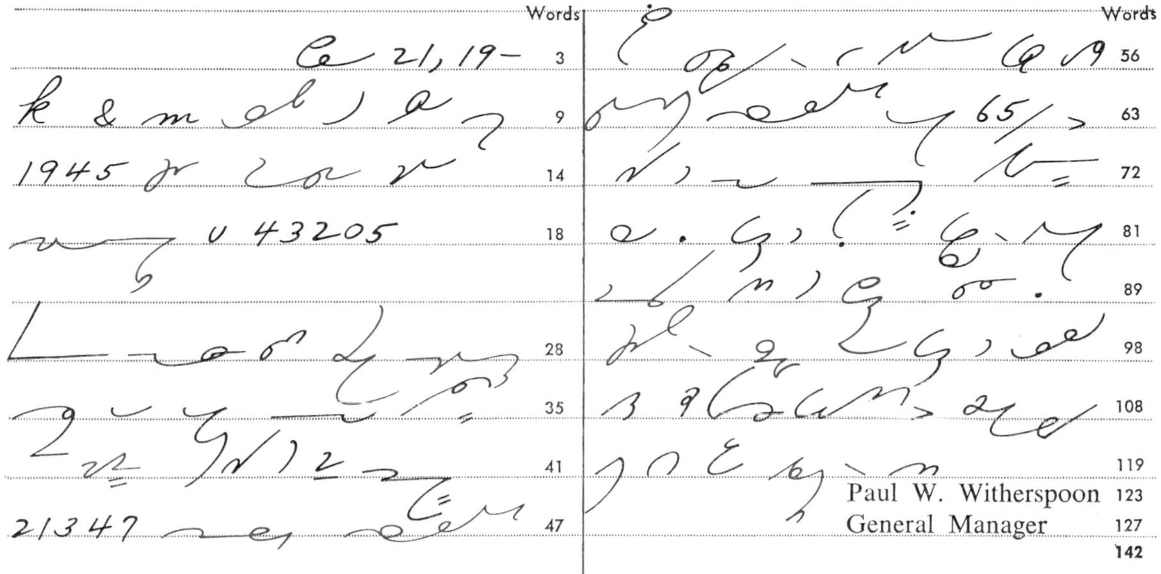

[Shorthand notes with word counts: 3, 9, 14, 18, 28, 35, 41, 47 in left column; 56, 63, 72, 81, 89, 98, 108, 119 in right column]

1945 — 43205 — 2 / 347

Paul W. Witherspoon 123
General Manager 127
142

Dictionary and Spelling Preview

1. freight, suite, antique
2. bookkeeping, proportionately, eliminating
3. guarantee, acknowledge, receipt
6. tinned, reverse

Preview of New Dictation Material

(1)  *[Shorthand notes]*

bedroom, vanity, suite, cherry, bench, antique, consisting, garden

Filing a Telegram. *Filing* a telegram means to get it into the hands of Western Union for transmission. A telegram can be filed in any one of several ways. It can be:

1. Given *over the counter* at the telegraph office.
2. Picked up by a Western Union messenger (summoned by telephone or special call box).
3. Sent on a teleprinter in the sender's office.
4. Sent by *Desk-Fax* or *Telefax* (special machines which instantly transmit a facsimile copy of a message from the sender's office directly to the Western Union office).
5. Filed by *telephone* (a frequently used method). Here is a typical telephone dialogue for filing a telegram:

Operator: Western Union.
Secretary: I would like to send a fast telegram.
Operator: To whom is it going?
Secretary: Statler Hilton Hotel.
Operator: Yes?
Secretary: Grand Circus Park at Washington Boulevard.
Operator: Yes?
Secretary: Detroit, Michigan.
Operator: Go ahead.
Secretary: Reserve single room—
Operator: Yes?
Secretary: —February 22 and 23.
Operator: Yes?
Secretary: Hold for late arrival and confirm.
Operator: Yes?
Secretary: Signed John A. Maher (M-a-h-e-r) 5101 Madison Road
Operator: To whom is it to be charged?
Secretary: South-Western Publishing Company.

Secretarial Responsibilities for Telegraphic Services. In addition to knowing the various classes of telegraphic services and their cost relationships and how best to prepare and file a telegraphic message, the secretary is expected to:

1. Give outgoing telegraphic messages priority in transcription and incoming telegrams priority in mail handling.
2. Select wisely the type of service to be used, keeping in mind differences in cost, speed of transmission and delivery, and time of day at the points of origin and destination.
3. Check the accuracy of the monthly statement (directly from the Western Union office or from the local telephone company on the regular telephone bill) by keeping a copy of each message sent.
4. Assist the employer in stating telegraphic messages as briefly, yet as clearly, as possible. Telegraphic language differs from letter language in that in well-prepared telegrams only important words and essential modifiers, prepositions, and conjunctions are included.
5. Be familiar with other telegraphic services such as *repeat-back service, report-delivery service, hotel-motel reservation service, Operator 25 service,* and *international telegraphic service.* Information on these special services is available from the local Western Union office.

Questions for Discussion and Office Practice Problems

1. What are the distinguishing features of each of the three classes of domestic telegraphic services, and what is the relative cost of each?
2. In telephoning a telegraphic message to Western Union, why is it sometimes desirable to spell certain names and words?
3. In what way are time zones throughout the country important when sending telegrams?
4. How should you indicate on a typewritten telegram that you want your address as well as your name transmitted?
5. What class of telegraphic service should be used in each of the following situations:

a. At 2:30 p.m. a secretary in Los Angeles, California, is given a 35-word message to send as quickly as possible to an office in Portland, Maine, which closes at 4:30 p.m.
b. At 10:45 a.m. a secretary in Chicago, Illinois, is given a 23-word telegram to be sent to a company in Dallas, Texas. A delay of a few hours is not important, but the telegram should be delivered the same day.

6. Rewrite each of the following telegraphic messages to bring them within the 15-word fast telegram basic rate:

a. I WILL ARRIVE IN ATLANTA ON DELTA FLIGHT 73 AT 7 O'CLOCK. JOIN ME FOR DINNER. I DEPART FOR MIAMI AT 10.
b. BECAUSE OF TROUBLE AT HOOVEN PLANT, CHANGE YOUR TRAVEL SCHEDULE TO JOIN ME THERE FRIDAY AFTERNOON. BRING YOUR COMPLETE SPECIFICATIONS FOR ENTIRE PROJECT.
c. TO BE ELIGIBLE FOR CONSIDERATION, YOUR BID ON PREASSEMBLED FORMS MUST BE IN OUR HANDS NO LATER THAN FRIDAY MORNING.

(2) [shorthand outlines]

bookkeeping, proportionately, very great, eliminating, will be made, as you can, understand

(3) [shorthand outlines]

we wish, plastic, clothespins, sturdy, durable, leaflet, popular

(4) [shorthand outlines]

this letter, hangers, Atlantic, specializes, stencil, you will receive, Columbus

(5) [shorthand outlines]

twin, bath, assured, with us, nicely, Alexander

(6) [shorthand outlines]

conversation, quotation, for your consideration, spools, reverse, confirmation, Argus, tinned, one year

Lesson **29** ⬡◯⬡◯⬡◯⬡◯⬡◯⬡◯⬡◯⬡◯⬡◯⬡◯⬡◯⬡◯⬡◯⬡

29A—Letters of Remittance, Claim, and Adjustment

A letter of remittance is a letter that accompanies a payment for merchandise or services. Such a letter states or explains the following:

1. The amount of the remittance
2. The form of the remittance (check, currency, coin, cashier's check, money order, bank draft, stamps, etc.)
3. What the remittance is in payment of (the specific order or service involved)

Oftentimes a letter of remittance is not sent if the statement of the amount owed is returned with the remittance.

A letter of remittance should be brief, but clear and complete.

Gentlemen:

We are enclosing our Corporation Franchise Tax return for 19--, together with our check for $150.10, which is the amount shown to be due.

Very truly yours,

Letter of Remittance

A good letter of claim or complaint is rather difficult to write because the one who must write such a letter is unhappy or irritated about something. The writer of such a letter should, however, try to be objective and courteous. The best procedure is to state briefly and clearly what the

Telegraphic, Postal, and Shipping Services

Lesson **116** ⬡⬡⬡⬡⬡⬡⬡⬡⬡⬡⬡⬡⬡⬡⬡

Telegraphic Services

Classes of Domestic Telegraphic Services. Just as the Post Office Department provides various classes of mail services, Western Union offers a choice of telegraphic services. The three classes of domestic messages are *fast telegrams, day letters,* and *night letters.*

Fast Telegrams. When speed of transmission and delivery is important, a *fast telegram* is used because it is sent immediately at any time, day or night; and it takes precedence over all other classes of domestic service. The minimum charge is based on 15 words; an additional charge is made for each additional word in the message.

Day Letters (DL). A *day letter* may be used at any time during the day or night. It is usually delivered the same day it is sent, although it is deferred until all fast telegrams have been transmitted. The minimum charge is for a message of 50 words; an additional charge is made for each additional group of 5 words or less. A 50-word day letter can be sent for approximately the same cost as a 25-word fast telegram.

Night Letters (NL). A *night letter* is an overnight service. The message can be sent at any time up to 2 a.m. for delivery the next morning. It is the least expensive class of service, a 50-word night letter costing less than a 15-word fast telegram. The minimum charge is based on a message of 50 words; an additional charge is made for each additional group of 5 words or less. This class of service is used when the message is dictated too late in the day to be received by the addressee the same day or when next-morning delivery is otherwise acceptable.

Preparing a Telegram. You must prepare a telegram carefully and accurately if it is to be delivered promptly and is to be clearly understood by the addressee. The following guides will help you:

1. Use Western Union telegraph blanks, obtainable free from any Western Union counter. You should prepare at least one carbon copy of each telegram, perhaps more.

2. Type an "X" in the appropriate service box (upper left-hand corner) opposite the type of service desired. If type of service is not indicated, the message will be sent and charged for as a fast telegram.

3. Type the message with double spacing and with capital and lower-case letters.

4. Indicate whether the message is sent *paid, collect,* or *charged.* If it is to be charged, type the name of the account below the heading "Charge to the Account of."

5. Type the point of origin and the date a double space below the last line of the printed heading.

6. Type in regular address form (exclusive of personal titles) the name and address of the addressee. When possible give the office or suite number. Spell out such words as "North" and "South"; do not use suffixes with street numbers (23 instead of 23rd Street).

7. Type the message clearly, with punctuation. Punctuation marks make the message clearer, and there is no charge for them.

8. Type your address and telephone number following the signature of the message. When typed directly beneath the signature, they are transmitted and charged for; when typed at the left margin, they are not transmitted and no charge is made for them.

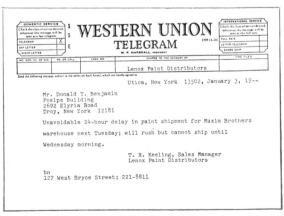

Correctly Typed Telegram

trouble is. All details necessary to enable the receiver of the letter to understand the situation should be given. Such details may include the date the merchandise or service was requested, the exact nature of the merchandise or service, the mistake that has been made, and the trouble or difficulty that has arisen from the mistake. The writer of the complaint should make a definite request for prompt adjustment—but courteously.

Gentlemen:

About May 15 of last year, I purchased a Rex swivel vacuum cleaner through the Grantly Hardware Company of Bismarck, North Dakota. That store obtained the cleaner from Binghamton Corporation, 791 North Broadway, Chicago, Illinois 60603.

This vacuum cleaner carried a guarantee of one year. Early this month, the flexible hose split open so that the cleaner could not be used. On April 10, I wrote to the Binghamton Corporation, asking whether we should return the defective part directly to them or send it somewhere else for replacement. We have had no response from that company. I am wondering whether you have a suggestion as to how this matter should be handled, since it is still under the one-year guarantee of your company.

Sincerely yours,

Letter of Claim

The letter responding to a complaint or claim should be made promptly. If the customer is obviously correct in his complaint, the letter of adjustment should reveal an eagerness to make amends. The complainant should be told what steps have already been taken or will be taken to correct the mistake. An explanation of how the mistake occurred often helps bring understanding. An expression of good will and desire to satisfy the customer is always in order. The customer should be told how the situation is to be remedied. It is well to express regret that he has been inconvenienced by the error.

"Fighting" words are all too often allowed to creep into letters regarding complaints. Such words as these are used: "you state," "you claim," "you neglected to," "you should have realized," "you failed to," etc. These words cause ill feeling and do not help solve the problem.

The person who answers a letter of complaint should do all the investigating he can in regard to the situation so that he will have a clear picture of the entire problem; then a settlement can be made in a minimum of time. Investigation may reveal that the customer is at fault, or that the manufacturer is at fault, or that the transportation company is in error. Perhaps the fault is shared by two or more of the parties concerned. Even though the customer is at fault, explanation of the error should be made in such a way that the customer remains friendly to the business firm.

Dear Mrs. Howard:

We regret to learn from your April 29 letter that the hose on your Rex swivel-top vacuum cleaner has split in so short a period of use.

Our Authorized Service Station in Grand Forks, North Dakota, is Wallace Electric Service at 3021 Glade Street. If you will take or send the defective hose to them, they will replace the hose section, using the original connectors, at no expense to you, under the warranty agreement. If you prefer, you may send the hose to our own Rex Electric Service Center in Sioux Falls, South Dakota; and your present hose will be replaced with a new, improved hose section.

Very truly yours,

Letter of Adjustment

Questions for Discussion

1. What information is usually included in a letter of remittance? When is it unnecessary to send one?
2. Why are letters of claim or complaint difficult to write well?
3. What are some points to remember in writing letters of claim or complaint?
4. What are some "fighting" words to avoid in writing letters of adjustment?
5. List some points to keep in mind in writing a letter of adjustment.

Office Practice Problem

Criticize the following letter. Rewrite it so that it follows the principles of good letter writing.

Dear Miss Shaw:

I thank you for the payment of $10.00, which pays for the glasses prescribed for you in July, excepting the State sales tax of .30¢ which I am not permitted to absorb as I used to.

The other $5.00 plus .15¢ sales tax was for a lens you broke in August, which I presume you forgot about.

Thanking you I am,

Sincerely,

Building Skill in Transcribing

Transcribing from Shorthand Notes

1. Write in shorthand Letter (1) given below.
2. Transcribe the letter from your notes as a 5-minute writing. Determine your *mwam*. If you complete the letter before time is called, repeat it from the beginning.
3. Transcribe Letter (2) as a 5-minute writing. Determine your *mwam* and compare it with your *mwam* on Letter (1).

(1)	Words
June 1, 19—	3

Miss Marie A. LeBlond	7
Coordinated Business Services, Ltd.	14
396 Tenth Avenue, S. E.	19
Calgary, Alberta, CANADA	24

Dear Miss LeBlond: 28

Thank you for requesting our recommenda- 36
tions for indexing special types of surnames. 45

Effective [1] indexing guides are easy to follow 54
and consistent in application for both per- 63
sonal and business [2] names. If simplicity and 72
consistency are carefully observed in devel- 81
oping and applying the guides,[3] everyone can 89
confidently and accurately file and find busi- 99
ness papers. 101

We therefore index a hyphened [4] surname 109
such as Dean-Allen as two units rather than 118
one, whether it occurs in a personal or in a [5] 127
business name. Likewise, we index a com- 135
pound surname such as St. John as two units 144
instead of one, to be [6] consistent with the 152
indexing of a geographic name such as St. 161
Paul in a business name. 166

Personal names for [7] which it is difficult to 175
determine the surname, as in Kosho Oshiro, 183
occur rarely in most business [8] offices. In- 192
stead of making a special rule for names 200
that rarely occur, it is better practice to fol- 210
low [9] the basic rule for personal names: 218
Consider as the surname the last word in 226
the written name and transpose the [10] other 234
words as the given names. 239

If you have other questions about filing, 248
please let us help you with them. (227) 255

Sincerely [11] yours, 258

280

(2)	Words
June 1, 19—	3

Dr. Jerry K. Rippey 7
Psychological Services, Inc. 12
1315 Ault View Avenue 17
Cincinnati, Ohio 45208 22

31
39
45
52
61
69
77
83
92
98
105
111
119
126
133
137
143
152
160
167
180
199

Transcribing from Dictation

Your teacher will dictate two letters to you for transcription. Prepare the letters for the signature of Jay K. Robbins, President, who does not use the company name in the closing lines.

Proportion Drill

Punctuation Preview

Rule 19: To indicate the possessive case, add *'s* to singular nouns and to plural nouns not ending in *s*. Add only an apostrophe to plural words ending in *s*.

For proper names ending in *s*, form the possessive singular by adding *'s*; for proper names ending in *s*, form the possessive plural by adding *'* only.

No apostrophe is used to indicate the possessive case of pronouns, i.e., *its, theirs, ours, yours, hers*.

Example: Our Sales Department's goal was to sell $20,000 worth of merchandise in the month. In the four weeks' intensive selling, the salesmen's efforts brought in $40,000, twice the original goal. As you can see, the Department was well pleased with the success of its campaign.

NOTE: In the following material, you will have to apply Rules 16-18, as well as the rule given above.

Terminal-Digit Filing. In a regular numeric system, the highest numbers are assigned consecutively to the most recently opened folders. Since the most recently opened folders are generally the most active, the filing and finding activities converge into the last sections of the file, causing file clerks to get in each other's way at the file cabinets. Terminal-digit filing was developed to overcome this crowded condition.

In terminal-digit filing, numbers are often divided into two-digit groups, reading from right to left. Thus, the number 302716 would be divided 30/27/16. The final group (16) indicates the number of the file drawer and the next group (27) indicates the number of the folder into which material so coded is filed. The next group (30) indicates the sequence of the item in the folder.

Terminal-digit filing has two major advantages: (1) it reduces filing errors caused by the difficulty of comparing solidly written numbers of four or more digits; (2) it provides a more even distribution of filed materials throughout the files.

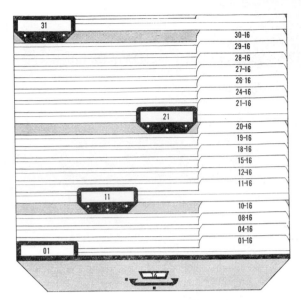

Portion of a Terminal-Digit File

Questions for Discussion

1. What are the basic differences in alphabetic, subject, geographic, and numeric filing?
2. Discuss two situations in which each of the aforementioned methods could be used to advantage.
3. What is a *relative index* and how is it used?
4. Why is it advisable to consult the supervisor and others who request filed materials before deciding the subject classifications to be used in a subject file?
5. In what order are individual items arranged in a miscellaneous folder in a subject file? in a geographic file?
6. How should you code a piece of correspondence for subject filing?
7. How should you code a piece of correspondence for geographic filing?
8. How should you decide which number to assign a new folder to be opened in a numeric file?
9. How should you decide with which number or letter to code a piece of correspondence to be filed in a numeric file?
10. What are the advantages of terminal-digit filing over consecutive-number numeric filing?
11. What is an *accession book* and how is it used?
12. In what order would the numbers 144610, 134810, and 124710 be filed in a terminal-digit system, assuming a two-digit group number division?

Office Practice Problems

1. Make a typewritten triple-spaced list of the letters *A-E*. Opposite the appropriate letter type the caption of the folder in which you would file the following items in the subject file illustrated on page 290.

a. A letter from Smith-Corona Marchant, Inc., giving information on the special features of the Marchant printing calculator.
b. A paid invoice for repairs on the A. B. Dick duplicator.
c. A price quotation from Royal for ten new typewriters.
d. An advertising brochure about the IBM Selectric typewriter.
e. A file copy of an order to Dictaphone Corporation for Dictaphone recording belts.

2. Using the procedure for Problem 1, indicate where you would file the following items in the geographic file illustrated on page 291.

a. A file copy of a price quotation to St. Joseph Academy, Chillicothe, Missouri.
b. A letter request from Manual High and Vocational School, Kansas City, Missouri.
c. A letter from William Chrisman High School, Independence, Missouri, that has been out of the file but is now returned for refiling.
d. A file copy of a statement sent to De La Salle High School, Kansas City, Missouri.
e. A letter which accompanied a check from Northeast High School, Kansas City, Missouri.

Practice Material for Building Fluency

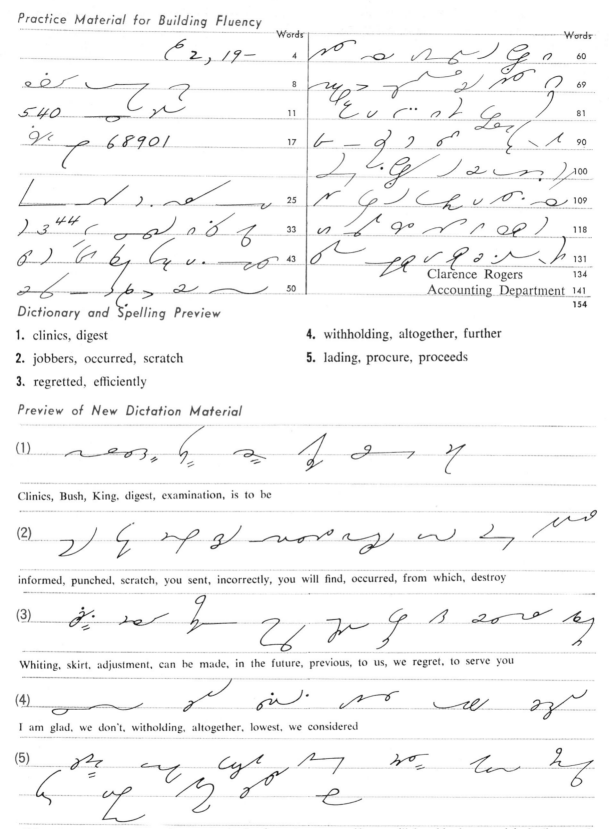

Words

4
8
11
17
25
33
43
50

60
69
81
90
100
109
118
131

Clarence Rogers 134
Accounting Department 141
154

Dictionary and Spelling Preview

1. clinics, digest
2. jobbers, occurred, scratch
3. regretted, efficiently

4. withholding, altogether, further
5. lading, procure, proceeds

Preview of New Dictation Material

(1)

Clinics, Bush, King, digest, examination, is to be

(2)

informed, punched, scratch, you sent, incorrectly, you will find, occurred, from which, destroy

(3)

Whiting, skirt, adjustment, can be made, in the future, previous, to us, we regret, to serve you

(4)

I am glad, we don't, witholding, altogether, lowest, we considered

(5)

Citizens, on our part, proceeds, too much, Southern, to procure, if you will be able, boxes, original, discovered, we doubt, national

Unit 6 · Lesson 29

The Nature and Uses of Numeric Filing. A numeric file is one in which numbers rather than letters or names are used for guide and folder captions. Numeric files are often used in professional offices such as those of lawyers in which each case is assigned a number; in contractors' offices in which each work project is assigned a number; and in departments where stock control is maintained by keeping records of numbered items of merchandise. Numeric filing is an indirect system because it is necessary to refer to a card index to determine the number assigned to a particular folder.

A numeric correspondence file consists of three parts: (1) a supplementary card index with names arranged alphabetically, showing for each name the corresponding folder number; (2) the numeric correspondence file in which guides and folders bear numeric captions; (3) a miscellaneous alphabetic correspondence file for papers about correspondents and subjects too inactive to justify the assignment of a number.

In a numeric correspondence file each important, active correspondent is given a separate folder with a numbered caption. The folders are numbered in sequence, beginning with 1 or 100, with no regard for the alphabetic order of names. When an individual folder is to be opened, that folder is given the first unassigned number. The number may be determined by consulting the folder and card supply or the *accession book* or *register* which gives a consecutive up-to-date list of all numbers that have been assigned.

The Arrangement of a Numeric File. In the illustration shown above, right, note that:

1. Primary guides are staggered in first and second positions.
2. Special guides, for very active folders, are placed in third position.
3. Individual folders are placed in last position.

In this system the guides are numbered by 10's to limit the number of folders behind each guide to ten. The folders are placed in the drawer in strict numeric order. The tabs of the folders bear only the numbers assigned to the various correspondents; names are not visible except on the special guides.

A supplementary card index accompanies this file to provide an alphabetic index of correspondents, each card bearing the matching folder number. The cards are prepared in the same manner as the one illustrated on page 261.

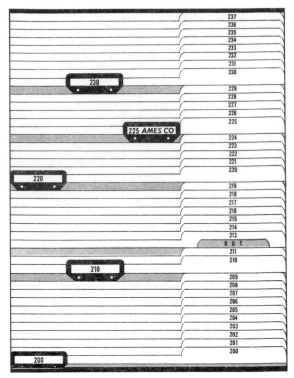

Portion of a Numeric Correspondence File

Numeric Filing Procedure. As for other methods of filing, numeric correspondence filing requires the accurate use of the five standard steps for processing materials to be filed.

The procedure for coding, however, is somewhat different. First, the name to be used as the basis for coding must be underlined, and other names that are to be used for cross-referencing must be marked also. Next, the card file must be checked for every name to be coded. If the name is listed in the card file, the number already assigned to that name must be clearly written in the upper right-hand corner of the letter. If no number has been assigned to the correspondent, the letter is coded by writing "M" in the upper right-hand corner to indicate that the letter is to be filed in the miscellaneous alphabetic file. Cross-references appear in the card file only, the cross-reference cards being prepared in the usual manner.

Sorting numerically coded materials is done first by hundreds, then by tens, and finally by units. All pieces marked "M" are placed in a separate pile to be filed at one time.

Materials are placed in individual folders by date, the most recent date in front. Materials are placed in miscellaneous folders alphabetically according to the names, then by date in each name group.

Lesson 30 ⬡⬡⬡⬡⬡⬡⬡⬡⬡⬡⬡⬡⬡⬡⬡⬡

30A—Letters of Credit and Collection

When a merchant buys merchandise from a jobber or a manufacturer, he usually buys "on credit." This term means that the manufacturer will send the goods to the merchant with the understanding that within a certain period of time, such as 30 days, the merchant will pay for the goods. This period of time enables the merchant to sell some of the merchandise to get money to pay the manufacturer. In similar manner, the manufacturer may buy raw materials on credit to use in making additional products that he will sell to jobbers or merchants.

When a businessman asks a firm to grant him credit, that firm will investigate to find out whether the businessman is a good "risk," that is, whether he can be relied upon to pay his bills when due. On the basis of what the firm learns, it may decide to grant him credit almost without limit, or grant him a limited amount of credit, or refuse to grant credit at all. Then the credit manager will write a letter explaining the decision. Such a letter is a "credit" letter. A letter that grants credit usually includes the following:

1. Statement of pleasure in granting request for credit
2. Statement regarding extent of credit allowed
3. Discussion of terms for payment
4. Expression of value of credit privilege

Dear Mrs. Stewart:

    Welcome to New Orleans!

    Pennington's would like to add a little additional warmth, so we have taken the liberty of opening an account in your name. Here is a courtesy card which will be your introduction for a charge in any of our departments.

    We cannot, in a few words, tell the story of a 60-year-old store with its cherished reputation for value, quality, and fashion correctness. But we can say that every member of our staff constantly strives to make Pennington's a friendly store.

    We shall welcome you as a Pennington and Company customer with an earnest effort to merit your goodwill and patronage.

            Very truly yours,

        Letter Granting Credit

A letter refusing credit should give the following:

1. Explanation of refusal
2. Expression of regret
3. Suggestion regarding some temporary plan for purchasing (such as cash deposit or c.o.d.) until better credit rating can be made
4. Statement leaving "door open" for reconsideration later

Dear Mr. O'Malley:

    We appreciate your letter of February 3, expressing interest in opening a charge account with our store.

    The sources of information available to us so far do not appear to warrant our granting your application. We do want to be of as much service to you as possible, however. May we suggest that you permit us to send your selections C.O.D. or that we be permitted to reserve them for you, to be taken within ten days on a cash basis?

    Perhaps at a later date we may be able to offer you credit. In the meantime, be assured that we would welcome your purchases on one of the above-mentioned bases.

            Sincerely yours,

        Letter Refusing Credit

Some businessmen always pay their bills when due; some pay them a little tardily occasionally; and some postpone payment as long as they can. When bills are overdue, the credit department must take steps to collect what is due. Letters in which an attempt is made to collect money owed are called "collection" letters. Such letters are difficult to write. They require considerable skill, for it is easy to offend or embarrass those who are delinquent. Collection letters should contain the following:

1. Explanation of the situation
2. Statement of details of the particular case
3. Statement of responsibility of the debtor

A positive approach appealing to self-respect, pride, cooperativeness, fairness, or friendship is best. Sometimes appeals to standing in the community, competition, or self-esteem are effective. The negative approach, using a tone of pity, anger, scolding, or ridicule, should be avoided.

Geographic Filing

The Nature and Uses of Geographic Filing. A *geographic file* is one in which the guide captions are based primarily upon the locations of correspondents. A wide variety of geographical classifications are in use: by territories, states, and cities for correspondence of national scope; by counties and cities for correspondence limited to one state; by districts, zones, and streets for local correspondence. The classification chosen for a particular file depends upon the geographical areas in which correspondents are located, upon the type of business activity, and upon the use that is to be made of filed materials.

Geographic filing offers advantages for certain types of businesses and for certain departments of many businesses. It is often employed by mail-order houses, publishing companies, transfer and storage companies, and many other sales and service organizations.

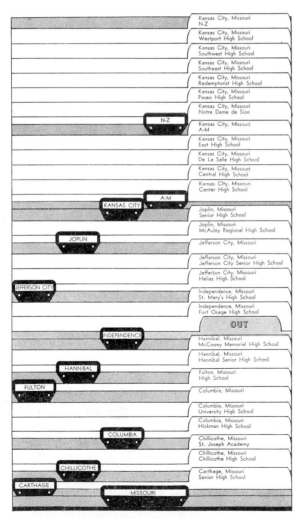

Portion of a Geographic File

The Arrangement of a Geographic File. The geographic file illustrated at the left below is that of a printer of school annuals. As you study it, you will see three kinds of guides:

1. A primary guide in third and fourth positions bearing the caption MISSOURI.
2. A series of special city guides in first, second, and third positions.
3. Two auxiliary guides in fourth position to divide KANSAS CITY correspondence into two alphabetic ranges, *A-M* and *N-Z*.

As you study the folders, all of which are in fifth (extreme right) position, note that:

1. Each city name guide has behind it one or more individual folders bearing the names of the city and state on the top line of the tab and the name of the school on the second line.
2. The city name guides COLUMBIA and JEFFERSON CITY each has behind the last of its individual folders a miscellaneous folder. The one behind the COLUMBIA guide houses all correspondence from Columbia schools for which there are no individual folders. The one for JEFFERSON CITY serves the same purpose for that city.
3. The city name guide INDEPENDENCE has behind it an OUT guide to indicate the temporary removal of one of the individual folders.
4. Each of the auxiliary guides *A-M* and *N-Z* behind the KANSAS CITY guide has behind it several individual folders and one miscellaneous folder. Note that each miscellaneous folder is captioned to show not only the city and state names but also the alphabetic range of material filed in it.

Geographic Filing Procedure. Materials to be filed geographically must be inspected, coded, cross-referenced (when necessary), sorted, and placed in appropriately labeled folders. Coding is often done by underlining the major geographic subdivision and circling the name of the correspondent. Rough sorting is done by major geographic subdivisions, such as state names; fine sorting, by progressively minor subdivisions, such as city names and names of correspondents.

Materials are placed in individual folders according to date, the most recent date in front. Within miscellaneous folders, items are arranged first alphabetically according to names of correspondents, then by date in each name group.

Dear Mr. Mayberry:

   We are greatly disappointed not to have received a remittance from you covering the statement that we sent you for your purchases of April 10 for $150.

   If the merchandise has proved unsatisfactory or if there is some misunderstanding regarding terms of payment, please let us know. If, on the other hand, the goods have been satisfactory and our terms clear, we should appreciate your mailing a remittance today. Won't you please cooperate with us by sending either a check or an explanation of the delay?

   We value your business; and we are confident that you, in turn, value your credit standing.

                          Sincerely yours,

Letter of Collection

Sometimes a series of letters (called follow-ups) is necessary to induce the debtor to pay. Each succeeding letter is more firm than the preceding one. The first letter may be mere notification, taking the point of view that the debtor has overlooked the bill. The second letter may seek to find a reason for the delay and express a wish to help if circumstances are explained. The third may be worded more strongly—perhaps implying risk to credit rating through nonpayment. The fourth may indicate that legal action is about to be taken.

In recent years, more firms are writing letters of appreciation to those customers who have paid their accounts promptly. Such a letter promotes goodwill.

Dear Mr. Folsom:

   Two years ago today you opened an account with us, and your payments have always been on time! We want to express our appreciation for the splendid manner in which you have handled your account.

                          (Continued)

Should you ever wish to refer to us in connection with a credit rating, we shall be happy to recommend you.

                          Sincerely,

Letter of Appreciation

Questions for Discussion

1. What is meant by the term "buy on credit"?
2. What does a credit manager do when he receives a request for credit?
3. What should a letter that grants credit include? that refuses credit?
4. Define "collection letters."
5. What type of information should collection letters contain?

Office Practice Problem

   Criticize the following letters; then rewrite them so that they follow the principles of good business correspondence:

1. Dear Mr. Swanson:

   We are enclosing a New York draft for $2,500.

   Will you please acknowledge receipt of this draft and credit the above amount to our account.

                          Yours truly,

2. Gentlemen:

   This is just a friendly reminder that the invoice listed below amounting to $40.50 is unpaid.

   No doubt nonpayment of this account is the result of oversight. In this event may we now request your giving the matter early attention.

   Thank you for your check which we hope will reach us by return mail.

                          Very truly yours,

30B—Building Speed in Taking Dictation

Repetitive Phrase Builder

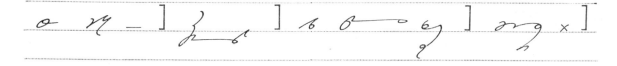

Subject Filing

The Nature and Uses of Subject Filing. A *subject file* is one in which the guide and folder captions are based upon subject titles instead of names of correspondents. Subject filing is used when it seems desirable to have all correspondence about one subject grouped in one place or when subject titles rather than names of correspondents are generally used to request filed materials. Subject files are typically maintained for individual departments or for specific executives rather than for the company as a whole.

In determining the subject classifications by which to set up a subject file, it is important to work closely with those individuals who will request filed materials. Furthermore, since it is difficult to standardize the subject titles by which materials may be requested by different persons or by the same person at different times, it is often necessary to set up a *relative index* (a cross-reference card system that lists all captions under which material *may be filed* or by which it *may be requested*).

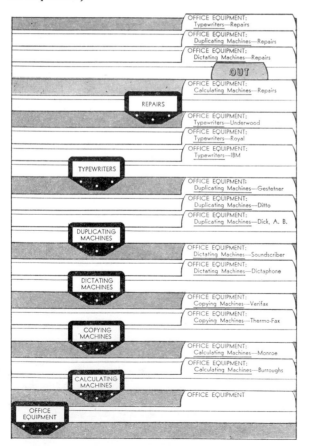

Portion of a Subject File

The Arrangement of a Subject File. The subject file illustrated at the left below contains:

1. A primary guide in first (extreme left) position bearing the caption OFFICE EQUIPMENT.
2. A series of special guides in second position to show subdivisions of the primary guide. These are captioned: CALCULATING MACHINES, COPYING MACHINES, DICTATING MACHINES, DUPLICATING MACHINES, and TYPEWRITERS.
3. An auxiliary guide in third position bearing the caption REPAIRS to show a further subdivision of the office equipment section.

The file also contains, in fourth and fifth positions:

1. Following the primary guide OFFICE EQUIPMENT a miscellaneous folder bearing the same caption. This folder houses all material for which individual folders are not provided.
2. Following the special guide CALCULATING MACHINES two individual folders. Each folder bears the primary and special guide captions. In addition, the first is subcaptioned *Burroughs* to indicate that material about Burroughs equipment is filed in that folder; likewise, the second is subcaptioned *Monroe*.

Each of the other special guides has filed behind it two or more individual folders, each captioned to indicate the subject of its contents.

Behind the auxiliary guide REPAIRS are individual folders for correspondence about repairs for each type of equipment.

In addition, an OUT guide in fourth and fifth positions indicates that one of the individual folders for repairs has been removed temporarily.

Subject Filing Procedure. Materials to be filed by subject must be processed through the five standard steps: inspection, coding (by underlining the subject title or by writing the title at the top or in the upper right-hand corner), cross-referencing, sorting, and placing materials in the appropriate folders.

When materials are filed by subject, correspondence with several persons or companies is often filed in a single subject folder. Within such a folder, individual items are arranged first alphabetically according to personal or business names, then by dates within each name group, the most recent date at the front of each group.

Rule 20: Use a comma before *namely, viz., i.e., for instance,* and *that is* if the material following is short; use a semicolon, a colon, or a dash if the material is long and a more definite break is desired.

Example: Two persons, namely Smith and Barrett, were on the committee. They made an intensive investigation of the entire situation; that is, they examined the background events, the current problem, and the possible solutions. The committee then made several observations: for instance, some people seemed unwilling to cooperate, and others gave biased information. The committee accused three people of obstructing the investigation--namely, Gordon, Price, and Donahue.

NOTE: In the following material, you will have to apply Rules 16-19, as well as the rule given above.

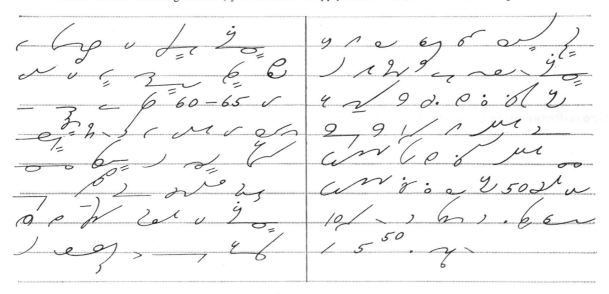

Practice Material for Building Fluency

	Words
	4
	7
	13
	18
	27
	34
	38
	45
	53
	60
	68
	76
	86
	93
	100
	110
	118
	126
Frieda Howells	130
	144

Cross-Referencing Guide 7: Names of Newspapers and Periodicals

Newspapers. The name of a newspaper is indexed under the name of the city in which the newspaper is published, whether the city name appears as the first word in the newspaper name or must be inserted before the name for indexing purposes. In the latter case, a cross-reference card may be prepared under the name of the newspaper.

Original Card	Cross-Reference Card
Dallas Times Herald	(No cross-reference necessary)
Denver: Rocky Mountain News	Rocky Mountain News See Denver: Rocky Mountain News

Periodicals. Since the name of a periodical is used in indexing, a cross-reference should be prepared for the name of the publisher.

Original Card	Cross-Reference Card
Barron's	Dow Jones & Company, Inc. See Barron's
Life	Time Inc. See Life

Cross-Referencing Guide 8: Similar Names

Since a number of surnames are similar in pronunciation but different in spelling, cross-reference cards should be made for each of the various spellings.

Cramer, see also Kraemer, Kramer, Kremer
Kraemer, see also Cramer, Kramer, Kremer

Cross-Referencing Guide 9: Names of Businesses That Are Known by More Than One Name

Sometimes a business is known by more than one name. For example, a business may have a long name that is shortened for convenience; or a business that is a subsidiary of another company may have its own name; or a branch of a large company may have its own distinctive name. In any of these situations, it is wise to prepare a cross-reference card for the full name of the business.

Original Card		Cross-Reference Card
Johnson's		Johnson Wholesale Paint and Varnish Manufacturing Company See Johnson's
Korman Store		Suburban Specialty Shops, Inc. See Korman Store

Long Beach Boys' Store
Mobile Boys' Store
	Two individually named stores owned and operated by Boys' Sportswear Mfg. Co., Inc.	Boys' Sportswear Manufacturing Company,
		    Incorporated
		See Long Beach Boys' Store
		    Mobile Boys' Store

Office Practice Problems

1. Prepare original and cross-reference cards for the following names. Use the original card number followed by an "x" when you type the cross-reference card number.

   171. General Electric Company (often referred to as GE)
   172. Ballou-Comfortair Service Co.
   173. Christian Science Monitor (published in Boston)
   174. Taylor Gift & Specialty Shop (commonly referred to as Taylor's)

2. Of the 170 cards that you have prepared in preceding lessons, prepare cross-reference cards for Nos. 17, 43, 110, 111, 120, 134, and 168.

3. Combine the cross-reference cards prepared in Problems 1 and 2 with Cards 1 through 174 into a single alphabetic file. Prepare an answer sheet and submit it to your teacher for checking.

Dictionary and Spelling Preview

1. profession, commend, accessories, distinctive
2. refinancing, unavoidably
3. nominal, delinquency
4. partial, recommend

Preview of New Dictation Material

(1) *[shorthand]*

Felber's, we hope you will, distinctive, to shop, commend, few minutes, apparel, revolving, choice, accessories, cordially

(2) *[shorthand]*

to your letter, refinancing, funds, unavoidably, as soon as

(3) *[shorthand]*

effected, delinquency, we have received, accordingly, presume, numerous, indicating, to provide, nominal

(4) *[shorthand]*

which has been, at this time, to submit, in which you can, we recommend, remainder

(5) *[shorthand]*

let us say, in a position, six months, alternative, you desire, kindly, in full

(6) *[shorthand]*

upon receipt, communication, we have your letter, proposal, invoice

Cross-Referencing Guide 3: Firm Names Composed of Combined Surnames

If two or more individual surnames compose a business name, a cross-reference card should be prepared for each surname other than the first.

Original Card	Cross-Reference Card
Carlson-Jones, Incorporated	Jones-Carlson, Incorporated See Carlson-Jones, Inc.
Gaines, Hart, (and) Smith Drugstore	Hart, Gaines, (and) Smith Drugstore See Gaines, Hart, and Smith Drugstore
	Smith, Gaines, (and) Hart Drugstore See Gaines, Hart, and Smith Drugstore
Adams, Howard (&) Towns, Larry, Architects	Towns, Larry (&) Adams, Howard, Architects See Howard Adams & Larry Towns, Architects

Cross-Referencing Guide 4: Names Composed of or Containing Initials and Abbreviations

The names of some companies and associations, such as the American Automobile Association (AAA) and Radio Corporation of America (RCA), are often referred to by the initial letters of the important words in the names. The original card for such a name should be made out for the full name of the company or association, and a cross-reference card should be made out for the initials referring to the name.

Original Card	Cross-Reference Card
American Automobile Association	AAA See American Automobile Association
American Records Management Association	ARMA See American Records Management Association
Radio Corporation (of) America	RCA See Radio Corporation of America
Young Men's Christian Association	YMCA See Young Men's Christian Association

Cross-Referencing Guide 5: Names Composed of Combined Surnames and Coined Names

If a business name consists of a surname and a coined name, a cross-reference card should be prepared for the coined name because the coined name rather than the surname may be the one by which material is requested.

Original Card	Cross-Reference Card
Larson-Goodfoods, Incorporated	Goodfoods-Larson, Incorporated See Larson-Goodfoods, Incorporated
Monteith C-Thru Plastics	C-Thru Plastics, Monteith See Monteith C-Thru Plastics
Mooney Easy-Run Electric Tools	Easy-Run Electric Tools, Mooney See Mooney Easy-Run Electric Tools

Cross-Referencing Guide 6: Names of Clubs and Service Organizations

If the name of an organization is filed according to the most distinctive word rather than the first word in the name, a cross-reference card should be prepared so that the name will appear in the file in the order in which it is written.

Original Card	Cross-Reference Card
Moose, Loyal Order (of)	Loyal Order (of) Moose See Moose, Loyal Order of
Pythias, Knights (of)	Knights (of) Pythias See Pythias, Knights of
International Affairs, Royal Institute (of)	Royal Institute (of) International Affairs See International Affairs, Royal Institute of

Building Speed in Taking Dictation

Lesson **31** ⬡⬡⬡⬡⬡⬡⬡⬡⬡⬡⬡⬡⬡⬡⬡⬡⬡⬡⬡

31A—Brief-Form Practice

Directions. The following paragraph has 32 brief forms and brief-form derivatives. If you can read it in 30 seconds, your reading rate will be 120 words a minute.

31B—Theory Review

The word ending -*ings* is expressed by a disjoined *s* placed in the position of the *ing* dot.

The months of *March, April, May, June,* and *July* are written in full; the others are written in abbreviated form.

The prefix *self-* is expressed by the left *s* above the line. The word ending -*self* is expressed by *s*. The word ending -*selves* is expressed by *ses*.

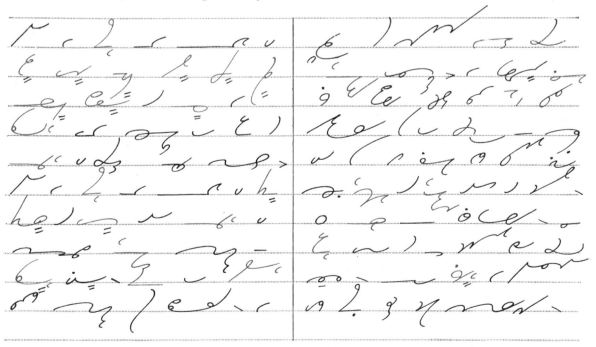

Cross-Referencing

Certain names, whether they appear in a card file or in a regular filing system complete with folders and guides, may present problems because they are made up of units that are not always thought of in the same order when different persons call for materials from the files. Names that most frequently fall into this category are:

1. Unusual names of individuals
2. Names of married women
3. Firm names composed of combined surnames
4. Names composed of or containing initials and abbreviations
5. Firm names composed of combined surnames and coined names
6. Names of clubs and service organizations
7. Names of newspapers and periodicals
8. Similar names
9. Names of businesses that are known by more than one name

When such names appear in a correspondence filing system, they are cross-referenced as described and illustrated on page 264. In a card filing system, however, either of two methods may be used to cross-reference the names to enable the files operator to locate them more quickly and easily:

1. The index form of a name is used as a basis for filing the original card, and a second card is prepared for the same name in another form. This second card is called a *cross-reference card*.

2. The most important name on the original card is used for filing, and names of secondary importance that might be associated with the original name are used on cross-reference cards. An example of this situation is a magazine, *Business Education Forum*, once called the *UBEA Forum*, published by the National Business Education Association. The original card and the cross-references are made as follows:

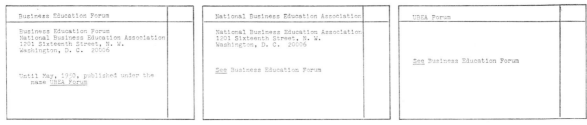

| Original Card | First Cross-Reference | Second Cross-Reference |

Cross-Referencing Guide 1: Unusual Names of Individuals

Because material filed under an unusual name may be requested by the name as usually written as well as by the name in transposed index order, two file cards should be prepared. The original card is prepared in transposed index order; the cross-reference card, in natural (written) order. For the name *Kosho Oshiro*, as an example, prepare the cards as follows:

Original Card
Oshiro, Kosho

Cross-Reference Card
Kosho Oshiro
See Oshiro, Kosho

Cross-Referencing Guide 2: Names of Married Women

Since the legal name of a married woman appears on the original file card, a cross-reference card should be prepared for her husband's name followed by "Mrs." in parentheses.

Original Card
Collins, Ruth Gaines (Mrs.)
(Mrs. Gary M. Collins)

Cross-Reference Card
Collins, Gary M. (Mrs.)
See Collins, Ruth Gaines (Mrs.)

Rule 21: Use a comma to set off a brief quotation, but use a colon to introduce a long quotation. Place a period or a comma always before a quotation mark. Place a colon or a semicolon always after the quotation mark. Put any other mark of punctuation before the quotation when it is a part of the quotation and after when it refers to the entire sentence of which the quotation is only a part. A quotation within a quotation is enclosed by single quote marks.

Example: The chairman said,"I'll read the text of the message." Then he proceeded to read the following: "Due to an oversight, we printed the folders without the words 'Restricted information' on the front cover. We are indeed sorry that the omission was made." A motion was made to change the title from "A Critical Situation" to "Urgent Business"; it was seconded quickly.

NOTE: The following material requires the application of Rule 16, as well as Rule 21.

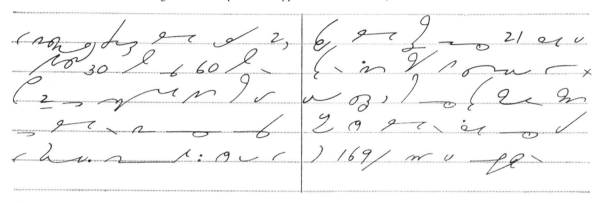

31D—Practice Material for Building Fluency

	Words		Words
	3		64
	6		71
	11		78
	15		85
			94
	23		100
	30		109
	40		116
	49		123
		James T. Bradford	129
	57		141

31E—Dictionary and Spelling Preview

1. etchings, charcoal

2. desirable, gatherings

3. buckwheat, reorder, inconvenience

5. recently, dandelion, eradicating

Office Practice Problems

1. Arrange the following names in correct alphabetic order, typing each name in transposed index order.

   a. Marine Inspection
      Coast Guard
      Treasury Department
      Cleveland, Ohio
   b. Board of Health
      Cuyahoga County
      Cleveland, Ohio
   c. Board of Commissioners
      Park Department
      Cincinnati, Ohio
   d. Civil Division
      Sheriff's Office
      Cuyahoga County
      Cleveland, Ohio
   e. Asphalt Plant
      Highway Maintenance Division
      Cincinnati, Ohio
   f. State Bureau of Motor Vehicles
      Hartford, Connecticut
   g. District Director of Internal Revenue
      Treasury Department
      Cleveland, Ohio
   h. National Advisory Council
      Office of Vocational Rehabilitation
      Department of Health, Education, and Welfare
      Washington, D. C.

2. The following subject titles are used in the filing system of the Klain-Lawrence Company. Type these subject titles in alphabetic order on a full sheet of paper. Leave eight blank lines after each title.

   Office Equipment Companies
   Office Stationery and Supply Companies
   Office Cleaning Services
   Sales Material Printers
   Office Equipment Repair Companies

   The names of the firms with which the Klain-Lawrence Company does business are given below and at the top of the next column. Indicate the order in which the folders for these firms would appear in the file by typing the names in correct alphabetic sequence under the appropriate subject titles on the sheet you have already prepared.

   We-Do-It-All Cleaners
   J B Promotional Publishers, Inc.
   Standard Letterhead Suppliers Co.
   Rite-Away Typewriter Repair Company
   All-Metal Desks, Inc.
   Jackson-Bardwell Sales-Print Company

   Gilmore Mimeo Supplies
   Multi-Brand Duplicating Machines, Inc.
   Paper Shop, Inc.
   Citywide Window Cleaners, Inc.
   Sit-Rite Chair Mfrs.
   Jacks' Business Forms, Inc.
   Quality Business Interiors
   Wall Washing & Cleaning Services Co.
   Office Equipment Fixit Service
   City Typewriter Mart

3. Listed below are 20 names. Type each one in index order on a 5 by 3 file card. Then, a triple space below, type the name in address order. Type the number representing the name in the upper right-hand corner of the card for that name. When all cards have been typed, arrange them in alphabetic order according to the names. Prepare an answer sheet similar to the one on page 271 and submit it to your teacher for checking.

   151. Fire Dept., Port Arthur, Texas
   152. La Grange Christian Church
   153. Porto Alegre Boat Club
   154. Mount Pleasant High School, Providence, Rhode Island
   155. Lake Erie College
   156. Water Works Dept., Lansing, Michigan
   157. Pleasant Ridge Methodist Church
   158. High School, Port Huron, Michigan
   159. Health Department, Lawrence, Massachusetts
   160. Police Department, El Cerrito, California
   161. Port Royal Industries, Inc.
   162. Mount Clemens Realty Corp.
   163. Paul Quinn College
   164. University of Puerto Rico
   165. Lake City Transit Co.
   166. Fishery Commission, Puget Island, Washington
   167. Lake's End Resort Dwellers Club
   168. Pre-eminent Order of Typographers
   169. Peace Baptist Church
   170. Mountain View Inn

4. Combine cards 131-170 into a single alphabetic card file. Prepare an answer sheet and submit it to your teacher for checking.

5. Combine cards 1-170 into a single alphabetic card file. Prepare an answer sheet and submit it to your teacher for checking. Keep the cards for use in Problem 3, Lesson 113, page 289.

31F—Preview of New Dictation Material

(1) *[shorthand outlines]*

Jennings, etchings, charcoal, specific, self-confident, self-reliant

(2) *[shorthand outlines]*

Hastings, around, various, findings, so many, listings

(3) *[shorthand outlines]*

forwarded, postage, too much, buckwheat, route, if you wish, pure, we hope this will not, you can give us

(4) *[shorthand outlines]*

calendar, to impose, appointment, we know, pad, prior

(5) *[shorthand outlines]*

introduced, eradicating, assistance, dandelion, Edwards, St. Paul, we shall see, if you need, benefit, ideas, derive, hundreds

Lesson 32 ⬡⬡⬡⬡⬡⬡⬡⬡⬡⬡⬡⬡⬡⬡⬡⬡⬡⬡

32A—Phrase Builder

There are 14 phrases in the following paragraph.

[shorthand outlines]

Names (Natural Order)	Alphabetic Index Order

Licking River Pumping Station
Kenton County Water Commission
Forest Hills, Kentucky
	Kenton, County
	  Water Commission
	  Licking River Pumping Station
	  Forest Hills, Kentucky

Bureau of Motor Vehicles
State of Ohio
Columbus, Ohio
	Ohio, State
	  Motor Vehicles Bureau
	  Columbus, Ohio

Child Welfare Consultation
Division of Social Administration
Department of Public Welfare
State of Ohio
Cincinnati, Ohio
	Ohio, State
	  Public Welfare Department
	  Social Administration Division
	  Child Welfare Consultation
	  Cincinnati, Ohio

NOTE 1: Two titles are often sufficient for identifying state, county, and city names because these names are usually less complex than those in the Federal Government.

NOTE 2: If the key name does not appear on the material as a part of the name, write it in for filing purposes.

Guide 25: Subjects as Primary Titles

When a subject title indicates more clearly than a correspondent's name the most important element for consideration, file the material under the subject title. If the subject title does not appear on the material, write it in. Use the name of the correspondent as the second and subsequent indexing units.

a. File applications for employment, bids, and similar names according to the subject titles rather than by names of correspondents. Within each such classification, arrange the names of correspondents alphabetically.

Alphabetic Index Order

Names	UNIT 1	UNIT 2	UNIT 3	UNIT 4	UNIT 5
Mary Anne Jones	Applications (Employment)	Jones	Mary	Anne	
Harold Loftus	Applications (Employment)	Loftus	Harold		
John C. Mason	Applications (Employment)	Mason	John	C.	
Johns Construction Co.	Bids (Construction)	Johns	Construction	Company	
West Side Builders	Bids (Construction)	West	Side	Builders	
Broder Moving and Storage Co.	Bids (Moving Equipment)	Broder	Moving (and)	Storage	Company
Larry Dean & Sons, Inc.	Bids (Moving Equipment)	Dean	Larry (&)	Sons	Incorporated
Kirk-Lowell Transportation Co.	Bids (Moving Equipment)	Kirk-	Lowell	Transportation	Company

b. When there is only limited correspondence with radio and television stations, index the names of stations by call letters and file them alphabetically throughout the files. (An example of this method is shown on page 274 in the illustrative examples following Guide 10.) When there is correspondence with many radio and television stations, however, index the names of the stations by call letters but file them according to the subject titles "Radio" and "Television" rather than by the names of the stations. Within each subject classification arrange the call letters alphabetically.

Alphabetic Index Order

Names	UNIT 1	UNIT 2	UNIT 3	UNIT 4	UNIT 5
WFMF	Radio	W	F	M	F
WJVA	Radio	W	J	V	A
WWVA	Radio	W	W	V	A
WLEX	Television	W	L	E	X
WSAZ	Television	W	S	A	Z
WTVP	Television	W	T	V	P

32B—Theory Review

The word ending *-ship* is expressed by a disjoined *sh*.

Short forms are used to express some amounts, quantities, and dimensions. *Hundreds* is expressed by *n* underneath the figure; *thousand*, by the over *th*; *dollars*, by *d*; *percent*, by right *s* slightly below the line; *o'clock*, by the *o* hook above the line; *million*, by *m* close to the figure on the right, *feet*, by *f*; *pounds*, by *p*; *billion*, by *b*.

32C—Punctuation Preview

Rule 22: Capitalize proper nouns, including days of the week, the months, political parties, governmental bodies, governmental departments, institutions, historical events and eras, documents, geographical names, buildings, all words pertaining to Deity, and personification. Do not capitalize words that have been derived from proper names if they are in common use. Capitalize *Federal* when it refers to the United States Government; capitalize *State* when it refers to a specific state.

Example: A group of Federal employees visited the special display of World War II mementos on Wednesday, October 15. The employees were members of the Republican Party who were employed in the Statistical Department of the Bureau of Mines. The mimeographed sheet of explanations helped them get the most out of the trip. Next month they plan to see an exhibit of various artists' interpretations of "The Lord's Supper" at the Art Museum.

NOTE: Rules 16, 17, and 21 are to be applied in the following material, as well as Rule 22.

Alphabetizing Other Names (Concluded)

Because of the extensive use of business facilities and services by the United States Government, as well as by state and city governments, many business firms have a large volume of correspondence with federal, state, county, and local government agencies. For this reason it is necessary for the files operator to be familiar with the rules for filing such correspondence. The following rules will give you that familiarity; their consistent use will make for uniformity in indexing procedure.

Guide 23: Federal Government Offices

Consider the parts of the name of a Federal Government office in the following order: (a) United States Government (three indexing units), (b) the principal words in the name of the executive department, (c) the principal words in the name of the bureau, and (d) the principal words in the name of the division.

Names (Natural Order)	Alphabetic Index Order

Military Liaison Committee
Atomic Energy Commission
	United States Government
	   Atomic Energy Commission
	   Military Liaison Committee

Armed Forces Policy Council
U. S. Department of Defense
	United States Government
	   Defense Department
	   Armed Forces Policy Council

National Security Agency
U. S. Department of Defense
	United States Government
	   Defense Department
	   National Security Agency

Bureau of Medical Services
Public Health Service
Department of Health, Education, and
   Welfare
	United States Government
	   Health, Education, and Welfare Department
	   Public Health Service
	   Medical Services Bureau

Urban Renewal Administration
Housing and Home Finance Agency
	United States Government
	   Housing and Home Finance Agency
	   Urban Renewal Administration

NOTE: If the key name (*United States Government*, for example) does not appear on the material as a part of the name, write it in for filing purposes.

Guide 24: Political Subdivisions

Consider the parts of the name of an office in a state, county, city, or other political subdivision in the following order: (a) the principal word or words in the name of the political subdivision, followed by its classification, such as "State," "County," or "City," and (b) the principal words in the name of the department, board, or office.

Names (Natural Order)	Alphabetic Index Order

Municipal Housing Commission
Covington, Kentucky
	Covington, City
	   Municipal Housing Commission
	   Covington, Kentucky

Traffic Division
Police Department
Covington, Kentucky
	Covington, City
	   Police Department
	   Traffic Division
	   Covington, Kentucky

Kenton County Tax Commissioner
Forest Hills, Kentucky
	Kenton, County
	   Tax Commissioner, County
	   Forest Hills, Kentucky

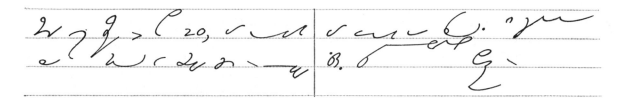

32D—Practice Material for Building Fluency

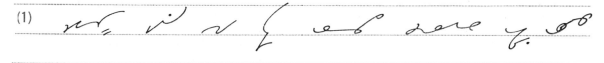

	Words		Words
	3		66
	10		72
	14		79
	20		86
	29		95
	38		101
	45		110
	51		120
	58		133
		Harold A. Cooper	137
			153

32E—Dictionary and Spelling Preview

1. secretaries, shorthand, shortened

2. shipshape, sponsorship, Commerce

3. connection, acquainted, premiums, reception

4. judgment, faultless, certificate

32F—Preview of New Dictation Material

(1)

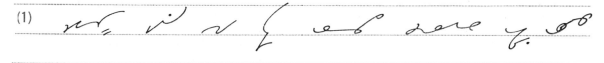

Stockton, shorthand, court, by which the, remedy, secretaries, reporting, right now

(2)

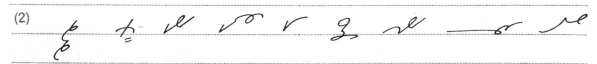

shipshape, Chamber of Commerce, shortest, shortcake, shorten, I shall send you, contest, many other, entries

2. Arrange the names in each of the following groups in correct alphabetic sequence, typing each name in index order.

(a) 1. Dr. Delman's Health Club
2. Dr. Alvin C. Delmar
3. Della's Beauty Shop
4. Del Rosa Transfer Co.
5. Delman-Walsh, Inc.

(b) 1. The Monacle
2. Mrs. Snyder's Candies
3. Muller Travel Service
4. Mary's Cupboard
5. Hotel Morraine

(c) 1. 32nd Street Medical Center
2. Thrifti-Mart, Inc.
3. Jas. A. Thielman & Associates
4. The Three Sisters Beauty Salon
5. Thermo-Fax Sales Co.

(d) 1. St. Louis Postage Meter Co.
2. Edward L. St. John
3. Ann Marie Saint
4. San Jose Hardware
5. St. Louis Post-Dispatch

(e) 1. Albert C. Jann, 1210 Eighth Street, Boston
2. Jann & Albert of Cincinnati
3. J. and B. Products Co.
4. Albert C. Jann, 2 Eilerson Place, Boston
5. Jann & Albert of Cleveland

(f) 1. Lee-LaRue Associates
2. Le Grand Sportswear Co.
3. Lawrence A. Lee-LaRue
4. Leggett Towel Supply Co.
5. Lyle Lee

(g) 1. Powers' Youth Club
2. Power Bros. Hardware
3. Power Transmission Service
4. Roy Powers, M.D.
5. Association of Power Tool Mfrs.
6. Powers-Royce Toy Kit Mfrs.
7. Powermatic Brake Co.
8. Roy Powers Language School
9. Ronald Powers & Sons, Inc.
10. Power-Pack, Inc.

(h) 1. Carlsbad High School
Carlsbad, New Mexico
2. Oceanside-Carlsbad College
Oceanside, California
3. Carlsbad Chamber of Commerce
4. Bow & Arrow Club of Carlsbad
5. Mid High School
Carlsbad, New Mexico
6. Buttons & Bows Sewing Circle
7. Carlsbad Community College
8. Carlsbad Baptist Church
9. Carlsbad High School
Carlsbad, California
10. Carlsbad Retailers Association

3. Listed below are 20 names. Type each one in index order on a 5 by 3 file card. Then, a triple space below, type the name in address order. Type the number representing the name in the upper right-hand corner of the card for that name. When all cards have been typed, arrange them in alphabetic order according to the names. Prepare an answer sheet similar to the one on page 271 and submit it to your teacher for checking. Save the 20 cards for use in Problem 4, Lesson 112, page 286.

131. University of Kentucky
132. Goode & Goode, Attorneys
133. Carl A. Gracen, Sr.
134. Jackson-Sorter Printers, Inc.
135. Better Business Bureau of Knoxville
136. Brother Carl Harlen
137. Kith-n-Kin Restaurant
138. King's College
139. Kenwood Congregational Church
140. Carl A. Gracen, Jr.
141. Mrs. Harold (Jane Ella) De Grace
142. Kim Soong
143. High School, Kingston, New York
144. Good Will Industries, Inc.
145. KNX Radio
146. Kneseth Israel Congregation
147. "King" William Jazz Band
148. James Allen Harle-Stewart
149. Jackson Hdwe. Co., Inc.
150. Kirby Road School, Cincinnati, Ohio

4. Combine cards 1-130 into a single alphabetic card file. Prepare an answer sheet and submit it to your teacher for checking. Keep the cards for use in Problem 4, Lesson 112, page 286.

(3) *[shorthand outlines]*

Bancroft, suite, ultimate, in connection, Anson, quarters, assistants, assistance, acquainted, Mason City, prosperity, cordial

(4) *[shorthand outlines]*

suggestions, faultless, Timeless, illustrated, judgment, nationally, certificate

Lesson 33 ⬡◇⬡◇⬡◇⬡◇⬡◇⬡◇⬡◇⬡◇⬡◇⬡◇⬡◇

33A—Potential Rate Builder

There are 16 words in the following sentence.

[shorthand outline]

33B—Theory Review

The word beginning *re-* is expressed by *r* before a downstroke or a vowel.

Some long words can be abbreviated by dropping the endings, such as *-ology, -ntic,* and *-bute.*

[shorthand outlines]

Alphabetic Index Order

Names (Natural Order)	UNIT 1	UNIT 2	UNIT 3	IDENTIFYING ELEMENT
Main Street Merchants	Main	Street	Merchants	
Men's Club of Omaha	Men's	Club (of)	Omaha	
Mental Health Association Cincinnati	Mental	Health	Association	(Cincinnati)
Mental Health Association Cleveland	Mental	Health	Association	(Cleveland)
Mental Health Association Columbus	Mental	Health	Association	(Columbus)
Merchants Club of Detroit	Merchants	Club (of)	Detroit	
Methodist Youth Fellowship	Methodist	Youth	Fellowship	
Miami Country Club	Miami	Country	Club	
Montgomery War Veterans	Montgomery	War	Veterans	
Loyal Order of Moose	Moose	Loyal	Order (of)	

NOTE: If the name of an organization consists of several words of importance and if the name is indexed according to a word other than the first, the name should be cross-referenced (as illustrated on page 288) so that it will appear in the file in address form also.

Office Practice Problems

1. Arrange the names in each of the following groups in correct alphabetic sequence, typing each name in index order.

(a)
1. Warren School
   Cleveland, Ohio
2. Barrett Junior High School
   Columbus, Ohio
3. Euclid Park School
   Cleveland, Ohio
4. Myers Park High School
   Charlotte, North Carolina
5. Lake School
   Cleveland, Ohio
6. Fred A. Cochran Junior High School
   Charlotte, North Carolina
7. West High School
   Cleveland, Ohio
8. Grandview Heights High School
   Columbus, Ohio
9. Hickman High School
   Columbia, Missouri
10. Newton Baker High School
   Columbus, Georgia

(b)
1. Springdale Teachers College
2. University of Springfield
3. Springfield State University
4. Spring-Dawson Business College
5. Springerville Commercial College
6. Spring City Institute of Music
7. Spring & Lyons Secretarial School
8. Stillwater Junior College
9. Springs School of Commerce
10. St. John College

(c)
1. Church of the Saviour
2. Chardon Methodist Church
3. Cedar Temple
4. Chapel of St. Clare
5. Calvary Baptist Church
6. Church of Christ
7. Cleveland Christian Church
8. Church of the Ascension
9. Cathedral of St. John
10. Covenant-First Presbyterian Church

(d)
1. EEE Confraternity
2. Exalted Order of Columbians
3. Benevolent and Protective Order of Elks
4. Evadale Men's Club
5. The Emma Long Dietitians' Club
6. Eager Beaver Society of Clark School
7. Eldred Playhouse Society of Chicago
8. Eva-More Stay-Fit Club
9. Evagreen Country Club
10. Elder Statesmen's Fraternity

(e)
1. Granger Road Retailers' Assn.
2. Brave Order of Grenadiers
3. Association of Greenhouse Operators
4. Green Hills Country Club
5. Grace Episcopal Church
6. Greenbrier Military School
7. GTX Society
8. Howard Grace's Athletic Club
9. Green-Leaf Florists, Inc.
10. Garinger High School, Charlotte, North Carolina

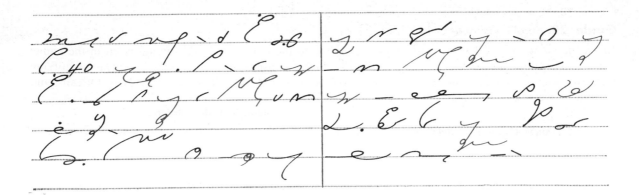

33C—Punctuation Preview

Rule 23: Use a colon after an introductory expression to indicate that something follows. Capitalize the first word following a colon when that word begins a complete sentence.

Example: Here is what I want you to do: Compare the progress of the West with that of the North, considering machinery in farming and industry. You will need to make notes of the following: number and kinds of machines used; number of people engaged in farming or industry; and volume of business.

NOTE: In the following material, Rules 16-18, 21, and 22 will need to be applied, as well as Rule 23.

33D—Dictionary and Spelling Preview

1. specialty, refrigerators, receipt

2. resentful, reprimand, threatened

3. reciprocate, current

4. evidently, shareholders, frankfurters

Guide 20: Colleges and Universities

Index the name of a college or a university according to the most clearly identifying word in the name. Unless city names are part of the college names, do not consider the city names except as identifying elements when identical college names are involved (as in Loyola University of New Orleans and Loyola University of Chicago).

Alphabetic Index Order

Names (Natural Order)	UNIT 1	UNIT 2	UNIT 3	IDENTIFYING ELEMENT
Massachusetts Institute of Technology	Massachusetts	Institute (of)	Technology	
Massachusetts School of Art	Massachusetts	School (of)	Art	
University of Massachusetts	Massachusetts	University (of)		
Massey Business College Birmingham	Massey	Business	College	(Birmingham)
Massey Business College Houston	Massey	Business	College	(Houston)
Massey Business College Jacksonville	Massey	Business	College	(Jacksonville)
Memphis State College	Memphis	State	College	
Merrill-Palmer School	Merrill-	Palmer	School	
Miami University	Miami	University		
Milwaukee School of Engineering	Milwaukee	School (of)	Engineering	
Mary Washington College	Washington	Mary	College	
Washington University	Washington	University		
Wayland Baptist College	Wayland	Baptist	College	
Western College for Women	Western	College (for)	Women	
College of William and Mary	William (and)	Mary	College (of)	

Guide 21: Churches and Synagogues

Index the name of a church or a synagogue in the order in which it is written unless some word other than the first word more clearly identifies the organization. If the name of the denomination is part of the name of the church, use that name as the first indexing unit. For example, in the name "Third Presbyterian Church," index the name under "Presbyterian" rather than under "Third." The word "Church" is never used as the first indexing unit.

Alphabetic Index Order

Names (Natural Order)	UNIT 1	UNIT 2	UNIT 3
Fairview Baptist Church	Baptist	Church	Fairview
Fairmount Temple	Fairmount	Temple	
Franciscan Monastery Chapel	Franciscan	Monastery	Chapel
Church of the Society of Friends	Friends	Society (of)	Church (of the)
Faith Lutheran Church	Lutheran	Church	Faith
Friendship Methodist Church	Methodist	Church	Friendship
First Presbyterian Church	Presbyterian	Church	First
St. Anthony Friary	Saint	Anthony	Friary
Cathedral of St. Francis	Saint	Francis	Cathedral (of)
St. Francis Church	Saint	Francis	Church
Sholom Temple	Sholom	Temple	

Guide 22: Clubs and Service Organizations

Index the name of a club or a service organization according to the most clearly identifying unit in the name. Treat a city name appearing in the name of an organization as an indexing unit. Otherwise, do not consider city names unless organization names in two or more cities are alike; in this case consider the city names last as identifying elements.

33E—Practice Material for Building Fluency

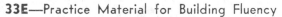

(shorthand outlines with word counts)

Words		Words
		80
4		89
7		96
11		103
17		110
24		118
32		125
41		132
52		140
63		148
72	Miriam Mitchell	154
		167

33F—Preview of New Dictation Material

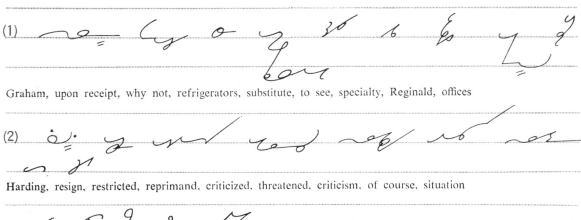

(1) *(shorthand outlines)*

Graham, upon receipt, why not, refrigerators, substitute, to see, specialty, Reginald, offices

(2) *(shorthand outlines)*

Harding, resign, restricted, reprimand, criticized, threatened, criticism, of course, situation

(3) *(shorthand outlines)*

periodic, average, if we can, during the past year, any information, reciprocate, confidential, courtesy

(4) *(shorthand outlines)*

evidently, frankfurter, juice, novel, shareholders, tender, housewife, laboratory, Pickering, pineapple, swanky, about which

Guides for Alphabetic Indexing and Filing

Lesson **III** ⬡◯⬡◯⬡◯⬡◯⬡◯⬡◯⬡◯⬡◯⬡◯⬡◯⬡◯⬡◯⬡

Alphabetizing Other Names

Many names, such as those of schools, colleges and universities, churches and synagogues, and clubs and service organizations, may be satisfactorily filed according to either of two plans: (1) under the name as written or (2) under the most clearly identifying word in the name. Some offices file such names under the first plan, while others find the second plan better suited to their needs.

Because of the confusion such names often create, they, along with government names and names filed under subject titles, are presented here under the heading "Other Names." Although more than one method would be acceptable for filing them, the following widely used rules are given to provide consistency in the filing of names that create these special problems.

Guide 19: Elementary and Secondary Schools

Index the names of elementary and secondary schools (1) according to the names of the cities in which the schools are located and (2) according to the most distinctive words in the names of the schools. When the name of the city is the first word of the school name, use the city name only once in indexing. Do not consider state names unless city names in two or more states are alike, in which case consider state names second as identifying elements.

	Alphabetic Index Order			
Names (Natural Order)	UNIT 1	UNIT 2	UNIT 3	UNIT 4
Cartersville High School Cartersville, Georgia	Cartersville	High	School	
Central High School Cincinnati, Ohio	Cincinnati	Central	High	School
Cincinnati Country Day School Cincinnati, Ohio	Cincinnati	Country	Day	School
Kennedy Elementary School Cincinnati, Ohio	Cincinnati	Kennedy	Elementary	School
Lotspeich School Cincinnati, Ohio	Cincinnati	Lotspeich	School	
St. John School Cincinnati, Ohio	Cincinnati	Saint	John	School
Robert Taft High School Cincinnati, Ohio	Cincinnati	Taft	Robert	High
Holmes High School Covington, Kentucky	Covington	Holmes	High	School
High School Crescent City, Florida	Crescent	City	High	School
Dayton High School Dayton, Kentucky	Dayton (Kentucky)	High	School	
Lincoln Elementary School Dayton, Kentucky	Dayton (Kentucky)	Lincoln	Elementary	School
Allen Elementary School Dayton, Ohio	Dayton (Ohio)	Allen	Elementary	School
Roosevelt High School Dayton, Ohio	Dayton (Ohio)	Roosevelt	High	School
Deland High School DeLand, Florida	DeLand	High	School	
Manual High School Denver, Colorado	Denver	Manual	High	School
North High School Denver, Colorado	Denver	North	High	School

34A—Proportion Drill

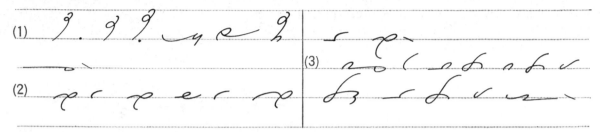

(1)

(2)

(3)

34B—Theory Review

The endings *-icle* and *-ical* are expressed by a disjoined *k*.

Some compound words are expressed by simply joining the two separate shorthand outlines. In some cases, the outline is modified slightly to make a better joining, as in words involving "ever."

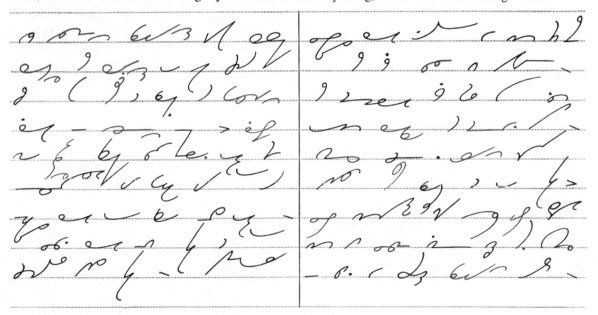

34C—Punctuation Preview

Rule 24: Use parentheses to enclose matter that has no direct relationship to the rest of the sentence or to enclose notation of authorship.

Example: An important feature of the report is the summary (page 25) that highlights the vital statistics.
These statistics will appear in a new book entitled <u>Business Cycles</u> (Bonner and Clark).

NOTE: The material at the top of page 97 requires application of Rules 16-19 and 21-23, as well as Rule 24.

Building Skill in Transcribing

Transcribing from Shorthand Notes

1. Write in shorthand Letter (1) given below.
2. Transcribe the letter from your notes as a 5-minute writing. Determine your *mwam*. If you complete the letter before time is called, repeat it from the beginning.
3. Transcribe Letter (2) as a 5-minute writing. Determine your *mwam* and compare it with your *mwam* on Letter (1).

	Words
(1) May 25, 19—	3

	Words
Miss Clára Herzog	6
Head, Filing Department	11
Security Insurance Company	16
384 West Eighth Street	21
Flagstaff, Arizona 86001	26
Dear Miss Herzog:	30

I am glad to have the opportunity of clarify- 39
ing the procedure for filing names [1] that 47
involve foreign particles or prefixes. 55

A foreign particle or prefix, such as *du*, 64
Van, El, and *La*,[2] in a personal or firm name 74
is not a separate indexing unit. It is, in- 83
stead, combined with the word [3] that fol- 91
lows and indexed as one unit. 97

At one time a prefix or a foreign particle 106
in a firm name was [4] indexed as a separate 114
unit; whereas, in a personal name a prefix 123
or a foreign particle was [5] considered a part 131
of the surname. These seemingly contradic- 140
tory procedures created confusion in [6] the 148
minds of filing personnel; consequently, the 157
rules were revised to eliminate the con- 165
fusion. 167

It is [7] likely that some of you file clerks 176
studied filing methods when separate rules 184
for personal names and for firm names [8] 192
were being taught, while others may have 200
learned the new rule. This perhaps accounts 209
for the lack of uniformity in [9] filing such 217
names in your department. 223

I shall be pleased if you will let me help 231
you with any other filing problems [10] that 239
may arise. (211) 242

Sincerely yours, 245
268

	Words
(2) May 25, 19—	3
Mrs. Marsha D. Lewis	7
Haskins & Sheldon	10
Navajo Building, Suite 31	16
Phoenix, Arizona 85002	20

Transcribing from Dictation

Your teacher will dictate a letter and an inter-office memo to you for transcription. Prepare the letter for the signature of R.D. Moore, Rules Consultant, who uses the company name in the closing lines.

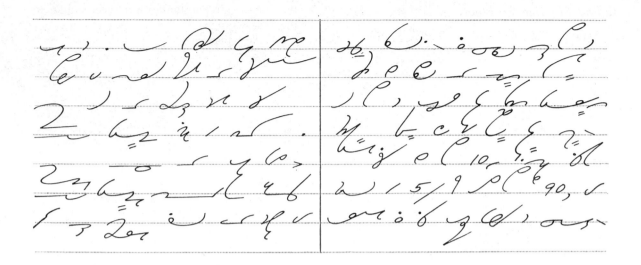

34D—Practice Material for Building Fluency

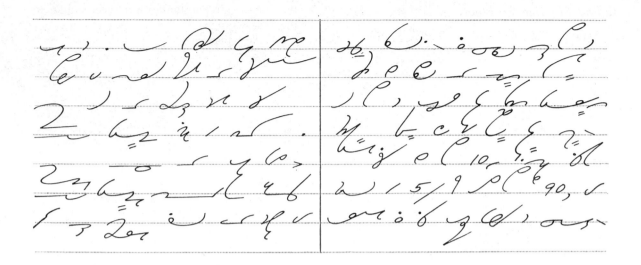

Words

4	79
9	86
14	97
21	101
	108
29	118
35	126
43	135
50	141
57	148
65	155
73	164
	166

34E—Dictionary and Spelling Preview

1. fanatical, concentrate, nontechnical

3. pamphlets, graphic, superintendent

4. unfortunate, expendable, movable

Unit 7 · Lesson 34

Office Practice Problems

1. Arrange the names in each of the following groups in correct alphabetic sequence, typing each name in index order.

   (a) 1. Latonia Camera Shop
        2. Las Vegas Advertising Agency
        3. J. C. Landis, Inc.
        4. LaRose Pharmacy
        5. Carl Lasher, Ltd.

   (b) 1. Sandalwood Cabinet Co.
        2. St. Paul Mattress Company
        3. Santa Barbara Barber Shop
        4. Sand Springs Record Shop
        5. Edward St. John, Inc.

   (c) 1. Robert Dunn & Associates
        2. Dun-Rite Laundry
        3. W. C. Dunn-Allyn Company
        4. DuPont Sales Corp.
        5. Du Quoin Transfer Co.

   (d) 1. Candlewax Smokeless Fuel Co.
        2. Candle Light Tearoom
        3. C & E Lighting Fixtures
        4. Candl-Glo Inn
        5. Candlelight Cafe

   (e) 1. Aaron Welding Co.
        2. Aarons' Appliance Co.
        3. A. J. Aarons and Co.
        4. Aaron's Portrait Studio
        5. A-1 Multi-Print, Inc.

   (f) 1. Co-op Stores, Inc.
        2. Co-ordinate Decorators
        3. Cooper Refining Co.
        4. Cooper-Excel Mining Co.
        5. Cooperative Mills, Inc.

   (g) 1. Bader Brothers, Springfield, Ill.
        2. Bader Brothers, Springfield, Mo.
        3. B & B Market, 1039 Elm Street
        4. Bader Brothers, Springfield, Mass.
        5. B & B Market, 450 Fifth Street

   (h) 1. Smith & Smith, Inc.
        2. Smith-Carpenter Termite Control Co.
        3. Smithers' Home Laundry
        4. L. N. Smith & Co.
        5. Smith's Awning Company

   (i) 1. Wm. Pitcher & Sons
        2. Albert J. Pitchon, Inc.
        3. Pi-Co Carry Out
        4. Pico Box Lunch Co.
        5. Pitch-N-Putt Golf Course

2. In the next column are 50 names. Type each one in index order on a 5 by 3 file card. Then, a triple space below, type the name in address order. Type the number representing the name in the upper right-hand corner of the card for that name. When all cards have been typed, arrange them in alphabetic order according to the names. Prepare an answer sheet similar to the one on page 271 and submit it to your teacher for checking.

   81. A. L. McCarty & Sons
   82. Queen City Motor Co.
   83. Portable Pools, Inc.
   84. D & M Plastering Company
   85. C. W. Rymer, Inc.
   86. Newtown Garage
   87. Hanna Printing Company
   88. 60 Second Shops, Inc.
   89. La Crosse Products Co.
   90. Chester T. Fitz-Hugh
   91. John Perkins, Portland, Michigan
   92. U. S. Welding Company
   93. R & Y Refrigeration Co.
   94. Groves Plumbing Company
   95. John Perkins, Oklahoma City, Oklahoma
   96. Laco Beauty Salon
   97. Oelsner's Colonial Inn
   98. S P Manufacturing Corporation
   99. Darwin Equipment Co.
   100. Point Pleasant Lacquer Co.
   101. N & N Tailors, Ltd.
   102. Porter Cable Company
   103. Forthright Loan Company
   104. Edwin A. Piper, 3721 Marvin Street, Akron, Ohio
   105. 6 Mile House
   106. Alan MacAuley-Ames Co.
   107. 9th Street Building
   108. New Brunswick Terminal
   109. Fort Mitchell Hardware
   110. Kosho Oshiro and Co.
   111. Arthur MacAuley & Joseph Ames
   112. O'Neill's Produce Co.
   113. The Rymer Canning Co.
   114. 400 Club
   115. N-A-Jiffy Lunch Room
   116. The Radio Shack
   117. Edwin A. Piper, 4187 Norris Street, Akron, Ohio
   118. San Diego Florist
   119. Port Arthur Luggage Shop
   120. Hanna-Osmer, Inc.
   121. R. J. Oelsner and Son
   122. Sanborn Hair Styling
   123. 19th Hole Sandwich Shop
   124. Albert Le Fevre & Associates
   125. Elder Street Market
   126. O K Bearing Company, Inc.
   127. A. R. Mackey Building Supplies
   128. 1 Hour Valet, Incorporated
   129. New York Central System
   130. Arthur MacAuley, Inc.

3. Combine cards 66-130 into a single alphabetic card file. Prepare an answer sheet and submit it to your teacher for checking. Keep the cards for use in Problem 4, Lesson 111, page 283.

34F—Preview of New Dictation Material

(1) *[shorthand outlines]*

to permit, uninformed, language, fanatical, to convince, Tuesday morning, reactions, mechanical, concentrate, somehow, everybody

(2) *[shorthand outlines]*

McCann, obstacles, last night, colorful, so many, spectacle

(3) *[shorthand outlines]*

health, specifically, graphic, adult, content, pamphlets, Documents, population, diseases, generally, Superintendent, stimulate

(4) *[shorthand outlines]*

rubber, shortcomings, expendable, stamps, you will be able, intervals, excessive, unfortunate, attached

Lesson 35 ⬡⬡⬡⬡⬡⬡⬡⬡⬡⬡⬡⬡⬡⬡⬡⬡

35A—Repetitive Phrase Builder

[shorthand outlines]

35B—Theory Review

The writing of one character through another (intersection) is sometimes useful, as in *p.m.*

In geographical expressions, *-ville* is expressed by *v*; *-ington,* by the disjoined *ten* blend; *burg* by *b*; *-ingham*; by *m.*

[shorthand outlines] 12:30 *[shorthand outlines]*

Guide 16: Compound Foreign Names

a. Index as one unit each separately written word (such as *Rio, San,* and *Santa*) in a compound foreign name.

b. Combine a foreign article or particle (such as *De, Des, Di, Du, El, La, Las, Le, Les,* and *Los*) with the word that follows it, and index the particle and its stem as one unit.

Alphabetic Index Order

Names (Natural Order)	UNIT 1	UNIT 2	UNIT 3	UNIT 4
Corpus Christi Book Co.	Corpus	Christi	Book	Company
Di Luca Building Supply Co.	DiLuca	Building	Supply	Company
El Capitan Motel	ElCapitan	Motel		
Elgin Tool Corporation	Elgin	Tool	Corporation	
La Jolla Men's Store	LaJolla	Men('s)	Store	
Los Angeles Gourmet Shop	LosAngeles	Gourmet	Shop	
Rio Grande Shipping Co.	Rio	Grande	Shipping	Company
San Marino Shoe Store	San	Marino	Shoe	Store
Santa Paula Desk Mfrs.	Santa	Paula	Desk	Manufacturers

Guide 17: Titles in Business Names

Consider a title in a business name as a separate indexing unit, and index it in the order in which it appears in the name. The titles "Mr." and "Mrs." are indexed as they are written rather than as they might be spelled in full.

Alphabetic Index Order

Names (Natural Order)	UNIT 1	UNIT 2	UNIT 3	UNIT 4
Colonel Johnson's Bakery Products	Colonel	Johnson('s)	Bakery	Products
Dr. Osborn's Magic Capsules	Doctor	Osborn('s)	Magic	Capsules
Madame Collette's Beauty Salon	Madame	Collette('s)	Beauty	Salon
Mr. Hunter's Gun Shop	Mr.	Hunter('s)	Gun	Shop
Mrs. Carson's Candy Company	Mrs.	Carson('s)	Candy	Company
Sister Kenney Foundation	Sister	Kenney	Foundation	

Guide 18: Identical Business Names

When the names of two or more businesses are identical, use addresses, not as indexing units, but as identifying elements (a secondary means of determining alphabetic sequence). In this situation consider the identifying elements in this order: (1) city names, (2) state names, (3) street names, and (4) numeric order of building numbers. (The name of the building in which the business is located is not considered unless the name of the street is not provided.)

Alphabetic Index Order

Names (Natural Order)	UNIT 1	UNIT 2	UNIT 3	IDENTIFYING ELEMENT	IDENTIFYING ELEMENT
Simpson Motor Sales, Ames	Simpson	Motor	Sales	(Ames)	
Simpson Motor Sales, Des Moines	Simpson	Motor	Sales	(Des Moines)	
Stag Sportswear, Portland, Maine	Stag	Sportswear		(Portland)	(Maine)
Stag Sportswear, Portland, Oregon	Stag	Sportswear		(Portland)	(Oregon)

Stimson Brothers
   Oakdale Building, 1050 Oak Street
   Portland, Oregon

Stimson Brothers
   Suite 15, Simms Bldg.
   Portland, Oregon

Stimson Brothers
   415 South Street
   Portland, Oregon

Stimson Brothers
   805 Walnut Street
   Portland, Oregon

Stimson Brothers
   5640 Walnut Street
   Portland, Oregon

Stimson Brothers
   200-206 Western Avenue
   Portland, Oregon

→ Order is determined by street names, which are third identifying elements in these examples, and by building numbers, which are fourth identifying elements. (The building name is used only when the street name is not given, as in the second example at the left.) The city names are the first identifying elements, and the state names are the second.

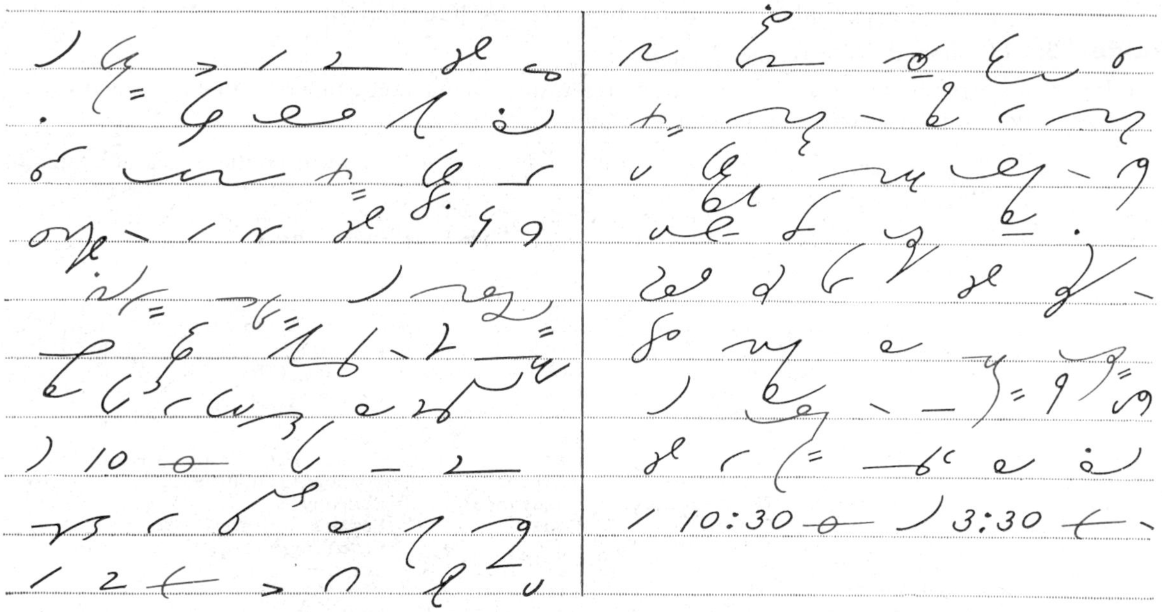

35C—Punctuation Preview

Rule 25: Use a dash to indicate a sudden change in the structure of a sentence. A dash is made by two hyphens with no space between, before, or after.

Example: `The consensus is--and I have the official vote right here--that we should postpone action until a later date.`

NOTE: In the following material, Rules 16-25 need to be applied.

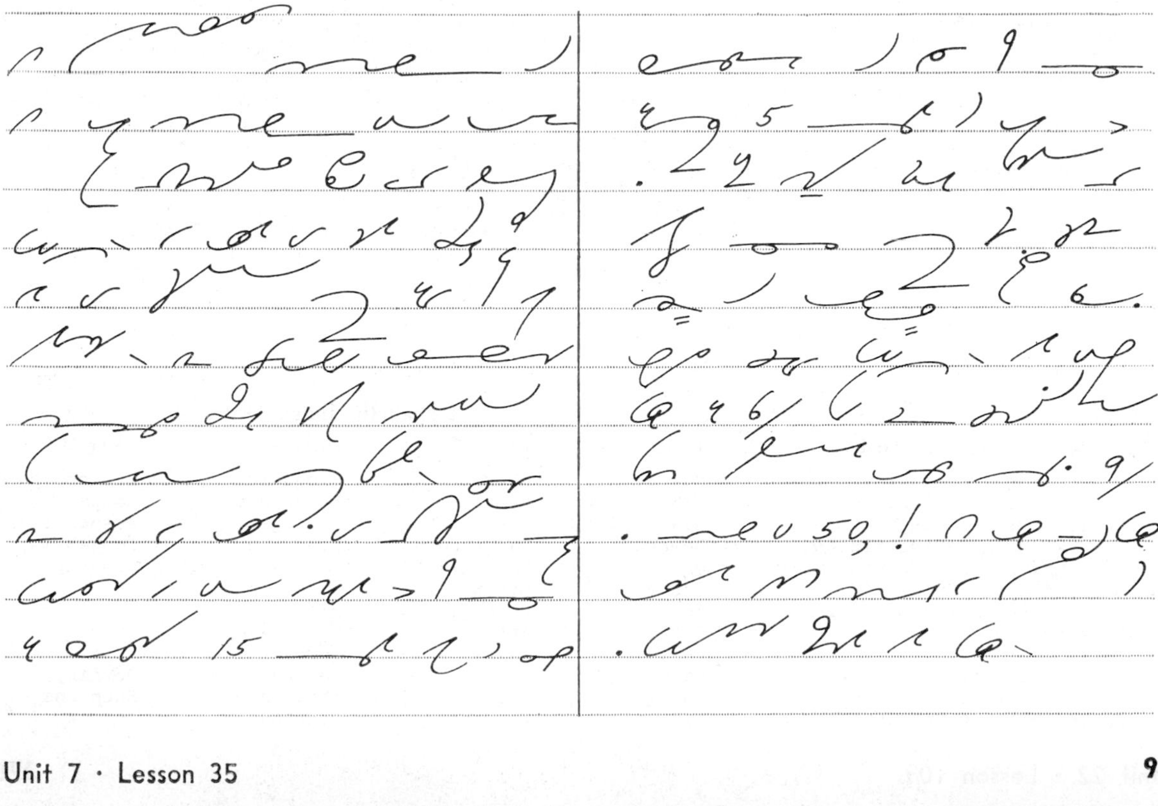

Alphabetizing Business Names (Concluded)

Guide 13: Hyphened Words and Names

a. Index as a separate indexing unit each part of a business name consisting of actual or coined names, words, or word substitutes combined with a hyphen.

b. Index as one unit a *single word* written with a hyphen. (Such a word contains a prefix such as *anti-, bi-, co-, de-, trans-, tri-*.)

Alphabetic Index Order

Names (Natural Order)	UNIT 1	UNIT 2	UNIT 3	UNIT 4
T-Shirt Mfg. Co.	T-	Shirt	Manufacturing	Company
Take-Out Pizza Palace	Take-	Out	Pizza	Palace
Taylor-Made Records, Inc.	Taylor-	Made	Records	Incorporated
The Neal Taylor Co.	Taylor	Neal	Company (The)	
Techni-Craft Corp.	Techni-	Craft	Corporation	
The Tecnifax Company	Tecnifax	Company (The)		
Hotel Terry-Derek[1]	Terry-	Derek	Hotel	
Third-Area Trust Bank	Third-	Area	Trust	Bank
The Tractor-Trailer Corp.	Tractor-	Trailer	Corporation (The)	
Trans-Oceanic Insurance Co.	Trans-Oceanic	Insurance	Company	
Howard Trevor-Roper, Ltd.	Trevor-	Roper	Howard	Limited
Tri-Us Printing Co.	Tri-	Us	Printing	Company
Tri-City Delivery Service	Tri-City	Delivery	Service	
Tru-Fit Glove Company	Tru-	Fit	Glove	Company
Try-Ur-Luck Fisheries	Try-	Ur-	Luck	Fisheries
Tulsa Drive-In Theater	Tulsa	Drive-	In	Theater

NOTE 1: If the word "Hotel" or "Motel" appears first in the name, it is transposed to follow the most clearly identifying word. This rule also applies to services or departments located in the hotel and using the hotel name.

Guide 14: One Versus Two Units

When separate words in a business name (such as *Good Will* Products Co. or *South Eastern* Furniture Co.) may be written as one word, consider them as one indexing unit.

Alphabetic Index Order

Names (Natural Order)	UNIT 1	UNIT 2	UNIT 3	UNIT 4
Hartwell Air Port Authority	Hartwell	AirPort	Authority	
Hartwell Baking Company	Hartwell	Baking	Company	
D. W. Hartwell Corp.	Hartwell	D.	W.	Corporation
Intercity Bus Company	Intercity	Bus	Company	
Inter City Parcel Delivery, Inc.	InterCity	Parcel	Delivery	Incorporated
Leathercraft, Inc.	Leathercraft	Incorporated		
Northwestern Development Company	Northwestern	Development	Company	
North Western Paper Mills	NorthWestern	Paper	Mills	
Rail Road Supply Company	RailRoad	Supply	Company	
Hotel South-West Restaurant	South-West	Hotel	Restaurant	

Guide 15: Compound Geographic Names

Index as a separate unit each word in a compound geographic name.

Alphabetic Index Order

Names (Natural Order)	UNIT 1	UNIT 2	UNIT 3	UNIT 4
McKees Rocks Products, Inc.	McKees	Rocks	Products	Incorporated
New Mexico Petroleum Co.	New	Mexico	Petroleum	Company
N. Y. Savings Assn.	New	York	Savings	Association
Newark Gas and Electric Co.	Newark	Gas (and)	Electric	Company
Oak Park Savings Company	Oak	Park	Savings	Company
Oakmont Motor Sales	Oakmont	Motor	Sales	
Pt. Comfort Building Company	Point	Comfort	Building	Company
Port Arthur Curio Shop	Port	Arthur	Curio	Shop
Portal Paint Co.	Portal	Paint	Company	
St. Cloud Realty Company	Saint	Cloud	Realty	Company
St. Louis Wholesale Supplies	Saint	Louis	Wholesale	Supplies
Salina Milling Company	Salina	Milling	Company	

35D—Practice Material for Building Fluency

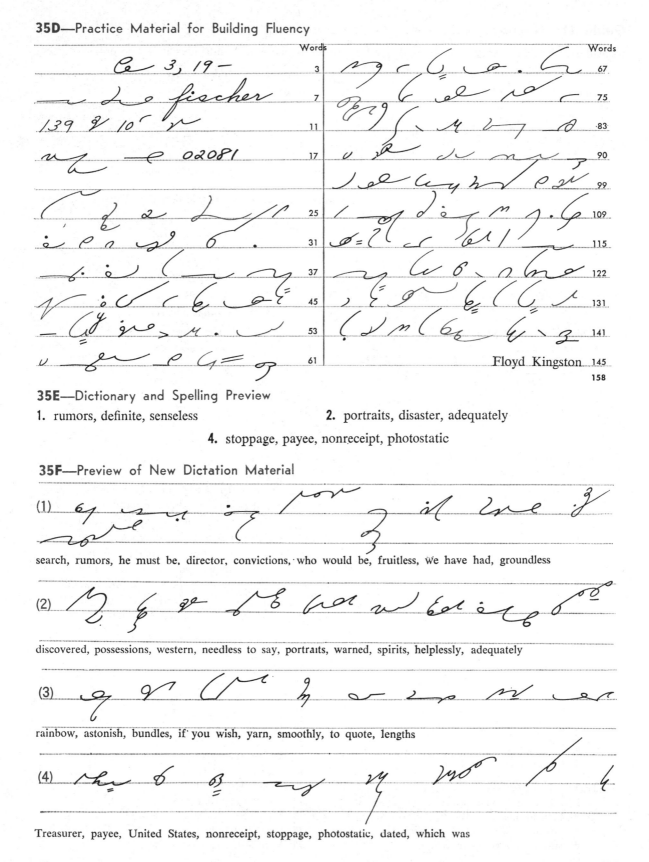

Words

3
7
11
17
25
31
37
45
53
61

67
75
83
90
99
109
115
122
131
141

Floyd Kingston 145

158

35E—Dictionary and Spelling Preview

1. rumors, definite, senseless

2. portraits, disaster, adequately

4. stoppage, payee, nonreceipt, photostatic

35F—Preview of New Dictation Material

(1)

search, rumors, he must be, director, convictions, who would be, fruitless, we have had, groundless

(2)

discovered, possessions, western, needless to say, portraits, warned, spirits, helplessly, adequately

(3)

rainbow, astonish, bundles, if you wish, yarn, smoothly, to quote, lengths

(4)

Treasurer, payee, United States, nonreceipt, stoppage, photostatic, dated, which was

Guide 11: Numbers

Consider a number in a firm name as if it were written as one word, and index it as one unit.

Alphabetic Index Order

Names (Natural Order)	UNIT 1	UNIT 2	UNIT 3	UNIT 4
A 1 Laundry Company	A	One	Laundry	Company
A to Z Electric Shop	A (to)	Z	Electric	Shop
18th Street Garage	Eighteenth	Street	Garage	
100 Club for City Improvement	One hundred	Club (for)	City	Improvement
101 Motel	One hundred one	Motel		
Poll Takers for 50 States	Poll	Takers (for)	Fifty	States
Route 66 Restaurant	Route	Sixty-six	Restaurant	
20th Century Theater	Twentieth	Century	Theater	

NOTE: Even though you consider a number as a word in indexing, you write it in figures if that is the form in which it is commonly used.

Guide 12: Possessives

When a word ends in *apostrophe s* ('s), do not consider the final *s* as part of the word for indexing purposes. When a word ends in *s apostrophe* (s'), however, consider the final *s*.

Alphabetic Index Order

Names (Natural Order)	UNIT 1	UNIT 2	UNIT 3	UNIT 4
The Little Boy's Toy Shop	Little	Boy('s)	Toy	Shop (The)
Little Boys' Play School	Little	Boys'	Play	School
Michael's Art Studio	Michael('s)	Art	Studio	
Michaels' Archery Range	Michaels'	Archery	Range	
Michaelson's Men's Store	Michaelson('s)	Men('s)	Store	
Michaelsons' Ice Skating Rink	Michaelsons'	Ice	Skating	Rink
Michener's Hotel	Michener('s)	Hotel		

Office Practice Problems

1. Arrange the names in each of the following groups in correct alphabetic sequence, typing each name in index order.

(a) 1. A. Betts
  2. A. A. Betts Company
  3. Donald G. Bettner
  4. Bettner Bottling Company
  5. A. A. Betts

(b) 1. Desmond & Casson
  2. Design Art Corp.
  3. D'Esposito Restaurant
  4. George F. DeSilver
  5. Desmond Bros. Insurance

(c) 1. E. G. Eaton & Associates
  2. E Z Loan Company
  3. Eastern Hills Stationery Co.
  4. E & M Sewing Center
  5. Eastman and Brock, Ltd.

(d) 1. 5 Point Grocery
  2. Edward's Bowling Lanes
  3. 11th Frame Soda Bar
  4. Edwards' Automotive Repair
  5. 8th Avenue Body Shop

2. Type each of the following names in index order on a 5 by 3 file card. Then, a triple space below, type the name in address order. Type the number representing the name in the upper right-hand corner of the card for that name. When all cards have been typed, arrange them in alphabetic order according to the names. Prepare an answer sheet similar to the one on page 271, and submit it to your teacher for checking. Keep the cards to be used in Problem 3, Lesson 109, page 278.

66. 7th Street Garage
67. Van Engineering Co.
68. The Charles W. Rymer Co.
69. Smith Upholstering Co.
70. United Display Corp.
71. Chas. Rymer & Son
72. 10 Pin Bowling Lanes
73. S & T Food Market
74. Van Deren Grocery
75. United Parcel Service
76. Rybolt Heating Co.
77. S O S Television Service
78. Vance Seed Co.
79. Safeway Credit Corp.
80. Van de Camp Restaurants, Inc.

Kinds of Business Letters

Lesson **36** ⬡ ⬡ ⬡ ⬡ ⬡ ⬡ ⬡ ⬡ ⬡ ⬡ ⬡ ⬡ ⬡ ⬡ ⬡ ⬡

36A—Sales Letters

Sales letters are, perhaps, more fun to write than any other type of letter. If you are attempting to sell some goods or services, you are probably enthusiastic about what you have to sell—you want others to have the pleasure of owning or using whatever the product or service is. This enthusiasm causes you to sit down and think about the qualities or characteristics that you think your prospective customer would be interested in. To know what these qualities or characteristics would be, you must know your product or service thoroughly; and you must know what your customer is like so that you know what would appeal to him. Once you have these points well in mind, you are ready to begin drafting your sales letter. Your sales letter should be developed in three basic stages:

1. Get attention. You can get attention in many different ways. The first attention-getter should be the appearance of the letter itself. Your choice of quality, color, and size of stationery may do the trick. Perhaps the use of colored ink or illustrations or an attractive letterhead design will catch the reader's eye. The arrangement of the letter on the page may be unusually pleasing. The second attention-getter will be your opening paragraph. It may be in the form of a question, a quotation, a humorous story, mention of a current news story, or something else.

2. Arouse interest and desire. When you have the reader's attention, you are ready to arouse his interest in your product or your service. By your sales message you seek to turn that interest into active desire to possess the product or to enjoy the benefits of the service. Here you use your knowledge of what you have to sell and of the prospective customer's characteristics. You emphasize the qualities of your product that will appeal to that particular type of customer. You give specific details through facts, figures, samples, testimonials, etc. You can arouse his desire to own or use the product or service by appealing to his emotions—the pleasure and satisfaction that will result from ownership.

3. Bring about action. To get the reader to act at once, make it easy for him to respond. Use business reply cards or envelopes so that there is a minimum of effort needed to send in for more information. Offer special inducements to act quickly by giving a time limit, by offering a special discount, by offering a free trial or payment at a later date.

In writing sales letters, you should be careful to be honest in your statements and promises. Don't use so many superlatives that you create doubt in the reader's mind about your sincerity or honesty. On the other hand, choose your words carefully so that they do justice to your product or service and carry the right appeal to your reader.

```
Dear Mr. Herbert:

     When harvest time comes around, you are
going to be busy.  We are going to be busy.
Everybody . . busy.

So let's
        get
           down
               to
                  the
                     point
                          now
                             and that's
                                       COMBINES!

     There's no need to tell you that combine
harvesting is low-cost, PROFITABLE harvesting.
But it's mighty important to have the right
size and type of combine.  It's like buying a
pair of shoes--no matter how well made or how
big a bargain the shoes may be, they are worth-
less unless they fit your feet.  That's why we
say, "Get the right kind of machine to fit
your needs."

     We believe the Powermaster 10 is the right
answer.  This engine-operated combine has
proved to be one of the most satisfactory ma-
chines ever introduced into this locality.  It
has been tried and tested on farms very much
like your own.  Available in 8-foot and 10-foot
cutting widths, the No. 10 is neither too large
nor too small for the average farm.  It gives
you all the advantages of the larger combines
without more weight or capacity than you need.

     Come in and let us tell you more about
this practical, economical machine NOW before
the harvest season rush is on.

          Yours very truly,
```

Sales Letter

Alphabetizing Business Names

Guide 8: Order of Indexing Units

a. Consider the units of a business name in the order in which they are written when they do not contain the complete name of an individual.

b. When the business name includes the complete name of an individual, consider the units in the individual's name in the same order as if that name stood alone. Sometimes, however, a business name containing the name of an individual (*Thom McAn Shoe Stores,* for example) is so well known that to transpose the units in the individual's name would cause confusion. In such a situation, consider the name in the order written and cross-reference it in transposed order.

Alphabetic Index Order

Names (Natural Order)	UNIT 1	UNIT 2	UNIT 3	UNIT 4
Thoburn Glass Company	Thoburn	Glass	Company	
Thoden Hotel	Thoden	Hotel		
Tholl Grocery Company	Tholl	Grocery	Company	
T. C. Tholl Corporation	Tholl	T.	C.	Corporation
Tholl Television Service	Tholl	Television	Service	
Thom McAn Shoe Stores	Thom	McAn	Shoe	Stores
Thomasville Trust Company	Thomasville	Trust	Company	
Walter Thompson Repair Shop	Thompson	Walter	Repair	Shop

NOTE: The indexing unit that determines the alphabetic order of business names is the first unit that is different in the names.

Guide 9: Disregarded Words

Generally, do not consider minor words—English articles, conjunctions, and prepositions (*the, and, &, of, for, on, by*)—as units for indexing purposes. Place them in parentheses when writing names on cards and folders. When, however, a preposition is the first word of a name (as in *In Town Club*), consider the preposition as a separate indexing unit. When "The" is the first word in the firm name, write it in parentheses at the end of the name.

Alphabetic Index Order

Names (Natural Order)	UNIT 1	UNIT 2	UNIT 3	UNIT 4
Imperial Products of the Berkshires	Imperial	Products (of the)	Berkshires	
Imperial Products Company	Imperial	Products	Company	
Imperial Products Company of Dayton	Imperial	Products	Company (of)	Dayton
Imperial Savings & Loan Association	Imperial	Savings (&)	Loan	Association
In Town Club	In	Town	Club	
The Intercity Cab Company	Intercity	Cab	Company (The)	
John Irwin (&) Hugh Long	Irwin	John (&)	Long	Hugh
Ives and Martin Associates	Ives (&)	Martin	Associates	

Guide 10: Abbreviations and Single Letters

a. Consider an abbreviation in a firm name (even when it consists of a single letter without a period) as though it were written in full.

b. Consider a single letter in a firm name, including an abbreviation for a word that is unknown and cannot be ascertained, as a separate indexing unit. It precedes all names in the same unit beginning with that same letter.

Alphabetic Index Order

Names (Natural Order)	UNIT 1	UNIT 2	UNIT 3	UNIT 4
M & A Candy Co.	M (&)	A	Candy	Company
M C A Supplies	M	C	A	Supplies
M.D. Name Plates	M.	D.	Name	Plates
Marshall Furniture Mfrs.	Marshall	Furniture	Manufacturers	
Chas. Newton & Sons	Newton	Charles (&)	Sons	
The A. and J. Noble Co.	Noble	A. (and)	J.	Company (The)
Noble and Westbrook, Ltd.	Noble (and)	Westbrook	Limited	
RS Mfg. Co.	R	S	Manufacturing	Company
RCA	Radio	Corporation (of)	America	
Raycraft Industries, Inc.	Raycraft	Industries	Incorporated	
WLW Radio	W	L	W	Radio

NOTE: Spacing between the single letters in a business name is of no significance.

Questions for Discussion

1. Why is it necessary to know your product or service thoroughly?
2. Why should you know something about the kind of person who is to receive the sales letter?
3. What are the three basic stages in writing a good sales letter? Explain.

Office Practice Problem

Criticize the letter at the right. Rewrite it so that it will be a more effective sales letter.

Gentlemen:

We take pleasure in submitting to you photographs of our Spring and Summer buttons for your consideration.

We would like to point out that one of the new trends is the use of heart buttons, and we refer you to the No. 648 in the 10-cent group and No. 520 in the 25-cent group.

May we take this opportunity to thank you for past favors, and we now look forward to the further pleasure to be of service.

For your convenience an order form is enclosed to facilitate your selection.

Yours very truly,

36B—Building Speed in Taking Dictation

Brief-Form Practice

Directions. There are 27 brief forms and brief-form derivatives in the following paragraphs. If you can read the paragraph in 20 seconds, you will be reading at the rate of 147 words a minute.

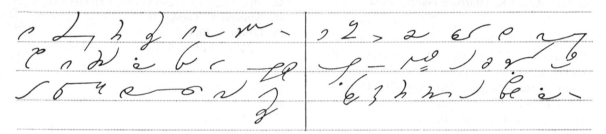

Writing of Numbers

Rule 26: Always spell out a number that begins a sentence. When one number immediately follows another, it is better to spell out the smaller one and to express the larger in figures. When unrelated groups of figures come together, separate them by a comma.

Example: In 1961, 1,283 hats were sold by the department. The top-ranking saleswoman sold an average of ten $5 hats per week. Fifty percent of the hats were sold on a credit basis.

Office Practice Problems

1. Type vertically the numbers 1 to 10. Opposite the number "1" type the letter representing the name that would appear first if the following names were arranged alphabetically. Opposite the number "2" type the letter representing the name that would appear second, and so forth.

a. Hugh Doyle, Jr.
b. Henry J. Durant
c. Dolores DuFrain
d. H. A. Doyle
e. Henry DuFrain, II
f. Hugh Doyle
g. Henry DuFrain
h. Hugh A. Doyle, Jr.
i. Henry DuFrain, III
j. Hugh A. Doyle, Sr.

2. Arrange the following names in alphabetic order, typing each name in transposed (index) order. Underline the letter that determines the position of each name in the list.

a. Mr. George H. Lind
b. Mrs. Walter J. (Alfreda Jones) Linde
c. Mrs. Arlene Linde
d. Mrs. George H. (Zelma Jean) Lind
e. Mrs. Alfred K. (Barbara Hardy) Lind

3. Type vertically the numbers 1 to 10. Opposite the number "1" type the letter representing the name that would appear first if the following names were arranged alphabetically. Opposite the number "2" type the letter representing the name that would appear second, and so forth.

a. A. J. McNeil
b. Martin Phillips
    305 Broad Street, Columbus, Ohio
c. Joseph MacIntosh
d. Jeffrey O'Neil
e. Martin Phillips
    14 Dalton Street, Dayton, Ohio
f. Neil C. McIlroy
g. Martin Phillips
    3210 River Road, Dayton, Kentucky
h. Martin Phillips
    1575 Akron Avenue, Dayton, Ohio
i. Louise Phillips
j. Raymond Oleski

4. In the next column are 40 names. Type each name in transposed order on a 5 by 3 file card. (See the illustration on page 271.) Then, a triple space below, type the name in address order. Type the number representing the name in the upper right-hand corner of the card for that name. When all cards have been typed, arrange them in alphabetic order according to the names.

Prepare an answer sheet similar to the one illustrated on page 271 and submit it to your teacher for checking.

26. Hubert C. LaCrosse
27. Joseph H. NeCamp
28. Miss Maria D'Andrea
29. Armond C. Oleski
30. Professor Charles A. Harlow

31. John Perkins, Portland, Oregon
32. P. D. Porter
33. Mrs. Robert L. (Florence Lee) Madaris
34. Lee Won
35. Mr. Dino Di Luca

36. Robert L. Mackenzie
37. John Perkins, Waurika, Oklahoma
38. Christopher Fitz-Hugh, Jr.
39. Carlos Montoya
40. Dr. Jos. R. Patterson

41. Miss Gladys Jacobson
42. Eduardo El Greco
43. Mrs. Philip G. (Jean Groves) Hanna
44. Armond C. Oleski, II
45. Edwin A. Piper
    2346 Marlow Avenue, Akron, Ohio

46. Father Patrick Fitzgerald
47. Jose A. Noriega, M. D.
48. Mr. Leslie Porter
49. H. W. LeGrande
50. John Perkins, Tulsa, Oklahoma

51. Chester B. Fitz-Hugh
52. Mrs. Elizabeth Lacy
53. Byron W. O'Neil
54. Christopher Fitz-Hugh, Sr.
55. Edwin A. Piper
    1368 Norris Street, Akron, Ohio

56. Robert O. MacKenzie
57. Wm. C. Hanna
58. Mrs. Edward J. (Rosie Lee) Patterson
59. Ted Narleski
60. J. Hugh Jackson

61. John Perkins, Portland, Maine
62. Dr. Arthur E. Kaufman
63. A. J. Oleski
64. John C. Jackson
65. Miss Maureen O'Callahan

5. Combine cards 1-65 into a single alphabetic card file. Prepare an answer sheet and submit it to your teacher for checking. Keep the cards for use in Problem 4, Lesson 111, page 283.

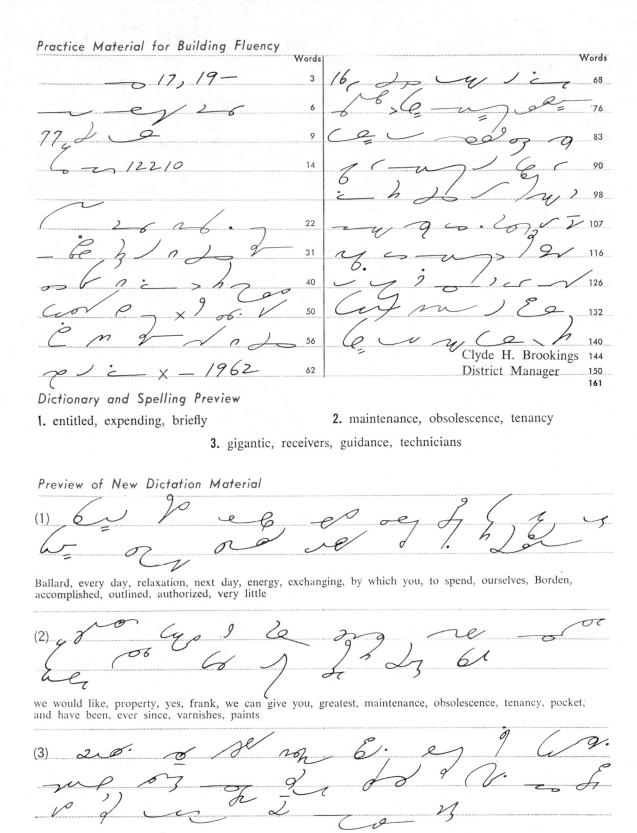

Words

3
6
9
14
22
31
40
50
56
62

68
76
83
90
98
107
116
126
132
140

Clyde H. Brookings 144
District Manager 150
161

Dictionary and Spelling Preview

1. entitled, expending, briefly

2. maintenance, obsolescence, tenancy

3. gigantic, receivers, guidance, technicians

Preview of New Dictation Material

(1)

Ballard, every day, relaxation, next day, energy, exchanging, by which you, to spend, ourselves, Borden, accomplished, outlined, authorized, very little

(2)

we would like, property, yes, frank, we can give you, greatest, maintenance, obsolescence, tenancy, pocket, and have been, ever since, varnishes, paints

(3)

we are writing, quite dissatisfied, unusual, expanding, television, huge, broadcasting, installation, technicians, manpower, facilities, gigantic, devoting, not only, expansion, shortly, supervision, locality, interfere, employment, stations

Alphabetizing Names of Individuals (Concluded)

Guide 5: Identical Personal Names

When the full names of two or more individuals are identical, use addresses, not as indexing units, but as identifying elements (a secondary means of determining alphabetic sequence). In this situation consider the identifying elements in this order: (1) city names, (2) state names, (3) street names, and (4) numeric order of house or building numbers. (The name of the building should not be considered unless the name of the street is not provided.)

Alphabetic Index Order

Names (Natural Order)	Names (Transposed)	UNIT 1	UNIT 2	IDENTIFYING ELEMENT
Dale Johns, Dallas	Johns, Dale (Dallas)	Johns	Dale	(Dallas)
Dale Johns, Houston	Johns, Dale (Houston)	Johns	Dale	(Houston)
Dale Johns, Springfield	Johns, Dale (Springfield)	Johns	Dale	(Springfield)

Edmund R. Watson
321 Grant Street, Philadelphia, Pa. 19113

Edmund R. Watson
7385 Independence Avenue, Philadelphia, Pa. 19149

→ Order is determined by street names, which are third identifying elements in these examples. The city names are the first identifying elements, and the state names are the second.

Guide 6: Seniority Titles in Identical Names

Consider a designation of seniority, such as "Junior" or "Senior," or "II (Second)" or "III (Third)," not as an indexing unit, but as an identifying element for the name (a secondary means of determining alphabetic sequence).

Alphabetic Index Order

Names (Natural Order)	Names (Transposed)	UNIT 1	UNIT 2	IDENTIFYING ELEMENT
David Langston	Langston, David	Langston	David	
David Langston, Jr.	Langston, David (Jr.)	Langston	David	(Junior)
Peter LaPorte, Jr.	LaPorte, Peter (Jr.)	LaPorte	Peter	(Junior)
Peter LaPorte, Sr.	LaPorte, Peter (Sr.)	LaPorte	Peter	(Senior)
Lawrence Larson	Larson, Lawrence	Larson	Lawrence	
Lawrence Larson, II	Larson, Lawrence (II)	Larson	Lawrence	(II)
Lawrence Larson, III	Larson, Lawrence (III)	Larson	Lawrence	(III)

Guide 7: Names of Married Women

Use the legal name of a married woman (if it is known) for filing purposes. (The legal name consists of the given first name and maiden surname with the husband's surname, or the given first and middle names with the husband's surname.) Place "Mrs." in parentheses at the end of the name but do not consider it in filing. Place the husband's name, preceded by "Mrs.," in parentheses below the woman's legal name. Names of married women are cross-referenced as illustrated on page 287.

Alphabetic Index Order

Names (Natural Order)	Names (Transposed)	UNIT 1	UNIT 2	UNIT 3
Mrs. Gary M. (Ruth Gaines) Collins	Collins, Ruth Gaines (Mrs.) (Mrs. Gary M. Collins)	Collins	Ruth	Gaines (Mrs.)
Mrs. H. H. (Mary Chase) Dickens	Dickens, Mary Chase (Mrs.) (Mrs. H. H. Dickens)	Dickens	Mary	Chase (Mrs.)
Mrs. Thomas (Wilma Marie) Dickens	Dickens, Wilma Marie (Mrs.) (Mrs. Thomas Dickens)	Dickens	Wilma	Marie (Mrs.)
Mrs. R. R. (Winona May) Dickens	Dickens, Winona May (Mrs.) (Mrs. R. R. Dickens)	Dickens	Winona	May (Mrs.)

```
                    1429 Western Boulevard
                    Los Angeles, California  90024
                    April 25, 19--


Miss Helen T. O'Neal, Manager
Employee Relations Department
Hanover Insurance Company
3460 Wilshire Boulevard
Los Angeles, California  90014

Dear Miss O'Neal:

     Miss Roland, head of the Business Department in our high
school, has suggested that I might qualify for the secretarial
position that is vacant in your department.  I should like to
be considered an applicant.

     Next month I shall be graduated from Rawley High School.
So far in my work I have earned an overall average of "B."
I am completing the secretarial training program.  For the past
three summers, I have worked in the offices of Lee and Healy.
As a substitute for various employees who were on their vaca-
tions, I have gained experience in several different kinds of
office work, including typing reports from rough draft, taking
dictation and transcribing, filing, and operating calculators.
Last summer I served as a receptionist for three weeks, which
gave me some practice in handling callers and telephone calls.

     The enclosed data sheet gives detailed information about
me and my qualifications.  I should be glad to come to your
office for a personal interview.  My telephone number is
925-6207.

                    Sincerely yours,

                    Josephine C. Bayliss

                    Josephine C. Bayliss

Enclosure
```

Letter of Application

```
                    JOSEPHINE C. BAYLISS

PERSONAL

    Address:  1429 Western Boulevard, Los Angeles, California  90024
    Telephone:  925-6207
    Age:  18
    Date and Place of Birth:  May 11, 1946, Des Moines, Iowa
    Height:  5 feet 4 inches
    Weight:  116 pounds
    Nationality:  American
    Physical Defects:  None

EDUCATION

    Will graduate May, 1964, from Rawley High School, Los Angeles

    Dictation Rate:  100 words a minute
    Transcribing Rate:  30 words a minute
    Straight-Copy Typing Rate:  70 words a minute

    Skilled in Operating:  Key-driven calculator, mimeograph, and
                           ten-key adding-listing machine

EXPERIENCE

    Three summers, substitute employee, offices of Lee and Healy

    Editor of Rawley Hi, school paper, senior year

    Student assistant for principal, junior and senior years

REFERENCES

    Mr. O. P. Grant, Treasurer; Lee and Healy; 6934 Columbia
        Parkway; Los Angeles, California  90020; 981-6423

    Mr. Donald F. Burns, Principal; Rawley High School; 4632
        Ferguson Road, Los Angeles, California  90020; 421-5981

    Miss Angeline T. Roland, Head; Business Department;
        Rawley High School; 4632 Ferguson Road; Los Angeles,
        California  90020; 421-5981
```

Data Sheet

Unit **8**

Lesson **37** ◇○◇○⬡○◇○⬡○◇○⬡○◇○◇○⬡○◇○⬡○◇○◇○

37A—Application Letters, Data Sheets, and Follow-Up Letters

A letter of application is, in a sense, a sales letter, for you are trying to "sell" your abilities to some businessman or firm. You remember that to write a good sales letter you must know your product thoroughly and know the type of person whom you are trying to interest in your product. The same thing is true in writing a good application letter. You must know what you have to offer, and you must know what firms can use the type of abilities you have. Keep the following points in mind:

1. Give careful attention to the appearance of your letter. Your letter is *you*. It must be neat and attractive in appearance. A carefully prepared typewritten letter is best. There must be no typographical errors, and the typed material must be well arranged on the page. Be sure to include your address in the heading, and be sure to sign the letter.

2. Explain how you learned of the position. You may have heard about the opening from an advertisement in the newspaper, from a friend, or from a teacher, for instance. Indicate the source of your information, then state definitely that you are applying for the position.

3. Give your understanding of the nature of the position. Your knowledge may be only general, but state what you understand to be the requirements or the nature of the work that you would be expected to do.

Office Practice Problems

1. Type vertically the numbers 1 to 10. Opposite the number "1" type the letter representing the name that would appear first if the following names were arranged alphabetically. Opposite the number "2" type the letter representing the name that would appear second, and so forth.

a. Meyers	**f.** Mier
b. Meiers	**g.** Meyer
c. Miers	**h.** Miele
d. Mieth	**i.** Miesert
e. Meier	**j.** Mielke

2. Arrange the following names in correct alphabetic order, typing each name in transposed indexing order. Underline the letter that determines the position of each name in the list.

a. Kay L. Miller	**f.** John E. Miller
b. A. J. Miller	**g.** Robert Evan Milar
c. Robert E. Milar	**h.** Arnold J. Miller
d. John Jay Miller	**i.** Ruth Ann Millar
e. Nelson Millar	**j.** John Eric Miller

3. Study the following illustration of a correctly typed file card. Note that the name is typed in transposed order a double space from the top and three spaces from the left edge of the card. The name is repeated in address order a triple space below. The number representing the name is typed in the upper right-hand corner of the card.

```
┌─────────────────────────────────┬─────┐
│  McKinley, Norma Jean (Miss)     │  1  │
│                                  │     │
│  Miss Norma Jean McKinley        │     │
│  412 North Plainville Road       │     │
│  Veneta, Oklahoma  97487         │     │
│                                  │     │
└─────────────────────────────────┴─────┘
```

Properly Typed File Card

At the top of the next column are 25 names. Type each name in transposed order on a 5 by 3 file card. Then, a triple space below, type the name in address order. Type the number representing the name in the upper right-hand corner of the card for that name. When all cards have been typed, arrange them in alphabetic order according to the names.

1. Miss Clara Jean MacAuley
2. Miss Helen Lamar
3. Virgil Lambert, D. D.
4. Professor Keith V. Odell
5. Father Michael
6. Mrs. Anita L. LaMay
7. Bob MacAuley-Ames
8. Benjamin Wright
9. Kevin G. McCarthy
10. Sister Bernadette Marie
11. Paul Lewis LeMasters
12. Miss Frances VanDeren
13. Miss Margaret O'Connell
14. Albert Patrick Macauley
15. William VonderStrasse
16. Dr. Edward St. Francis
17. Mr. Wing Chou
18. Mrs. Roberta VanDam
19. Mr. Evelyn McCarty
20. James Vanderbilt
21. Mr. Marion O'Dea
22. Kenneth Mayfield
23. Miss Alice St. John
24. Edwin R. McCarthy
25. Dick Lamar

Prepare an answer sheet similar to the one shown below. List on the answer sheet the numbers of the cards in the order in which you have them arranged. Submit this answer sheet to your teacher for checking. Save the 25 cards for use in Problem 5, Lesson 107, page 273.

```
┌──────────────────────────────────────────────┐
│  STUDENT'S NAME  Bleier, Barbara               │
│  DATE       2/14/--                            │
│  LESSON NO.    106    PROBLEM NO.              │
│                                                │
│   1.  17        9.          17.                │
│   2.   5       10.          18.                │
│   3.           11.          19.                │
│   4.           12.          20.                │
│   5.           13.          21.                │
│   6.           14.          22.                │
│   7.           15.          23.                │
│   8.           16.          24.                │
│                             25.                │
│                                                │
└──────────────────────────────────────────────┘
```

Sample Answer Sheet

4. Show how you are equipped for the position. Give specific information regarding your education, training in school, and experience. If you use a data sheet (described below and illustrated on page 104), you will limit this discussion in your letter to certain facts that you think would appeal particularly to the employer. You might want to tell something of your part-time work experience, for example.

5. List references. Give the name and address of at least three people who can tell something of your ability or personality. *Be sure* you have obtained permission to use their names.

6. Request an interview. It is well to close your letter with an expression of willingness to come for an interview. Indicate how you can be reached—telephone number or mail address.

7. Enclose a recent photograph. It is a good idea to enclose a recent photograph, attached to the data sheet if you use one; otherwise, attach it to your letter. On the back of the photograph write your name and the date on which the photograph was taken.

8. Be accurate and thoughtful in your statements. Your application papers will become part of your personnel record after you are employed.

A data sheet is an excellent way to present details of yourself, your education, experience, etc. The data should be so organized that it can be read easily. If a data sheet is used, the letter accompanying it should discuss only points you wish to emphasize—points of interest that would catch the employer's attention, points other candidates might not have to offer.

Some firms have printed application forms for an applicant to fill in. In filling in such a form, be sure to give information in every blank. If you have no information for some blank, indicate that fact by a dash or by some appropriate word such as "None." Do not leave it blank, for then the reader does not know whether you have no information for that point or whether you overlooked it.

If you have not heard from the company within a week or ten days, you may write a follow-up letter. In this letter you may express continued interest in the position and offer to supply additional information if it is needed.

When you accept a position with one firm, you should write a letter to any other firm with which you have filed an application asking them to remove your name from their active files because you have accepted another position.

Printed Application Form

Questions for Discussion

1. Why is the appearance of an application letter so important?
2. What points should be covered in a letter of application?
3. What is a data sheet? How does a letter that accompanies it differ from an application letter that does not have a data sheet attached?
4. What topics should be discussed in an application letter?

Office Practice Problem

Criticize the following letter of application. Rewrite it if your teacher so directs.

Dear Mr. Abott:

I would like to apply for the secretarial position that you have open. I heard about it through the newspaper.
I think I can fulfill the requirements for the job, as I can take shorthand at 90 words a minute and can type very accurately.
Some more of my qualifications that will help me perform the job are listed on the enclosed data sheet.
The people who will be glad to give me a reference are listed on the data sheet also.
In school I am always on time for all my classes, and my grades are always above average.
By the enclosed photograph, you can see that I always am well-groomed and try to dress in accordance with business.
I can come for an interview at any time that is convenient for you.
Sincerely yours,

Guide 2: Surname Particles or Prefixes

Consider a surname particle (sometimes called "prefix") as part of the surname, not as a separate indexing unit. Among the common particles are: *D', Da, De, Del, Des, Di, Du, Fitz, La, Le, Mac, Mc, O', Van, Vander, Van der, Von, Vonder, Von der.* In some cases the first letter of a particle is not capitalized, but this has no significance in indexing the names.

		Alphabetic Index Order		
Names (Natural Order)	**Names (Transposed)**	UNIT 1	UNIT 2	UNIT 3
Mario D'Allesandro	D'Allesandro, Mario	D'Allesandro	Mario	
Shirley Ann Dalton	Dalton, Shirley Ann	Dalton	Shirley	Ann
Antonio de la Luz [1]	de la Luz, Antonio	delaLuz	Antonio	
Lisa Marie DeLancy	DeLancy, Lisa Marie	DeLancy	Lisa	Marie
Joseph Delaney	Delaney, Joseph	Delaney	Joseph	
Gerald Mark DelGrossa	DelGrossa, Gerald Mark	DelGrossa	Gerald	Mark
Richard DuBois	DuBois, Richard	DuBois	Richard	
Albert Duboise	Duboise, Albert	Duboise	Albert	

NOTE 1: Ignore the spacing between the particle and its stem (the surname), as it is not significant, and index the particle exactly as it is spelled.

Guide 3: Initials and Abbreviations

a. Consider an initial in an individual's name as an indexing unit. Within the same unit an initial precedes all names beginning with the same letter as the initial.

b. Consider an abbreviated first or middle name or a nickname as if it were spelled in full if the full name is known. Briefed names or what seem to be nicknames, however, are often the full given names; when thus used, they must be indexed as written.

		Alphabetic Index Order		
Names (Natural Order)	**Names (Transposed)**	UNIT 1	UNIT 2	UNIT 3
J. D. Roberts	Roberts, J. D.	Roberts	J.	D.
John A. Roberts	Roberts, John A.	Roberts	John	A.
Donald J. Robertson	Robertson, Donald J.	Robertson	Donald	J.
"Dick" Robertson	Robertson, "Dick"	Robertson	Richard ("Dick")	
Chas. Robinson	Robinson, Chas.	Robinson	Charles	
Charles A. Robinson	Robinson, Charles A.	Robinson	Charles	A.
Terry B. Robinson	Robinson, Terry B.	Robinson	Terry	B.

Guide 4: Titles

a. As a general rule, do not consider a personal or professional title (such as *Miss, Mr., Dr.,* or *Professor*) or a degree (such as *Ph.D., D.D.,* or *LL.D.*) in determining the alphabetic order of names. Write such a title in parentheses at the end of the name for identification purposes.

b. Index as written a name consisting of a personal or professional title or a title of royalty followed by a given name only.

c. Index as written a religious title (such as *Father, Brother,* or *Sister*) followed by one or more given names. (A religious title is not considered in filing if it precedes a name that includes a surname; however, it is retained in parentheses for identification purposes.)

		Alphabetic Index Order		
Names (Natural Order)	**Names (Transposed)**	UNIT 1	UNIT 2	UNIT 3
Father James Davis	Davis, James (Father)	Davis	James (Father)	
Father John	Father John	Father	John	
Dr. Kenneth Flanders	Flanders, Kenneth (Dr.)	Flanders	Kenneth (Dr.)	
Martin E. Kendall, D.D.	Kendall, Martin E. (D.D.)	Kendall	Martin	E. (D.D.)
Professor A. J. Marlow	Marlow, A. J. (Professor)	Marlow	A.	J. (Professor)
Mr. Edward O'Malley	O'Malley, Edward (Mr.)	O'Malley	Edward (Mr.)	
Mrs. Eva O'Malley	O'Malley, Eva (Mrs.)	O'Malley	Eva (Mrs.)	
Miss Evelyn O'Malley	O'Malley, Evelyn (Miss)	O'Malley	Evelyn (Miss)	
Princess Margaret	Princess Margaret	Princess	Margaret	
Sister Andrea	Sister Andrea	Sister	Andrea	
Sister Marion Marie	Sister Marion Marie	Sister	Marion	Marie
Sister Mary Margaret	Sister Mary Margaret	Sister	Mary	Margaret

Phrase Builder

There are 11 phrases in the following paragraph.

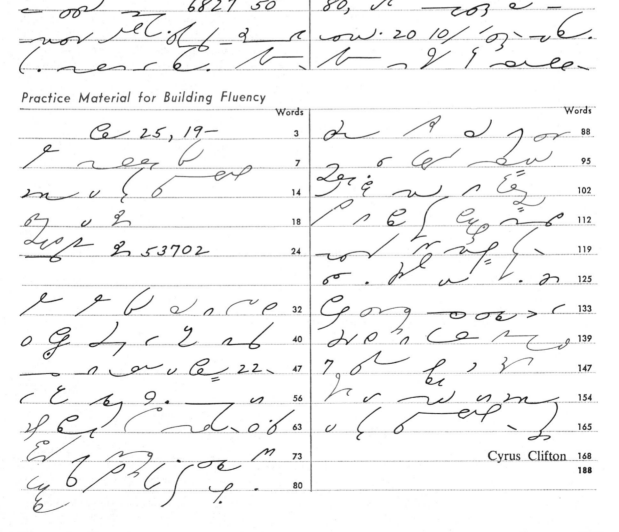

Punctuation Preview

Rule 27: Capitalize only the names of specific departments.

Example: Our Sales Department reports a 10 percent increase in sales during the past month. Any sales department would be proud of that record.

NOTE: The following material requires the application of Rule 26, as well as Rule 27.

Practice Material for Building Fluency

	Words		Words
	3		88
	7		95
	14		102
	18		112
	24		119
			125
	32		133
	40		139
	47		147
	56		154
	63		165
	73	Cyrus Clifton	168
	80		188

Guides for Alphabetic Indexing and Filing

Lesson **106** ◇◯◇◯◇◯◇◯◇◯◇◯◇◯◇◯◇◯◇◯◇◯◇

Alphabetizing Names of Individuals

The alphabetizing of names is simply the process of arranging names in A-to-Z sequence. The telephone directory and the dictionary are examples of this process.

The name "Allen" is listed before "Barton" in an alphabetic arrangement because the first letters in the two names are different. "Barton" is listed before "Beckman" because the second letters in the two names are different. These examples are illustrations of the basic alphabetizing rule that *the first letter that is different in any two names in an alphabetic arrangement is the letter that determines the order of the names.* To apply this rule, however, two preliminary steps must be taken:

Step 1: Determine what makes up each part, or *unit*, of the name. For example, the alphabetic order of the names "DeAngelo" and "Dean" depends upon whether the particle "De" is considered to be a separate unit of the name or if it is considered to be a part of the surname. In filing practice a surname particle or prefix is considered to be an inseparable part of the surname; therefore, "Dean" comes before "DeAngelo" in an alphabetic arrangement.

Step 2: Determine the index order of the units of each name. The *index order* is the order in which the units of the name should be considered for alphabetizing. The position of the names "Alan Young" and "Robert Bell" in an alphabetic list depends upon whether the first or the last names are considered first. Since the last name (the surname) is the more important, it is considered first in filing. The name "Robert Bell" therefore appears first in the list.

The purpose of the following guides is to help you determine what makes up each unit in a variety of names and the index order of those units. They are, therefore, often called "indexing and filing" rules. Their consistent use will make filing and finding easier.

Guide 1: Order of Indexing Units

Each part of an individual's name is an indexing unit. To determine the alphabetic order of names of individuals, consider the parts in this order: (1) surname or last name, (2) first name, (3) middle name.

a. Determine the alphabetic order of the names of individuals by the surnames alone when those names differ in spelling.

b. When the surnames of individuals are alike, determine the alphabetic order of the names of those individuals by first names.

c. When the first names as well as the surnames are alike, determine the alphabetic order by middle names.

In each example the underline indicates the letter of the unit that determines the alphabetic sequence.

Alphabetic Index Order

Names (Natural Order)	Names (Transposed)	UNIT 1	UNIT 2	UNIT 3
Lloyd Johnsen	Johnsen, Lloyd	Johnsen	Lloyd	
Albert Johnson	Johnson, Albert	Johns<u>o</u>n	Albert	
Alexander Kennedy	Kennedy, Alexander	<u>K</u>ennedy	Alexander	
Arthur Kennedy	Kennedy, Arthur	Kennedy	A<u>r</u>thur	
John Kennedy	Kennedy, John	Kennedy	<u>J</u>ohn	
John Edward Kennedy	Kennedy, John Edward	Kennedy	John	<u>E</u>dward
Alan Jay Kent	Kent, Alan Jay	Ken<u>t</u>	Alan	Jay
Kosho Oshiro [1]	Oshiro, Kosho	<u>O</u>shiro	Kosho	
Evan Rynn-Davis [2]	Rynn-Davis, Evan	<u>R</u>ynn-	Davis	Evan
Roy St. John [3]	St. John, Roy	<u>S</u>aint	John	Roy

NOTE 1: When it is difficult or impossible to decide which part of a name (such as *Kosho Oshiro*) is the surname, consider the last part of the name as written to be the surname.

NOTE 2: Hyphened (compound) surnames, such as *Rynn-Davis,* are unusual. When they do occur in filing, disregard the hyphen and consider each word as a separate indexing unit.

NOTE 3: In a compound surname such as *St. John,* consider "St." to be the first indexing unit (in spelled-out form) and "John" to be the second unit.

Dictionary and Spelling Preview

1. dissertation, professorship

2. reluctance, grateful, sabbatical, morale

Preview of New Dictation Material

(1) [shorthand outlines]

faculty, regulation, I shall be, references, Administration, candidate, wife, advancement, University, dissertation, professorship, session, very much

(2) [shorthand outlines]

reluctance, sabbatical, in view, institution, officials, to become, upon his

(3) [shorthand outlines]

furthermore, graduates, desperate

Lesson **38** ⬡⬡⬡⬡⬡⬡⬡⬡⬡⬡⬡⬡⬡⬡⬡⬡⬡⬡⬡

38A—Letters of Recommendation and Introduction

You will probably not need to write letters of recommendation or introduction until you have been in the business world for some time. However, it is well for you to know now what they are like, since some may be written about you when you are trying to obtain a position.

A letter of recommendation is a letter in which the writer tells what he knows about you that might help the employer decide whether you are qualified for the position for which you have applied.

A general letter of recommendation (one which usually begins "To Whom It May Concern") is not of much value; it does not carry much weight, especially if carried by the applicant. A recommendation sent directly to a specific employer by the person making the recommendation is likely to be read more carefully and given more consideration.

A letter of recommendation usually discusses personal qualities of the person being recommended about which the prospective employer might like to know—promptness, dependability, initiative, etc., as judged by the writer. Your teacher, for example, might be able to say that she believes you would be prompt in getting to work because you are never late to class. She might say that she thinks you would be a dependable employee because you always hand in your assignments neatly and completely done when due. She might indicate that you assumed full responsibility for the advertising for the class play, thus proving that you have initiative.

A letter of recommendation is considered confidential, and the person who is being recommended does not see the letter—and should never ask to see it. A letter of recommendation is shown on page 108.

Transcribe the following letter (modified block style with blocked paragraphs and with the date ending even with the right margin; mixed punctuation) as a 5-minute writing. Determine your *mwam*. Compare this rate with your *mwam* rate on the plate notes transcribed in Lesson 101. If you complete the letter before time is called, start again from the beginning.

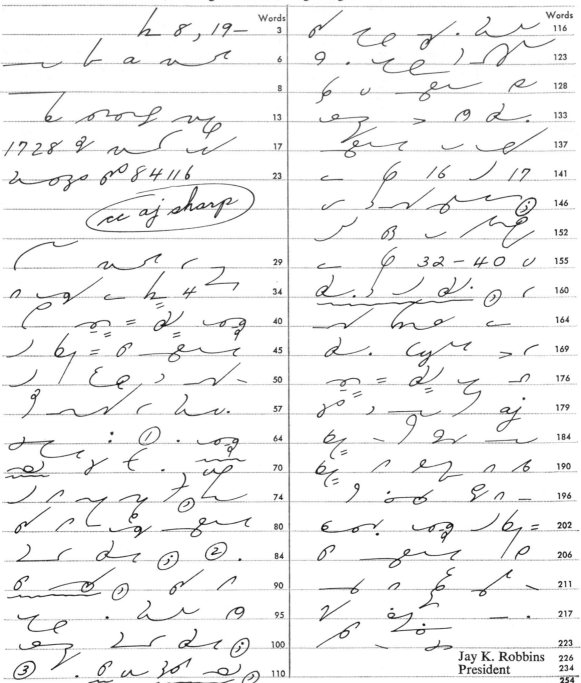

105C—Transcribing from Dictation

Your teacher will dictate Letters (1) and (2) to you for transcription. Do not use the company name in the closing lines. Prepare the letters for the signature of Jay K. Robbins, President.

Dear Dean Wright:

First of all, I want you to know that Ken Danby is one of my good personal friends. We shared an office at the Alabama State College when we were working on our doctorates. Our families are close friends. We exchange visits every summer. I am telling you this for two reasons: first, so that you will know that I am biased in his favor; and second, so that you will know that I think well of him and his family.

Ken's character is excellent. He is honest, active in civic affairs, and a member of the Methodist Church.

If I were in a position of hiring faculty, I should be glad to have him as a member of my staff.

Sincerely yours,

Letter of Recommendation

A letter of introduction is a letter that serves to introduce you to someone you have never met. Perhaps you are going to work in a town some distance from your home town, and you know no one there. Your teacher or your minister or a business friend of your family might give you a letter of introduction to someone he knows in the town to which you are going. You present this letter to the addressee, and that person may help you meet other people in that town or in some way help you "get settled."

Such a letter usually introduces the individual by telling who he is, what his line of business and interests are, some facts about the individual, and expresses appreciation for any courtesies that may be extended.

The person who carries the letter of introduction should present it as soon as practicable after arriving in town. He should be appreciative of any efforts of the individual to whom he presents the letter, but he should not expect that person to

look after him and devote a lot of time to him. The responsibility for adjustment to living in a new town belongs to the person who goes there. Care must be taken not to impose on someone because of a letter of introduction.

Dear Mr. Bryant:

The bearer of this letter, Frank Proctor, is a close friend of our family. He has accepted a position with Cyerson's, Inc., in your city.

Mr. Proctor was graduated from our local high school in June, where he was an outstanding student. He has been an active member of the young people's groups in the Baptist Church. He was an assistant Boy Scout leader during his senior year.

Mr. Proctor will, I am sure, be an asset to your community.

Cordially yours,

Letter of Introduction

Questions for Discussion

1. What is a letter of recommendation? Whom might you ask to write one for you?
2. What is a general letter of recommendation?
3. Name some topics that might be covered in a letter of recommendation.
4. What is the purpose of a letter of introduction?
5. Who might write one for you?

Office Practice Problems

1. Write a letter of recommendation for one of your classmates, assuming that he is applying for a job in a local business firm.
2. Write a letter of introduction for a friend of yours, assuming she is going to a town where you have a close friend living.

38B—Building Speed in Taking Dictation

Potential Rate Builder

There are 11 words in the sentence.

Follow-Up Methods. The nature of the material borrowed and the policy of the company determine how long papers may be retained by the borrower. In any case, a definite schedule must be followed in checking charge-outs and in locating papers that have been kept out longer than the allowed time.

If the filing department is small, it is easy for the file clerk to check the due dates of the borrowed materials on the requisition cards or out sheets in the files. If the department is large, however, it is simpler to use a follow-up or tickler file like that illustrated on page 266. Note that the file consists of a guide for each month and for each day of the month. The current month guide is always placed in front, and the day guides are arranged in chronological order behind the current month only.

When a tickler file is used, a duplicate is made of the requisition card or out sheet, and the duplicate is filed in the tickler according to the date on which the borrowed material is due to be returned. The tickler is checked each day to see what materials are due back in the filing department, and the borrower is notified. If the materials are still needed, the due date may be extended; otherwise, the materials are returned.

When borrowed materials are returned, the charge against the borrower must be canceled. This is done by removing the out guide or substitution card from the files and destroying the requisition card held in the pocket of the guide or card. The tickler-file copy of the requisition is also removed and destroyed.

A special situation arises when the original borrower of filed material transfers it to someone else in the office for attention. When this is done, a *transfer slip* is sent to the filing department to indicate to whom the material has been transferred. This information is then noted on the requisition card in the filing department so that the correct charge appears there.

Questions for Discussion

1. Name the four basic systems for filing business papers and give the distinguishing characteristics of each.
2. What basic knowledges and skills must a secretary possess in order to file proficiently?
3. What is the function of each of the following filing materials:

   a. Primary guide
   b. Auxiliary or special guide
   c. Individual folder.
   d. Special folder
   e. Miscellaneous folder
   f. Cross-reference sheet
   g. Requisition card

   h. Tickler file
   i. Out guide
   j. Out folder
   k. Carrier folder
   l. Out or substitution card
   m. Out sheet
   n. Transfer slip

4. What is the purpose of special systems for requesting, charging out, and following up filed materials?
5. How can a piece of correspondence that is to be released for filing be coded to indicate that it will be needed on a definite future date?
6. What kinds of information are given on a requisition card?
7. How may a charge for filed materials be canceled by the filing department?
8. Why is it essential to send a transfer slip to the filing department when borrowed material is transferred to someone else?

Office Practice Problem

The following incoming letter is ready to be filed. As a check on your understanding of filing procedure and terminology, answer the questions given below the letter.

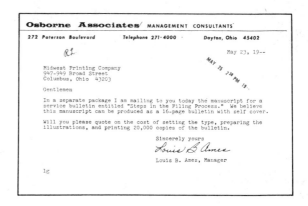

1. What is the name on the label of the individual folder in which you would file this letter?

2. Which of the two dates shown on the letter would you use in placing the letter in the file folder?

3. What are the initials of the person who released the letter for filing?

4. What is the first word you would consider in finding the folder in which this letter should be placed?

Punctuation Preview

Rule 28: Hyphenate compound numerals from 21 to 99 when written out.

Example: `About twenty-five complaints were filed yesterday.`

NOTE: Rules 26 and 27 need to be applied in the following material, as well as Rule 28.

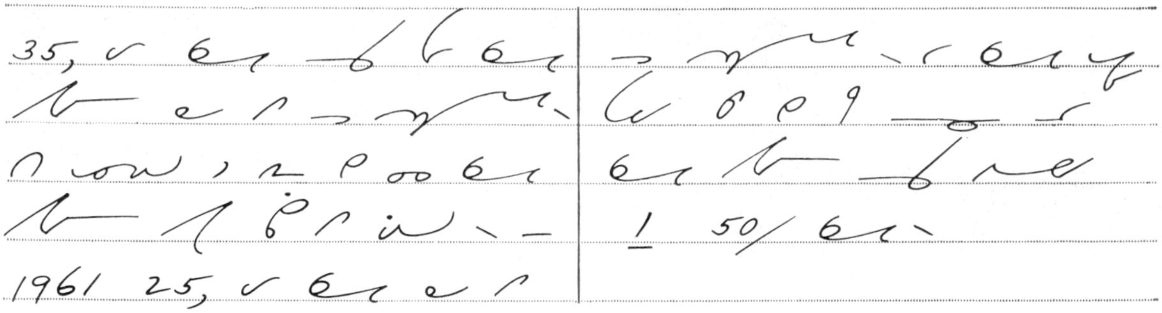

Practice Material for Building Fluency

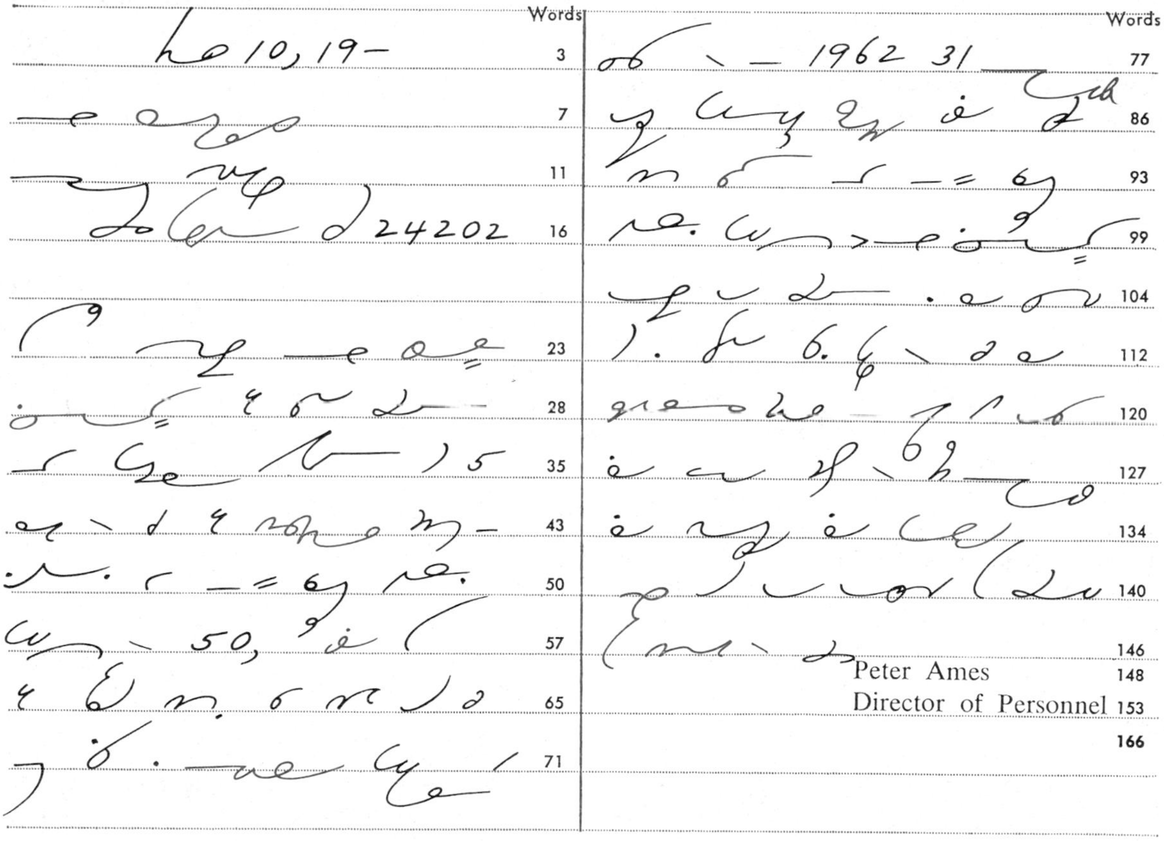
Words
3
7
11
16
23
28
35
43
50
57
65
71
Words
77
86
93
99
104
112
120
127
134
140
146
Peter Ames 148
Director of Personnel 153
166

Dictionary and Spelling Preview

1. initiative, derogatory, definitely
2. cordially, intellectual, aloof
3. pursuing, dissertation, facilities
4. handicapped, thorough, barrier

Requisition Card Tickler

Out Guide

Charge Methods.

Charge Methods. The methods used for charging out filed materials differ from office to office and according to the nature of the request. Two types of requests are frequently made: (1) for the entire contents of a folder and (2) for a single paper from a folder.

Folder Requests. Ordinarily when a request for filed materials is received in the filing department, the folder with its entire contents is removed from the files and in its place is inserted a marker known as an *out guide.* An out guide is a pressboard guide on the tab of which is printed the word "Out." This tab is visible when the guide is placed in the file drawer. One type of out guide has on the front near the top a pocket into which is inserted the requisition card showing the name on the tab of the folder, the name of the borrower, the date of the request, and the date the folder is due to be returned to the files. Another type, called a *cumulative out guide,* provides on the front a form for recording this same information for a series of borrowers. It thus provides a history of how the records have been used and by whom.

In some offices an *out folder* is used to replace a borrowed folder of material. It serves the same purpose as the out guide and, in addition, provides a place for filing any new papers that arrive while the original folder is on loan.

In still other offices the contents of a requested folder are placed in a *carrier folder* and sent to the borrower while the original folder remains in the files.

Single-Paper Requests. When the request is for a single paper or for only part of the contents of a folder, an *out* or *substitution card* or an *out sheet* may be used to show to whom the material is charged.

An *out* or *substitution card* (illustrated below) is similar to an out guide, but it is designed to be placed inside the folder to replace the material that is removed. It may have a pocket for inserting a requisition card or it may provide a cumulative record form to show a history of the requests for specific papers.

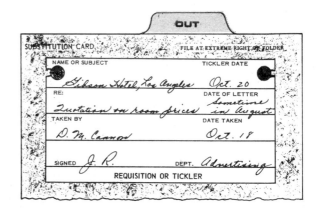

Out or Substitution Card

The procedure for the *out-sheet* method is much the same as that for the card-requisition method. A request for filed material is made on an out-sheet form which shows the same general kind of information as that included on the requisition card. When the requested material is removed from the folder, this sheet is placed in the folder to substitute and charge for the material that is removed. If an out folder is substituted for the original folder, the out sheet is placed in the out folder.

Preview of New Dictation Material

(1)

Rathbone, South Carolina, I have known, attitude, sincerity, derogatory, shortcomings, commendable, initiative, reliability, unknown, to me

(2)

cordially, earned, economics, intellectual, honesty, aloof, Stanford, scholar, exceptionally, classified, brilliant, atmosphere

(3)

bearer, of this letter, pursuing, we do not have, adequate, trustworthy, it has been, graduate, engaged, research, assistance, dissertation, I hope that

(4)

Lincoln, handicapped, unproductive, industrious, conservation, ambition, agricultural, nationality, barrier, endeavor, to consult, striking, thorough

Lesson **39** ⬡⬡⬡⬡⬡⬡⬡⬡⬡⬡⬡⬡⬡⬡⬡⬡⬡

39A—Letters of Notification, Invitation, and Confirmation

Letters of notification are letters that inform a person of (a) his appointment or election to an office or committee, (b) his employment with a firm, (c) a meeting that he is expected to attend, or some similar point. Care should be taken in writing this kind of letter to give all the pertinent facts. In the case of an appointment, the specific position should be given, an indication of the responsibility involved in it should be made, and an expression of the honor that has been bestowed should be included.

Dear Mr. Grissom:

On Tuesday evening at 7:30, August 3, the California Merchant Plumbers will meet in Mr. K. S. Brady's office at 513 North Sixth Avenue for their regular monthly meeting.

Matters of great importance will be discussed at this meeting; you will want to make every effort to attend. If you cannot be with us, will you please let me know as soon as possible.

Yours very respectfully,

Letter of Notification

Questions for Discussion

1. Why should all incoming correspondence be time stamped to indicate the date and time it was opened by the mail clerk?
2. Some offices follow the practice of coding in red the name that is to be the basis for filing and of coding in black the name to be used for the cross-reference. What is the purpose of using different colors?
3. Why should a specific position, such as the upper left-hand corner, be used for the initials of the person releasing the correspondence for filing?
4. Why is the date of the item being cross-referenced given on the cross-reference sheet in the illustration?
5. Why is the name Records Management Association shown first on the cross-reference sheet, rather than *Filing Forum*?

104B—Transcribing from Dictation

Your teacher will dictate to you for transcription a letter and an interoffice memorandum. The letter is to be signed by A. C. Rippey, Sales Assistant, Quick-Find Filing Systems, Inc. If you transcribe the letter and the memorandum before time is called, repeat the transcription of the letter.

Office Practice Problem

Prepare in typewritten form a cross-reference sheet blank similar to the one in the illustration on page 264. Using the information given below, fill in the necessary data.

a. The cross-reference was authorized by Jean Jones on May 18, 19—.
b. The original letter was prepared on the letterhead of *The Balance Sheet* published by South-Western Publishing Company.
c. The date of the original letter is May 15, 19—.
d. The letter outlines the policy of the magazine in not accepting product advertisements since it is a service magazine, not a subscription magazine.

Lesson 105 ◇ ◇ ◇ ◇ ◇ ◇ ◇ ◇ ◇ ◇ ◇ ◇ ◇ ◇ ◇ ◇ ◇

105A—Basic Correspondence Filing Procedures

Systematically placing materials in the files is only a means to an end. The real purpose of filing is the quick finding of filed materials when they are needed. It is, therefore, necessary to be equally systematic in requesting material from the files, in charging the material accurately to the one who requests it, and in following up to see that the material is returned promptly and restored to the appropriate place in the files. To aid in this work, special requisition, charge-out, and follow-up methods have been devised.

Requisition Methods. The secretary can request material from the filing department in either of two ways. In some offices she uses a *requisition card*, similar to the one illustrated at the right, which provides space to identify the material requested and the person making the request, and to note the date of the request and the date on which the material is to be delivered. In other offices she requests material by telephone or in person. In this case the requisition card is made out by someone in the filing department.

Date Due *Feb. 25, 19--* Charge Date *Feb. 23, 19--*
MATERIAL REQUESTED FROM FILES
Name or Subject *Johnson & Smith, Inc.*
Address *Detroit, Michigan*
Date of Material *January 27, 19--*
Regarding *Error in Jan. invoice*
Requested by
Name *Gerald S. Lang*
Department *Accounting* Date of Request *Feb. 23, 19--*

Requisition Card

Sometimes it is known when the material is coded and released for filing that it will be needed again on a certain date. This information can be noted on the material itself by using one of the following codes: "Follow-Up," "Pending," or "Tickler" with the date when the material is again desired. When the file clerk sees such a notation, she makes out the requisition card and places it in a *tickler* or *follow-up file* similar to the one illustrated on page 266.

Dear Mr. Gale:

I am delighted to inform you that you have been elected to membership in the Transcription Supervisors' Association of Delaware.

We are looking forward to greeting you Wednesday, July 11, at 6 p.m. at the L. & K. Restaurant at 61 Seventh Avenue, for our regular monthly meeting.

Sincerely yours,

Dear Miss Wendt:

After a very thorough study of your application, I regret that we do not have a vacancy at this time in which we can utilize your particular skills and training.

I want you to know, however, that we greatly appreciate the interest you have shown in our Company.

Yours truly,

Letters of Notification

Letters of invitation may be of several different types. The invitation may be to attend or participate as a speaker in a meeting or conference to be held. It may be to attend a purely social affair. The invitation might be to join an organization; it might be to utilize the services of a business firm.

Such letters must include all essential facts—what, who, when, where. If participation is requested, the exact nature of the performance wanted must be explained in order that the recipient of the invitation will know what he is accepting or rejecting.

Dear Mr. Leyburn:

Thank you for your letter of August 10, inviting me to attend the meeting of the Taxation Committee in Denver on October 5. I am making plans to attend.

Do you have information about the entire program and the procedure for reserving hotel rooms? I shall appreciate any information you can give me.

Yours very truly,

Dear Mr. Wertz:

How about having lunch with me Wednesday, May 5? I expect to be in St. Louis that day and should enjoy very much having an opportunity to talk with you.

I'll call your office early Wednesday morning to see whether you can join me and to select the time and place.

Cordially yours,

Letters of Invitation and Response

Letters of confirmation notify a person that certain arrangements have been made or that certain action has been taken. Confirmation letters commonly used are ones sent by hotels regarding reservations. Frequently this type of confirmation is sent in card form. Some business firms send a letter of confirmation of a telephone call or of a telegram. A confirmation of a telephone call puts in writing the agreements reached orally so that they become a matter of record. A letter confirming a telegram usually contains a restatement of the telegraph message and a further explanation of some aspect of the transaction involved.

Dear Miss Reynolds.

We are pleased to confirm your reservation for a single room at the Grande Hotel on February 20.

Please notify us if you expect to arrive late, since reservations are not held later than 6 p.m. unless we have been notified.

We shall look forward to having you as our guest, and we will do our best to make your stay a pleasant one.

Sincerely,

Dear Mr. Bernhard:

This letter will confirm the agreement we reached in our telephone conversation this morning. We shall ship the 150 yards of Green DX-140 this afternoon by express collect.

As I mentioned to you, this color is slightly different from the Green DY-140 you have been using; but I think you will find it even more suitable for your purposes.

Sincerely yours,

Letters of Confirmation

Questions for Discussion

1. List some types of notifications that might be sent by letter.
2. What are some important points to be included in a letter of invitation?
3. What are letters of confirmation?
4. Why might a letter confirming a telegram be desirable?

Office Practice Problems

Write the following letters:

1. To a businessman inviting him to speak at your assembly next Wednesday at 10 a.m.
2. To the Southland Jazz Band confirming a tentative agreement to play for the Junior-Senior Prom on May 10 from 8 to 11 p.m.
3. To a teacher informing him that he has been chosen sponsor of the class for the current year.

the item (1) writes that name in the margin of the correspondence, or if the name appears in the item, underlines it and writes an "x" in the margin, and (2) prepares a *cross-reference sheet* to be filed under that name.

Cross-referencing permits the original correspondence to be filed where most persons are likely to look for it. At the same time, the cross-reference sheet, filed according to another name or subject, refers the person to the original correspondence if he has looked for it under another name.

Study the illustrations given below. The one on the left shows a letter that is time stamped, marked for release, coded, and marked for cross-referencing. The one on the right shows a properly prepared cross-reference sheet for the letter.

Sorting. Sorting is the preliminary arrangement of materials in preparation for placing them in the files. To simplify the job of sorting, special trays, folders, or compartments are used. If such equipment is not available, the materials may be sorted on a desk or table. For this type of sorting, three steps should be followed: (1) sort the materials into small piles according to the first letters of the first filing units, for example, A-C, D-H, I-M, N-S,

T-Z; (2) sort the materials in each of these piles into single alphabetic groups (A, B, and C for the first group); (3) sort the materials in each pile in alphabetic order.

Placing Correspondence in Folders. After the correspondence has been sorted alphabetically, it is filed in appropriate folders. This procedure consists of three steps:

1. Locate the appropriate file drawer by examining the drawer labels. These labels are marked to show the alphabetic range of materials filed in a particular file drawer.

2. Scan the guides in the drawer to locate the guide that introduces the alphabetic section in which a particular piece of material should be filed.

3. Check to see whether there is an individual or special folder for the letter. If so, file the letter in it with the letterhead facing left front. If not, file the letter in the miscellaneous folder.

Items in an individual folder are arranged in date order, the most recent date at the front. In a miscellaneous folder, however, items are arranged first alphabetically according to name, then by date if there is more than one piece of correspondence filed according to the same name.

Incoming Letter Properly Time Stamped, Marked for Release, Coded, and Marked for Cross-Referencing

Properly Prepared Cross-Reference Sheet for the Letter Illustrated at the Left

39B—Building Speed in Taking Dictation

Proportion Drill

(1)

(2)

(3)

Writing of Numbers

Rule 29: Spell out street names that are numbers from one through ten. State house numbers in figures except for the house number *One*.

Example: He lives at One East Street in Alexandria; he used to live at 3 West 25th Street.

NOTE: The following material requires the application of Rules 26-28, as well as Rule 29.

Practice Material for Building Fluency

	Words
	3
	8
	13
	16
	21
	29
	39
	49
	62
	71
	77
	84
	91
	100
	106

Office Practice Problem

Make a typewritten, double-spaced list of the numbers 1 to 10. Opposite the appropriate number type the caption of the folder in which you would file the following items in the correspondence file illustrated on page 262:

1. A letter from Bordon Co. dated March 4.
2. A letter from the Apex Construction Company.
3. The file copy of a letter written to Brancroft Engineering Company.
4. A report dated July 15 from Audiphone Co.
5. A paid invoice dated May 31 from Bradley Freight.
6. A copy of a purchase order issued to the Andrews Motor Sales Co.
7. A file copy of a letter to Airways Canteen Company.
8. A letter dated April 3 from Automatic Sprinkler Corp.
9. A letter from American Roofing Co.
10. A file copy of a letter dated March 12 to Bankers Trust Co.

103B—Transcribing from Dictation

Your teacher will dictate Letters (1), (2), and (3) to you. The letters are to be signed by A. C. Rippey, Sales Assistant, Quick-Find Filing Systems, Inc., whose letters contain the company name in the closing lines.

Transcribe all three letters, using the same letter and punctuation styles as in 101B.

Lesson 104 ○ ○ ○ ○ ○ ○ ○ ○ ○ ○ ○ ○ ○ ○ ○ ○ ○ ○ ○

104A—Basic Correspondence Filing Procedures

When incoming mail is received in the business office, the mail clerk opens and stamps each piece with a *time stamp* (a rubber stamp or machine) to mark the date and time it was opened. After the mail is stamped by the mail clerk, it is sorted and delivered to the proper offices or persons for attention.

When a letter has been answered, the secretary who types the reply prepares the original incoming letter and a carbon copy of the reply for filing. She writes or stamps her initials or those of her employer in the upper left-hand corner of the original letter to indicate that it has been released for filing. This notation is known as a *release mark*. A release mark is not needed for a carbon copy of an outgoing letter.

Five steps should be observed by the secretary who is responsible for filing correspondence. These steps are known as: (1) inspection, (2) coding, (3) cross-referencing, (4) sorting, and (5) placing materials in the files.

Inspection. The first step in filing is to inspect each piece of incoming correspondence to see that it has been released for filing. This step is not necessary, of course, for carbon copies of outgoing materials.

Coding. The second step is to mark, or code, the correspondence to indicate its proper placement in the file. This is most often done by drawing a line under the entire name and a second line under the first word that is to serve as the basis for filing. If the name or subject under which the item is to be filed does not appear on the letter, the name or subject should be written at the top or in the upper right-hand corner of the paper.

The name of a business firm is usually coded when it (1) is part of the letterhead, (2) appears in the heading or as part of the signature of a letter written on plain paper, (3) appears in the inside address of an outgoing item, (4) is mentioned in the body of the letter and is the most important name in the letter.

An incoming letter of a personal nature is coded by using the name of the person by whom it was written; the file copy of an outgoing letter is coded by using the name of the addressee.

If a special folder for a special subject is provided in the file, all correspondence pertaining to that subject is coded with the special folder caption, regardless of who wrote the communication.

Cross-Referencing. If a piece of correspondence may be called for by a name other than the one under which it is to be filed, the person who codes

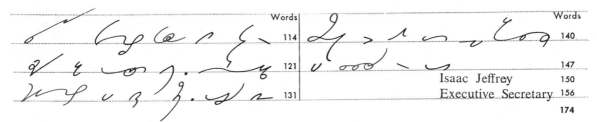

	Words		Words
	114		140
	121		147
	131	Isaac Jeffrey	150
		Executive Secretary	156
			174

Dictionary and Spelling Preview

1. cancellation, indebtedness **2.** seasonal **3.** ultramodern, discriminating

Preview of New Dictation Material

(1)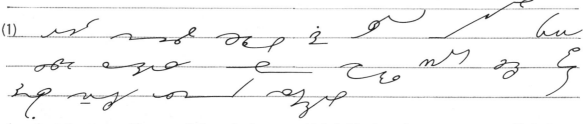

throughout the, communities, cancellation, who is not, entitled, indebtedness, borrower, announce, illustrate, maximum, compulsory, wonderful, we can say, expensive, subscribing, qualified, recommend, careful consideration

(2)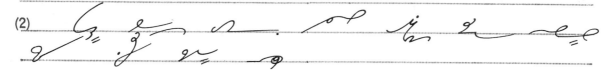

Bruce, telegram, of this morning, decoration, and hope you can, seasonal, Christmas, assorted, we have had, Easter, inquiries

(3)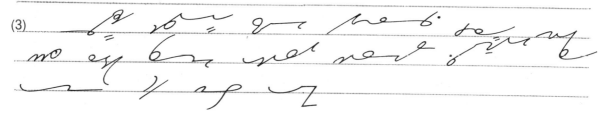

Midwest, Statler, assortments, discriminating, Chicago Illinois, cordial, worthwhile, irresistible, bargains, restaurants, ultramodern, headquarters, welcome, forward, you may have, luncheon

Lesson **40** ⬡⬡⬡⬡⬡⬡⬡⬡⬡⬡⬡⬡⬡⬡⬡⬡⬡⬡

40A—Letters of Congratulation, Appreciation, Praise, Sympathy, and Greeting

Letters of congratulation, appreciation, praise, sympathy, and greeting are letters that are easy to write in that they should be short; they are difficult to write in that correct tone of the letter is not easy to attain. In these types of letters—perhaps even more than in some others—the writer must be able to put himself in the place of the person who is to receive the letter. He must say to himself, "What would I appreciate in this situation?" "What thoughts would bring me consolation?" "What words would mean the most to me at a time like this?" The keynote of these letters is sincerity. Genuine interest must be reflected. "Gushiness," overenthusiasm, flowery expressions must be avoided. Hackneyed phrases easily creep into letters dealing with human emotions.

102B—Transcribing from Dictation

Your teacher will dictate Letter (1) to you in office style, Letters (2) and (3) at a controlled rate. The dictator of Letter (1) is Jay K. Robbins, President, whose letters do not contain a company name in the closing lines. The dictator of Letters (2) and (3) is John C. Kelso, Sales Manager, Quick-Find Filing Systems, Inc., who does use the company name in his letters.

Transcribe all three letters, using the same letter and punctuation styles as in 101B.

Lesson 103 ◯◯◯◯◯◯◯◯◯◯◯◯◯◯◯◯◯◯

103A—The Nature of Correspondence Filing

Correspondence filing consists of the systematic arrangement of original incoming correspondence and carbon copies of outgoing correspondence in vertical or drawer files. A correspondence file drawer, like a card file, is divided into convenient sections by stiff pressboard cards called *guides*. On the *tabs* of these guides are printed the name, letter, or number *captions* representing the sections into which the drawer is divided. Lightweight and somewhat flexible file *folders* are placed in correct order behind the guides. The folders, are cut with tabs on which appropriate name, letter, or number captions can be typed.

Folders are placed vertically in the file drawer with the fold at the bottom of the drawer. The open end (with the tab) stands upright so that a person looking at the drawer can read the tab captions at a glance.

Correspondence Guide　　　**Folder**

Primary guides indicate the principal sections into which the file drawer is divided. *Auxiliary* or *special guides* indicate the location of material of a special nature, such as applications, or of unusually heavy correspondence with the same company. They speed filing and finding by calling attention to the important subsections of the file.

Guides are usually placed in staggered arrangement in first, second, and third positions from left front to back right. The basic principle to keep in mind in placing guides in a file drawer is that *a primary guide always precedes all other material in a section, including special guides, special folders, individual folders, and miscellaneous folders, that falls within the range covered by that primary guide.*

Folders can be classified as individual, special, and miscellaneous. An *individual folder* is used to file material to, from, or about one company or one individual when such correspondence is active, regular, or important. A *special folder* holds material that relates to a special subject, such as branch office or applications. A *miscellaneous folder* houses correspondence to, from, or about several companies or individuals with whom correspondence is not frequent and whose names have first indexing units that fall into the range indicated by the caption on the folder.

Study the following illustration of an alphabetically indexed file. Note the arrangement of:

1. A-Z index guides
2. Special name guides
3. Individual name folders
4. Chronological folders
5. Miscellaneous folders

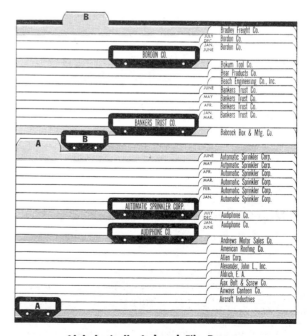

Alphabetically Indexed File Drawer

Dear Mr. Patton:

Again, let me express my appreciation for your kindness in presenting the Greater Oklahoma City Plan to the Rotary Club at the Monday luncheon. It was a subject of much interest to our group.

Please express my appreciation to Mr. Ferris, also, for his participation.

                    Yours very truly,

Letter of Appreciation

Dear Thomas:

As you celebrate your thirtieth service anniversary, it is my pleasure to send you this note of congratulations.

Our Company has always taken great pride in its capable and efficient group of long-service employees, and I feel that a large measure of the success which our Company has achieved can be attributed to the support of this fine group.

Please accept my sincere good wishes for your future health and happiness.

                    Yours very truly,

Letter of Congratulation

Dear Belle:

All the employees of Goodheart deeply regret the passing of your father, John Porter. He was respected and admired by his co-workers, and his advice was sought frequently in time of trouble.

If we can be of any help during this difficult time, be sure to let us know.

                    Most sincerely yours,

Letter of Sympathy

Dear Mr. Briscoe:

This is that happy time of the year when we pause to thank our customers for giving us the opportunity to serve them during the past 12 months. It is a pleasure to do business with a firm like yours.

We look forward to working with you in the New Year just ahead.

                    Yours very truly,

Letter of Greeting and Appreciation

Questions for Discussion

1. Why are letters of congratulation, appreciation, praise, sympathy, and greeting rather difficult to write? Which do you think is the most difficult?
2. What can you do to give yourself the right perspective in writing the types of letters discussed?
3. Name some hackneyed phrases that you should be careful to avoid using.

Office Practice Problems

Write the following letters:

1. Congratulating a cousin on earning state honors in basketball competition.
2. Expressing appreciation for a gift from a relative who lives in a distant city.
3. Extending holiday greetings to a friend in another city.

40B—Building Speed in Taking Dictation

Repetitive Phrase Builder

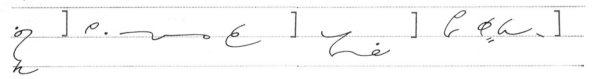

Punctuation Preview

Rule 30: Do not use abbreviations when they stand alone. In tabulations in business correspondence or in invoices, units of measurement when accompanied by figures, and names of states (except Alaska, Hawaii, Idaho, Iowa, Maine, Ohio, Texas, and Utah) when accompanied by cities may be abbreviated.

Examples: Will you please ship us 20 pounds of 8-8-8 fertilizer.

5 bu. @ $1.15 a bu., f.o.b., Chicago, Ill.

The sign will be 20 feet high and 35 feet long.

NOTE: Rules 26-29 will need to be applied in the material on page 115, as well as Rule 30.

102A—The Nature of Card Filing

The secretary must have a systematic plan for filing and finding the material that her employer requests and expects to have before him within a minute or two.

Different offices may require the secretary to file a wide variety of materials. The filing and finding of cards and correspondence, however, constitute the major part of her filing responsibility.

The *alphabetic card file* is one of the simplest and most frequently used types of files in the modern business office. It consists of a file box or cabinet in which cards that contain such information as names and addresses of persons, businesses, and organizations are filed in alphabetic order.

Standard-sized file cards are 5″ x 3″, 6″ x 4″, and 8″ x 5″. They are often ruled and typed as shown in the following illustration. Thus, the needed information is recorded in the least time and in a minimum space. The cards are placed in the file box or drawer so that the names are arranged in alphabetic order from front to back.

```
Anderson, Charles L.

Mr. Charles L. Anderson
6970 Lester Road
Cincinnati, Ohio  45213
```

Properly Typed File Card

consist of letters of the alphabet, names, or a combination of letters and numbers.

Study the arrangement of the following illustration of an alphabetic card file. Note (1) the alphabetic sections into which the guides divide the file, (2) the staggered arrangement of the guide tabs, and (3) the placement of the card for Milton Anderson behind the appropriate guide.

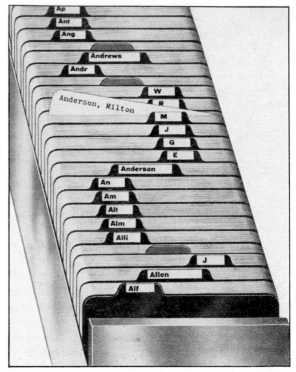

—*Shaw-Walker Co.*

Alphabetic Card File

Special cards, or partitions, known as *guides* are used to divide the file drawer into convenient alphabetic sections. These card guides are made of heavy cardboard. They have projecting *tabs* on which *captions* are printed. The captions indicate the alphabetic sections into which the guides divide the cards. The tabs of the guides vary in position so that they are staggered across the file drawer from left to right. This staggering of tab positions enables the secretary to read the captions more easily.

Cards are filed behind appropriate identifying guides. The captions on the card guide tabs may

Office Practice Problem

Type the following list of names vertically on a sheet of plain paper. Opposite each name type the guide-tab caption behind which you would place each name if you were filing it in the alphabetic card file illustrated above.

1. Allen, Frank
2. Allen, John
3. Allison, Henry
4. Allyn, George
5. Alsworth, Jay
6. Anastasio, Maria
7. Anderson, Edward
8. Andres, Paul
9. Andrews, Jean
10. Anhofer, Hugo

(Gregg shorthand outlines)

Practice Material for Building Fluency

	Words		Words
l 16, 19—	4		93
	8		101
972	12		109
10031	17		114
	25		123
	33		128
	42		137
	47		143
2	55		149
	62		155
	67		164
	75		173
	86		184
			191
		Allen Bryan	196
			210

Transcribe the following letter (modified block style with blocked paragraphs and with the date ending even with the right margin; mixed punctuation) as a 5-minute writing. Determine your *mwam*. Use this rate as your transcription goal for the week. As you transcribe the new letters in this section, try to attain this rate. (This letter may also be used from time to time as supplementary transcription practice as your teacher directs.)

QUICK-FIND FILING SYSTEMS, INC.
M. J. Wright, Personnel Director

101C—Transcribing from Dictation

Your teacher will dictate Letters (1) and (2) to you. The dictator of both letters is M. J. Wright, Personnel Director, Quick-Find Filing Systems, Inc., who uses the company name in the closing lines.

Transcribe the letters, using the same letter and punctuation styles as used in 101B. In transcribing from your own notes, try to attain the rate at which you transcribed the plate notes given above.

Dictionary and Spelling Preview

1. vacuum, patronage   **3.** analyze, fiscal   **4.** relinquishing, privilege

Preview of New Dictation Material

(1)

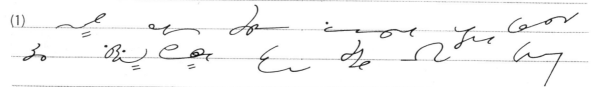

Curtis, years ago, vacuum, homemakers, repeaters, predict, subsequently, Household Appliance, popular, faithfulness, endeavor, patronage

(2)

Kirkland, between the, reflection, we hope that, demonstrate, pledge, helpful, entrusted, to serve you, expanding, thanks, ahead, prosperous

(3)

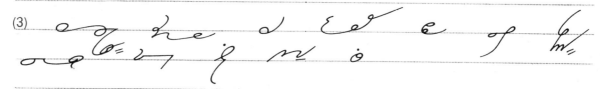

Arganbright, fiscal year, I want, splendid, easier, whenever, Beechwood, analyze, so much, it has been, to quote, highly

(4)

Pickett, it has, relinquishing, active, thoughts, associations, I have had, thus, this note, participation, privilege, retirement, to say, luck

(5)

moment, World, I should have been, and was, activities, relieved, to know, publicity, startled, I wondered, standpoint, congratulations

Getting Acquainted with Office Files

Lesson **101** ◇ ○ ◇ ○ ◇ ○ ◇ ○ ◇ ○ ◇ ○ ◇ ○ ◇ ○ ◇ ○ ◇ ○ ◇ ○

101A—Requirements of the Filing Job

Office activity requires a constant flow of papers: letters, memorandums, telegrams, checks, statements, invoices, purchase orders, statistical and accounting records, catalogs, price lists, and hundreds of other papers. Some of them come from outside the organization; others come from within. These materials are used daily as the basis for making business decisions.

Filing is the process of classifying, arranging, and storing such materials systematically so that they can be located quickly and easily when needed. No one person or group of persons can remember the details of all the events that take place as a firm conducts its business. A filing system that systematically stores this information acts as a "giant brain" or "memory" for that firm.

There are four basic systems for filing business papers: (1) alphabetic, (2) subject, (3) geographic, and (4) numeric.

In alphabetic filing, cards and other business records are arranged in alphabetic sequence according to the letters in the names to be filed. In subject and geographic filing, materials are arranged alphabetically according to subject titles and geographic names, respectively. In numeric filing, however, materials are placed in the files according to preassigned numbers.

The types of records kept, the procedures for filing and finding them, and the filing equipment used vary from company to company and from office to office within a single organization. Regardless of where she works, however, the secretary is required to do some filing. To perform this task well, she must have the following knowledges and skills:

1. She must know alphabetic and numeric sequences. All filing systems are based on alphabetic or numeric sequences, or on some combination of the two. The secretary, therefore, must be able to indicate immediately what letter comes before or after any other letter in the alphabet; she must know, likewise, what number comes before or after any other, whether the sequence is expressed in units, tens, hundreds, or thousands.

2. She must be able to read quickly and accurately. The secretary is required to read a letter or document in whole or in part to determine where it should be filed. Of special importance is the ability to read accurately and quickly the names and numbers that appear in a letter or report since these often determine how the paper will be filed.

3. She must be familiar with common abbreviations. The secretary must be able to recognize readily the common abbreviations that appear in business correspondence. In addition, she must know how to spell the names for which such abbreviations stand.

4. She must know the basic rules for alphabetic indexing. The secretary must know thoroughly the rules for alphabetic indexing and must follow them consistently. These rules with illustrative examples are presented in the next two units.

In addition to these knowledges and skills, the secretary must possess manual dexterity so that she can handle papers and cards quickly. She must have good eyesight to be able to read quickly and accurately the papers that must be filed; and, if the filing system utilizes color, she must be able to tell one color from another. The secretary must possess a good memory so that she unfailingly remembers the indexing rules and filing procedures. She must also be accurate so that the papers she files can readily be found when they are needed.

Office Practice Problems

1. Make a typewritten copy of the following list of abbreviations. Opposite each abbreviation type the word or words for which the abbreviation stands. Use a secretarial handbook or a dictionary as a reference.

a. Co.	**f.** Corp.	**k.** Ore.
b. Inc.	**g.** R.R.	**l.** Md.
c. St.	**h.** Rev.	**m.** R. I.
d. Ltd.	**i.** Supt.	**n.** Minn.
e. Ave.	**j.** Secy.-Treas.	**o.** N. J.

2. Ask one or more secretaries in your town what filing duties they perform on the job, such as:

a. How much time they spend daily in filing and finding business papers

b. What kinds of business papers they file

c. What filing system or systems they use: alphabetic, numeric, subject, or geographic

d. What their most difficult filing problems are

Building Speed in Taking Dictation

Lesson **41** ⬡⬡⬡⬡⬡⬡⬡⬡⬡⬡⬡⬡⬡⬡⬡⬡⬡⬡

41A—Brief-Form Practice

Directions. The following paragraph has 33 brief forms and brief-form derivatives. If you can read it in 30 seconds, your reading rate will be 130 words a minute.

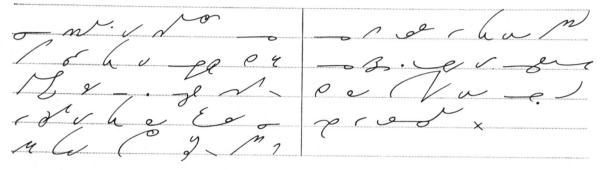

41B—Theory Review

A vowel following a long *i* is expressed by a small circle within the large circle.

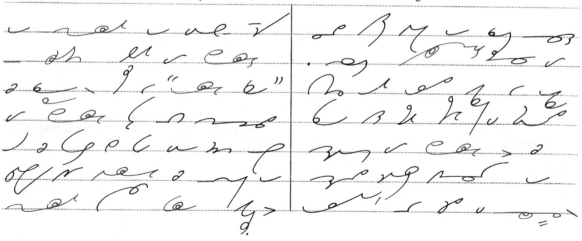

41C—Word Spellings and Meanings

Some words that sound alike or similar are spelled differently and have different meanings. Three such words are given below. Study their spellings and meanings so that you will use them correctly; they occur in the dictation. Read the shorthand copy, indicating the proper spelling of each of these three words.

    to—indicates direction or introduces an infinitive

    too—in addition, more than enough, to such a degree

    two—second in number

100C—Transcribing from Dictation

Directions. Again you will take office-style dictation. Use modified block style with centered date and indented paragraphs; mixed punctuation.

The dictator of the first letter is Warner F. Knopf, Manager; of the second letter, Mildred P. Sweet, Reservation Manager; of the third letter, Irving O. Longstreet, Chief Accountant.

PUNCTUATION REMINDER: Use a semicolon between clauses of a compound sentence that are joined by a conjunctive adverb, such as *so, therefore, hence, however, otherwise, yet, still,* and *furthermore.*

100D—Supplementary Transcription

Directions. Transcribe from Lesson 25, page 68, as directed by your teacher.

100E—Transcriber's Guide

Typewriter Ribbons. When you purchase typewriter ribbons, you will need to indicate to the salesperson the make of typewriter you are using, what inking you want, of what material you want the ribbon to have been made, and the color. Ribbons are made of nylon, cotton, acetate, or silk. The recommendation of the manufacturer of your machine and your own experience will help you make a decision on the matter of material. Medium-inked ribbons are usually preferred for regular office work. When possible, the number of yards of ribbon on a spool should be ascertained. Sometimes ribbons on special sale actually have fewer yards on the spool than others. Black is the color most commonly used. Specialty companies some-times use a letterhead stationery with a colored design and then use a matching color in the typewriter ribbon. Black-and-red ribbons are available for use when two-color work is to be done.

The technique for changing ribbons is not the same for all machines, but in no case is it particularly difficult. Every secretary should be able to change her typewriter ribbon. The following illustrations show how to change the ribbon on several makes of typewriters. The first step in changing any ribbon (except the new Royal ribbon with disposable spools) is to notice whether the ribbon goes around the front or the back of the spool and how it is threaded.

Nonelectric (Underwood)

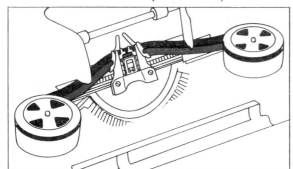

Path of the Ribbon As It Winds and Unwinds on the Two Spools

Electric

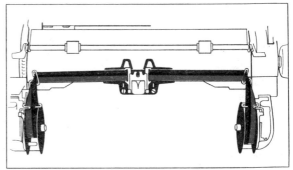

IBM Fabric Ribbon

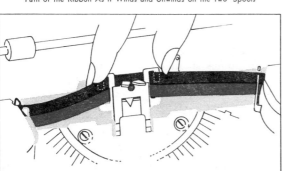

Ribbon Threaded Through the Ribbon-Carrier Mechanism

IBM Carbon Ribbon

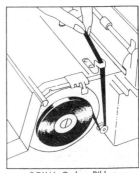

ROYAL Carbon Ribbon

[Shorthand practice material — two lines at top]

41D—Practice Material for Building Fluency

	Words
(1) *[shorthand]* 21, 19—	3
[shorthand]	7
418 *[shorthand]*	11
6 *[shorthand]* 94302	17
[shorthand] 30 *[shorthand]*	25
[shorthand]	34
[shorthand]	41
[shorthand]	47
[shorthand]	52
[shorthand]	61
[shorthand]	66
[shorthand]	75
[shorthand]	84
[shorthand]	91
[shorthand]	99
[shorthand]	107

	Words
[shorthand]	112
Avery Randall	115
(2) Vice-President	119
	132
[shorthand] kavanaugh	5
[shorthand] woodard	10
[shorthand] 3, 19—	14
[shorthand]	23
[shorthand]	30
[shorthand]	36
[shorthand]	43
[shorthand]	48
[shorthand]	56
[shorthand]	65
[shorthand]	77
[shorthand]	83
[shorthand]	90
[shorthand]	99

41E—Dictionary and Spelling Preview

1. jewelry, clientele, proprietor, craft, scientific, bracelet

2. definition, termites, stitch

4. mimeograph, hectograph, offset

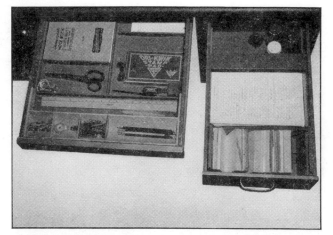

Center Drawer; Top Side Drawer

Note that the shallow *center drawer* contains supplies that are frequently used by the secretary, such as pencils, erasers, paper clips, rubber bands, scissors, transparent tape, ruler and dictation notebooks.

At the extreme right of the illustration the *top side drawer* is often used for card files, for work that is currently in process, and for such supplies as ink, correction fluid, and a stapler.

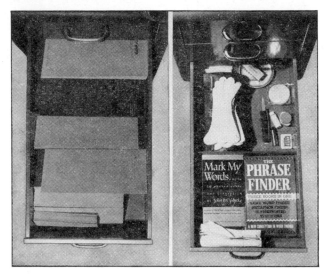

Middle Side Drawer; Bottom Side Drawer

The *middle side drawer* (often called the *stationery* drawer) is usually equipped with sloping pockets for stationery supplies. This type of drawer is arranged for the efficient assembling of letterhead sets. Envelopes are stacked vertically in the front of the drawer.

The secretary's personal articles (gloves, purse, etc.) are kept in the *bottom side drawer*. She may also keep her reference books there. If the drawer is of the deep file-drawer type, the secretary can use it to file folders containing current and reference materials.

One Secretary's Arrangement of Supplies and Work in the Desk

Lesson **100** ⬡⬡⬡⬡⬡⬡⬡⬡⬡⬡⬡⬡⬡⬡⬡⬡⬡⬡

100A—Punctuation and Theory Review

(1) *[shorthand outlines]*

(2) *[shorthand outlines]*

100B—Vocabulary Preview

[shorthand outlines]

41F—Preview of New Dictation Material

(1)

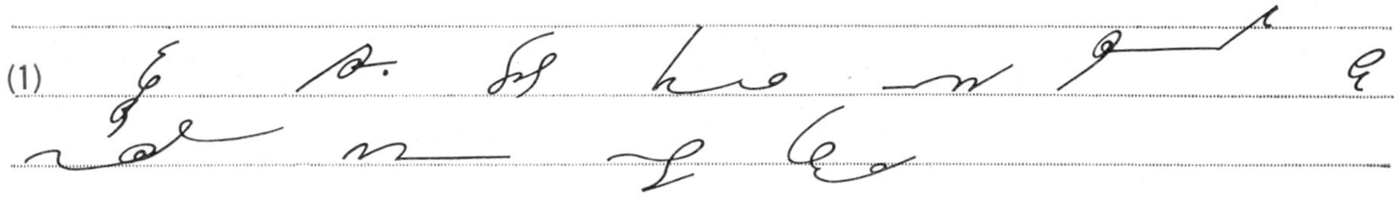

specialize, designing, beautiful, jewelry, uncut, diamonds, I was, clientele, workmen, craft, bracelet

(2)

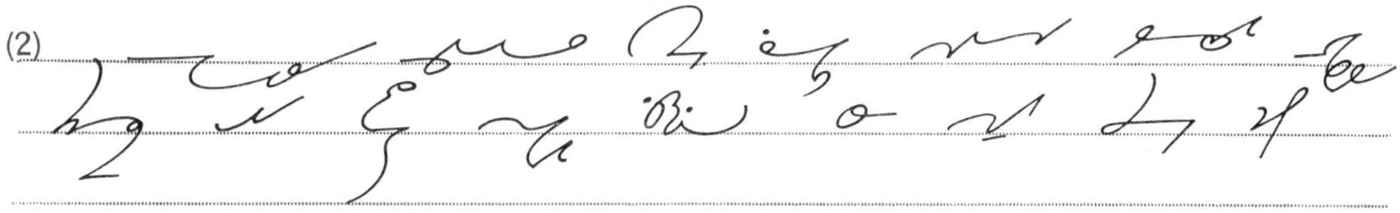

employed, naturally, definition, help us, contract, termites, in the past year, have you given, thought, expensive, carpets, household, why not, quotation, very much, stitch

(3)

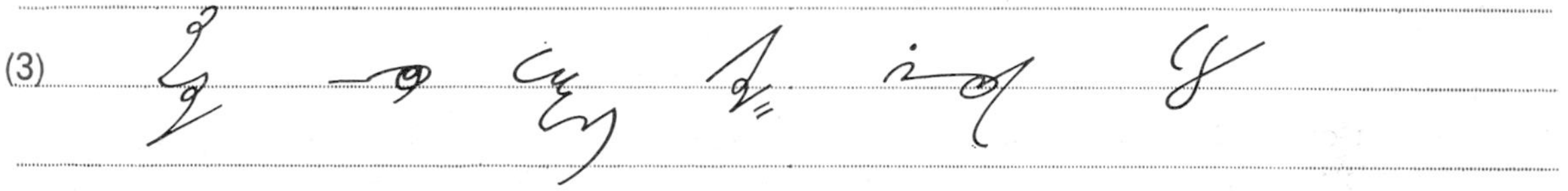

we have received, inquiries, prospective, Digest, who might be, postpaid

(4)

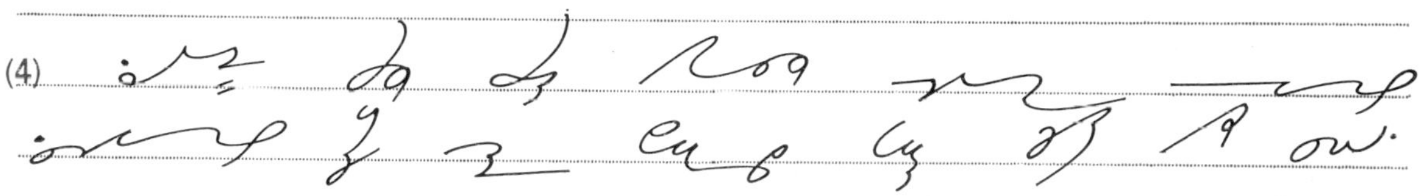

Henderson, vacation, various, duplication, instructional, mimeograph, hectograph, offset, consume, approximately, processes, we do have, decision, according

Lesson 42

42A—Phrase Builder

There are 13 phrases in the following paragraph.

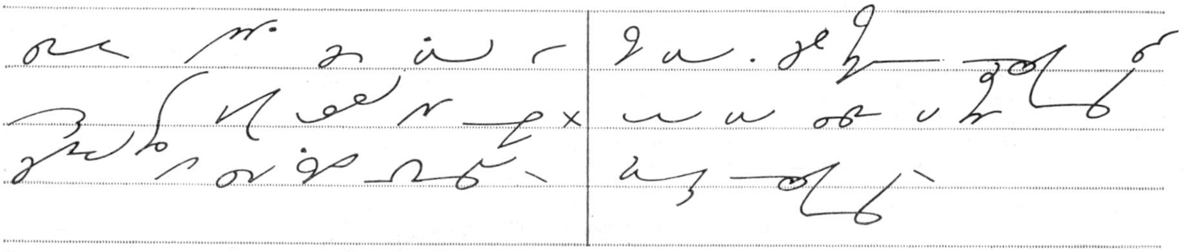

99B—Vocabulary Preview

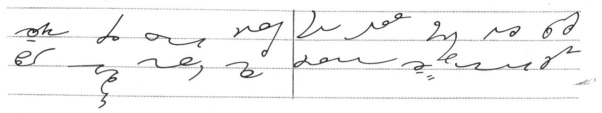

99C—Transcribing from Dictation

Directions. Your teacher will give you office-style dictation. Use the same letter and punctuation styles as in Lesson 98.

The dictator of the first letter is Rodney P. Love, Sales Director; of the second letter, Jack S. Nunnally, Sales Department.

PUNCTUATION REMINDER: A comma is used to indicate the omission of words necessary for the completeness of a sentence.

99D—Supplementary Transcription

Directions. Transcribe from Lesson 24, page 66, as directed by your teacher.

99E—Transcriber's Guide

Organization of Work. The secretary handles so many details that careful organization of her work is essential to satisfactory performance of her duties.

1. Supplies and work in process must be arranged in and on the desk so that there is a minimum of lost time and motion. Frequently used supplies should be where they are readily available —in the front of the drawers and in the top drawers. Less frequently used supplies should be in the lower drawers and in the back part of those and top drawers. Study the illustration below for suggested desk arrangement.

2. Work in process should be placed in folders that are accurately tabbed as to contents so that it can be found at a moment's notice. The secretary may need to keep a "pending" file in her desk or in her file cabinet. A tickler, or follow-up, file in card form may be utilized to good advantage as a reminder of duties to be performed on certain days. A file of frequently called telephone numbers or of frequently used mailing addresses may save time in handling callers or correspondence. The use of special files is discussed at greater length in Lessons 101-115.

3. The top of the desk should be kept looking neat. If possible, only the material being worked on at the moment should be on the desk. At the end of the day all papers and supplies should be placed inside the desk so that the top of the desk is clear.

4. The notations on the calendar or appointment pad should be checked frequently to be sure that no commitments are forgotten and no duties overlooked.

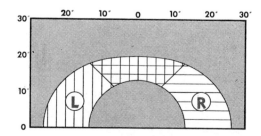

Visualize the top of the desk as an open rectangular working space. The typewriter will be on an extension to one side. Notice the arc-shaped working areas in the diagram. The horizontally ruled area (R) is the reach of the right hand and should be reserved for items used by the right hand, such as pencils, fountain pen, stapler, calendar, and memo pad. The vertically ruled area (L) is the reach of the left hand and should be reserved for items the left hand can use, such as the telephone, work organizers, and letter trays. The crosshatch area includes the reach of both hands. The small clear semicircle is the area in which the forearms move and should be kept free.

Arrangement of Work on the Desk

42B—Theory Review

The sounds of *ea* and *ĭa* are expressed by a large circle with a dot within it.

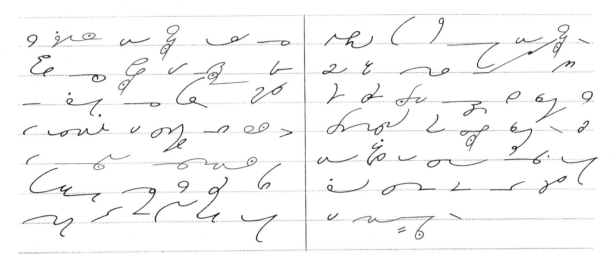

42C—Word Spellings and Meanings

affect—to influence, to modify, to assume artificially (verb)

effect—an immediate result or general impression (noun); to accomplish or bring about (verb)

NOTE: The following material includes words presented in Lesson 41, as well as those given above.

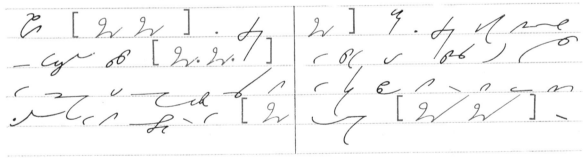

42D—Practice Material for Building Fluency

		Words			Words
(1)	1, 19—	3			23
		7		34 04	29
	721	10			36
	12866	17			41

98D—Supplementary Transcription

Directions. Transcribe from Lesson 23, page 63, as directed by your teacher.

98E—Transcriber's Guide

The Stenographic Pool. Many large business firms have a stenographic pool, which is an office in which clerical, stenographic, and secretarial work is performed for various departments of the organization. The work is coordinated by a supervisor, who receives the jobs to be done and distributes them to the workers in the pool.

Sometimes calls are received for stenographers to go to other offices to take dictation. They then usually return to the pool to do the transcription.

Occasionally, they serve as "relief" when secretaries are on vacation or are ill.

The Service Order. If considerable work is sent to the stenographic pool to be handled, the company usually has a printed service order on which the person wanting work done fills in directions for the typist or stenographer to follow. The directions are usually about the kind and size of stationery, number of carbon copies, date wanted, etc.

INSTRUCTIONS FOR
STENOGRAPHIC WORK
(THIS SHEET SHOULD ACCOMPANY WORK UNTIL
COMPLETION AND THEN BE RETAINED FOR
STENOGRAPHIC FILE)

WORK FOR _____
COMPLETE
PREFERABLY_____
BUT
NOT LATER THAN _____

CHARGE: JOB NO. _____ CO. _____

NO. OF
COPIES _____ CARBONS ☐ TYPE
DITTO ☐ PICA ☐
DUPLIMAT ☐ ELITE ☐
KIND AND
PAPER SIZE _____ MARGIN _____

_____ SHEETS NUMBERED YES ☐ SPACE SINGLE ☐
NO ☐ DOUBLE ☐

TYPIST	PROOFREADER	COMPTOMETER	APPROVED	DEL'D.

TYPE OF COVER _____

PUT IN SETS YES ☐ STAPLE YES ☐
NO ☐ NO ☐

DESCRIPTION _____
_____
_____
(OVER)

SPECIFIC INSTRUCTIONS

KEEP THIS RECORD WHEN RECEIVING AID WITH WORK
WHICH HAS BEEN ASSIGNED TO YOU.

TYPED BY	COMPARED WITH	COMPS.	DUP.	DEL'D.

A Service Order

Anyone sending work to a pool should be sure to give **specific, detailed** instructions; otherwise, work may have to be done over at a considerable cost of time, effort, and materials.

Lesson **99** ◇ ◇ ◇ ◇ ◇ ◇ ◇ ◇ ◇ ◇ ◇ ◇ ◇ ◇ ◇ ◇ ◇ ◇ ◇

99A—Punctuation and Theory Review

(1) [shorthand outlines]

(2) [shorthand outlines]

Words | 51
57
64
71
80
87
95
100
110
118
124

S. M. Palmer 127
Credit Manager 130
144

(2) ____ 3
9

Words | 13
18
10005
12469 27
33
235 40
51
59
66
76
85
2876 91
130073 99
106

Philip Jones 109
Accounting Department 113
129

42E—Dictionary and Spelling Preview

2. quadruplicate, deleting, returnable

4. brochure, farther, comprehensive

5. inasmuch, authorization, approximation, capacity, receipt, pipeline

42F—Preview of New Dictation Material

(1)

traffic, enthusiastically, we hope that this, award, ability

(2)

effective, thereafter, overstock, textbooks, upon request, quadruplicate, you wish, retained, deleting, returnable, Village, as they are

98A—Punctuation and Theory Review

(1) *[shorthand outlines]* 3 ~ 15 ~ *[shorthand]*

5 1648 *[shorthand outlines]*

(2) *[shorthand outlines]*

98B—Vocabulary Preview

[shorthand outlines]

98C—Transcribing from Dictation

Directions. Your teacher will dictate Letter (1) to you in office style. Transcribe Letter (2) from the notes given below, then transcribe Letter (1) from the notes taken from your teacher's dictation. Use block style and open punctuation.

The dictator of Letter (1) is Christopher Small; of Letter (2), Henry Wadsworth.

PUNCTUATION REMINDER: Commas are used to set off words of direct address.

(2)
April 11, 19--

Mr. Don Leland
Planters Building
Birmingham, Alabama   35202

cc aw wrenn

[shorthand notes]

(3) 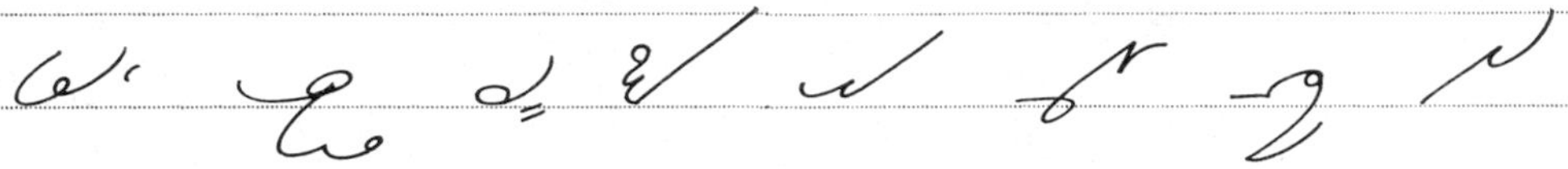 *[shorthand outlines]*

printings, library, Aunt, exhausted, reorder, in addition to the, in the event, don't

(4)  *[shorthand outlines]*

brochure, useful, yearly, appropriate, if so, farther, otherwise, in response, at this time, comprehensive, variety, unusually, considerably, indicated, to spend, circular

(5) 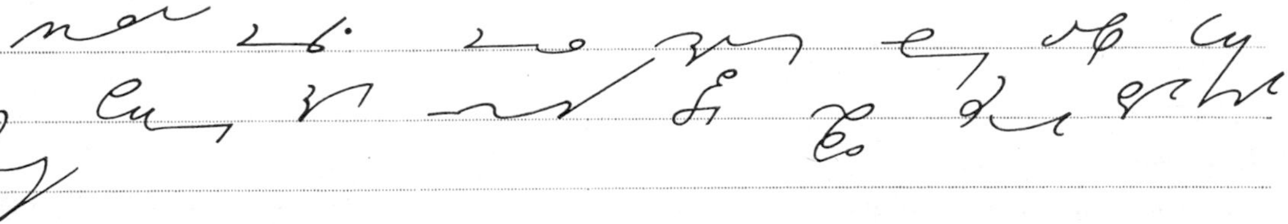 *[shorthand outlines]*

to your letter, submitting, summary, construction, inasmuch, authorization, projects, involved, approximation, substantial, included, expansion, capacity, facilities, assistance

Lesson 43 ⬡⬡⬡⬡⬡⬡⬡⬡⬡⬡⬡⬡⬡⬡⬡⬡⬡⬡⬡

43A—Potential Rate Builder

There are 14 words in the sentence.

[shorthand outline]

43B—Theory Review

The sound of *ort* is expressed by *ot*.

The sound *sume* is expressed by *sm;* the sound *sumption* is expressed by *[shorthand symbol]* .

[shorthand outlines]

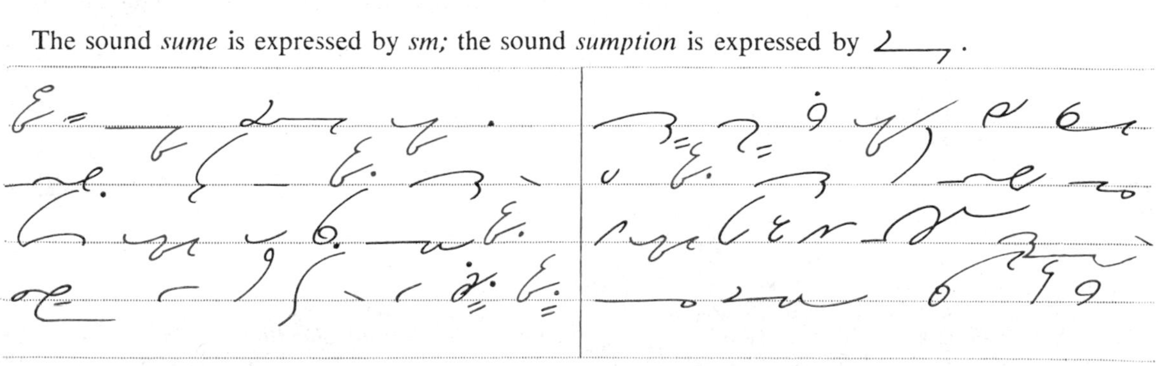

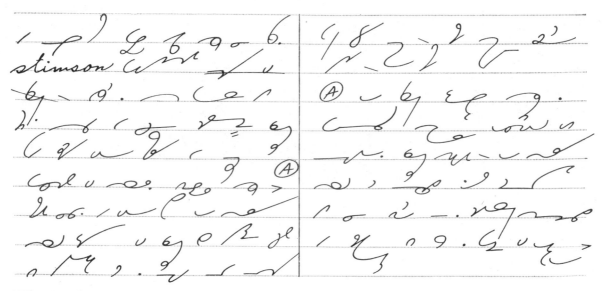

97D—Supplementary Transcription

Directions. Transcribe from Lesson 22, page 60, as directed by your teacher.

97E—Transcriber's Guide

Reference Books and Correspondence Manuals. A secretary needs to have authorities whom she can consult when she is in doubt about the correct form or procedure. The advice of these authorities is available in reference books and correspondence manuals.

Some business firms have a correspondence manual that has been prepared within their own firm for the use of their employees. Such a correspondence manual may give information about such subjects as the history of the firm, names of the executives, procedures for handling incoming and outgoing mail, a list of technical words peculiar to that firm's business, how to report conferences, and a summary of rules of grammar, punctuation, spelling, and use of figures. The manual may give specific directions about letter styles to be followed, methods of sending telegrams, routing telephone calls, and the uses to be made of each kind of stationery provided.

Some firms use a secretarial handbook that has been published for general use. A handbook of this type covers more topics than a company correspondence manual. It may, for instance, give complete information about the typing of business papers used in all kinds of businesses. It may give pointers about how to buy various kinds of office supplies and equipment. Such a book may discuss problems in human relations in the office, filing rules, duplicating methods, or the setting up of itineraries and making reservations. A secretary should have a secretarial handbook whether or not she is given a correspondence manual of the firm for which she works.

Many other reference books are available for the secretary's use, either in the business firm or in the public library. Some of those books are: atlases and gazetteers, **biographies of noted people,** business etiquette, dictionaries, encyclopedias, directories, style manuals, shipping and mailing guides, word usage and quotation manuals, statistical abstracts, and indexes. A partial list is:

Etiquette by Emily Post
Familiar Quotations by John Bartlett
Hotel Red Book by American Hotel
    Association Directory Corporation
The Industrial Arts Index
International Business Dictionary by Frank Gaynor
National Associations of the United States (published
    by U. S. Department of Commerce)
Patterson's American Educational Directory
Poor's Register of Directors and Executives
Rand McNally-Cosmopolitan World Atlas

Readers' Guide to Periodical Literature
Roget's Thesaurus
Standard Handbook for Secretaries
    by Lois Hutchinson
Statistical Abstract of the United States (published by
    U. S. Department of Commerce)
Thomas' Register of American Manufacturers
Webster's Third New International Dictionary (Un-
    abridged)
Who's Who in America
The World Almanac and Book of Facts

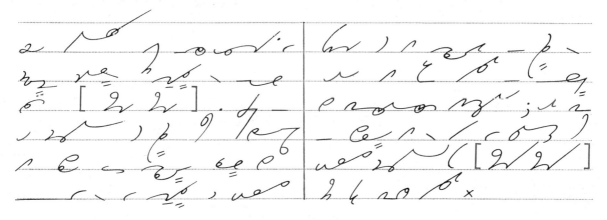

43C—Word Spellings and Meanings

there—in or at that place (adverb) used to introduce a sentence or clause

their—of or belonging to them (possessive adjective)

NOTE: The following material includes words presented in Lessons 41 and 42, as well as those given above.

43D—Practice Material for Building Fluency

	Words		Words
(1) 28, 19	3		27
	7	25	34
1001	11		43
71280	17		48

96D—Supplementary Transcription

Directions. Transcribe the memo from Lesson 21, page 59, as directed by your teacher.

96E—Transcriber's Guide

Office-Style Dictation. If a considerable revision is to be made, a capital letter may be inserted at the point where the correction begins; and the revised dictation (with a corresponding capital letter) may be inserted below the dictation given just prior to the correction. Care should be taken to indicate the end of the inserted matter so that you will know how much of your shorthand belongs to the insert.

If information is to be checked on a certain point, a wavy vertical line may be drawn down the outside edge of the page to remind you to do so before beginning **transcribing**. Some secretaries use a paper clip to indicate points to be checked.

Lesson **97** ⬡⬡⬡⬡⬡⬡⬡⬡⬡⬡⬡⬡⬡⬡⬡⬡⬡

97A—Punctuation and Theory Review

(1) [shorthand notes]

(2) [shorthand notes]

97B—Vocabulary Preview

[shorthand notes]

97C—Transcribing from Dictation

Directions. Your teacher will dictate Letter (1) to you in office style. Transcribe Letter (2) from the notes given below, then transcribe Letter (1) from the notes taken from your teacher's dictation. Use the same letter and punctuation styles as in Lesson 96.

The dictator of Letter (1) is Clyde A. Turner, Sales Department. The dictator of Letter (2) is Roy E. Waterman, District Sales Manager.

PUNCTUATION REMINDER: A comma (or commas) is used to set off words in apposition.

(2)   November 14, 19--

Mr. Tracey O. Planter
8312 North Euclid
Phoenix, Arizona   85003

[shorthand notes]

	Words		Words
	57		26
	65		34
	75		41
	80		49
	87		55
	94		62
	101		66
	111		76
	117		84
	128		92
Bruce Cabot	131		100
Credit Manager	137		109
	151		115
(2)	3		
cantrell	7		
	13	Bob Tyler	117
2-7607	19	Manager	121
			137

43E—Dictionary and Spelling Preview

1. timesaver, packaged, sorter

2. Residence, tenants, receipt, Cashier

3. sponsoring, cosponsor, campaign, financially, certificate

43F—Preview of New Dictation Material

(1)

it has been, that there is, sorter, on the market, packaged, line of business, understand, obtainable, New York City

(2)

Residence, receipt, payable, Cashier's Administration, Iowa, delinquent, up to date, vacate, withdrawn, we wish

Transcribing Office-Style Dictation

Lesson **96** ⬡⬡⬡⬡⬡⬡⬡⬡⬡⬡⬡⬡⬡⬡⬡⬡⬡⬡⬡⬡

96A—Punctuation and Theory Review

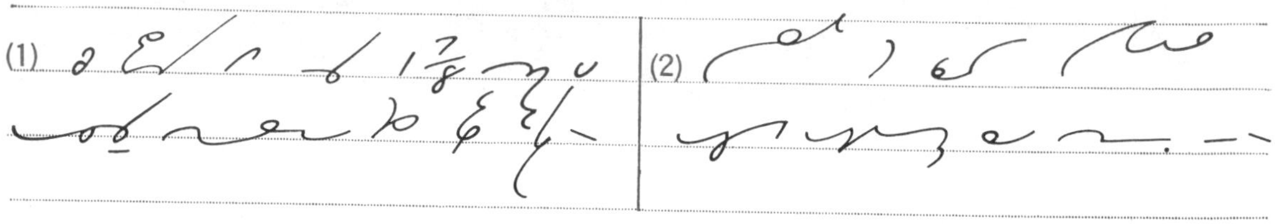

(1) *[shorthand notation]*

(2) *[shorthand notation]*

96B—Vocabulary Preview

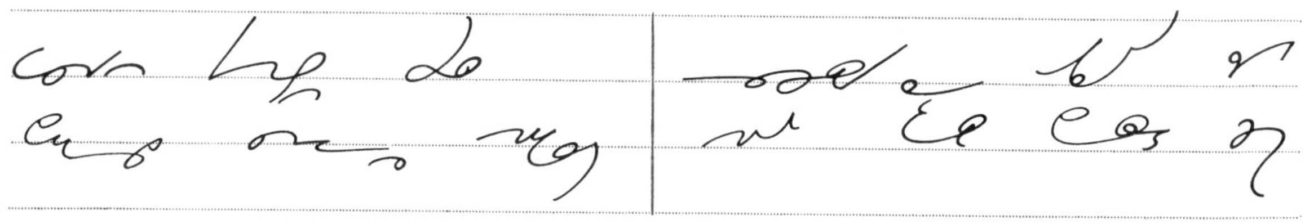

[shorthand notation]

96C—Transcribing from Dictation

Directions. Your teacher will dictate Letter (1) to you in office style. Transcribe Letter (2) from the notes given below, then transcribe Letter (1) from the notes taken from your teacher's dictation. Use modified block style with date ending at the right margin and no paragraph indention; open punctuation.

The dictator of the first letter is Tim McCoy, Manager, Variety Distributors, Inc. The dictator of the second letter is Claude S. Cantrell, Purchasing Department.

PUNCTUATION REMINDER: Either a clause of reason introduced by *for* or *as* or a clause of concession introduced by *though* or *although* is separated from the main clause by a comma.

(2)   August 21, 19--

Mr. T. F. Jacobs
Urbana Variety Store
1001 Second Street
Urbana, Illinois   61805

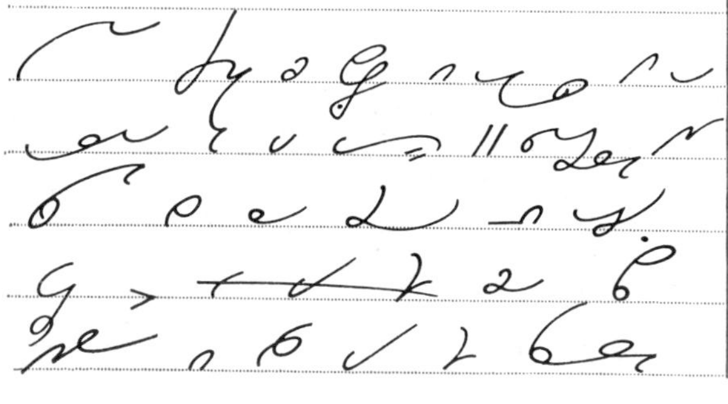

[shorthand notation]

(3)

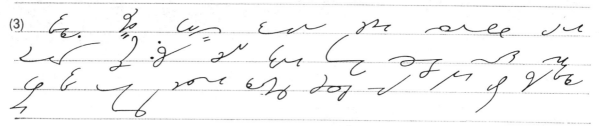

sponsoring, Safety, Program, slaughter, citizens, carelessness, authorities, for a long time, you have been, has had, window, posters, bumper, campaign, courteous, cosponsor, prevention, support, will be made, stickers, certificate, financially, in order, donation, whatever, afford

Lesson 44 ⬡⬡⬡⬡⬡⬡⬡⬡⬡⬡⬡⬡⬡⬡⬡⬡

44A—Proportion Drill

(1)

(3)

(2)

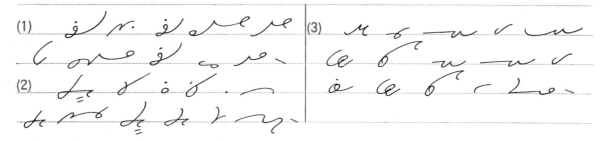

44B—Theory Review

The word endings *-tial* and *-cial* are represented by *sh*. The word ending *-cient* is expressed by *sht*; the ending *-ciency*, by *shse*.

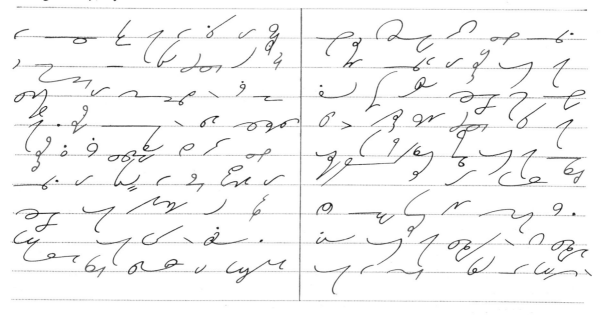

We have begun the process of assembling such material, but we cannot complete our informational booklet until the [cap] Engineering department has finished its final testing of [stet] [stet] the equipment. When ~~we~~ this final testing has been completed, we will be able to distribute our material in a few days' time.

Thank you very much for your nice compliment about our public relations program, which we regard as one of great importance. I hope that we can live up to your expectations.

Very sincerely,

Sam Grunther

95C—Supplementary Transcription

Directions. Transcribe the memorandum in Lesson 20, page 57, if your teacher so directs.

95D—Transcriber's Guide

Office-Style Dictation. Review the pointers given in Lessons 16-19 about handling office-style dictation and transcription.

Deciding on the proper setup for a letter containing many changes will be more difficult than it has been for dictation without changes. Your skill will improve as you gain experience. Here are a few pointers that may help you if, after starting a letter, you realize that you have misjudged the letter's length.

"Shortening" a Letter. If you find that the letter is actually taking more space than you anticipated, you may be able to "shorten" it by the following procedures:

1. Using the variable line spacer, allow a little less than a double space between paragraphs—just a fraction of a vertical space. If you have several paragraphs, you will soon have saved a full space.

2. Use three instead of four spaces between the complimentary close and the dictator's name (or between the company name and dictator's name).

3. Type the dictator's title on the same line as the name.

4. Type the reference notation on the same line as the last closing line.

"Lengthening" a Letter. If you find that the letter will require less space than you anticipated, you may be able to "lengthen" it by the following procedures:

1. Using the variable line spacer, allow a little more than a double space between paragraphs.

2. Use a little more than a double space between the body of the letter and the complimentary close.

3. Use five instead of four spaces between the complimentary close and the dictator's name.

4. Type the dictator's title on the line below his name.

5. Type the reference notation three instead of two spaces below the last closing line.

The Short Letter. If you know a letter is going to be very short, you can lengthen it in appearance by double spacing the body of the letter or by using a 10- or 15-space indention for paragraphs. The space from the top of the paper to the date line or between the date line and the inside address can be increased.

44C—Word Spellings and Meanings

later—after a lapse of time

latter—the second of two things or persons

NOTE: The following material includes words presented in Lessons 41-43, as well as those given above.

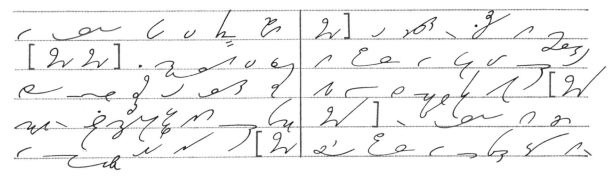

44D—Practice Material for Building Fluency

	Words
(1) ... 10, 19—	3
	7
203 ... 110 ...	12
... 48197	17
... sb ragan	22
	31
	35
	42
	49
	55
	61
	71
	79
	88
	96
	106

	Words
	115
	122
	131
	143
	151
	161
Harry Simmons	164
	178
(2) ... 15, 19—	3
	8
15—19 ...	11
... 37208	17
	25
	31
	39
	48

Directions. Retype each letter, making the corrections indicated, so that it can be mailed.

PUNCTUATION REMINDER: Use a comma to separate two consecutive parallel adjectives modifying a single noun. If the adjectives are not parallel, no comma is used. Ordinarily, parallel adjectives can be identified by the fact that they might be connected with *and*.

(1)

September 2, 19--

Mr. K. A. Olson, Manager
Olson Enterprises
Saginaw, Michigan   48604

Dear Mr. Olsen:

We are very happy to announce another mile stone in the rapid, continued growth of our company.

In order to achieve this goal, we have had to have the continued support and encouragement from our customers.

The good will of our customers is, we realize our most valuable asset.

Our new building provides us with one of the largest plants in our industry; it is also one of the most modern plants. Increased space and facilities for production, shipping, and administration will enable us to help you better serve the rapidly growing market for stationary, tablets and envelopes, and school supplies.

We appreciate the cooperation you have given us; and it is our earnest desire to continue to serve you with quality products, outstanding packaging and aggressive merchandising programs.

Very truly yours,

Kenneth S. Hemingway

(2)

October 4, 19--

Mr. Stanley Post, Editor
News of the Week
102 East Nebraska Street
Wichita, Kansas   67203

Dear Mr. Post:

Realizing your interest in the intalations we have made resently, we will send you the material your requested about our new newly completed compressor stations just as quickly as possible.

(Continued)

(shorthand outlines) Words
58
65

Words
79

Rodney Porter 82
Sales Department 89
102

44E—Dictionary and Spelling Preview

1. facial, complexion, beneficial, endorsed   **2.** knowledge, either, inconvenience, courtesies

3. electronic, processing, conform

44F—Preview of New Dictation Material

(1) *(shorthand outlines)*

we are having, facial, tissues, you will find, endorsed, one of the, on the market, complexion, prompt, for which

(2) *(shorthand outlines)*

Watson, president, decided, dictating, it was, decision, to handle, too many, consequently, I will not be able, sincerely, inconvenience, any way, courtesies, hesitate

(3) *(shorthand outlines)*

continued, install, electronic, processing, system, faster, warehouse, to speed, in order, to set up, it is necessary, to change, so that they, conform, numbering, attached, accordingly, who would be, with these, invoices, one of our, of these

Lesson **45** ◇○◇○◇○◇○◇○◇○◇○◇○◇○◇○◇○◇

45A—Repetitive Phrase Builder

(shorthand outlines)

94C—Transcription from Dictation

Directions.· Letter (1), which will be dictated to you by your teacher, is to be transcribed in the semiformal style with mixed punctuation on 7¼ by 10½ stationery. Then retranscribe the letter on 8½ by 5½ stationery, using modified block style with centered date and indented paragraphs; mixed punctuation.

Transcribe Letter (2), which will be dictated to you, on 8 by 10 stationery, using the same letter style and punctuation style as for your second typing of Letter (1).

The dictator of Letter (1) is Emory P. Nugent, Manager; of Letter (2), William A. Rodgers, New Accounts Division, Small and Small, Inc.

PUNCTUATION REMINDER: Use a comma to set off an introductory phrase beginning with a participle (verbal adjective). No comma should follow an introductory phrase beginning with a gerund (verbal noun).

94D—Supplementary Transcription

Directions. Transcribe the memorandum in Lesson 19, page 53, as directed by your teacher.

94E—Transcriber's Guide

Proofreader's Marks. Sometimes a transcript is corrected with proofreader's marks, which the secretary must be able to interpret correctly in retyping the transcript. The most commonly used proofreader's marks are those given below. Study them so that you can type the corrected copy in Lesson 95.

‖ Align type; set flush	ˣˣˣ/ Insert ellipses	⌐ Move up; raise
c+sc Capitals and small capitals	···/ Insert leaders	¶ Paragraph
⊂ Close up space	⊙ Insert period	No¶ ⌐ No new paragraph
℘ Delete; take out	?/ Insert question mark	↰ Run in material
℘ Delete and close up	⟨⟨ ⟩⟩ Insert quotation marks	run in Run in material on same line
⋀ Insert (caret)	;;/ Insert semicolon	cap or set in capitals
# Insert space	ital Italic, change to	lc or set in lower case
⸣ Insert apostrophe	stet Let type stand	sp Spell out
: ⊙ Insert colon	⌊⌋ Move down; lower	tr ⋃ Transpose letters or words
⸝/ Insert comma	⌐ Move to left	(?) ⟨?⟩ Verify or supply information
	⌐ Move to right	

Lesson 95 ⬡⬡⬡⬡⬡⬡⬡⬡⬡⬡⬡⬡⬡⬡⬡

95A—Punctuation and Theory Review

(1) [shorthand outlines] 35 [shorthand outlines] (2) [shorthand outlines]

The word beginnings *enter-*, *intr-*, and *inter-* are expressed by *n* above the line.

The ending *-rd* is expressed by *r* with an upward turn at the end. The ending *-ld* is expressed by *l* with an upward turn at the end.

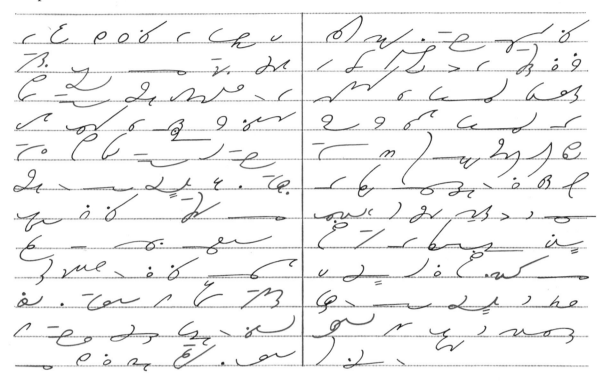

45C—Word Spellings and Meanings

it's—the contraction for *it is*
its—possessive pronoun (possessive of *it*)

NOTE: The following material includes words presented in Lessons 41-44, as well as those given above.

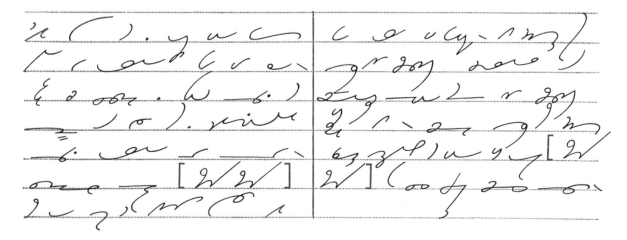

93C—Transcribing from Dictation

Directions. You are to transcribe from "cold" notes—those that you took from dictation in the preceding period. Use the modified block style with indented paragraphs and centered date, and use the mixed punctuation style.

The dictator is Horace P. Twining.

PUNCTUATION REMINDER: To set off an introductory **adverbial** phrase containing a verb, use a comma.

93D—Supplementary Transcription

Directions. Transcribe from letters in Lesson 18, page 49, as directed by your teacher.

93E—Transcriber's Guide

Semiformal Style of Letter. This letter style is used to create a more personal effect than the standard styles. The letter should be folded as for a No. 10 envelope. The size of stationery most often used for this style of letter is 7¼ by 10½. The size of envelope that should be used with this stationery is 3⅞ by 7½.

Other sizes smaller than 8½ by 11 that are sometimes used are 8½ by 5½ and 8 by 10.

PHONE 321-1121

maxims   DEPARTMENT STORE
AMBERLY SQUARE
MEMPHIS, TENNESSEE 38110

February 8, 19--

Dear Mrs. Blair:

We are having our annual Presale of women's summer suits and dresses from Monday through Friday, February 12 to 16. This Presale is for the benefit of our regular customers; it gives them an opportunity to have first choice from the many beautiful styles and fabrics we selected when we were at the New York markets last fall.

The lines and colors of the new styles are especially flattering this year. Emphasis is on the practical with the feminine touch.

We hope to see you next week.

Cordially yours,

Barbara Carnell

Mrs. Paul T. Blair
496 Rosita Drive
Memphis, Tennessee 38108

MODEL E: Semiformal Style

Lesson **94** ⬡⬡⬡⬡⬡⬡⬡⬡⬡⬡⬡⬡⬡⬡⬡⬡⬡⬡⬡

94A—Punctuation and Theory Review

(1) [shorthand outlines]

(2) [shorthand outlines]

94B—Vocabulary Preview

[shorthand outlines]

45D—Practice Material for Building Fluency

	Words		Words
(1) *[shorthand]* 8, 19 —	4	(2) *[shorthand]* 10, 19 —	4
[shorthand]	7	*[shorthand]*	7
193 *[shorthand]*	9	*[shorthand]*	12
[shorthand] 40203	15	*[shorthand]* 85282	16
[shorthand]	23	*[shorthand]*	24
[shorthand]	29	*[shorthand]* 50	32
[shorthand]	37	*[shorthand]*	41
[shorthand]	44	*[shorthand]* 51	47
[shorthand]	51	*[shorthand]*	56
[shorthand]	59	*[shorthand]*	61
[shorthand]	68	*[shorthand]*	68
[shorthand]	74	*[shorthand]*	75
[shorthand]	85	*[shorthand]*	85
[shorthand]	93	*[shorthand]*	94
[shorthand]	101	*[shorthand]*	104
[shorthand]	108	*[shorthand]*	111
[shorthand]	115	*[shorthand]*	118
[shorthand]	124	*[shorthand]*	126
O. D. Kelly	126	Clifton Wilson	129
	138	President	132
			144

45E—Dictionary and Spelling Preview

1. expert, economy, evident

2. recruiting, assistance

3. unanswered, scholastic, scene

92B—Vocabulary Preview

92C—Transcription from Dictation

Directions. Your teacher will dictate a letter to be transcribed in the AMS Simplified Letter Style. The dictator is Paul A. Wiseheart, Sales Manager.

PUNCTUATION REMINDER: Use a semicolon between coordinate clauses that are joined by a conjunction when these clauses contain commas.

92D—Supplementary Transcription

Directions. Transcribe letters from Lesson 17, page 46, as directed by your teacher.

92E—Transcriber's Guide

Care of the Typewriter. The typewriter is the secretary's "best friend" in the office. A machine that is well cared for will help her turn out neat, attractive transcripts; and work will not be delayed while the serviceman repairs a machine that is out of order because of carelessness of the operator. Here are some pointers that may help you keep your typewriter in the best possible working order:

1. Clean the type at least once a day. Use a stiff brush designed for cleaning keys. Brush the keys toward you and not from left to right. Plastic type cleaner can be used to lift off all loose fibers and ink after the keys have been brushed. If a liquid cleaner is used, it should be sparingly applied; too much liquid will make the keys "gummy."

2. At the end of each working day brush all erasure crumbs out of the machine. Depress the margin release and move the carriage to the extreme left and right to make sure that you remove all crumbs from the carriage rails. Use a long-handled brush—not your type brush. Brush crumbs from the platen, under the hood, and on the keyboard. Wipe off the table or platform on which your machine rests.

3. Keep the machine covered when not in use.

4. Oil the machine seldom and then sparingly.

5. If some part of the machine does not function properly, call the serviceman. Don't exert undue pressure on any part; you may break or damage it.

Lesson 93 ⬡⬡⬡⬡⬡⬡⬡⬡⬡⬡⬡⬡⬡⬡⬡⬡⬡

93A—Punctuation and Theory Review

93B—Vocabulary Preview

(1)

Weatherford, Council, entrance, Airport, for the purpose, Interior, length, expert, I hoped, reactions, economy, interpret, evident, summary, glossy

(2)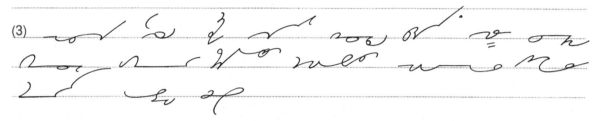

Professor, with our, recruiting, brochure, outlining, organization, graduates, assistance, men and women

(3)

in regard, postcard, sufficient, contents, unanswered, outstanding, Cohen, I am sure, this means, of this month, if you would like, scholastic, normally, to complete, from the time, let us know, we may be

Unit **10**

Secretarial Duties

Lesson **46** ⬡⬡⬡⬡⬡⬡⬡⬡⬡⬡⬡⬡⬡⬡⬡⬡⬡⬡

46A—Handling Incoming Mail

In handling incoming mail, you should remember to observe the following suggestions:

Handle Mail in Order of Urgency. Handle mail in the following order of urgency: first, telegrams, special-delivery, registered, and airmail letters; second, personal mail; third, regular first-class mail; fourth, advertisements, newspapers, and magazines. To handle mail in this fashion, you must first sort the mail into the aforementioned classifications. Stack each kind in an orderly pile.

Use a Minimum of Motion, Effort, and Time in Opening the Mail. Be sure your aids are arranged for ease and speed in using: letter opener, time stamp, paper clips, stapler, transparent tape, and others.

Each piece of mail should be time stamped as shown in the illustration. Paper clips and stapler

CONSOLIDATED EQUIPMENT COMPANY   423-2150

1213 West Third Street • Detroit, Michigan 48205

November 17, 19--

NOV 18 3 11 PM 19

Mr. William C. Campbell
Carlson Products Corporation
819 Northern Boulevard
Lansing, Michigan 48906

Dear Mr. Campbell:

Thank you very much for your order of November 12. The materials have been shipped by express as you requested.

Time-Stamped Letter

In typing a long quotation, indent the quoted matter five spaces from each margin and do not use quotation marks.

The letter was dictated by George C. Ulrich, Office Organization Representative.

PUNCTUATION REMINDER: A comma (or commas) should be used to set off parenthetical expressions if a definite pause is indicated.

91D—Supplementary Transcription

Directions. Transcribe letters from Lesson 16, page 43, as directed by your teacher.

91E—Transcriber's Guide

Simplified Letter Style. More than one "simplified" letter style has been advocated at various times, but the one that has received most attention in recent years is the form recommended by the Administrative Management Society (formerly National Office Management Association).

The principal argument for any simplified letter style is, of course, the saving of time in transcribing. Note in the illustration given at the right the absence of a salutation and a complimentary close, the use of a subject line, and the use of the block arrangement.

MODEL D: AMS Simplified Style

Observe that the subject line is a triple space below the address; the first line of the body, a triple space below the subject line. The dictator's name is in solid caps (but not his title) and is four spaces below the body. If an attention line is used, it is typed a double space below the inside address.

```
                                                          Phone 688-1150

        KEYSTONE PRODUCTS INCORPORATED
     KEYSTONE BUILDING · 1213 MERTON AVENUE · DENVER, COLORADO 80203

        March 12, 19--


        City Power & Light Company
        Brazer Building
        Boulder, Colorado  80306

        CATALOG NO. 61A:  KEYSTONE CARBON RINGS

        Our representative, Mr. W. C. Ring, sent us a
        report of his pleasant visit with you on March 8.
        We are glad to send you a copy of Catalog No. 61A,
        which describes our Keystone Carbon Rings.

        The catalog not only gives general specifications
        about the various sizes of carbon rings we have
        available, but also describes the uses to which
        these rings have been applied.

        We appreciate your interest in our Keystone Carbon
        Rings, and we hope to receive an order from you
        soon for rings to meet your particular needs.

        Benjamin L. Crain
        BENJAMIN L. CRAIN - Regional Sales Manager

        ls
```

Lesson 92 ⬡⬡⬡⬡⬡⬡⬡⬡⬡⬡⬡⬡⬡⬡⬡⬡

92A—Punctuation and Theory Review

(1) [shorthand outlines]

(2) [shorthand outlines]

will come in handy for fastening enclosures to the letter they accompany. Transparent tape may be needed to repair tears or cuts in the mail.

Handle Each Piece of Mail with Care. Here are a few cautions:

(a) Never open personal mail. If you do so by mistake, seal the envelope with tape, write on the flap "Opened by mistake," and sign your initials.

(b) Remove material carefully from an envelope. If enclosures are indicated in the letter but are not in the envelope, make a note of that fact on the letter. If some item is being sent in a separate envelope or package, keep a record of the expected item. You may have a Mail Register that is provided for your use in keeping a record of such items or of insured and registered mail that has been received.

(c) Do not dispose of the envelope. Your employer may want you to clip it to the letter, or he may want you to keep the envelope until the correspondence has been answered. Sometimes the name or address of the writer is given only on the envelope.

The postmark on the envelope or a notation stamped on it by the Post Office may show that there has been a delay in mailing or delivery. Such a fact may be important in the proper handling of a business transaction.

(d) If a mechanical letter opener is used, be sure to jog the contents of an envelope into the bottom of the envelope before opening in order to avoid cutting the letter itself or some enclosure such as a check.

(e) If an incoming letter refers to previous correspondence, your employer may want you to get

	Wellen, Incorporated
	TRANSMITTAL SLIP

Date ___11/15/--___
To _John Rayburn_
From _Ted Sanders_

☐	Note and Return	☐	Investigate and Report
☐	Note and See Me	☐	Get More Details
☐	Note and File	☒	Take Appropriate Action
☐	Note and Discard	☐	Please Answer
☐	For Your Approval	☐	For Your Signature
☐	Per Your Request	☐	Prepare Reply for Me

Comments _Please return correspondence after action has been taken. Make a record of action taken for file purposes._ _T.S._

Transmittal Slip

Sometimes your employer will want to refer a piece of correspondence to someone else for investigation, for signature, or for preparation of a reply rather than answer it himself immediately. If so, he may ask you to attach a transmittal slip to that piece of correspondence and make certain notations.

the previous correspondence from the files and attach it to the letter.

(f) Arrange the mail neatly on your employer's desk or in a tray or drawer if he has designated one for that purpose. If he is not at his desk, place the top item face down so that it cannot be read by anyone passing by his desk.

MAIL REGISTER   Name _Sally Leeds_

RECEIVED		FROM Name/Address	DATED	ADDRESSED TO		DESCRIPTION	SEP. COV. RECEIVED	REFERRED		WHERE FILED
Date	Time			Dept.	Person	Kind of Mail/Enc./Sep. Cov.		To	Date	
3/17	8:30 a.m.	G. Patterson, Boston	3/15	Pers.		Request for conf. schedule		Pers.	3/17	
3/19	11 a.m.	Monroe Mach. Co. Monroe	3/14		DGP	Spec. del. letter		DGP	3/19	
3/22	2:30 p.m.	A. Hughes, Austin, Minn.	3/19	Adv.		Descriptive list being sent	3/24	Adv.	3/24	Adv.
3/23	1 p.m.	T. L. James Co. Local	3/22	Acctg.		Sample forms enclosed		Acctg.	3/23	Acctg.
3/25	10 a.m.	H. A. Bolt Local	3/24		J. Givens	Red Cross Drive material enc.			3/25	
3/27	3 p.m.	J. Semon, Los Angeles	3/24		DGP	Adm. manual sent sep. cov.	3/28		3/28	
3/29	9 a.m.	Peterson, Inc. Local	3/28	Acctg.		Tax forms enc.		Acctg.	3/31	
3/31	2 p.m.	M. K. Sheppherd New York	3/28		DGP	Tickets—TV Broadcast Enc.	—	DGP	3/31	
3/31	1:15 p.m.	M. Spears New Orleans	3/30		OGF	Annual Rept. being sent				

Mail Register

90D—Supplementary Transcription

Directions. Transcribe letters from Lesson 15, page 39, as directed by your teacher.

90E—Transcriber's Guide

Second-Page Headings. An appropriate heading should begin second and succeeding pages of a letter. Then if the pages become separated, they can be reassembled with a minimum of difficulty. The minimum information that should be included in a second-page heading is: the name of the addressee, the page number, and the date.

Some firms who have considerable correspondence that requires more than one page have special stationery for their continuation sheets with at least the name of the company on it. Some printed continuation sheets are illustrated at the right.

Second-Page Heading Styles

```
Mr. O. J. Pressley          2          May 10, 19--

     10.  This area gives a fine view to the south.  The
immediate area to the south has a thick growth of sumac,
pine, and oak.  More permanent trees should be inter-
planted in such a way as to frame a view to the south.
```

```
Mr. O. J. Pressley
Page 2
May 10, 19--

     10.  This area gives a fine view to the south.  The
immediate area to the south has a thick growth of sumac,
```

Unit **19**

Transcribing Letters with Special Problems

Lesson **91** ⬡○⬡○⬡○⬡○⬡○⬡○⬡○⬡○⬡○⬡○⬡○⬡○

91A—Punctuation and Theory Review

(1) [shorthand] 24 [shorthand] 6 4 [shorthand] .10/ [shorthand]   (2) [shorthand]

91B—Vocabulary Preview

[shorthand notes]

91C—Transcribing from Dictation

Directions. Your teacher will dictate a long letter to you for transcription. Use modified block style with centered date and paragraph indentions; mixed punctuation. Make an extra carbon copy for Mr. Gregory.

Questions for Discussion

1. In what order should mail be handled?
2. Suggest an arrangement of aids that would speed up handling the mail.
3. What are some cautions to be observed in handling the mail?

Office Practice Problem

In a form similar to that shown in the illustration for a Mail Register, record the essential facts about the following:

a. Mr. Horace Appleby writes that he is sending a newspaper in a separate package.

b. Miss Harriet Blaine states in a letter that she is sending a short story by registered mail.

c. Graves Printing Company has announced that it has returned some defective merchandise by express collect.

d. Mr. Claude Brown has wired that he is sending complete details of his contract by special-delivery letter.

46B—Building Speed in Taking Dictation

Brief-Form Practice

Directions. The following paragraph has 32 brief forms and brief-form derivatives. If you can read the copy in 30 seconds, you will be reading at the rate of 120 words a minute.

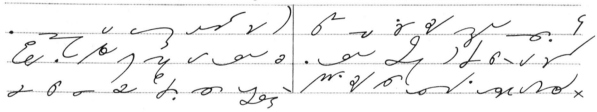

Word Spellings and Meanings

guarantee—to insure the performance of (v.)
    an agreement that insures performance, genuineness, reliability (n.)

guaranty—an agreement that insures performance, genuineness, reliability (n.)
    (this spelling never used as a verb)

NOTE: The following material includes words presented in Lessons 42-45, as well as those given above.

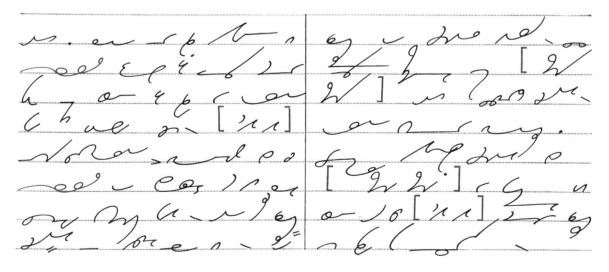

If a great deal of multiple-copy typing is done, the typist may be given a hard platen to use in her machine; or she may be given a backing sheet made of very hard material to place at the back of the carbon pack.

Carbon sheets that are not suitable for continued use in carbon packs may still be satisfactory for use in making only one carbon copy of typed material.

Lesson 90 ⬡○⬡○⬡○⬡○⬡○⬡○⬡○⬡○⬡○⬡○⬡○⬡○

90A—Punctuation and Theory Review

90B—Vocabulary Preview

90C—Transcribing from Dictation

Directions. Use the same letter and punctuation styles as in Lesson 89. Letter (1) will be dictated; transcribe (2) from the plate notes. Make two carbon copies of each letter.

The dictator of the first letter is R. C. Layton, Rodney Layton Company. The dictator of the second letter is H. L. McMasters, Meisler Brokerage Company.

PUNCTUATION REMINDER: Commas are used to set off words, phrases, or clauses used in a series.

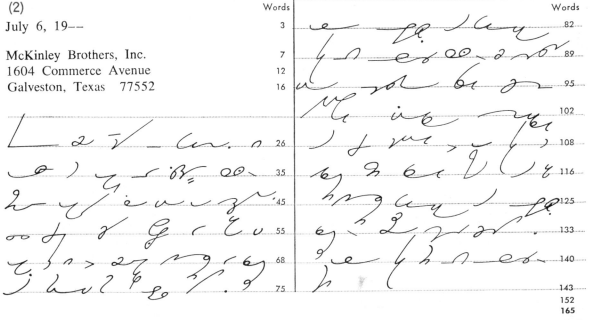

	Words
(2)	
July 6, 19--	3
McKinley Brothers, Inc.	7
1604 Commerce Avenue	12
Galveston, Texas 77552	16
	26
	35
	45
	55
	68
	75

	Words
	82
	89
	95
	102
	108
	116
	125
	133
	140
	143
	152
	165

Practice Material for Building Fluency

	Words
(1)	

[Shorthand outlines throughout this section]

(1) ⟨shorthand⟩ 8, 19— — 3

⟨shorthand⟩ — 7

631 ⟨shorthand⟩ — 11

⟨shorthand⟩ 60085 — 16

⟨shorthand⟩ — 26

⟨shorthand⟩ — 32

8½ (5½) 9½ (6 — 36

⟨shorthand⟩ — 44

⟨shorthand⟩ — 51

⟨shorthand⟩ — 57

⟨shorthand⟩ — 66

4/ ⟨shorthand⟩ — 71

⟨shorthand⟩ 360 ⟨shorthand⟩ — 78

⟨shorthand⟩ — 86

⟨shorthand⟩ — 94

⟨shorthand⟩ — 104

⟨shorthand⟩ — 112

Raymond Prescott — 115
Sales Department — 119
— 132

(2) ⟨shorthand⟩ 12, 19— — 4

⟨shorthand⟩ rb amberg — 7

⟨shorthand⟩ — 11

⟨shorthand⟩ 46135 — 16

⟨shorthand⟩ — 23

⟨shorthand⟩ — 30

⟨shorthand⟩ — 36

⟨shorthand⟩ — 45

⟨shorthand⟩ — 53

⟨shorthand⟩ — 60

⟨shorthand⟩ — 70

Gladys Gordon — 75
— 87

Dictionary and Spelling Preview

1. faille, bullion, broadcloth, tissue

2. Lilac, congestion, lessening, patrons

3. accordance, secretary, envelopes

4. re-cover, anniversary, craftsmanship, tapestry, reweb

Preview of New Dictation Material

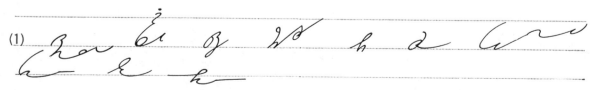

(1) ⟨shorthand⟩

thank you for your letter, husband's outfit, if you decide, tissue, faille, broadcloth, bullion, tassel, measurement

89D—Supplementary Transcription

Directions. Transcribe letters from Lesson 14, page 37, as directed by your teacher.

89E—Transcriber's Guide

Assembling a Carbon Pack. In assembling papers when one or more carbon copies are to be made, considerable time and motion can be saved by having the stationery arranged as shown in Lesson 80 on page 220. When stationery is so arranged, the papers are assembled as they are pulled from the drawer. The first illustration below shows the assembly of the original and first carbon copy sheets; the second, the addition of succeeding carbon and copy sheets.

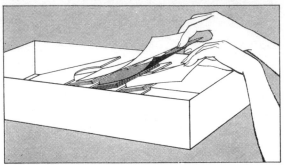

First Step in Assembly

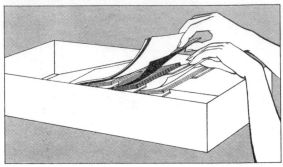

Second Step in Assembly

Rotating Carbon Sheets. If you are typing a number of copies of a long report, you can insure the clearest possible copies by "rotating" your carbon sheets. Suppose you were making five carbon copies and had decided that five typings was the maximum use you could make of a sheet of carbon paper and still have a clear fifth copy. As you disassemble the copies of a typed page, lay aside the carbon sheet that had been used to make the *first* carbon copy. In assembling the pack for the next page, put a new sheet of carbon paper into position for the *last,* or fifth, copy. The other four sheets are then moved forward one copy from where they were in the previous pack. Continue this procedure for each succeeding typed page. This method is used because the closer the carbon sheet is to the original copy the greater the force with which the keys are hitting the paper; therefore the most-used sheet should be nearest the front of the pack.

320 EUCLID AVENUE   DES MOINES, IOWA 50307   351-6866

Century Equipment Company

August 21, 19--

Mr. L. J. Herrera
1614 Langston Drive
Kansas City, Kansas 66120

Dear Mr. Herrera

Thank you very much for your partial payment of August 18, which we have credited to your account.

In order that we may cooperate with you in your efforts to complete payment, will you please let us know what arrangements you would like to make for handling the remaining balance.

We are enclosing an envelope for your convenience in writing us. Your prompt reply will be greatly appreciated.

Very truly yours

Peter A. Hanson
Credit Department

kd

Enclosure

MODEL C: Block Style

(2) *[shorthand]*

Minton, Lilac, parent, downtown, at least, congestion, patrons

(3) *[shorthand]*

in accordance with your, to send the, directly, Township

(4) *[shorthand]*

reweb, bottom, re-cover, wing, tapestry, cushion, dining, discount, Anniversary, expert, craftsmanship, yard

Lesson 47 ⬡○⬡○⬡○⬡○⬡○⬡○⬡○⬡○⬡○⬡○⬡○⬡○⬡○⬡

47A—Handling Outgoing First-Class Mail

Wholly or partially typed letters or cards are sent by first-class mail, which is the speediest postal service. First-class mail may be sent by "regular" mail service (train or car) or by airmail service, which is faster for long distances than regular. If there is no postal air service directly from your town to the town to which you are sending mail, regular mail may be as speedy as airmail, especially if the distance involved is not very great. When in doubt, check schedules with the post office because there is no point in spending extra money for airmail service if it will not effect quicker delivery.

Some special services in speeding delivery or in guaranteeing delivery are available upon payment of a fee:

Special Delivery. A letter that has been sent special delivery will be delivered upon its arrival to the address given if the destination is within one mile of a delivery station (post office or substation) if it arrives before 11 p.m.

Registered Mail. A letter may be "insured" by registering it at the post office. To obtain this service, you must fill in a form on which you place the address of the person who is to receive the letter, your own address, the nature of the contents, and its value. The sender may obtain a receipt as evidence of delivery by marking the envelope "Return Receipt Requested" and paying an additional fee.

A fee will be charged, and you will be given a slip to retain as evidence of the registration.

If the registered letter is not delivered within a reasonable time, you then take steps to have the letter traced by the post office.

REGISTERED NO. 12285	POSTMARK
Value $18.00 Spec. del'y fee $	CINCINNATI, OHIO NOV 20 19
Fee $.75¢ Ret. receipt fee $.10¢	
Surcharge $ Rest. del'y fee $	
Postage $.16¢ ☐ Airmail	
Postmaster, By CRF	
From Paul Lowry Cincinnati, Ohio	
To Joseph Gage Chicago, Illinois	
POD Form 3806 c48—16—70493-8	

Receipt for Registered Mail

Lesson 89 ⬡⬡⬡⬡⬡⬡⬡⬡⬡⬡⬡⬡⬡⬡⬡⬡⬡⬡

89A—Punctuation and Theory Review

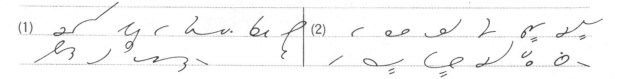

89B—Vocabulary Preview

89C—Transcribing from Dictation

Directions. Use block style and open punctuation (Model C, page 242). Letter (1) will be dictated; transcribe (2) from the plate notes.

The dictator of the first letter is Chauncey L. Harris, Director, Public Relations. The dictator of the second letter is J. R. Merman, Personnel Assistant.

PUNCTUATION REMINDER: A clause that is essential to the meaning of a sentence is restrictive and is not set off by commas; a clause that is not essential is set off by commas.

	Words		Words
(2)　　　　　　April 2, 19--	3		71
			78
Miss Margaret Hardy	7		85
Robinson Hall	10		
University of Missouri	14		94
Columbia, Missouri　65201	19		103
	30		110
	38		119
	45		131
	55		138
	62		147
			163

Certificate of Mailing

Certificate of Mailing.
If you want proof that you have mailed a letter, you can get a certificate of mailing. This certificate does not insure or speed delivery in any way; it merely is evidence that you did mail a certain item, such as an income tax return, on a specific date. There is a charge for this service.

Recalling a Letter. If you mail a letter and then want it back, you may be able to get it from the post office before it is delivered. The proper procedure is to go to the local post office and give the clerk the complete address and time the letter was posted. There may or may not be a charge for this service, depending on what is involved in retrieving the letter.

Forwarding a Letter. If you wish to forward a letter to another address, cross out neatly the old address and write the new one on the envelope. No additional postage is required. If the letter had been sent by special delivery, however, you would have to pay the special-delivery fee to have the letter handled by special delivery at the second address.

Foreign Mail. If a letter is to go abroad, the amount of postage needed may be different from that needed for domestic mail. Check your *Postal Manual* or inquire at your local post office.

Certified Mail. For a fee of 20 cents the post office will provide a numbered receipt so that the delivery of a letter can be traced. This service is called certified mail.

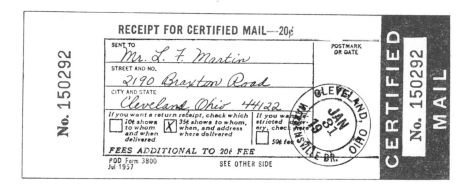

Receipt for Certified Mail

The gummed stub at the right-hand end carries the same number as the receipt and is attached to the face of the envelope.

Questions for Discussion

1. What is first-class mail?

2. What should you consider in deciding whether to send a letter by regular mail or airmail?

3. What service do you get when you send a letter by special delivery? by registered mail? by certified mail?

4. What is the purpose of a certificate of mailing?

5. What is the procedure for recalling a letter you have mailed? for forwarding a letter?

Office Practice Problem

According to the *Postal Manual*, how much will it cost to send each of the following:

a. Letter weighing 3 ounces, regular mail.

b. Letter weighing 5 ounces, airmail.

c. Letter weighing 4 ounces, airmail and special delivery.

d. Letter weighing 3 ounces with a declared value of $100, regular mail registered.

e. Letter weighing 6 ounces to go by regular mail and for which you are to obtain a certificate of mailing.

Words

(2)   July 20, 19--   3

6

Dr. Victor Goff   9
Child Guidance Center   14
318 North 14th Street   18
Chicago, Illinois   60620   23

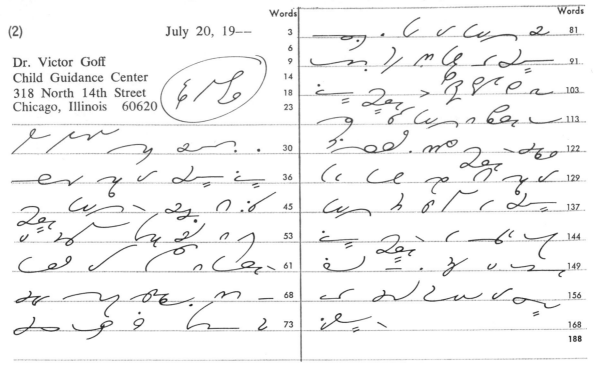

Words

81

91

103

113

122

129

137

144

149

156

168

188

88D—Supplementary Transcription

Directions. If time permits, transcribe the letters in Lesson 13, page 34, as directed by your teacher.

88E—Transcriber's Guide

Carbon Paper—Kinds and Care of. Carbon papers differ in quality, size, color, weight, and hardness and thickness of finish. The lightest weights of paper are the most desirable for multiple copies because they keep the thickness of the pack at a minimum. The hardest finish is also the most desirable for multiple copies. Black is the color preferred for most office work. The better the quality of carbon paper the less trouble you will have with smudges on carbon copies.

Carbon paper that is 8½ by 11½ size and has cut corners is best to use with 8½ by 11 stationery because it enables you to disassemble papers more easily and also keep your fingers clean.

Be careful in handling carbon paper to avoid wrinkling or tearing the edges because wrinkled or torn edges are difficult to "line up" with the edges of your copy paper so that the papers are straight in the machine. If the papers are not straight, you may have wrinkles in your carbon paper that will make "trees" on your carbon copies.

Keep the carbon paper face down in a folder or stationery slot of your desk drawer. Replace carbon sheets carefully after use. Keep them away from heat.

If a sheet of carbon paper does get wrinkled, lay it face down on plain paper and rub the wrinkle gently with your thumb nail.

After a carbon sheet has been used, you can sometimes get more wear out of it by cutting a thin strip off one end.

For special types of jobs, one-time carbon is sometimes used. This one-time carbon may be attached to single copy sheets or a pack may be preassembled.

Phrase Builder

There are 17 phrases in the following paragraph.

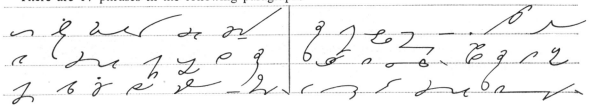

Word Spellings and Meanings

device—a clever plan, contrivance, or invention (n.)

devise—to make a new arrangement of parts or a new application of principles (v.)

NOTE: The following material includes words presented in Lessons 43-46, as well as those given above.

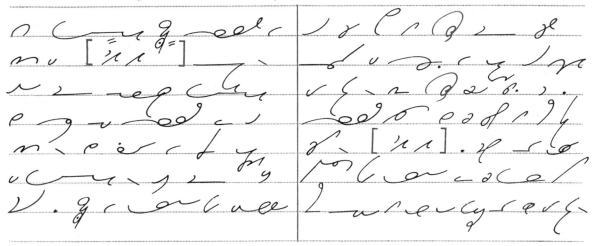

Practice Material for Building Fluency

	Words		Words
... 7, 19	3	...	49
... farr	7	...	58
... 18 6 ...	13	...	64
... 6 15220	20	...	72
		...	80
...	28	...	87
...	34	...	95
		Walter Sumner	99
...	41		115

Dictionary and Spelling Preview

1. incised, aluminum
2. automatic, defective
3. nonsupervisory, nontechnical, maintenance, reappraised

Personal Notation. If a personal letter is sent to a business address, the word *PERSONAL* is typed on it so that it will be delivered unopened to the addressee. This notation is placed in the same position on the envelope as an attention line—in the lower left-hand corner. It may or may not be typed on the letter itself; if it is typed, it is placed the same as an airmail notation.

Hold for Arrival Notation. Sometimes the possibility exists that a letter may arrive at a destination before the addressee does; for instance, at a hotel. The notation *Hold for Arrival* in the lower left-hand corner of the envelope tells the person handling the mail that the addressee will be arriving and that the letter should be held for him.

```
ILLINOIS EXTENSION CENTER
CHAMPAIGN, ILLINOIS  61820

                                           AIRMAIL
                                    SPECIAL DELIVERY

              Dr. Victor Goff
              Child Guidance Center
              318 North 14th Street
              Chicago, Illinois  60610


  PERSONAL
```

Airmail, Special Delivery, and Personal Notations on Envelope

Lesson 88 ⬡⬡⬡⬡⬡⬡⬡⬡⬡⬡⬡⬡⬡⬡⬡⬡⬡⬡

88A—Punctuation and Theory Review

(1) *[shorthand outlines]*

(2) *[shorthand outlines]*

88B—Vocabulary Preview

[shorthand outlines]

88C—Transcribing from Dictation

Directions. Use the same letter and punctuation styles as in Lesson 86. Your teacher will dictate Letter (1), which is to be signed by Henry C. Burwell, President. Transcribe Letter (2) from the plate notes. It is dictated by Norma Brumage, Home Demonstration Agent.

Postscripts are typed below the last special notation (reference, enclosure, or carbon-copy notation). A postscript may be typed with or without "P. S." at its beginning. See the illustrations below.

```
reputation in our line and are proud of the job we
are doing.

We hope that you are now successfully established
in the packing industry; we look forward to hearing
from you in the very near future.

              Very truly yours,

              Henry C. Burwell

              Henry C. Burwell, President

ed

P. S.  Are you aware of our new free telephone
order plan?
```

```
Thank you for the assistance that you are giving us with
the program; your appearance will guarantee a worthwhile
conference.

              Sincerely,

              Norma Brumage

              Norma Brumage
              Home Demonstration Agent

ls

Enclosure

Please keep this copy of the program for your use during
the Farm Home Conference.  The meetings will be held in
a suite of rooms on the second floor of the Anchor Hotel.
```

Postscripts

Preview of New Dictation Material

(1)

I have your letter, standardized, incised, painted, aluminum, to consider, entrance, we should like, some of the, let us have, typical, in order that, we may have, upon receipt, of such

(2)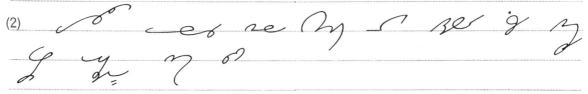

automatic, on the market, one year, defective, intention, to start, has yet, to invite, preview, Rochester, you can be, with us

(3)

Freeman, out of these, recognized, employees', nontechnical, nonsupervisory, recommendations, advisory, maintenance, Denver, Los Angeles, assist, Council, president, summarized, bulletin, award, photographs, contributors, during the year, reappraised

Lesson 48 ◇○◇○◇○◇○◇○◇○◇○◇○◇○◇○◇○◇○

48A—Telephone Usage

A great deal of business is transacted over the telephone; and you, as a secretary, can gain or lose customers by your telephone technique. Here are some general suggestions on effective use of the telephone:

1. Talk directly into the mouthpiece in an ordinary tone of voice. The transmitter should not be more than an inch from your lips.

2. Have nothing in your mouth such as candy, pencil, or cigarette to blur your speech.

3. Be courteous and cheerful; the other person's impression of you, your employer, or your company is based on your tone of voice and choice of words. "Please" and "thank you" are words used frequently by thoughtful callers.

4. Do not cover up the mouthpiece with your hand to say something to another person in the room that you don't want the individual on the other end of the wire to hear. Your hand will not always screen out what you say. If you must get a message to him, do it by hand signal or by writing a note for him to read.

5. Answer the telephone as quickly as possible. The ringing may disturb others in the office, and the delay may irritate the person who is calling.

6. Don't use a business telephone for personal calls.

7. If you have a long list of numbers to call, don't call one right after the other. Allow a few minutes between calls so that others can use the line or incoming calls can be received.

The dictator of Letter (1) is Harold Burns, Account Executive; the dictator of Letter (2) is John A. Brown, Policy Consultant. Make a carbon copy of Letter (1) for Richard Fanske and a carbon copy of Letter (2) for Floyd Harrell.

PUNCTUATION REMINDER: When two independent clauses are joined by a coordinating conjunction, the clauses are separated by a comma.

```
If at some future time the Red Star coverage should
be made available to our billed-at-home subscribers,
we shall be happy to receive an application from
you.

                        Sincerely yours,

                        John A. Brown

                        John A. Brown
                        Policy Consultant

vs

Enclosure

cc Floyd Harrell
```

Enclosure and Carbon-Copy Notations

87D—Supplementary Transcription

Directions. If time permits, transcribe the letters in 12D—Practice Material for Building Fluency exercise in Lesson 12, page 32.

87E—Transcriber's Guide

Airmail Notation. If a letter is sent by airmail, the word *AIRMAIL* may be typed on both the envelope and on the letter. Typing the notation on the letter reminds the transcriber how the letter is to be sent and serves as a record of how it was sent. It tells the receiver how the letter was sent. Typing the notation on the envelope helps insure that the person who stamps the letter will use the right amount of postage and helps the Post Office Department handle the letter.

Please Forward Notation. If the sender thinks that the addressee may have changed his address, he can have the words *Please Forward* typed in the lower left-hand corner as a request to the Post Office Department or to the person who accepts the mail at the old address to forward it to the new address.

Special Delivery Notation. A letter sent by special delivery is delivered by special messenger. The notation *SPECIAL DELIVERY* is typed on the letter and on the envelope in the same manner as an airmail notation. If both an airmail notation and a special delivery notation are needed, they may be typed as shown in the illustration at the right.

```
                                    October 20, 19--

AIRMAIL

Carson Fruit Company
Hyde Park Building
1431 East 25th Street
San Francisco, California  94105

Gentlemen:

Last year we had an exchange of letters.  At that
time you informed us that you were planning to
```

Airmail Notation on Letter

```
BURWELL COMPANY
LOS ANGELES, CALIFORNIA  90002

                                            AIRMAIL

          Carson Fruit Company
          Hyde Park Building
          1431 East 25th Street
          San Francisco, California  94105

Please Forward
```

Airmail and Please Forward Notations on Envelope

```
                                    July 20, 19--

AIRMAIL - SPECIAL DELIVERY

Dr. Victor Goff
Child Guidance Center
318 North 14th Street
Chicago, Illinois  60610

Dear Dr. Goff:

We are enclosing a marked copy of the Farm Home
Conference program.  We are sending this ahead of
```

Airmail and Special Delivery Notation

TELEPHONE MESSAGE

FOR __Mr. Lockman__

DATE __2/14/--__   TIME __11 a.m.__

WHILE YOU WERE OUT

Mr. __Davidson__

FROM __Davidson Brothers__

PHONE NO. __522-7080__

TELEPHONED		X	PLEASE PHONE
RETURNED YOUR CALL			WILL CALL AGAIN
CAME TO SEE YOU			WANTS TO SEE YOU

MESSAGE __Re Adamson Towers contract__

TAKEN BY TJC

Telephone Call Slip

8. Have telephone call slips at hand and a note pad. If your employer is not in, jot down on the call slip all pertinent information—person calling, time of call, message, any specific directions for returning the call.

9. If someone is to answer the incoming call on another instrument, be sure he has picked up the handpiece before gently replacing yours.

10. If your employer is busy on another line, ask the caller if he wishes to hold the line, call back, or be called. If he wants to wait, report back to him at least every sixty seconds so that he'll know he has not been forgotten. He may decide to talk to someone else or to call back later.

11. Be sure of the correctness of any number you call. The telephone directory has two sections —alphabetic and classified. The alphabetic lists subscribers by alphabet regardless of whether the number is a home or a business number. The classified section lists businesses by type of service or product they provide. If certain numbers are called often, you may wish to list those in a special notebook or card file where they can be easily found.

12. Don't play guessing games on the telephone. Identify yourself or your firm quickly.

13. Replace the receiver gently when the call has been completed—don't drop it or slam it onto the set.

The Key Set. This type of set enables a person to handle more than one call at a time on the same instrument. Assume that a call comes in to the PBX operator from Mr. Gandy for Mr. Jones in the Contract Division. Here is the procedure, using the keyed illustration below:

PBX operator signals secretary in the Division by ringing a free line. Let us say it is Line 1001 (lamp lights under button on key set).

Secretary depresses button (1) on Line 1001, picks up earphone and says, "Contract Division."

Operator: I have a call for Mr. Jones.

Secretary: Just a moment, please.

Secretary depresses "Hold" button (2), then depresses "Local" button (3), then dials "3," which is Mr. Jones' line. His phone rings.

Mr. Jones: Jones speaking.

Secretary: You have a call on Line 1001.

Mr. Jones depresses Line 1001 button on his instrument, picks up earphone, and talks to Mr. Gandy. When connection is made, Secretary replaces earphone on cradle, which releases "Hold" and "Local" buttons. Light remains on Line 1001 button of her instrument until call is completed.

If another call comes in for someone else in the Division while this call is in progress, the operator will signal on one of the other lines that are free; then the procedure is repeated.

Many different arrangements are possible on the key set. For instance, all buttons may be extension lines. Also, the number of buttons may be less than six.

Use of a Key Set

Reference Notation. Most offices prefer that identification of the transcriber be given on a letter. The most common practice is for the initials of the transcriber to be typed flush with the left margin and a double space below the last closing line. In many cases, the initials of the dictator are typed before the transcriber's initials.

Occasionally, a dictator may want his name instead of his initials typed as part of the notation.

If the dictator and the signer are not the same person, the reference notation may so indicate. Some firms use numbers instead of initials, particularly if the dictator is not the signer but that fact is to remain unknown to the addressee.

RB:SF   rb/sf   sf   Russell Blair/sf   2:4

Enclosure Notation. If anything is enclosed with a letter, a notation of that fact is usually made in the left-hand corner a double space below the reference notation. Enclosure notations serve as a reminder to the transcriber and to the signer

that an enclosure is to be sent. The notation also tells the Mailing Department of the receiving company to look for an enclosure. Sometimes the enclosures are itemized; other times, not. It is good practice to use this notation when applicable.

Enclosure   Enclosures 2   Enc.   Enclosure: Catalog C

Carbon-Copy Notation. If a carbon copy of a letter is sent to one or more people other than the addressee, a notation to that effect is usually made below the reference notation (or the enclosure notation if there is one). It is considered a courtesy to let the addressee know who besides himself receives a copy. Once in a while the

signer of the letter may not wish to reveal that fact. In that case, the carbon copy is called a "blind carbon copy"; and the carbon-copy notation is made on the file copy but not on the original. It is not necessary, of course, to note carbon copies sent to people within the dictator's own firm.

cc Mr. J. B. Kildeer   CC J. B. Kildeer   bcc J. B. Kildeer

Lesson 87 ⬡⬡⬡⬡⬡⬡⬡⬡⬡⬡⬡⬡⬡⬡⬡

87A—Punctuation and Theory Review

87B—Vocabulary Preview

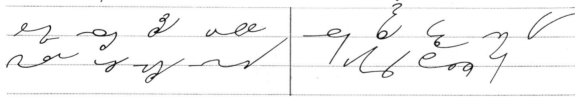

87C—Transcribing from Your Own Notes

Directions. Use the same letter and punctuation styles as in Lesson 86. Make appropriate enclosure and carbon-copy notations.

Questions for Discussion

1. Why is it important to use a "voice with a smile" on the telephone?

2. What information should you record on a telephone call slip?

3. What can you do if you need to say something to another person near you while you are engaged in a telephone conversation?

Office Practice Problems

1. While your employer was out, Mr. Clark of Weiss, Inc., called. He said that he needed to talk with your employer by 11. What would you put on the telephone call slip?

2. Under what title would you look in the classified section of the directory for: a surgeon, a taxicab, a firm doing repair work on plumbing, a firm handling carpenter's tools?

48B—Building Speed in Taking Dictation

Potential Rate Builder

There are 18 words in the sentence.

Word Spellings and Meanings

capital—a chief city, money or assets, upper-case letter

capitol—the building or buildings housing legislative bodies (capitalized when it refers to a specific capitol building)

NOTE: The following material includes words presented in Lessons 44-47, as well as those given above.

May 10, 19--

```
Mr. Thomas Jenkinson
Brewer College
St. Louis, Missouri  63109
```

```
School of Business and Economics
Schrader Polytechnic Institute
Evanston, Illinois  60203

Attention Dean M. K. Bancroft

Gentlemen:

        Subject:  Your Latest Catalog

Since I am now engaged in the reevaluation of the
business program at Brewer College, I would be most
```

```
School of Business and Economics

Schrader Polytechnic Institute

Evanston, Illinois  60203



Attention Dean M. K. Bancroft
```

Attention and Subject Lines in Letter   **Attention Line on Envelope**

86D—Supplementary Transcription

Directions. If time permits, transcribe the letters in 11D—Practice Material for Building Fluency in Lesson 11, page 29, using the same directions as for Letters (1) and (2) of 86C—Transcribing from Your Own Notes.

86E—Writing Shorthand from Print

Directions. Write the letters carefully in shorthand so that you can transcribe from your own notes in Lesson 87 or can take the letters from your teacher's dictation. Study the outlines given in the Vocabulary Preview of Lesson 87.

(1)

	Words
June 5, 19—	3
Kensington Hills Company	8
12 Boalsburg Road	11
Bowling Green, Kentucky 42101	17
Attention Mr. Quentin Schrader	24
Gentlemen:	26
Subject: Our Letter of June 1	32
Thank you for your telephone call of June 3.	41
We have carefully and [1] completely checked our files, and we find that we did receive $60.31 for last year.	50 58 63
This letter [2] may be used as a receipt for your income tax return. It is always a pleasure to be of service. (52)	71 79 85
Very [3] sincerely yours,	89
	120

NOTE: Observe that the attention line is typed a double space *above* the salutation; the subject line, a double space *below* the salutation.

(2)

	Words
June 7, 19—	3
Mrs. Earl S. Waters	7
140 East Second Street	11
Louisville, Kentucky 40209	17
Dear Mrs. Waters:	21
Subject: Change of Insurance Coverage in Policy 64321	29 32
Thank you for your [1] letter that notified us of your marriage. More information is needed before your husband can be included [2] on your contract.	40 48 55 61
Would you please pencil your husband's age and the date of your marriage at the bottom of this letter [3] and return it to our office immediately.	69 78 87 89
Your interest in Red Star coverage is appreciated.[4] That type of coverage is now offered only to persons who are employed where Red [5] Circle and Red Star are available to them.	98 106 114 122 125
If at some future time the Red Star coverage should be made available to our [6] billed-at-home subscribers, we shall be happy to receive an application from you. (125)	134 143 150 157
Sincerely yours,	161
	185

Practice Material for Building Fluency

	Words		Words
(shorthand)	3	*(shorthand)* 12	39
	7		45
	11		50
	16		59
	25		66
	33	Sidney Bishop	69
		Manager	73
			86

Dictionary and Spelling Preview

1. weight, paramount, choice, often, capital

2. embossed, quarterfolded, expedite, imprinted

3. endorsement, extension, premium, respectively, vehicles

Preview of New Dictation Material

(1) *(shorthand)*

if we can, electric wax, polisher, 8 pounds, several thousand, housewives, around, capital, any other, paramount, do you think

(2) *(shorthand)*

napkins, Fraternity, slightly, variety, authorized, embossed, basketweave, Greek, undoubtedly, we feel sure, individually, imprinted, economical, quarterfolded, accumulate, expedite, earliest, payable, at the time, you send, notification, it has been, requirements

(3) *(shorthand)*

we have had, during the past, damage, windstorm, vehicles, coverages, restriction, premium, at least, if you desire, to provide

Transcribing Letters with Special Problems

Lesson **86** ⬡⬡⬡⬡⬡⬡⬡⬡⬡⬡⬡⬡⬡⬡⬡⬡⬡⬡

86A—Punctuation and Theory Review

(1) *[shorthand]* (2) *[shorthand]*

86B—Vocabulary Preview

[shorthand]

86C—Transcribing from Your Own Notes

Directions. Use modified block style (Model B, at the right) with date ending at right margin and no paragraph indentions; mixed punctuation. Note the arrangement of subject and attention lines in the illustration on page 236.

Transcribe from the notes you wrote in 85D—Writing Shorthand from Print, page 233, or from notes taken from your teacher's dictation. If your teacher so directs, fold and insert the letters into the envelopes according to the directions on page 234.

The letters were dictated by Carl D. Orr, Executive Assistant.

PUNCTUATION REMINDER: When a dependent clause is used before an independent clause, set it off by a comma.

MODEL B: Modified Block Style with No Paragraph Indentions and Date Ending at Right Margin

3148 West Sixth Street

Denver, Colorado 80212

432-3469

AMERICAN MOTOR PARTS, INC.

October 5, 19--

Farmer-Bohn Company
149 East First Street
Denver, Colorado 80204

Gentlemen:

Recently you were presented with a copy of our latest catalog. We hope that by now you have had an opportunity to look through this catalog and to note the many beautiful lines of nationally advertised merchandise we have available for you and your customers.

Let us remind you that we have most of the merchandise shown in the catalog on display at our showroom in Denver at 3148 West Sixth Street. We invite you to visit this display room at your earliest convenience.

Sincerely yours,

Rodney P. Lange

Rodney P. Lange, Manager

ls

Lesson 49 ○○○○○○○○○○○○○○○○

49A—Procedure for Placing Local Calls

The procedure for placing local telephone calls is determined by the type of instrument—dial or manual—and by the presence or absence of a PBX board. A private exchange board is a central station through which all outside calls are channeled.

Dial Telephone—No PBX Board. A dial telephone number may have a name as a prefix, followed by a series of numbers, as ALpine 5-6821; or, two figures may be used instead of a name prefix, as 255-6821. You lift the receiver and dial the capital letters and then the figures; or in all-number dialing, you dial each digit of the number as given. If the line is busy, you will hear a repeated buzzing sound. Replace the handpiece and call again later. If someone answers, identify yourself immediately: "This is Jones & Company; Mr. King would like to talk with Mr. Waters."

Dial Telephone—PBX Board. Procedures may differ according to the type of switchboard installation. You may need to dial the operator and give her the number you want, or you may need to ask her for an outside line so that you can dial the number yourself, or you may be required to dial "9," which automatically gives you an outside line, and then dial your number. If you give the operator the number, give the full prefix word as follows:

NUMBER	YOU SAY
ALpine 5-6821	Alpine 5 (*pause*) six-eight-two-one
ALpine 5-1000	Alpine 5 (*pause*) one-thousand

If the line is busy, the operator will tell you so, and you will say, "Thank you," and replace the handpiece.

Manual Telephone. When you lift the receiver, the operator will say, "Number, please"; you will then give her the number as explained in the preceding paragraph. If the line is busy, she will tell you so; and you will say, "Thank you," and try again later.

49B—Procedure for Placing Long-Distance Calls

The procedure for placing long distance calls, like that for local calls, is determined by the presence or absence of a PBX board.

Dial Telephone—No PBX Board. Dial the long-distance operator as directed in your telephone book. Give the necessary information in the following order:

City and state to be called
Company name (if station-to-station call)
Person and company name (if person-to-person)
Telephone number if you know it
Your own number (and extension if you have one) when operator asks for it.

If the call is to be "collect," that is, paid by the other party, you should say "I'd like to make a collect call" before you give any other information to the operator.

When you make a station-to-station call, you are agreeing to pay for the call no matter whether the person you would like to talk to is there or not.

There is, therefore, a certain element of risk involved in making such a call. When you make a person-to-person call, there is no charge unless the operator reaches the person you want.

For station-to-station calls in certain cities, you can dial numbers directly. Each city that has "direct distance dialing" is assigned an area code number. To place a DDD call, dial the area code number first; then dial the regular telephone number.

Dial Telephone—PBX Board. Give the switchboard operator the information if she places long-distance calls. If she does not, she will connect you with a long-distance operator. In some cases, you dial "9," then dial the long-distance operator, and make the call yourself without the assistance of the switchboard operator in your firm.

If the party called cannot be reached, the operator will ask you whether you want her to try again later or whether you want to cancel the call.

Folding Letters. The illustrations below show the correct method of folding letters for small, large, and window envelopes.

Inserting Letters into Envelopes. The edge of the second fold is inserted first into a No. 10 envelope. The edge of the last fold is inserted first into a No. 6¾ envelope. In inserting letters into window envelopes, be sure that the complete address is visible through the window.

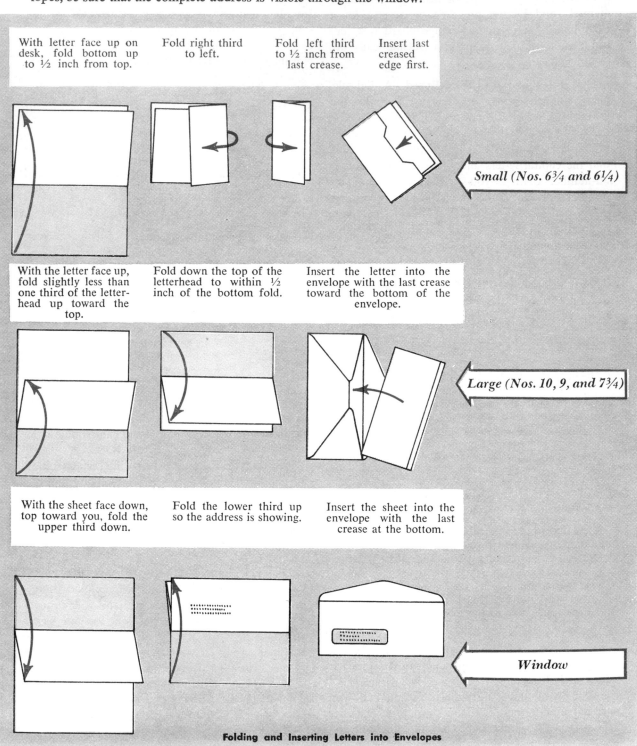

With letter face up on desk, fold bottom up to ½ inch from top.

Fold right third to left.

Fold left third to ½ inch from last crease.

Insert last creased edge first.

Small (Nos. 6¾ and 6¼)

With the letter face up, fold slightly less than one third of the letterhead up toward the top.

Fold down the top of the letterhead to within ½ inch of the bottom fold.

Insert the letter into the envelope with the last crease toward the bottom of the envelope.

Large (Nos. 10, 9, and 7¾)

With the sheet face down, top toward you, fold the upper third down.

Fold the lower third up so the address is showing.

Insert the sheet into the envelope with the last crease at the bottom.

Window

Folding and Inserting Letters into Envelopes

If there is no PBX board, when you pick up your telephone, identify yourself at once by saying, "King Heating Company, Mr. Burke's office." If the call has gone through the switchboard, the caller knows he has your company; and you say, "Mr. Burke's office, Miss Abrams speaking."

When Mr. Burke is not at his desk, you say something like, "Mr. Burke is not at his desk just now. May I have him call you?" or "Mr. Burke is not here just now. Can I help you?" When your employer is not available, be as specific as possible in answering but do not tell exactly where he is. Knowing where your employer is may give a caller some vital bit of information that should not be revealed.

Questions for Discussion

1. Explain the procedure for placing a local call from a dial telephone when there is no PBX board; when there is a PBX board.

2. Explain the procedure for placing a long-distance call when there is a PBX board and when there is not one.

3. What advantages and disadvantages can you see in all-number dialing? In direct distance dialing?

Office Practice Problem

Exactly what would you say

a. If your employer was out for a coffee break when a local call came in?

b. If your employer was out of the building when a long-distance call came in?

49D—Building Speed in Taking Dictation

Proportion Drill

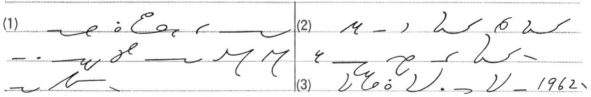

Word Spellings and Meanings

besides—in addition to, other than

beside—by the side of, separated from

NOTE: The following material includes words presented in Lessons 45-48, as well as those given above.

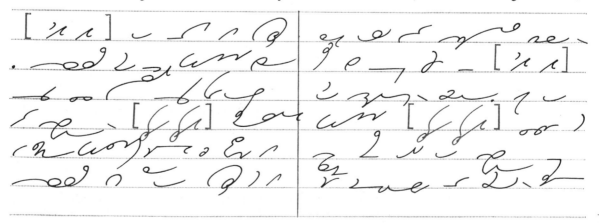

(2)

April 12, 19—

Mr. Timothy Moore
1230 Zenith Avenue
Indianapolis, Indiana   46205

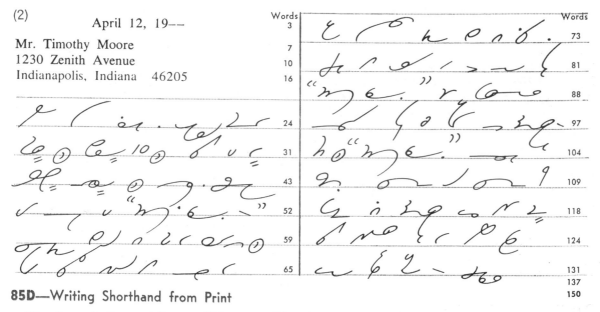

	Words
	3
	7
	10
	16
	24
	31
	43
	52
	59
	65
	73
	81
	88
	97
	104
	109
	118
	124
	131
	137
	150

85D—Writing Shorthand from Print

Directions. In Lesson 86, you will be transcribing from your own shorthand notes. Write in shorthand the letters given below. Your teacher may ask you to transcribe from those notes, or she may dictate the letters to you. Before writing the shorthand, study the outlines in the Vocabulary Preview in Lesson 86.

NOTE: The superior figures appearing in the copy are given to enable your teacher to dictate the letter to you if she so desires. The material is marked in groups of 20 standard words. Do not write the figures in your notes.

(1)

	Words
May 10, 19—	3
School of Business and Economics	9
Schrader Polytechnic Institute	15
Evanston, Illinois 60201	21
Attention Dean M. K. Bancroft	27
Gentlemen:	29
Subject: Your Latest Catalog	35
Since I am now engaged in the reevaluation	44
of the [1] business program at Brewer College,	52
I would be most grateful if you would have	61
a copy of your latest catalog [2] sent to me.	69
I would also appreciate being placed on the	78
mailing list to receive future bulletins.	87
I [3] shall be very happy to include you on the	96
mailing list for our bulletins that are	104
issued annually.[4]	107
Many thanks for your courtesies. (79)*	114
Sincerely yours,	117
	148

(2)

	Words
April 4, 19—	3
School of Business Administration	10
University of Akron	14
Akron, Ohio 44304	17
Attention Dean John E. Huntley	24
Gentlemen:	26
Subject: Business Curricula in Your School	35
We are conducting a study of business cur-	43
ricula [1] in collegiate schools of business.	52
Since your school has one of the outstanding	61
programs in the country, we should like [2]	69
very much to know more about it. Would	77
you please send us a copy of your most	85
recent catalog or bulletin [3] that describes	93
degree requirements and course offerings.	102
We should appreciate any other informa-	109
tion [4] that you could send us regarding the	118
business program in your school. (89)	125
Sincerely yours,	128
	156

* NOTE: The figure shown above in parentheses after the last line in the body of the letter is the number of 5-stroke words in the body of the letter. Use this figure in connection with the Placement Table on page 229.

Practice Material for Building Fluency

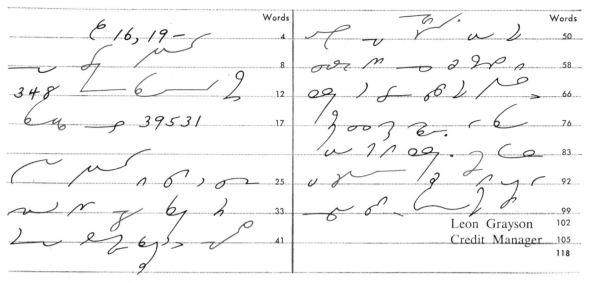

	Words
	4
	8
	12
	17
	25
	33
	41

	Words
	50
	58
	66
	76
	83
	92
	99
Leon Grayson	102
Credit Manager	105
	118

Dictionary and Spelling Preview

1. buzzer, similar, suite, unique
2. passbooks, transferred
3. eliminate, unusable, conserve, necessity, correspondence, excepted
4. recent, bookkeeping, cancel, volume
5. incidentally, subsequently, recovered, heretofore

Preview of New Dictation Material

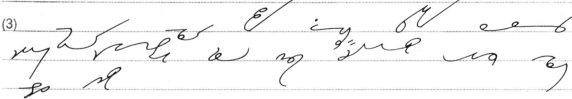

(1)

buzzer, is to be, installed, replacement, defective, one year, besides, suite, downtown, unique, as you can see, instruction, for your information

(2)

we received, this morning, transferred, passbooks, with this letter, entries, transaction

(3)

unfolded, insert, excepted, Home Office, adopted, eliminate, storage, stenographers', soiled, unusable, centralize, location, conserve, necessity, to type

85A—Punctuation and Theory Review

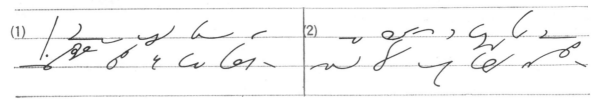

85B—Vocabulary Preview

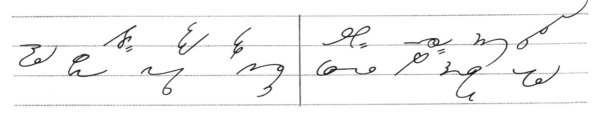

85C—Transcribing from Shorthand Notes

Directions. Follow the directions given in Lesson 83. Letter (1) has 143 words in the body; letter (2), 107.

There is no company name in the closing lines. Type the dictator's name, Alfred K. Henderson, four spaces below the complimentary close.

	Words
(1) October 22, 19--	3
Mr. Kirk S. Brand, Laboratory Director	11
Newspaper Research Institute, Inc.	18
P. O. Box 349	21
Indianapolis, Indiana 46204	27

35
42
50
59
67
73
83
92

100
109
115
123
132
141
147
153
160
168
173
181
186
209

(4)

in order that, bookkeeping, to cancel, possession, stamped, and return, will be made, to present, that will be, in this matter

(5)

heretofore, we find, instances, subsequently, recovered, incidentally, I might

Lesson 50 ⬡○⬡○⬡○⬡○⬡○⬡○⬡○⬡○⬡○⬡○⬡○⬡○⬡○⬡

50A—The PBX Board

By means of a private branch exchange board a firm can receive and make many more calls than would be possible otherwise. A secretary should understand how such a board is operated, even though she may not herself be an operator, because such knowledge will help her use her office telephone more efficiently.

There are PBX boards on which connections are made by means of cords. These cord-type switchboards are suitable for firms having a large number of calls. The cordless PBX boards have a limited capacity and are suitable for smaller business firms. A cord-type board with its various parts labeled is shown on page 145.

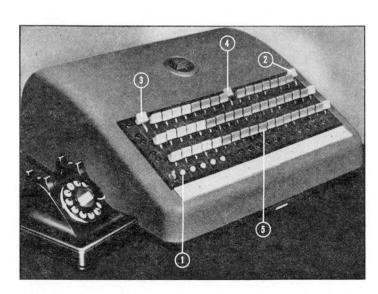

Cordless-Type Board

This is a small cordless switchboard capable of handling 5 incoming trunk lines and 12 extension lines.

Let us assume that Mr. Abrams calls in on an outside line (trunk) wanting to talk to Mr. Ames on Extension 5.

1. Light (1) comes on indicating incoming call on central trunk line.
2. Attendant removes receiver of switchboard telephone and operates attendant's talking key (2).
3. Attendant operates a trunk-connecting key (3) above the signal light, answering, "225-1006."
   MR. ABRAMS: Mr. Ames, please.
   ATTENDANT: Thank you, sir.
4. (a) Attendant operates extension key (4) on Ames's line and then (b) operates downward the ringing key (5) on the same vertical row.
5. When Mr. Ames answers, attendant restores attendant's key and replaces switchboard telephone.

Connection can be made also from extension to trunk (outside) or from extension to extension.

Example: Read the chapter entitled "Accounts Receivable" in PRINCIPLES OF ACCOUNTING; it was praised in the June issue of <u>The Office Manager</u>.

Dear Miss James:

Your request for a copy of "Principles of Economics" by Hammer and Caine was received this morning. The book is being billed to your account at a ten percent educational discount, making the price to you only $5.

We are confident that you will appreciate the many new features the authors have provided. Parts of the chapter entitled "<u>Price Theory</u>" were quoted in the last issue of the AMERICAN ECONOMIC REVIEW.

As your requested, the book is being sent to your home address at 3 East 9th Street. Will you please let us know what you think of the book as a possibly textbook for your introductory course in economics?

Cordially yours,

84E—Transcriber's Guide

Addressing Envelopes. The same information that is given in the inside address should appear in the envelope address. The placement of the lines of the address is determined by the size of envelope, the number of lines in the address, and the length of those lines.

The style of the address on the envelope should be the same as the style of the letter except that three-line addresses should be double-spaced. If only the name of the addressee, the city, and state are to be typed, the city is typed on the second line; and the state, on the third.

Addresses having average-length lines are well placed if started on the 12th line from the top of the envelope and five spaces to the left of center on small business envelopes (6½ by 3⅝ inches).

Addresses having average-length lines are well placed on No. 10 envelopes (9½ by 4⅛ inches) if they are started on the 13th or 14th line from the top edge of the envelope and at the approximate horizontal center. Short-line addresses should be placed somewhat farther to the right, and addresses having one or more long lines should be started farther to the left.

Many companies use window envelopes for part or all of their correspondence. When these are used, the letter must be folded so that the inside address shows through the "window," as shown on page 234.

Study the illustrations of correctly addressed envelopes below.

Correctly Addressed Envelopes

1. Extension jack into which cord is inserted to make a connection

2. Signal lamp that lights on when an extension wants service

3. Jack into which cord is inserted to connect on outside line

4. Signal lamp that lights on when outside call comes in

5. A pair of cords to connect two parties

6. A lamp that lights when operator rings; off when phone answers; on again when call has been terminated

7. A key matching the extension cord to enable operator to ring party wanted

8. A lever key which, when turned to the right, permits operator to talk with either party.

Let us assume that Mr. Haynes (outside caller) telephones Jones & Company to talk to Mr. Peters, whose extension is 1. Here are the steps in handling the incoming call:

1. When Haynes rings Jones & Company, signal lamp (4) lights above trunk jack (3).

2. Operator plugs left cord of a pair (5) into jack (3) and moves lever key (8) to the right, saying "Jones & Company."

   Haynes asks for Peters. Operator says "Thank you."

3. Operator picks up right cord of a pair (5) and plugs it into jack of Extension 1 (1) with one hand and with other hand depresses the extension ringing key (7) to ring the extension. As she rings, an extension light (6) goes on above that key and goes out when extension answers.

4. When light goes back on, call has been completed and she pulls out the cords.

If an extension line is busy, the operator hears a peculiar buzz as she touches the metal end of the cord to the jack; and she then tells the caller that the line is busy.

When an extension number wants to call another extension, the operator plugs in the *right* cord of a pair of cords to hear his order; and she uses the *left* cord to connect with the other extension. The lever key is turned to the right; and the extension ringing key is depressed to ring the extension number wanted.

When an extension number wants to call an outside number, the operator plugs in the *right* cord to hear the order and then uses the *left* cord to connect with an outside line. If the board is a manual board, the operator dials the desired outside number; if it is a dial board, the one wanting the outside number dials on his own instrument.

84C—Transcribing from Shorthand Notes

Directions. Follow the directions for letter style and punctuation style as given in Lesson 83. Letter (1) has 145 words in the body; letter (2), 80. Refer to the Placement Table on page 229 for suggestions on letter placement.

The dictator is Patrick O'Malley, Vice-President, Modern Furniture, Inc.

	Words
(1) May 8, 19--	2
Mr. Donald McBride, President	8
Kimberly Furniture Company	14
13 Howell Building	18
Evansville, Indiana 47702	23

(shorthand notes — left column)

31
39
46
54
61
66
72
77
84
91
98
104
112
119
126
132
142

(shorthand notes — right column)

151
160
167
174
181
189
195
200
221

(2) May 12, 19--	3
Bellview Furniture Company	8
1643 High Point Street	13
Terre Haute, Indiana 47802	18

28
34
42
47
54
62
69
75
83
91
101
107
115
130

84D—Proofreading Problem

Rule 35: Titles of books, booklets, magazines, and newspapers may be typed in solid capitals or in caps and lower case and underlined. In the example on page 231, the title of a book is shown in solid capitals; and the title of the magazine is shown in caps and lower case with underlining. It is a good idea to use one style for a book title and the other for a magazine title when both kinds of publications are listed in the same letter or report.

Titles of chapters in books and titles of articles in magazines are enclosed in quotation marks.

Questions for Discussion

1. What two principal types of PBX boards are used?

2. What are the holes called into which cords are plugged?

3. Which cord—front or back—is used to answer calls from the outside? from the inside?

Office Practice Problem

Assume that you are a switchboard operator of a cord-type PBX board. Explain the steps to follow in handling each of the following calls:

a. Mr. Bond (outside) wants to talk to Mrs. Wade on Extension 14.

b. Mrs. Wade wants to talk to Mr. Bond at 634-2631.

c. Mrs. Wade wants to talk with Miss Sims on Extension 30.

50B—Building Speed in Taking Dictation

Repetitive Phrase Builder

Word Spellings and Meanings

farther—refers to distance

further—refers to time, quantity, or degree

NOTE: The following material includes words presented in Lessons 46-49, as well as those given above.

Practice Material for Building Fluency

2. The setup for a certain length of letter may not always be the same. For instance, a 100-word letter may have tabulated material in it, may have an unusual number of paragraphs, or may have a subject or attention line. That letter would require a longer writing line than a 100-word letter with none of those features.

3. The left, right, and bottom margins of a letter should not be less than one inch in width.

4. If the letter is too long for one page, at least four lines of the body should be carried to the second page.

5. The first line of a paragraph should not be typed by itself at the bottom of a page or the last line of a paragraph typed by itself at the top of a page.

6. A letter of fewer than 90 words may be typed with double spacing in the body of the letter.

Letter Placement Table [1]

(For single-spaced letters on 8½- by 11-inch stationery)

5-Stroke Words in Body	Line Length (Pica or Elite)	Date on Line [2]	Blank Lines Between Date and Inside Address
Up to 100	45	16	6–3
101–150	55	15	6–3
151–200	60	14	6–3
201–300	65	13	5–3
301–350 [3]	{ 65 pica (2-page)	13	5–3
	{ 75 elite (1-page)	12	4–3

[1] The assumption has been made that the letter will have three lines in the inside address and will have closing lines consisting of: complimentary close, company name, and dictator's name or title. If the letter being transcribed has more lines in the inside address, more lines in the closing, or fewer lines in the closing, adjustment in the placement of the letter will have to be made by altering the writing line length or number of blank lines between date and inside address.

[2] If a fixed date line is used (for example, date on 12th line from top of page), increase the number of blank lines between the date line and the inside address.

[3] Letters over 350 words are usually 2-page letters for elite as well as for pica. The line length would vary from 60 to 65 for pica type and 70 to 80 for elite, depending on the letter length (i.e., letters just slightly too long for one page would be written with a 60-space line for pica and 70-space for elite, while letters considerably longer than one page would be written with a 65-space line for pica and 80-space for elite.)

Lesson 84 ○◇○◇○◇○◇○◇○◇○◇○◇○◇○◇○◇○

84A—Punctuation and Theory Review

(1) *[shorthand outlines]* 180

(2) *[shorthand outlines]*

84B—Vocabulary Preview

[shorthand outlines]

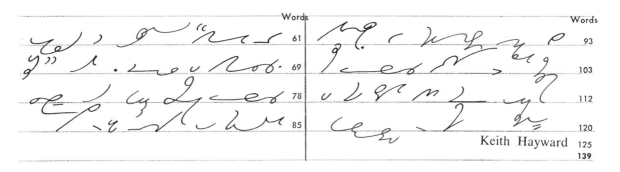

Keith Hayward

Dictionary and Spelling Preview

1. anticipation, confident, finance, devices
2. policyholder, Minnesota, decipher, embarrassing, incident
3. corporate, publicity, journalism, Albuquerque, principally

Preview of New Dictation Material

(1)

expand, further, mechanical, that have been, six months, Preview, Exhibits, anticipation, if we can, expansion, you may have, welcome

(2)

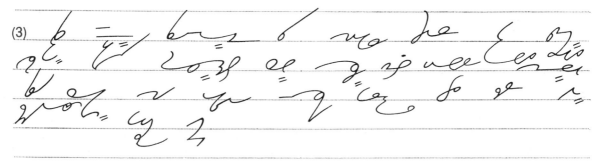

dictators, that there is, typewritten, notation, initials, years ago, Minnesota, decipher, had been, avoid, embarrassing, incident, instituted, outgoing, handwritten, signature, obscuring, observe

(3)

Jasper, New Mexico, Journalism, edit, corporate, veteran, publicity, University, thesis, obtained, Flagstaff Arizona, Gazette, one half, of last year, Commerce, joined, Albuquerque, court, reporter, engaged, principally, particularly, eastern, Texas, if you would like, professional, to furnish

Words

(shorthand outline) 44

(shorthand outline) 52

(shorthand outline) 59

(shorthand outline) 64

(shorthand outline) 69

(shorthand outline) 78

(shorthand outline) 85

(shorthand outline) 92

(shorthand outline) 99

(shorthand outline) 105

108

114

133

(2)

April 24, 19--   3

Mr. R. E. Austin   6
Central Purchasing Agent   11
C. W. Woodward Company   16
Trenton, New Jersey 08603   21

(shorthand outline) 31

(shorthand outline) 40

(shorthand outline) 47

(shorthand outline) 57

(shorthand outline) 65

(shorthand outline) 74

(shorthand outline) 82

(shorthand outline) 94

97
103
121

83D—Proofreading Problem

Rule 34: Spell out street names that are numbers ten and below. When a street has a number as its name, separate the house number from the street name by a hyphen with a space before and after it. The letters *th*, *d* and *st* may be added to the number that represents a street name, but they are often omitted. State house numbers in figures except for the house number *One*.

Examples:
```
The address is One East Fourth Street.
Our residence is 1241 West 24th Street.
```

```
Dear Mr. Temple:

    We have moved from Two South 10th Street to 46 West 31st
Street.  The move will mean a considerable saving for use be-
cause the rent is 20% less at the new location.  We have been
paying $260.00 a month.

    Will you please notify the various departments handling
our account of the address change.

                        Yours truly,
```

83E—Transcriber's Guide

Placement of Letters on the Page. To assist you in the placement of letters, a table is given on page 229. Do not memorize it, but refer to it until you become familiar with the space that is consumed by letters of various lengths. Keep in mind the following points whenever you use the table:

1. Practices vary in the vertical placement of the date line. Some companies use a fixed date line; i.e., a date line that is typed in the same place on every letter. Others use a "floating" date line, varying the placement according to the length of the letter.

Building Speed in Taking Dictation

Lesson **51** ⬡⬡⬡⬡⬡⬡⬡⬡⬡⬡⬡⬡⬡⬡⬡⬡⬡⬡⬡⬡

51A—Brief-Form Practice

Directions. The following paragraph has 37 brief forms and brief-form derivatives. If you can read it in 30 seconds, you will be reading at the rate of 116 words a minute.

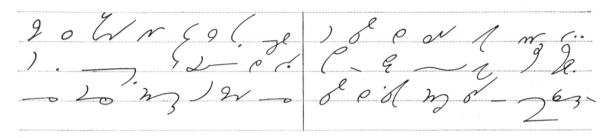

51B—Theory Review

The word beginning *ex-* is expressed by *es*. The prefix *electr-* or *electric* is expressed by *el* above the line.

Punctuation Styles. The most commonly used form of punctuation is *mixed*, illustrated at the right. In this form no punctuation is used after the date or lines of the inside address. A colon is used after the salutation; and a comma, after the complimentary close.

In *open punctuation*, illustrated at the right, no punctuation is used after any of the opening or closing lines of the letter except those ending with an abbreviation, in which case, of course, the period for the abbreviation must be used.

Mixed Punctuation   **Open Punctuation**

Lesson **83** ◇○◇○◇○◇○◇○◇○◇○◇○◇○◇○◇○◇

83A—Punctuation and Theory Review

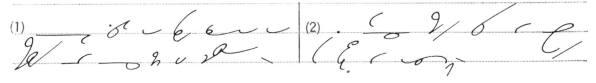

83B—Vocabulary Preview

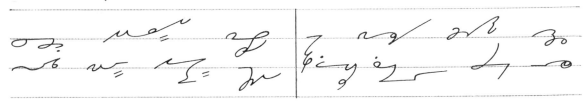

83C—Transcribing from Shorthand Notes

Directions. In transcribing the letters, use modified block style (Model A, page 226) with centered date line and indented paragraphs; mixed punctuation. The dictator is Harry Voorhies, Manager, Blackstone Company.

Start the date on the 16th line from the top of the page and use a 45-space writing line. Type the first line of the inside address on the 4th line down from the date. Whenever you transcribe a letter, make a file copy and address an envelope. Refer to the information on page 231 about addressing envelopes.

	Words		Words
(1) May 21, 19--	3		
Mrs. Esther Farmer, Motor Service	9		
American Red Cross	13		30
Eighth and Beech Streets	18		35
Toledo, Ohio 43602	22		

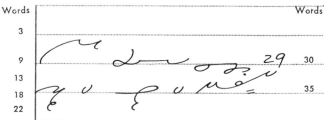

51C—Word Spellings and Meanings

stationary—fixed; not movable

stationery—paper on which letters are written

NOTE: The following material includes words presented in Lessons 47-50, as well as those given above.

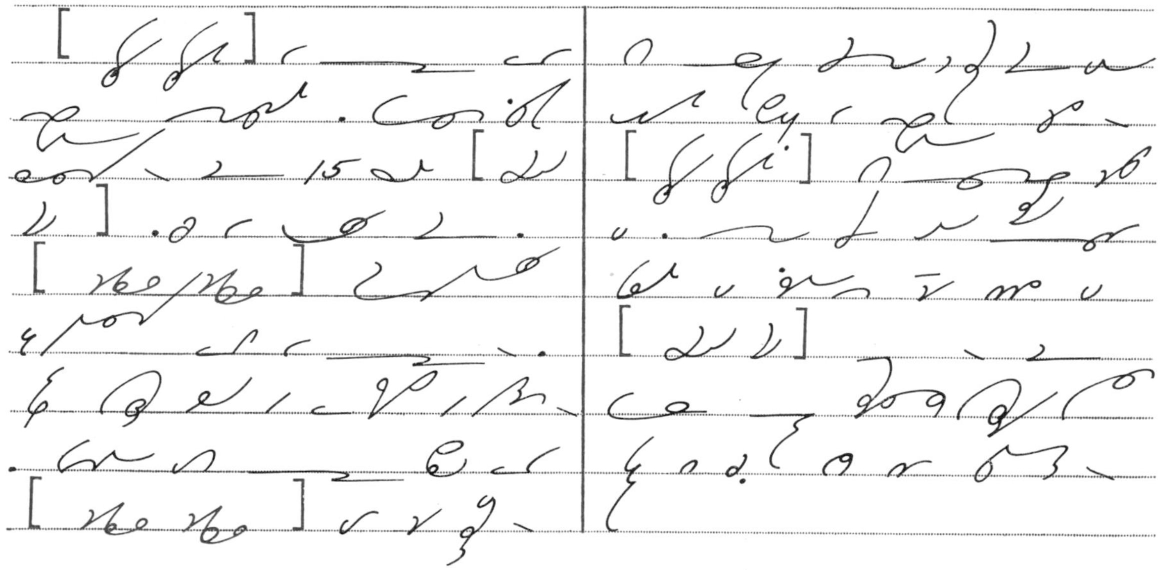

51D—Practice Material for Building Fluency

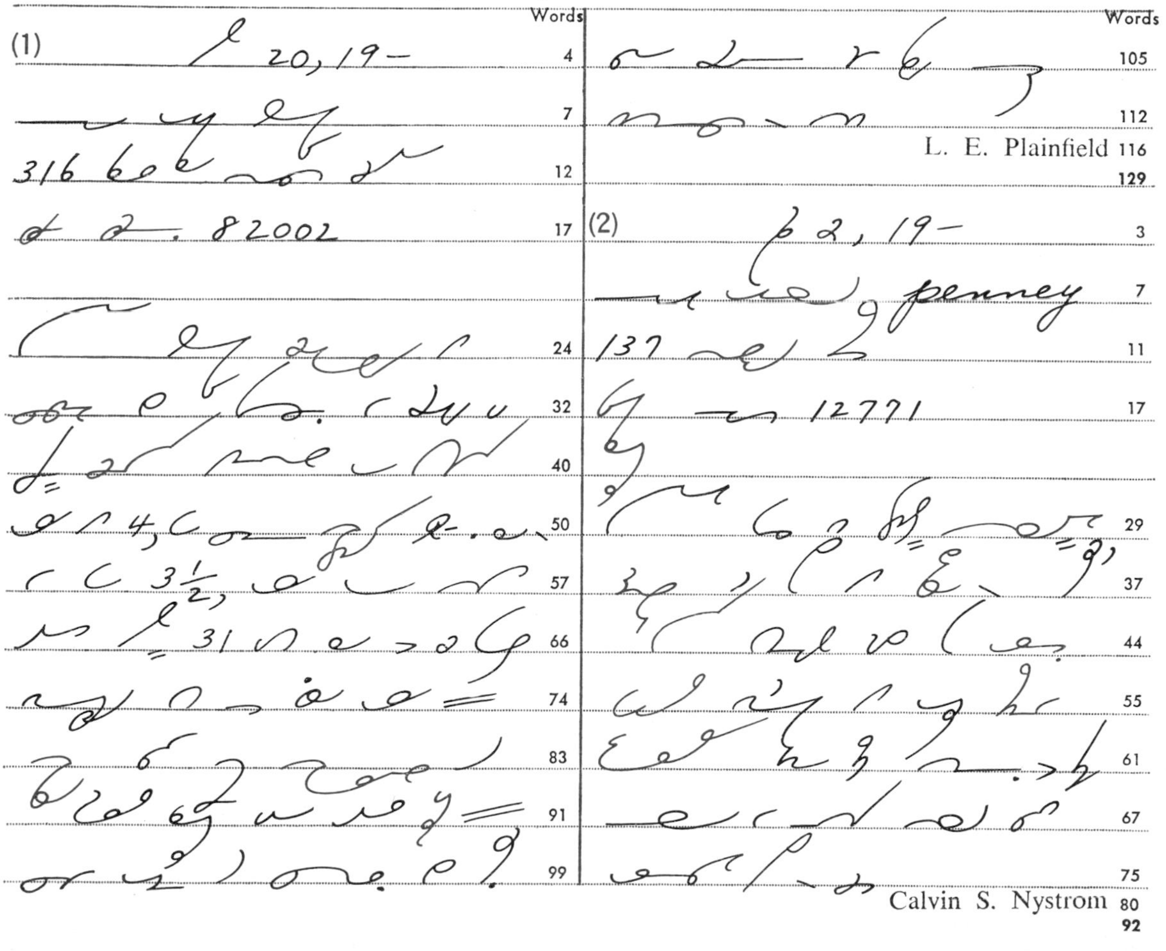

Words
(1)
4
7
12
17
24
32
40
50
57
66
74
83
91
99
Words
105
112
L. E. Plainfield 116
129
(2)
3
7
11
17
29
37
44
55
61
67
75
Calvin S. Nystrom 80
92

82D—Proofreading Problem

Rule 33: A period instead of a question mark is used after requests stated in the form of a question.

Example: `Will you please send in your report for February as quickly as possible.`

```
Gentlemen:

     There seems to be some mistake in our bill for the month
of May.  Our records show a balance do of $76.  The bill that
we received today from you shows a balance due of $76.50.  We
cannot account for the extra fifty cents.  Will you please ha-
ve your Accounting Department re-check it's records of our tran-
sactions?

     You might be interested to no that we have already sold
more then 60% of the business stationery we bought from you
on April 10.  The most popular item has been the twenty-pound
bond paper that measures 7¼ by 10 1/2 inches.

                              Sincerely yours,
```

82E—Transcriber's Guide

Business Letter Styles. The most commonly used letter style is *modified block*. This basic format has many variations. Some firms follow the practice of indenting paragraphs; some, of blocking them. Some firms center the date line; others have it placed to end even with the right margin; still others may type it directly under some line in the printed heading, such as below the address. Modified block format with centered date and indented paragraphs is shown at the right.

In the *block* style, shown on page 242, all lines of the letter begin flush with the left margin. The *simplified* and *semiformal* styles are shown on pages 245 and 247.

MODEL A: Modified Block Style with Indented Paragraphs and Centered Date

```
                                      115 Frost Pond Road      Phone 688-3270
                                      Syracuse, New York  13232


         STEVENS ARTE PUBLICATIONS, INC.

                    January 15, 19--


    Mr. Joseph L. Reed, Manager
    Blackburn & Blackburn Enterprises
    151 Lincoln Street
    Syracuse, New York   13210

    Dear Mr. Reed:

        We are pleased to announce a revision in our sales
    policy for individual art reproductions.  Now you can
    purchase Stevens Arte prints in assorted quantities.  As
    a result of this innovation, you can now select any amount
    of individual art reproductions at the same total quantity
    price.  Your minimum order, however, should be at least $5.
    It is also possible now to order less than fifty prints.

        We sincerely hope that Stevens Arte reproductions
    have been as enthusiastically received by your art patrons
    as they have been by so many others.

        If you have in mind any masterpieces that you would
    like to see reproduced, please let us know your choices.

                    Yours very truly,

                    STEVENS ARTE PUBLICATIONS, INC.

                    Henry B. Metcalf
                    Henry B. Metcalf, Sales Manager

    sd
```

51E—Dictionary and Spelling Preview

1. electrician, electronic, attendance
2. facilities, magnificent, library
3. imprinted, volume, friendship
4. projectors, piece, Penguin, probability

51F—Preview of New Dictation Material

(1)

extensive, exhibit, attendance, expand, electronic, journal

(2)

magnificent, official, expansion, educational, facilities, prouder, citizens, themselves, Rotary

(3)

valentines, streamlined, jumbo-size, imprinted, numerous, Friendship, bookstores

(4)

cameras, shooting, prospective, purchasers, projectors, in the market, Penguin, on the market, during the past, brilliant, probability, don't

Lesson 52 ⬡⬡⬡⬡⬡⬡⬡⬡⬡⬡⬡⬡⬡⬡⬡⬡

52A—Phrase Builder

There are 11 phrases in the following paragraph.

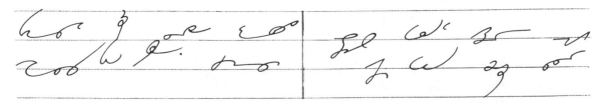

82C—Transcribing from Shorthand Notes

Directions. Transcribe Memorandum (1), following the same directions as for Lesson 81. When (1) is mailable, transcribe (2).

		Words
(1) To:	All Offices	3
From:	John L. Welch	8
Date:	May 22, 19––	12
Subject:	Reporting Long-Distance Calls	20

29
39
45
53
63
69
79
86
92
98
105
112
121
128
138
144

		Words
(2) To:	Miss Clara Lester	5
From:	John L. Welch	9
Date:	May 25, 19––	13
Subject:	New Printings of Price	19
	Lists A and B and Catalog C	25

36
41
45
54
62
68
74
82
89
98
103
110
116
120

52B—Theory Review

The following sounds are written by the *m-n* blend: *min-*, *men-*, *mon-*, *moun-*, and *mem-*.
The prefix *after-* is expressed by the same form used for the brief form, *aft*.

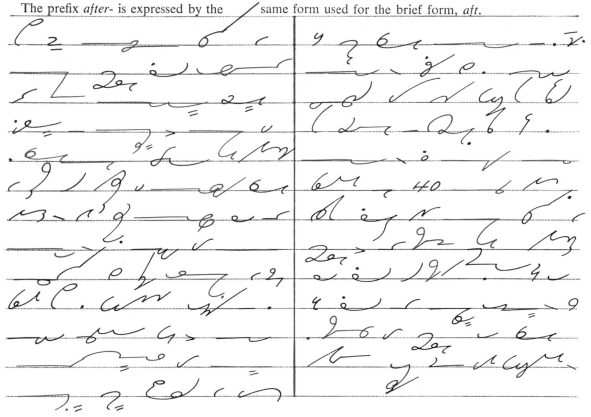

52C—Word Spellings and Meanings

council—a group of people called together for conference, consultation, or advice
counsel—advice or deliberation; person who gives legal advice

NOTE: The following material includes words presented in Lessons 48-51, as well as those given above.

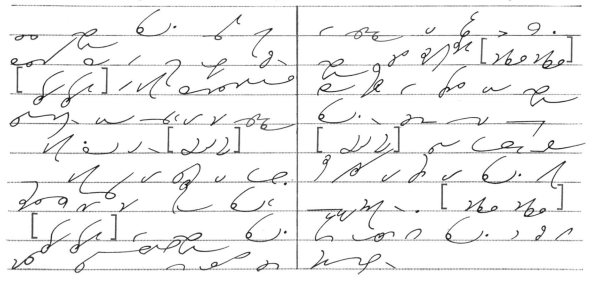

(2) To: Mr. Elmer Price
    From: John L. Welch
    Date: May 29, 19—
Subject: 25-Year Service Record

(shorthand outlines with word counts: 4, 8, 12, 19, 24, 32, 38, 46 on left; 54, 59, 70, 77, 83, 89, 95 on right)

81D—Proofreading Problem

Rule 32: Certain kinds of numbers are typed in figures whether they are above or below *ten* and whether they are definite or approximate. Some of these are: amounts of money, percentages, measures, weights, dimensions.

Examples: About 5 percent of the total would be $9.
The paper was 8½ by 11 inches and cost 25 cents.

Dear Mrs. White:

    We have just recieved your inquiry about our No. 614 fabric with a blue background. This material is 40 inches wide and is on sell for $1.00 a yard. It originally sold for $1.98 a yard. This saving of ninety-eight cents is a sizeable one.

    We have about twenty yards of these material still availa-ble, so rush us your order if you can use this fabric. All ready about 60% of the material we have on sale has been sold.

Very truly yours,

81E—Transcriber's Guide

Methods of Sending Interoffice Memos. Memos are usually distributed by the company's own mail service. If the mail is not confidential, it may be sent by any of the methods shown on page 16. If it is confidential, the memo is placed in a sealed envelope.

Lesson 82 ◇◇◇◇◇◇◇◇◇◇◇◇◇◇◇◇◇◇◇

82A—Punctuation and Theory Review

(1) *(shorthand outlines with 10 and 30)*

(2) *(shorthand outlines)*

52D—Practice Material for Building Fluency

[Shorthand outlines with word counts]

	Words
18, 19 —	3
	8
3 6 2	11
66802	16
	25
	32
	38
	45

	Words
	51
	58
	64
	71
	79
	87
	95
	102
	107
Alvin Elkins	112
	125

52E—Dictionary and Spelling Preview

1. reexamined, admitted

2. allot, monograph, handicapped, unanimously

3. geographical, inquiries, prevalent

4. symbol, artistic, reaction

5. throughout, benefit, manufacturers'

52F—Preview of New Dictation Material

(1) *[Shorthand outlines]*

membership, eliminated, reexamined, I remember, managed, to do so, prospective

(2) *[Shorthand outlines]*

Mental, allot, monograph, handicapped, nominated, unanimously, tremendous, creditable

(3) *[Shorthand outlines]*

geographical, forwarded, Louisville, inquiries, insects, prevalent, moth, termite

Introduction to Transcribing
Memorandums and Letters

Lesson **81** ⬡⬡⬡⬡⬡⬡⬡⬡⬡⬡⬡⬡⬡⬡⬡⬡⬡⬡⬡⬡

81A—Punctuation and Theory Review

Directions. The first sentence requires the application of rules on punctuation and writing numbers; the second sentence reviews several shorthand principles. There are 14 words in each sentence. Your teacher will time you for 30 seconds on each one. Can you make an accurate transcript?

81B—Vocabulary Preview

Directions. Type the list of words and phrases as many times as you can in one minute.

81C—Transcribing from Shorthand Notes

Directions. Transcribe the first memorandum, using the style shown in the illustration on page 222. Make a file copy of each memorandum or letter that you type in this and succeeding lessons. If time permits, transcribe the second memo. Punctuation marks are given in the shorthand notes.

		Words
(1) To:	All Executives, District	6
	Managers, and Branch Managers	12
From:	John L. Welch	16
Date:	November 20, 19--	21
Subject:	Appointment of New Branch	28
	Manager for Washington Area	34

Words: 77, 86, 94, 102, 111, 119, 127, 137, 142, 148

40, 46, 56, 60, 69

(4)

[shorthand symbols]

capital, proportion, brand, symbol, artistic, reaction, proposal, I believe

(5)

[shorthand symbols]

Convention, benefit, greatly, wonderful, in a position, many of the, throughout, at that time

Lesson 53 ○○○○○○○○○○○○○○○○○○○○○○

53A—Potential Rate Builder

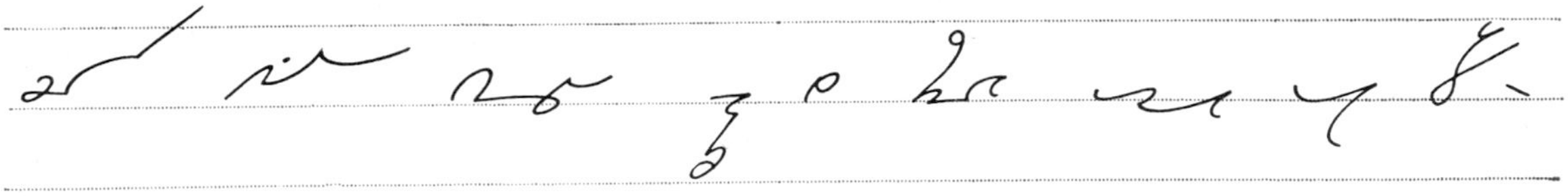

[shorthand symbols]

53B—Theory Review

The ending *-ful* is expressed by *f*. The ending *-ification* is expressed by a disjoined *f*.

The sounds *ded, det, dit,* and *ted* are expressed by a blend of *t* and *d*.

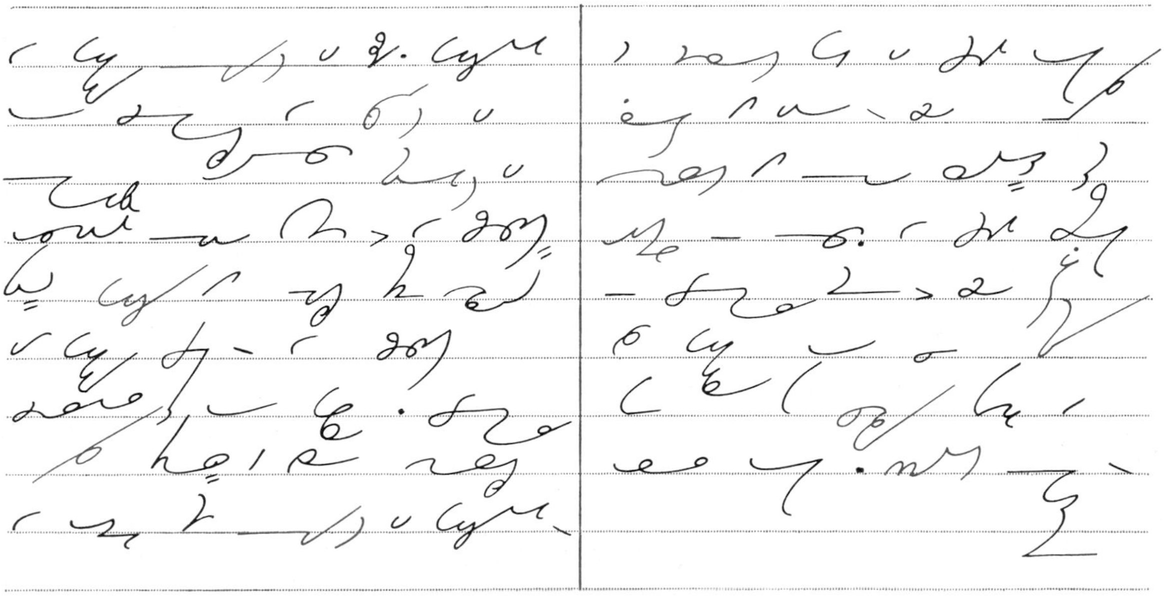

[shorthand outlines in two columns]

Dear Mrs. Kenilworth:

    About 10 days ago we send you some samples of our new fabric for draperys. This new fabric has an unusual guarantee, i.e., you get your money back if it fades within two years after purchase.

    The well known manufacture of this material tell us that its there newest and best product. Can we help you select patterns for your re-decoration?

                    Yours very truly,

80E—Transcriber's Guide

Interoffice Memorandums. Letters written within a firm are usually in the form of interoffice memorandums. This form saves time for the stenographer or secretary, as you can see by the illustration below.

Some firms have a greater volume of correspondence within the company than they do with other business firms. Although the memorandums may be called interbranch, interdepartmental, intracompany, or interorganization, we shall refer to all such correspondence as interoffice.

Most companies have special stationery for memos with such lines as "To," "From," "Date," and "Subject" printed on it. If, however, such printed stationery isn't available, just type the necessary headings on blank paper.

The most commonly used size of stationery is 8½ by 11, but many firms use 8½ by 5½ for short messages.

NOTE: As preparation for Lesson 81, review the rule given in the Punctuation Preview in Lesson 16, page 42.

GEORGIA SOUTHERN MANUFACTURING CO.

INTEROFFICE
CORRESPONDENCE

2100 peachtree road   •   atlanta, georgia 30305   •   413-4996

```
To:    New Members of the Stenographic Pool
From:  Lois A. Cole, Correspondence Supervisor
Date:  September 16, 19--

Subject:  Interoffice Correspondence

                        Triple-space
        The interoffice or interdepartment letterhead is used,
as the name implies, for correspondence between offices or
departments within the company.  The chief advantage of this
form is that it can be set up quickly.  Titles (Mr., Mrs.,
Dr., etc.), the salutation, the complimentary close, and the
formal signature are usually omitted.

        Triple-space between the last line of the heading and
the first line of the message.  Short messages of no more than
five lines may be double-spaced; single-space longer messages.

        Reference initials should be included.  When enclosures
are sent, the enclosure notation should appear below the refer-
ence initials.
    Double-space
lwn
```

One Style of Printed Interoffice Memorandum Stationery

53C—Word Spellings and Meanings

advice—recommendation (n.)
advise—to recommend or counsel (v.)

NOTE: The following material includes words presented in Lessons 49-52, as well as those given above.

[shorthand outlines]

53D—Practice Material for Building Fluency

	Words		Words
[shorthand] 31, 19—	4	[shorthand]	104
[shorthand] laughton	7	[shorthand]	110
[shorthand]	13	[shorthand]	117
54 [shorthand]	17	[shorthand]	121
[shorthand] 35904	22	[shorthand]	130
		[shorthand]	137
[shorthand]	31	[shorthand]	145
[shorthand]	39	[shorthand]	153
[shorthand]	49	[shorthand]	160
[shorthand]	57	[shorthand]	168
[shorthand]	65	[shorthand]	175
34 [shorthand]	71	[shorthand]	183
[shorthand]	78	[shorthand]	191
[shorthand]	86	[shorthand]	199
[shorthand]	92	[shorthand]	208
[shorthand]	97	[shorthand]	211
		Horace Tipton	214
		President	218
			236

80B—Vocabulary Preview

Directions. Transcribe each outline as many times as you can before the return is called.

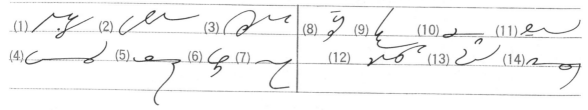

80C—Transcribing from Shorthand Notes

Directions. You will transcribe for 3 minutes. Compare your *mwam* rate with your rate from print.

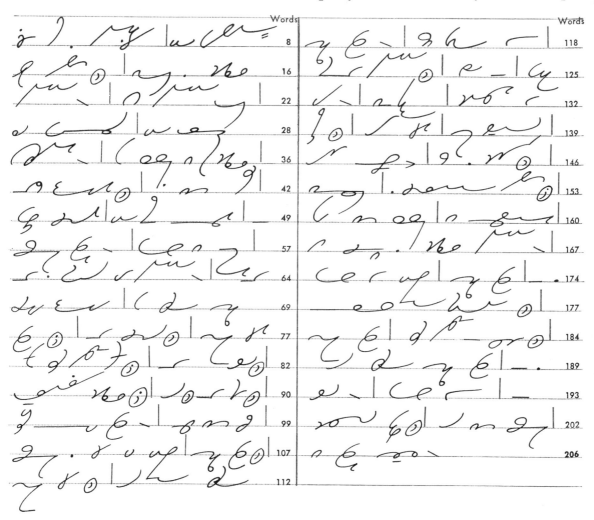

80D—Proofreading Problem

Rule 34: Definite numbers over *ten* are written in figures; *ten* and below are written in words. Approximate numbers (numbers preceded by such qualifying words as *about* or *approximately*) are written in words when they can be expressed in two or three words.

Examples: There were 50 people at the conference.
About fifty people attended the conference.

53E—Dictionary and Spelling Preview

1. photographs, dependable, convenience, specify

2. homemade, incident, thorough

3. parcel, scenes, metered, automatically

53F—Preview of New Dictation Material

wonderful, acceptance, illustrate, assist, photographs, bound, identification, to give you, dependable, attached, postcard, for your convenience, specify

Grayson, sought, homemade, bomb, thorough, incident, forced, occurred

parcel post, for example, metered, postage, minimizes, automatically, postmark, photos, smallest, stamping, device, behind, which is the, helpful, efficiency, and return

Lesson 54 ◇◇◇◇◇◇◇◇◇◇◇◇◇◇◇◇◇◇◇◇◇◇

54A—Proportion Drill

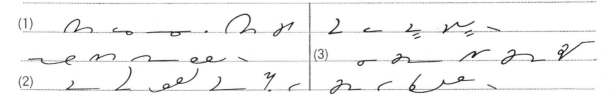

Lesson **80** ◇ ○ ◇ ○ ◇ ○ ⬡ ○ ⬡ ○ ⬡ ○ ⬡ ○ ◇ ○ ◇ ○ ⬡

80A—Typewriting from Printed Copy *(as directed in 76A, page 211)*

Words

Whether you have a drophead or pedestal-type desk, you will have a | 13
stationery drawer. This drawer will have either permanent or removable | 28
dividers. By arranging your stationery in these slots, you can save pre- | 42
cious seconds or even minutes in assembling papers. Place your envelopes | 57
in the front of the drawer. In the first slot put file copy paper; in | 71
the second, carbon sheets (face down); in the third, letterhead station- | 85
ery; and, in the fourth, interoffice memo paper. Now you can easily as- | 100
semble a set of original copy paper, carbon sheet, and file copy paper. | 114
As you pull them from the drawer, they are in proper order. One jostle | 129
straightens the edges, and the sheets can be twirled into the machine. | 143

As a student, you may not have a secretarial desk; but you can | 156
arrange your materials to simulate a stationery drawer. Place the origi- | 170
nal copy paper in a manila folder, carbon paper face down in another, | 184
and file copy paper in a third. Place them in staggered position, and | 198
you can assemble your papers quickly. | 206

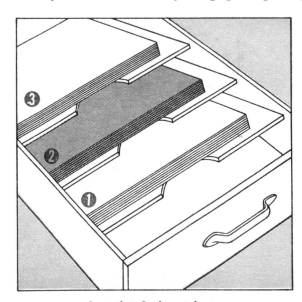

**Arranging Stationery in a
Stationery Drawer**

**Arranging Stationery in
a Set of Folders**

The prefix *sub-* is expressed by *s*. The prefix *trans-* is expressed by a disjoined *t* above the line. The prefix *under-* is expressed by the *oo* hook above the line.

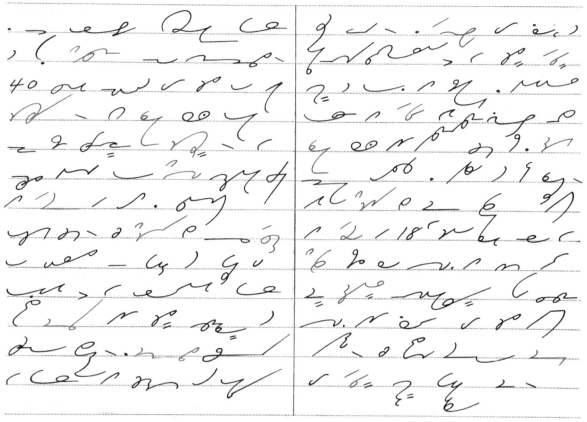

54C—Word Spellings and Meanings

least—smallest, shortest; in the lowest degree

leased—conveyed to another by a lease

NOTE: The following material includes words presented in Lessons 50-53, as well as those given above.

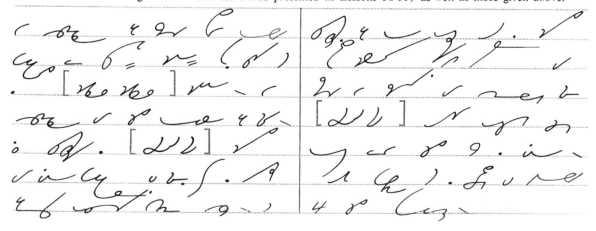

79D—Squeezing and Spreading in Correcting Errors

To insert a word in a space smaller than it would normally occupy, use the technique illustrated by the following procedure in changing "was" to "were."

Step 1. Erase the word "was."

Step 2. Move the carriage pointer to the space preceding the position of "w" in "was." Depress the space bar and strike the "w." Release the space bar and depress again. Type the "e." Proceed in a similar manner in typing the "r" and "e."

```
They was here.

They were here.
```

To insert a word in a space larger than it would normally occupy, use the technique illustrated by the following procedure in changing "where" to "when."

Step 1. Erase the word "where."

Step 2. Move the carriage pointer to the space formerly occupied by the letter "w." Depress the space bar and strike the letter "w." Release the space bar and depress it again. Type the letter "h." Proceed in a similar manner for each of the remaining letters.

```
He was there where class began.

He was there  when  class began.
```

NOTE: To spread or squeeze letters on an electric typewriter, hold the carriage at the right spot with one hand while you strike the correct key with the other, except on the Smith-Corona and Royal, which have half-space keys.

79E—Comparison Writing with Carbon Copy

Directions. Your teacher will time you for two 3-minute writings, one from the printed copy and one from the shorthand copy. Compare your *mwam* rates.

79F—Proofreading Problem

Directions. Proceed as for preceding proofreading problems. The punctuation rule included in this problem for special study is as follows:

Rule 33: Hyphen an adjective composed of two or more words if used before a noun. Do not hyphen these words if they follow the noun they modify unless the second part of the adjective is a word or suffix consisting of a noun plus -ed.

Examples:
```
Can you settle your past-due account?
Your account is past due.
A good secretary is never ill-mannered.
```

```
Dear Mr. Bauer:

     I believe the time has come when we must revise our fol-
lowup letters if we are to collect on our past-due accounts.
We have entirely too many that our past due.

     Mr. Nicols' recommendations have considerably merit; name-
ly, employ a letter writing consultant, employ a correspondence
supervisor, or conduct a clinic on letter writing under our
office managers direction.

     Other department heads have been asked for their suggest-
ions.  Theirs, your's, and Mr. Nichols's ideas will be discus-
sed at the Executive Boards' meeting Tuesday.

                    Sincerely yours,
```

54D—Practice Material for Building Fluency

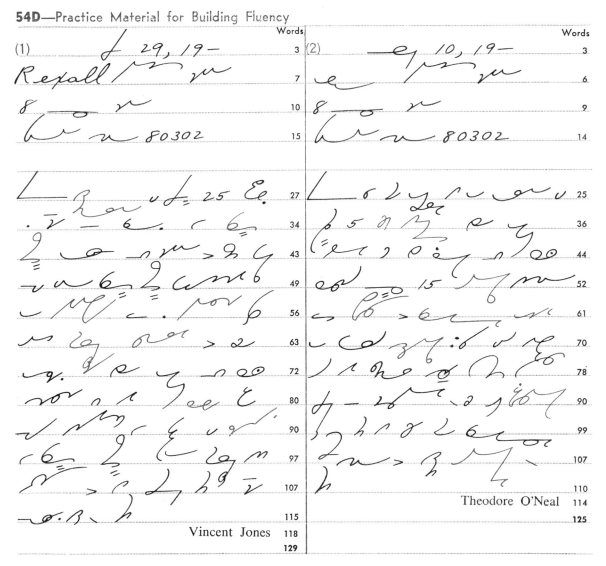

Words

(1) 29, 19— 3
Rexall 7
.... 10
80302 15

.... 25 E. 27
.... 34
.... 43
.... 49
.... 56
.... 63
.... 72
.... 80
.... 90
.... 97
.... 107
.... 115

Vincent Jones 118
129

Words

(2) 10, 19— 3
.... 6
.... 9
80302 14

.... 25
.... 36
.... 44
.... 52
.... 61
.... 70
.... 78
.... 90
.... 99
.... 107
.... 110

Theodore O'Neal 114
125

54E—Dictionary and Spelling Preview

1. financial, survey, adjustment, stoppage
2. substantiate, curfew, enforced, agency
3. popular, letterhead, companies
4. receiving, recently, lose

54F—Preview of New Dictation Material

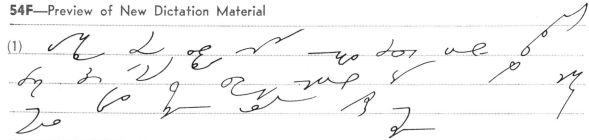

(1)

automobile, very well, inexperienced, continued, mostly, financial, always, I didn't have, pick up, subsequent, transformed, accomplished, installation, system, daily, stoppage, inventory, body, adjustment, rental, decisions, investment

If the dictator is at his desk when the transcribed letters are   111
placed on it, they can be presented face up, arranged in order of dicta-   125
tion. If he is not there, the letters should be placed face down, pref-   139
erably with a paper weight on top.   147

The file copies are usually kept in the secretary's desk until the   160
letters have been mailed; then they are filed.   170

It has been estimated that a letter costs between $1.70 and $2 to   183
dictate, transcribe, and mail. Will yours be worth that much?   195

79B—Vocabulary Preview

Directions. Your teacher will call the carriage return.

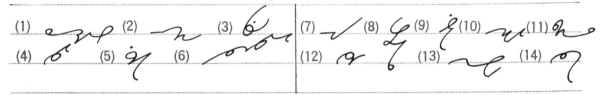

79C—Transcribing from Shorthand Notes

Directions. Set your machine for a 3-minute writing from the shorthand notes.

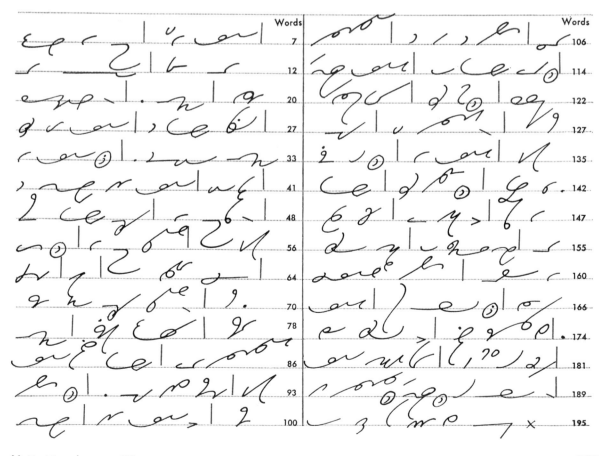

(2)

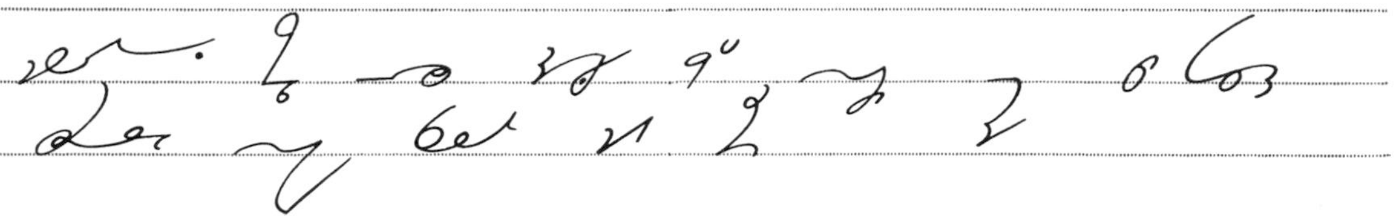

[shorthand outlines]

startling, agency, inquiry, substantiate, nine o'clock, curfew, enforced, outbreaks, violence, curbed, parents, station, civic

(3)

[shorthand outlines]

increasingly, popular, itself, we are sending you, we have made, next time, on us

(4)

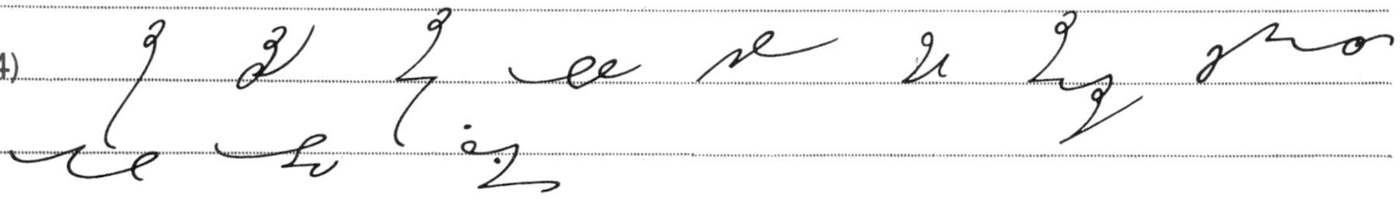

[shorthand outlines]

we have been, we find, we have not been, last year, to tell, if there is, we have not received, we do not like, will you please, let us know, hearing from you

Lesson 55 ⬡◯◯◯⬡◯⬡◯⬡◯⬡◯⬡◯⬡◯◯⬡◯⬡

55A—Potential Rate Builder

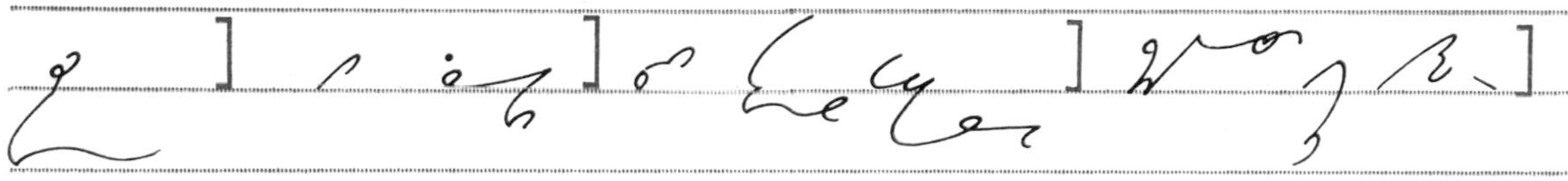

[shorthand outlines]

55B—Theory Review

The word ending -ther may be expressed by either the left or the right th, whichever joining is more facile. The sound of w within a word is expressed by a dash under the vowel.

The days of the week are written in abbreviated form.

[shorthand outlines in two columns]

78E—Comparison Writings with Corrections

Directions. Set your machine for a 3-minute writing from the copy on page 215, making an original and a carbon copy. You are to correct any mistakes you may make as you type. Next you will be timed for 3 minutes on transcribing from the notes on page 216. Compare your rates with those you made in Lesson 77.

78F—Proofreading Problem

Directions. Make a list of changes that should be made in the letter, or retype the letter if your teacher so directs. See if the following rule has been correctly applied; it is used in Lesson 79.

Rule 32: Use an apostrophe to indicate the possessive case of nouns. In the possessive singular form, the apostrophe precedes the *s*; in the possessive plural form, the apostrophe follows the *s*; in the possessive plural not ending in *s*, the apostrophe precedes the final *s*. No apostrophe is used with the possessive adjectives.

Examples: The secretary's desk should be kept neat at all times.
The secretaries' conference was well attended.
The committee held its meeting in the library.

Dear Mr. Blezek:

Its about time we reviewed this years' activities to see what changes should be made in our promotional program for the coming year. We should study the effectiveness of each of our competitor's programs as compared with our's. While we have no intention of copying any of theirs, we can learn something from analyzing then.

We have had several employee's suggestions turned in, i.e. a "give-away" TV program, a contest to rename one of our products, and a contest for salesman with a prise of $2,000 for the winner.

Your truly,

Lesson **79** ◇

79A—Typewriting from Printed Copy

(as directed in 76A, page 211)

	Words
Slip the envelope over the letter in the manner shown in the illus-	13
tration. An enclosure that is the size of the letter is placed behind	27
the letter; a small enclosure is clipped to the letter or possibly even	42
placed inside the envelope. Of course, the envelope address should be	56
checked to be sure that it is the same as the inside address. If an	70
enclosure has to be supplied after the letter has been placed on the	84
dictator's desk, a note to that effect should be clipped to the letter.	98

(Continued)

55C—Word Spellings and Meanings

complimentary—expressive of regard; of the nature of, or containing, a compliment

complementary—serving to fill out or complete

NOTE: The following material includes words presented in Lessons 51-54, as well as those given above.

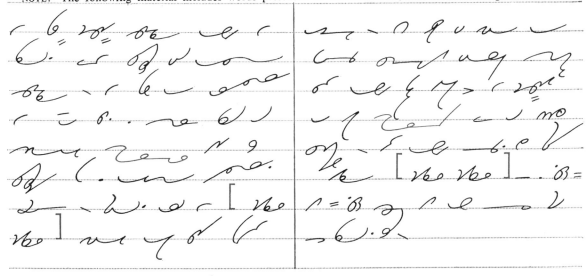

55D—Practice Material for Building Fluency

	Words
	3
	6
	11
	16
	24
	33
	40
	49
	55
	61
	68
	74
	82
	90
	98
	104
	111
	122
	127
	135
	145
	154
	163
	171
Edgar C. Dunbar	175
Vice-President	180
	193

78B—Vocabulary Preview

Directions. Your teacher will call the carriage return.

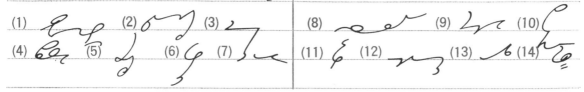

78C—Transcribing from Shorthand Notes

Directions. Transcribe for 3 minutes from these shorthand notes. Determine your *mwam*.

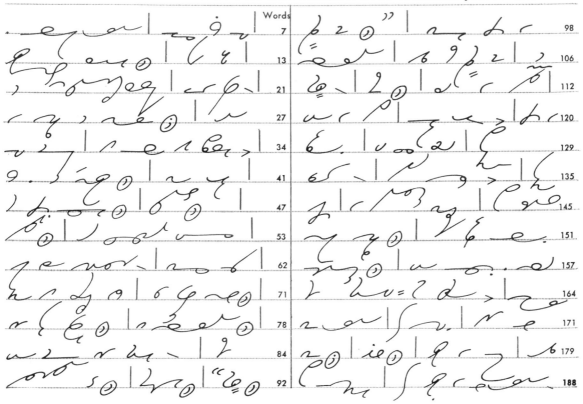

78D—Erasing and Correcting with Carbon Copy

If you have one or more carbon copies in the machine, your correction procedure is as follows:

Step 1. Move the carriage (as directed on page 214).

Step 2. Place a 5 by 3 card between the original and the carbon paper to prevent smudges from appearing on the carbon copy while the original is being erased.

Step 3. Remove as much of the ink as possible with plastic cleaner; then erase with light strokes of a typing eraser.

Step 4. Remove the card and place it between the first carbon sheet and the first carbon copy so that your fingers do not touch the carbon paper. If you have more than one carbon copy in the machine, put a second card immediately behind the first carbon copy to protect the other copies in the pack. Again, use plastic type cleaner or kneaded rubber to remove as much of the carbon impression as possible. Then erase with a soft or pencil eraser.

Step 5. When the error has been erased on all copies, position the carriage to the proper point and type the correct letter or letters.

55E—Dictionary and Spelling Preview

1. headquarters, quota, exceeded

2. neither, spurs, outfitting, knack

3. hospital, practice (n.), adjacent

4. preferable, occasional, movable, recommendation

5. Aeronautics, cordial, anytime

55F—Preview of New Dictation Material

(1)

headquarters, New York City, quota, equipment, right now, squad, projects

(2)

neither, leather, silver, spurs, cowboy, outfitting, after that, they'd, knack

(3)

proposal, Grand Forks, hospital, adjacent, adequate, objectively, prospects, medical, in the future, community, bitterly, opposed, young, attract

(4)

typewriter, preferable, vibration, occasional, movable, instruction, manufacturers', at least, to follow

(5)

Aeronautics, Government, cordial, inspection, invitation, to send you

Is the following rule applied correctly? This rule is applied in Lesson 78, too.

Rule 31: Use a comma to precede *namely*, *viz.*, *i.e.*, *for instance*, and *that is*. These words may be preceded by a semicolon, a colon, or a dash if the material is long or grammatically independent.

Examples: We expected to have three groups meet with us; i.e., Campfire Girls, Girl Scouts, and the "Y" girls.

The City Council cited two citizens, namely Mr. Bill Andrews and Mr. Harold McMann, for their outstanding contributions.

Dear Mr. Kantor:

It has occured to us that possible you might be interested in the growth if organizations for young boys in our city. We now have several Boy Scout troops. These troops have ever opportunity to grow, i.e. fine leaders, good fasilities, and there own enthusiasm.

We are greatly indebted to our director and co-director namely Mr. Jones and Mr. Brush for their efforts in building an organisation of which we can be mighty proud. We managed to retain their services for another year.

Sincerly yours,

Lesson 78 ⬡⬡⬡⬡⬡⬡⬡⬡⬡⬡⬡⬡⬡⬡⬡⬡⬡⬡⬡⬡

78A—Typewriting from Printed Copy *(as directed in 76A, page 211)*

	Words
A mailable letter not only has no typographical errors, but also	13
is attractively arranged on the page. The copy is clean; there are no	27
smudges to mar its appearance.	34
As a transcriber, you are responsible for checking names, addresses,	47
dates, and amounts of money to be sure they are correct. You may need to	62
verify these with previous correspondence, other business papers, your	76
calendar, or some other source. If the dictator says, for instance,	90
"Friday, February 2," you must check the calendar to see if February 2	104
is Friday. If not, either the date or the day must be wrong.	117
Check the spelling of any word about which you are not certain.	130
Don't guess.	133
Be sure to check the directions you received about extra carbon	146
copies, special mailing instructions, or making a card for the follow-up	161
file.	162
Complete one letter before going to the next one; i.e., type the	175
envelope and see about enclosures before typing the next letter.	188

Receptionist Duties, Travel Details, and Business Ethics and Etiquette

Lesson **56** ○○○○○○○○○○○○○○○○○○○○○○

56A—Receiving Callers

The size and type of business will determine whether a full-time receptionist is employed or whether the secretary handles receptionist duties as part of her work. Even if there is a receptionist for the firm, a secretary will find that she performs some such duties herself. Here are some basic rules for handling visitors.

1. Be pleasant, poised, and, when necessary, firm. Always be courteous and respectful. Do not adopt special manners to fit what you believe to be the importance of the visitor, being effusive for those you think are important and haughty and cold for those you believe to be unimportant. Do not judge people by their appearance or speech—you may make an embarrassing mistake.

one—perhaps a slip of paper on which you write the name and business connection of the caller and possibly the purpose of his call.

You will need to follow your employer's wishes in regard to scheduling appointments. He may wish to see everyone; on the other hand, he may wish you to check with him before you tell a visitor whether he can be admitted. If the latter is the case, when the visitor approaches your desk, you will attempt to find out the purpose of the call by saying something like, "May I tell Mr. Ames what you wish to see him about?" Should the visitor refuse to tell you, you may suggest that he write a note, which you will seal and take in to your employer who can then make the decision.

REGISTER OF CALLERS *Monday — January 14, 19--*

TIME	NAME AND AFFILIATION	PERSON ASKED FOR	PERSON SEEN	PURPOSE OF CALL
9:30	K. Nelson — Lowell Lighting	G. B.	✓	Salesman
10:15	M. Bell — Rowe Plumbing	J. R.	✓	Salesman
11:30	V. Geisler — Contr. on Carew Bldg. — for lunch appt.	G. B.	✓	Discuss progress
2:15	T. Resor — Woodflex Consultant	G. B.	J. R.	Hammer job
3:50	Messenger from Woodflex	—	✓	Brought samples

Register of Callers

2. Do not be sarcastic or "wisecrack" with visitors. You will lose control of the conversation if you do.

3. Keep adequate records of callers. The kind of record you keep depends on the type of business in which you are employed. In a doctor's office, for example, you would keep a register of callers. In another type of office, you might retain the business cards of callers to give your employer or to file for future reference when you want the name and address of the firm represented by the caller.

In still another office, you might keep a record of callers in an appointment book or on an appointment calendar.

The record you keep may be only a temporary

If the visitor has called before, you probably know whether to give him an appointment without inquiring into the purpose of his call.

If your employer is in conference and the caller will have to wait, you should suggest that he sit down and make himself comfortable. If he has a topcoat on, you should suggest that he remove it and hang it on the coat rack.

Should it become obvious that the person in conference with your employer has overstayed his time and you think that your employer is having difficulty terminating the conversation, you may be able to help by means of an interruption such as calling him on the telephone to remind him that the next visitor is waiting or by writing him a note and laying it on his desk.

77C—Transcribing from Shorthand Notes

Directions. You will be timed for 3 minutes. Determine your *mwam*.

77D—Erasing and Correcting Errors

To erase and correct a typographical error when you are typing only one copy, follow these steps:

Step 1. Depress the margin release key and move the carriage to one side so that the eraser crumbs will not fall into the machine. If the error is on the right half of the page, move the carriage to the right; if it is on the left half, move the carriage to the left.

Step 2. Erase the error with light strokes; *do not scrub.* Brush crumbs onto the table and away from the machine. If you have a new ribbon, plastic type cleaner or kneaded rubber may be used to take off most of the ink impression before using the eraser. An eraser shield may be used to prevent smearing letters adjacent to the error.

Step 3. Type the correct letter or letters, being careful not to use too much force.

77E—Comparison Writing with Corrections

Directions. Set your machine to type another 3-minute writing. This time you are to correct any mistakes you make as you type. You will be timed first on 77A—Typewriting from Printed Copy and then on 77C—Transcribing from Shorthand Notes. Compare your rates.

77F—Proofreading Problem

Directions. Proofread carefully the letter on page 215. Type a list of changes that should be made or retype the letter if your teacher so directs.

APPOINTMENTS FOR *Friday, January 18, 19--*		
Time	Engagements	Memorandums
9:00	*Mr. Petersen*	*Call J. M. Schulte re contract*
9:30		*Call Thornton re United Appeal Drive*
10:00	*Mr. Sherwood*	
10:30	*Retirement Plan Conference – 45 mins.*	*Prepare revised outline for this (7 copies)*
11:00		
11:30	*Dr. McDevitt*	*Trip to Chicago Saturday – tickets in safe*
12:00		
12:30	*Lunch – Mr. Townes Gibson Hotel*	*Work on Ch. of Commerce speech*
1:00		
1:30	*Mr. Carmichael*	

Appointment Calendar

1. What should be the secretary's manner in receiving callers?
2. What types of records may be kept of callers and appointments?
3. How can you help your employer terminate a conference when a visitor has definitely overstayed?

Office Practice Problem

How would you handle each of the following visitors: a member of your employer's family; a salesman that your employer has told you he does not want to see; a person who will not state his purpose in calling?

56B—Building Speed in Taking Dictation

Brief-Form Practice

Directions. There are 39 brief forms and brief-form derivatives in the following paragraphs. If you can read the material in 40 seconds, you will be reading at the rate of 130.5 words a minute.

Word Spellings and Meanings

sight—a view; the power of seeing; a small device through which objects are to be seen

cite—calling upon authoritatively to appear, as before a court; quoting authority or proof

site—local position, as of a town; the seat or scene of anything

NOTE: The following material includes words presented in Lessons 52-55, as well as those given above.

7. When a word is to be divided at a point where two vowels that are pronounced separately come together, these vowels should be divided into separate syllables.

    Right: gradu-ation   Wrong: gradua-tion

8. Compound words written with a hyphen should be divided at the hyphen only.

    Right: self-supporting   Wrong: self-sup-porting

9. Avoid, if possible, dividing a proper name or separating a title from the name. If a division must be made, follow these suggestions:

    Miss Rose - Mary Lautenbach
    Mr. Leon K. - Smith

10. Never separate a month from the date or "page" from the number of the page.

    Right: June 2 -   Wrong: June -2
    Right: page 12 -   Wrong: page -12

Directions. Assume that you needed to divide each of the following words if a correct division could be made. Type each word, indicating by a hyphen where you would divide it: important, service, above, transcribe, wouldn't, Mr. A. K. Dodds, self-addressed, about, page 22, situation, invaluable, reliable.

Lesson 77 ◯◯◯◯⬡◯◯⬡◯⬡◯⬡◯⬡◯◯◯⬡◯

77A—Typewriting from Printed Copy *(as directed in 76A, page 211)*

	Words
When you are asked to transcribe a letter, you are expected to	13
prepare it for mailing. It is your job to be sure that the letter is	27
mailable, not your employer's. To be sure that the letter is mailable,	41
you must proofread it carefully.	48
Some transcribers have the mistaken idea that they know when they	61
make errors and don't need to proofread. Unless an error causes you to	76
break the rhythm of your typing, you will not know that you made it.	90
Skimming is not proofreading. About the only error you will find	103
by skimming is one such as "extimate" for "estimate." You must read for	117
thought to detect such errors as these: "possible" for "possibly"; "if"	132
for "of"; punctuation errors; errors in capitalization or division of	146
words. Read the letter as though you were seeing it for the first time	160
and would have to tell someone what was in it.	170
The letter should be proofread while it is still in the machine so	183
that corrections can be made easily.	191

77B—Vocabulary Preview

Directions. Type each word or phrase as many times as you can before your teacher calls for the carriage return.

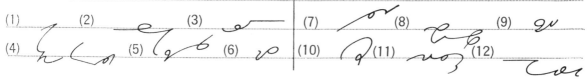

(1)   (2)   (3)   (7)   (8)   (9)
(4)   (5)   (6)   (10)   (11)   (12)

[shorthand outlines]

Practice Material for Building Fluency

	Words		Words
7, 19—	3	1986	32
	7	5	42
101	11	3	53
10020	16		62
			72
29	24	Maurice McGuire	76
			89

Dictionary and Spelling Preview

1. fulfill, floral, transistor
2. visitors, portable
3. photofinishing, laboratory, tracer
4. deluxe, congratulation

Preview of New Dictation Material

(1) *[shorthand outlines]*

illustrations, Linoleum, Hanover, tastes, handsome, floral, exclusive, distributors, transistors, one of those, fastest, announcement, colorings

(2) *[shorthand outlines]*

redecorate, interior, newly, blackboards, consultant, circular, conference, portable, yellow

(3) *[shorthand outlines]*

photofinishing, package, Lois, laboratory, consisted, from which, you have not received, tracer, no doubt, shortly, Post Office

Unit 12 · Lesson 56   163

Directions. This is a timed writing from shorthand notes. The copy is the same as that you typed in 76A—Typewriting from Printed Copy; use the same machine setup. Punctuation marks are given in the copy. When your teacher calls time at the end of 3 minutes, circle each error and make the necessary computations to determine your *mwam* rate. Record the information in the upper right-hand corner of your paper. Compare this rate with the rate you made when typing from print. The thought phrases are marked to help you transcribe.

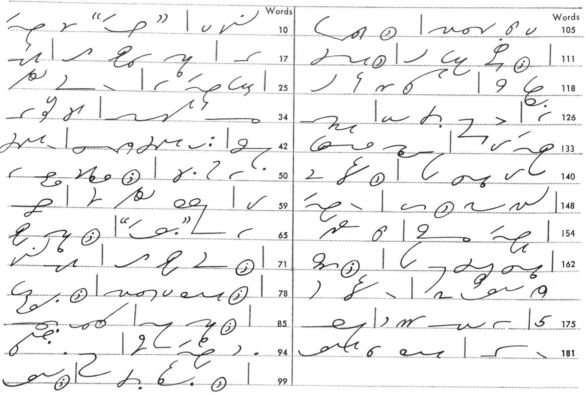

76E—Division of Words

Frequently in transcription the problem of correct division of a word at the end of a line will arise. Study the following brief summary of rules for the division of words.

1. Divide words only between syllables; therefore never divide a word of only one syllable. The contracted part of a word should not be separated from the remainder of that word (as in wouldn't or doesn't).

2. Try to put enough of the word at the end of the line to suggest to the reader what the word is. For that reason, avoid, if possible, putting a two-letter syllable at the end of the line. Never divide a five-letter word; and avoid, if possible, dividing a six-letter word.

3. If possible, avoid dividing words at the end of two or more consecutive lines. Never divide the last word on a page. Never divide the last word in a paragraph.

4. Never separate a syllable of one or two letters at the end of a word or a one-letter syllable at the beginning of a word. Avoid dividing a two-letter syllable at the beginning of a word.

   Right: lib-erty   Wrong: liber-ty
   Right: apart-ment   Wrong: a-partment

5. Divide at the point where a prefix or suffix joins the root word, provided such a division is not contrary to the syllabication.

   Prefixes: dis-agree com-pany prel-ude
   Suffixes: crit-ical mov-able abun-dance

6. When a word has three or more syllables and is to be divided at a one-letter syllable, the one-letter syllable should be typed on the first line.

   Right: sepa-rate   Wrong: sep-arate

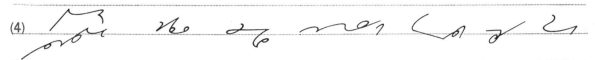

(4)

deluxe, stationery, sympathy, congratulation, punctuation, inside, flush, dictator's

Lesson 57 ⬡⬡⬡⬡⬡⬡⬡⬡⬡⬡⬡⬡⬡⬡⬡⬡⬡⬡

57A—Receiving Callers (Concluded)

Announcing Callers. Visitors may be announced to your employer in various ways. You may have an intercommunicating device by which you announce visitors. You may escort a caller to the door of your employer's private office or even to his desk. You may simply indicate to the visitor that your employer is ready to see him and direct him to the proper door without arising from your chair. Your employer will explain his preferences when you first assume your duties in his office.

In making introductions, business position rather than age or sex usually determines who is introduced to whom. The name of the person being honored is spoken first. The names may be spoken like this: "Mr. Ames (your employer), may I present Mr. Jensen?" "Mr. Ames, this is Miss Kane of Emery Industries."

If your employer should introduce you to a caller, he will say, "Mr. Oakley, this is my secretary, Miss Bates." You respond with a pleasant "How do you do, Mr. Oakley." If you are seated at your employer's desk or your own desk, you do not usually rise or shake hands. The introduction is not an invitation to join the conversation.

If your employer introduces you to his wife, of course you stand to acknowledge the introduction. Shake hands if she offers hers to you.

If your desk is back of a counter to which visitors come, you get up from your desk and go to the counter. Do not carry on conversations from several feet away.

Do not keep visitors waiting at a counter or at your desk while you complete work that you are doing. It is discourteous. Turn immediately from your work to greet the visitor and find out what you can do for him.

If a visitor persists in continuing a conversation with you after you have scheduled him for an appointment or have explained that you cannot do so, excuse yourself by some such remark as, "I'm sorry, but will you excuse me? I must get this report (or letter) completed as soon as possible." "Won't you have a chair over there? Mr. Ames will be with you in a few minutes."

Be careful to keep business papers out of sight of callers. A visitor can obtain some vital information he should not have just by seeing a name or a figure on a sheet of paper lying on your desk. Never leave anything uncovered in your typewriter when you step away from your desk. Slip a plain sheet of paper under the paper bail over the copy in the machine.

Do not make dates with visitors to the office. If someone wants to see you outside of office hours, he should call you at your home.

If your employer's superior comes to the office, he should, of course, be permitted to scc your employer at once. If there is someone in the office at that time, you should explain with whom your employer is in conference. Then your employer's superior will know whether to interrupt or return later.

Questions for Discussion

1. What determines the order of names in making introductions in business?

2. What can you say to visitors who persist in conversing with you?

3. Explain some ways in which callers may be announced to your employer.

Office Practice Problem

How would you handle each of the situations listed at the top of page 165?

The Nature of Transcription

Lesson **76** ⬡⬡⬡⬡⬡⬡⬡⬡⬡⬡⬡⬡⬡⬡⬡⬡

76A—Typewriting from Printed Copy

Directions. Set your machine for a 70-space line, double spacing, and 5-space paragraph indention. This is a straight-copy timed writing. When your teacher calls time at the end of 3 minutes, circle each error you have made. Determine your mailable-words-a-minute rate from the chart on page 374. Record it in the upper right-hand corner of your paper.

	Words
Transcription is the "translation" of shorthand notes into typewrit-	13
ten copy in the desired form. The transcription process in the office	28
situation includes many factors. Among these factors are: assembling	42
the necessary stationery; setting up the machine for the desired arrange-	56
ment of the typed copy; "translating" the shorthand notes into typed	70
form; proofreading; correction of errors; making required carbon copies;	85
addressing an envelope if the transcript is a letter; checking spelling,	99
punctuation, correct use of figures, and proper hyphenation; and such	113
other items as preparing enclosures or checking information.	126
The primary concern of the transcriber is not speed, but accuracy of	139
the transcript. Of course, you will want to turn out as many transcripts	154
as you can; but never sacrifice accuracy for speed. One letter that is	169
mailable is worth more than five letters with errors in them.	181

76B—How to Read Shorthand for Transcription

Directions. Efficiency in reading notes is a big factor in speed of transcription. By reading in thought phrases, you will not need to reread notes; and you will not misread notes because you will be getting the thought as you transcribe.

In the sentences below, the colored perpendicular lines mark the notes into thought phrases. Read the first phrase; then type it. Type each succeeding phrase in the same manner.

76C—Vocabulary Preview

Directions. Set your machine for single spacing. At the "Begin" signal, type the first word as many times as you can before the teacher calls "Return." Then return the carriage quickly and, without pause, begin typing the second outline. Continue in this manner until all the outlines have been typed.

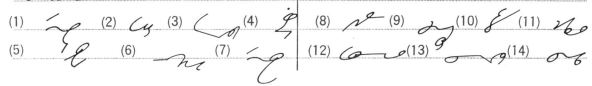

a. A salesman continues his conversation with you after you have said that your employer will see him in half an hour.

b. A visitor asks you what you are working on at your typewriter.

c. Your employer has said that he doesn't want to be disturbed while he is working on a report and his superior comes in to see him.

57B—Building Speed in Taking Dictation

Phrase Builder

There are 17 phrases in the following paragraph.

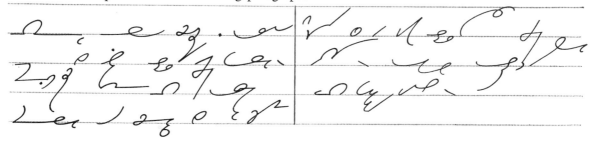

Word Spellings and Meanings

eraser—the implement with which one removes copy
erasure—the act of removing copy

NOTE: The following material includes words presented in Lessons 53-56, as well as those given above.

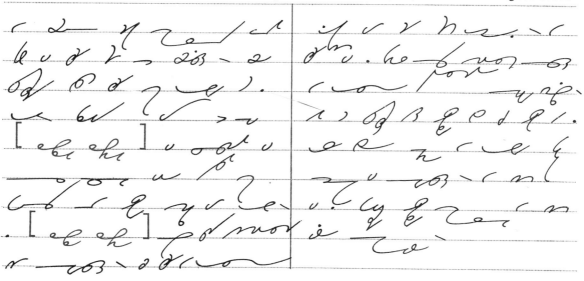

Practice Material for Building Fluency

75C—Acceleration Practice

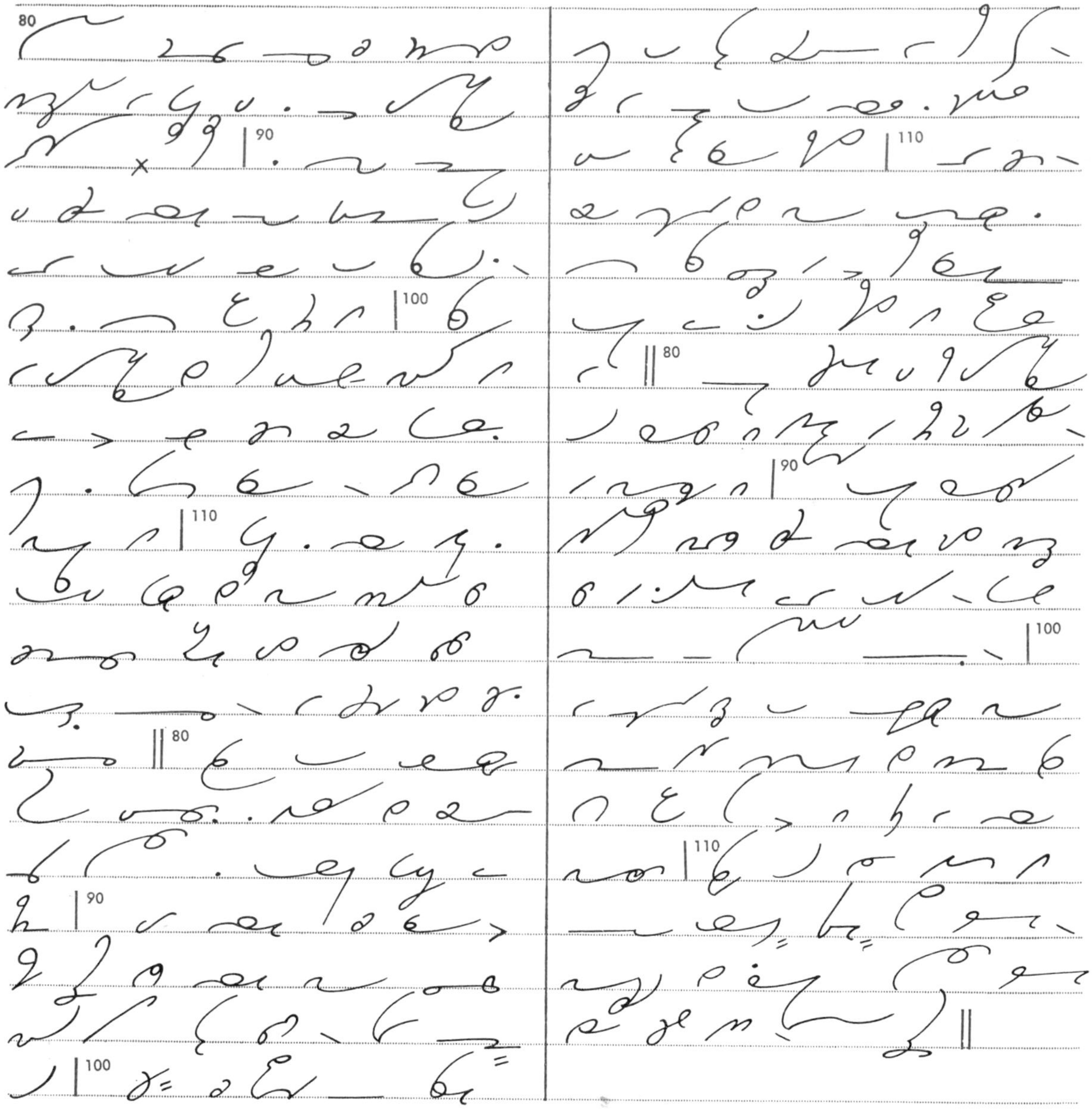

[shorthand outlines]

75D—Preview of New Dictation Material

[shorthand outlines]

nothing, we are not sure, apparel, apparent, necessity, surplus, wasteful, spoiled, antiquated, ancient, unmistakably, majority, yard, lengths, Economy, packages, beautifully, patterns, cellophane, self-service, carton, initial, variety, acquired, commented, progressive, circular, coupon

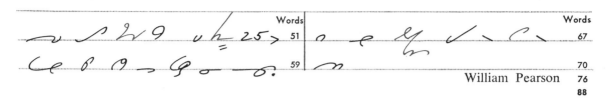

Words

51
59

Words

67
70

William Pearson 76

88

Dictionary and Spelling Preview

1. supervisor, sufficient, secretarial, career

2. anticipate, phase, inquiries, omissions

3. routine, messages

Preview of New Dictation Material

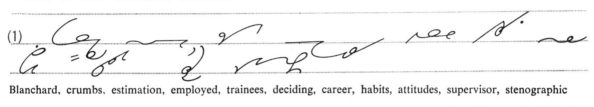

(1)

Blanchard, crumbs, estimation, employed, trainees, deciding, career, habits, attitudes, supervisor, stenographic

(2)

confirming, Junior, Eastbrook, omissions, confusion, instruments, anticipate, unpack, which has been, storage, upon the, simplest, enable, serviceman, with respect, Knoxville, inquiries, et cetera, anxious, repack

(3)

routine, telegrams, messages, Western Union, informed, earliest, sender

Lesson 58 ⬡ ⬡ ⬡ ⬡ ⬡ ⬡ ⬡ ⬡ ⬡ ⬡ ⬡ ⬡ ⬡ ⬡ ⬡ ⬡

58A—Travel

If your employer's responsibilities require his going to other cities, you may have some duties to perform in connection with his travel. These duties may involve selecting mode of travel, making up itineraries, preparing travel requisitions and expense vouchers, and making reservations for trips and for hotel accommodations.

Selecting Mode of Travel. You may be asked to check bus, train, and airplane schedules to see which type of transportation provides the best itinerary. If none of these provides a good schedule, your employer may go by company or personal car.

In checking schedules you may need to use a

75A—Review of Cities and States

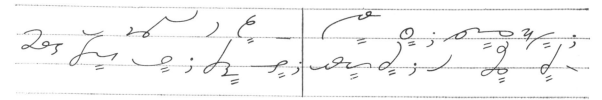

75B—Brief Forms and Derivatives

PACIFIC AIR LINES SCHEDULES — EFFECTIVE MARCH 1, 19 — All Times Shown are Local Times — AM—Light Face — PM—Dark Face		342 Daily DC-3	422 Daily Except Sun. & Hol. MARTIN	341 Daily DC-3	406 Daily Except Sun. & Hol. MARTIN	320 Daily DC-3	430 Daily MARTIN	732 Daily Except Sun. & Hol.	752 Daily Except Sun. & Hol.	428 Sun. & Hol. Only MARTIN	738 Sun. & Hol. Only	750 Sun. & Hol. Only	418 Daily MARTIN	758 Daily	756 Daily	734 Daily	486 Daily MARTINLINER AIR COACH	402 Daily MARTIN	344 Daily DC-3	326 Daily DC-3	336 Daily DC-3	764 Daily	704 Daily
SEATTLE	Ar						U1 46						U5 04									U11 19	
Portland	Ar						12 18						3 11									10 08	
MEDFORD	Ar/Lv					11 50 / 11 23							1 44							10 04 / 9 20			
CRESCENT CITY	Lv/Ar																						
Eureka-Arcata						10 55 / 10 10	10 50 / 10 36						1 20 / 1 12							8 50 / 7 56		8 45 / 8 28	
UKIAH	Lv																			7 00			
SANTA ROSA	Lv					.9 18	9 42													6 35			
Redding	Lv/Ar												3 08						7 05				
RED BLUFF	Lv						8 53						2 47						6 50				
CHICO	Lv						8 35												6 32				
MARYSVILLE-YUBA CITY	Lv						8 10						2 16						6 07				
Sacramento	Lv/Ar				10 13		7 48												5 45				
Stockton	Lv				9 49																		
Oakland	Lv/Ar					7 15	9 14															7 23	
San Francisco	Lv					7 00	9 00						12 00	1 45					5 00	6 00		7 00	
San Francisco	Ar	8 10	9 15					9 35	9 42	11 30	11 25	11 04		1 07	2 07				6 10			6 15	
San Jose	Lv/Ar	7 50		9 22	9 05						10 51			12 54		3 15			5 54			6 02	
Stockton	Lv	7 26																	5 26				
Sacramento	Lv	7 00																	5 00				
San Francisco	Lv			9 00																			
Monterey-Carmel (Ft. Ord)	Lv							9 08			10 58			1 40									
P'SO ROBLES-S. L. OBISPO	Lv		8 23							10 38													
SANTA MARIA (VANDENBERG A.F.B.)	Lv/Ar		8 00							10 15													
Bakersfield	Ar								8 36		9 47				11 48						4 55		
Las Vegas	Lv/Ar															2 06					3 30		
Santa Barbara	Lv							8 07		9 39	9 57				12 39								
OXNARD-VENTURA	Lv		7 24						9 39														
INYOKERN	Ar		8 07							8 04								6 37					
PALMDALE-LANCASTER	Ar																1 10						
BURBANK LOCKHEED A.T.	Lv				7 40						9 16							12 50	1 50				
Los Angeles International	Lv		7 00	7 20	7 15			7 30	7 40	9 15	9 20	9 00		11 00	12 00			12 30	1 30	5 45			

Airline Flight Schedule

printed time schedule, and you may need to consult passenger agents. In reading a timetable, remember that the light-face type gives morning time and bold-face type gives afternoon and night time. You need to determine not only departure and arrival time but also name of the transportation lines, changes to be made en route, stopovers, accommodations available, and days on which service is available.

Making Reservations. You will need to make reservations as soon as your employer has chosen his mode of travel and time schedule. There are usually regulations about the deadline for picking up and paying for reservations. There are also rules about confirming airplane reservations within a few hours of departure time.

In making train reservations there may be several choices of accommodations available—chair car, berth, roomette, compartment, or bedroom. On some busses and airplanes there are sleeping accommodations for overnight trips.

Types of Accommodations. You may need to make hotel or motel reservations. In writing for them, indicate the date for which you are requesting the reservation and type of accommodation wanted—single, double (double or twin beds), or suite. Expected arrival time should also be given, especially if it is after 6 p.m. A confirmation is usually sent, which your employer should take with him to present when he registers at the hotel or motel.

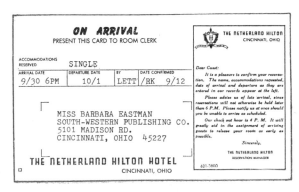

Confirmation of Reservation

74C—Acceleration Practice

74D—Preview of New Dictation Material

(1)

balloons, counter, extremely, round, shape, assorted, pictures, every day, inflating, why not

(2)

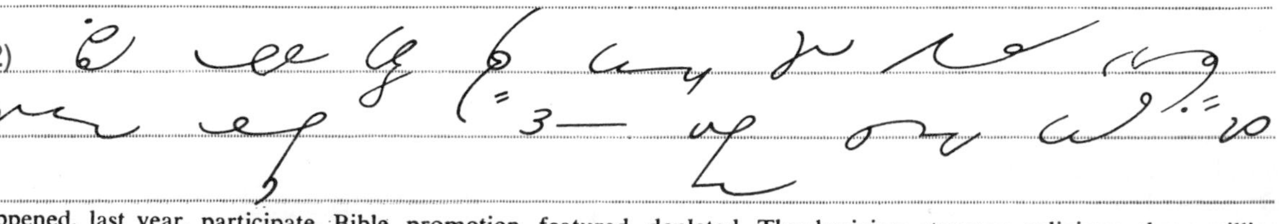

happened, last year, participate, Bible, promotion, featured, depleted, Thanksgiving, stronger, religious, three million, original, against, promptly, so that

```
                    MR. BROWN'S ITINERARY, FEBRUARY 8-18, 19--
                    New York - Upper Darby - Philadelphia - Baltimore

   FRIDAY--FEBRUARY 8 (ST. LOUIS TO NEW YORK)

   6:45 pm    Leave St. Louis airport on TWA 639 Jetliner Ambassador
              (tickets in TWA envelope).

   9:50 pm    Arrive Idlewild (16 miles from NYC). "Guaranteed-
              arrival" reservation at Park-Sheraton Hotel (con-
              firmation of reservation attached)

   SATURDAY--FEBRUARY 9 (NEW YORK)

   10:30 am   See Mr. John Archer, Sales Manager of Flair Products,
              Room 888, Seagram Building, 243 Park Avenue.

   12:30 pm   Lunch at New York Athletic Club, 61 Central Park South,
              with Mr. Thomas Lowell and Miss Anne Mastin of Apex
              Manufacturing, Inc. to discuss advertising promotion
              of Multiflex (Multiflex folder in briefcase).

   4:30 pm    Interview Mr. Donald Beagle for position as Production
              Manager, your room at the Park-Sheraton (application
              and job specification in briefcase).

   7 pm       Dinner with Mr. and Mrs. James Kilpatrick at
              68 East 72 Street.

   SUNDAY--FEBRUARY 10 (UPPER DARBY PLANT AND WEEKEND IN PAOLI)

   9:30 am    Leave New York, Pennsylvania Station, on PRR (no
              reservation; buy coach ticket at station).

   11 am      Arrive Philadelphia, 30 Street Station. Pick up Hertz
              Oldsmobile (arranged for) and drive to Upper Darby
              plant for rest of day. (File on plant proposals will
              be mailed to you at plant.)

              Drive to Paoli for weekend with sister. Turn in car
              at Hertz, 82 East Wilmington Drive, Paoli.

   WEDNESDAY--FEBRUARY 13 (PHILADELPHIA CONVENTION)

   8 am       Check in at Penn-Sheraton (confirmation of reservation
              attached). Check with hotel to see that charts to illus-
              trate talk have been received (will be mailed 11/1/--;
              return wrapping, postage, and labels in package).

              Convention opens.

   2 pm       Your speech (in briefcase; duplicate in package with
              charts).

   7 pm       Annual banquet. Tickets for dais guests will be given
              to you by secretary. White tie.
```

First Page of an Itinerary

Making Itinerary. It is well to prepare a typed copy of an itinerary for your employer's trip. On the itinerary will be included a chronological listing of arrival and departure times; mode of travel and accommodations; and possibly scheduled meetings.

Preparing Travel Requisition and Expense Voucher. In some firms, you will prepare a travel requisition on which is indicated an estimate of expenses. Upon the return of your employer, an expense voucher listing exact expenses is prepared for submission to the Accounting Department so that reimbursement can be made.

Questions for Discussion

1. In what way may you be able to help your employer select his mode of travel?

2. How do you make reservations for travel? for hotel or motel accommodations?

3. What information should be contained on an itinerary you type for your employer?

Office Practice Problems

1. Using the flight schedule on page 167, list the times and flights that would be followed in making the following trip:
   Your employer wants to leave Los Angeles as late as possible and yet have time to be in San Francisco for an airport luncheon with business associates at 12 noon. He will then spend the night in San Francisco, work the next morning, and take a flight out of San Francisco sometime after 11 a.m. for Redding.

2. Reserve a single room with bath for Mr. X at the Californian Hotel, Taylor and O'Farrell Streets, San Francisco, California 94102.

58B—Building Speed in Taking Dictation

Potential Rate Builder

There are 16 words in the sentence.

Word Spellings and Meanings

adopt—to put into practice as one's own; to accept, as a report; to take by choice into a relationship, as an heir

adapt—to adjust or to make suitable

adept—skillful

NOTE: The following material includes words presented in Lessons 54-57, as well as those given above.

Lesson 74 ⬡⬡⬡⬡⬡⬡⬡⬡⬡⬡⬡⬡⬡⬡⬡⬡⬡⬡

74A—Review of Cities and States

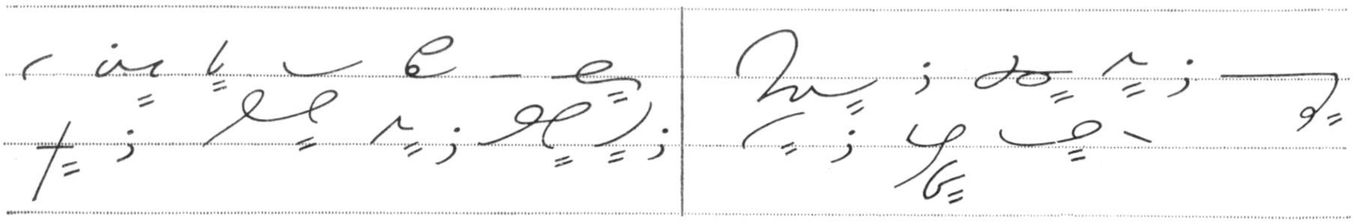

[shorthand outlines]

74B—Brief Forms and Derivatives

[shorthand outlines]

	15″	12″	10″
(1) *[shorthand]*	66	82	99
(2) *[shorthand]*	74	96	111
(3) *[shorthand]*	83	104	124
(4) *[shorthand]*	91	114	137
(5) *[shorthand]*	91	114	137

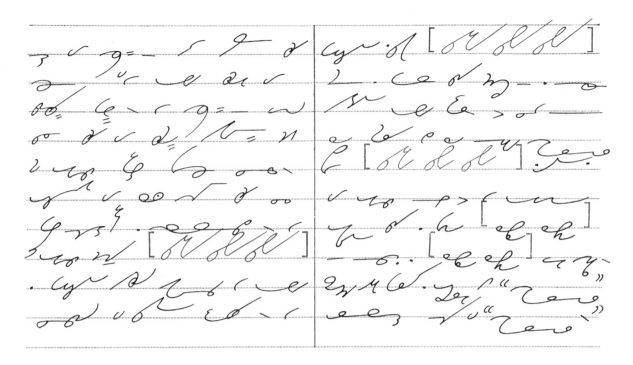

Practice Material for Building Fluency

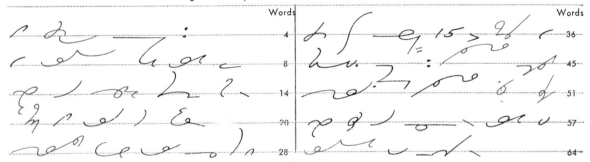

Words
4
8
14
20
28

Words
36
45
51
57
64

Dictionary and Spelling Preview

1. showroom, comprehensive, assistance
2. versatile, themes, eventually, sprightly, recreation
3. comments, resubmitted, signature
4. Memorial, Independence, Armistice, necessitate

Preview of New Dictation Material

(1)

to visit, showroom, for the purpose, furniture, comprehensive, personnel, weekdays, appointment, if it is, to bring, send them, introduction, we may be, assistance

73D—Preview of New Dictation Material

(1)

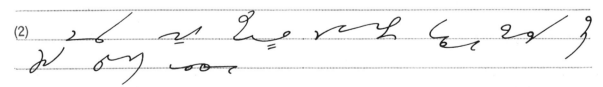

potential, cosmetic, during the past year, awarded, Achievement, issued, Institute, recognition, awareness, of what, exercising, choice, cherish, vitally, share, lucrative, initial, furnishing, specialized, upon request, extent, postal, extended

(2)

submitted, quotation, Waverly, stenographic, pencils, as requested, if you have, found, attractive, requirements

(2)

guest, promotional, versatile, eventually, timely, recreation, Scotchweave, aimed, useful, potential, user, greatest, postage, many thanks, meanwhile, sprightly

(3)

legal, document, identifying, rejected, director, comments, we should like, resubmitted, signature

(4)

holidays, Lincoln's Birthday, Washington's, Independence, Memorial, Columbus, Armistice, Thanksgiving, necessitate, emergency

Lesson 59 ⬡◇⬡◇⬡◇⬡◇⬡◇⬡◇⬡◇⬡◇⬡◇⬡◇⬡◇⬡◇

59A—Business Ethics

"Business ethics" is a term used to refer to accepted rules of conduct in the business world. These rules are concerned with what actions are morally right in carrying on business activities. A specific action might be *legally permissible* but not *ethically correct*. It is not ethical, for instance, to misrepresent facts, to be party to a dishonest transaction, to tell only part of the truth and thus mislead somebody in his belief or actions. Good business ethics require the following actions or attitudes on the part of a businessman or an employee:

1. He should be loyal to the firm for which he works. In being loyal, he will work for the best interests of the organization with which he is associated. He will not criticize the firm in the presence of people outside the firm. Neither will he give information about the firm's activities that would be helpful to competitors.

If an employee cannot feel loyalty toward the employer and be enthusiastic about the business enterprise with which he is associated, he is probably basically unhappy in his work. He should, in such a case, seek employment with an employer for whom he can feel loyalty and in a business enterprise about which he can feel enthusiastic.

2. He should be honest with other members of the organization and with other people or businesses with which he deals. As an employee, he should give a day's work for a day's pay. As a buyer, he should pay his bills; as a seller, he should not misrepresent his product or his services. Promises should be kept in business life just as they should be kept in personal life.

Claims about one's product or service should be true. To make untrue statements about a competitor or his product is unethical; for instance, it

Lesson 73

73A—Review of Cities and States

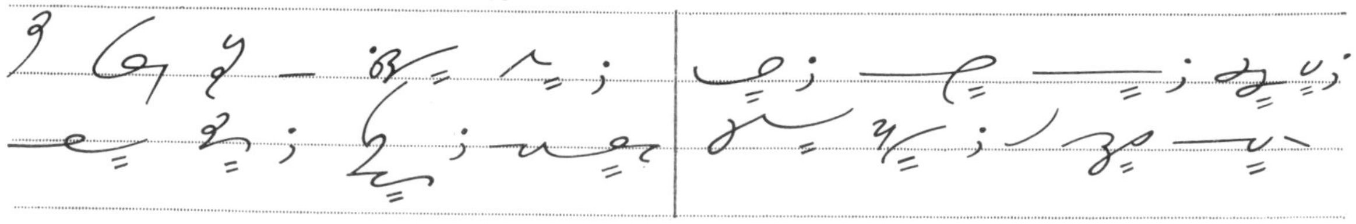

73B—Brief Forms and Derivatives

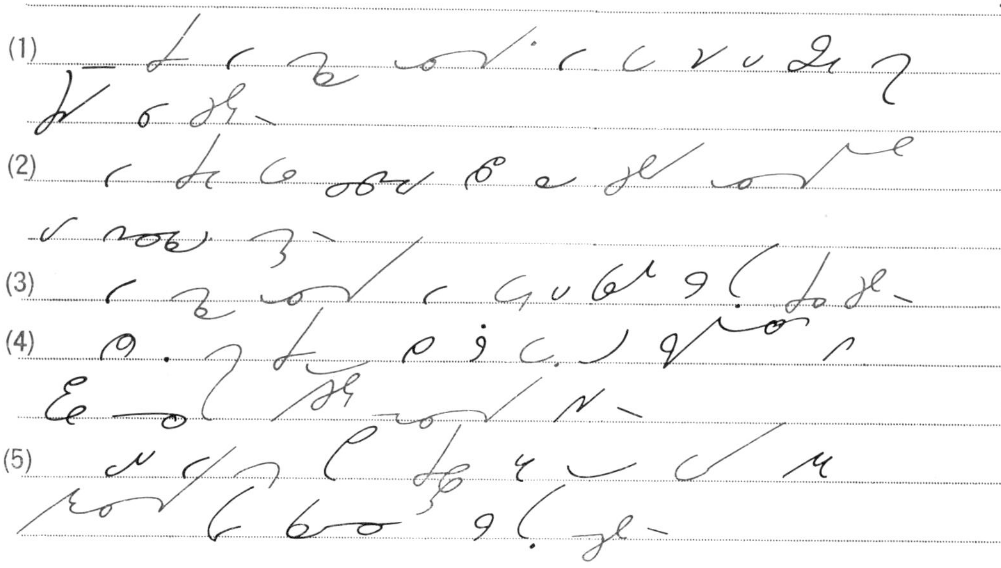

	20″	15″	12″
(1)	71	89	107
(2)	71	89	107
(3)	74	96	111
(4)	104	130	156
(5)	106	132	159

73C—Acceleration Practice

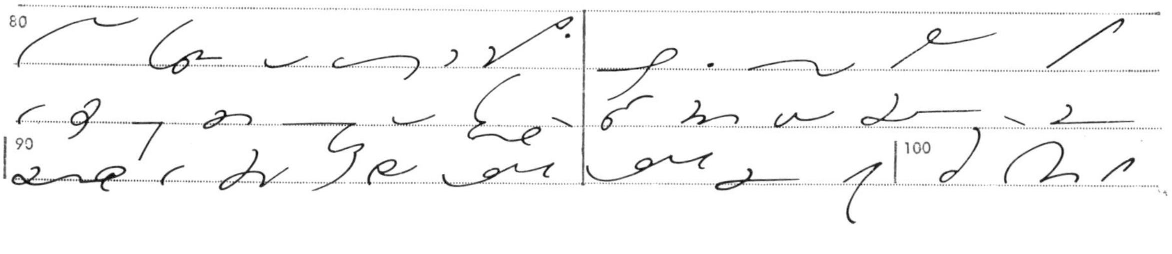

would be unethical for a businessman to try to sell his own product by telling customers that his competitor is going out of business and won't be able to service the product that he is selling.

3. He should be a responsible person. That means, for example, that as an employer he should give reasonable notice of intention to discontinue using the services of an employee so that the employee has an opportunity to find other work before he is "separated" or "laid off" by the firm. An employee, on the other hand, should give reasonable notice of intention to quit work so that the employer has an opportunity to find someone to fill the vacancy that will be created.

4. He should earn advancement in his chosen field by ability and work, not by "pull" or by criticizing the efforts of others. The repeating of rumors derogatory to another person in an effort to raise one's own standing is unethical.

Questions for Discussion

1. What does the term "business ethics" mean?

2. Is a "half truth" as unethical as a 100 percent falsehood?

3. What does being honest mean in being ethical?

4. What does being loyal involve?

5. Describe a "responsible person."

Office Practice Problem

Which of the following do you think is ethically correct? Be prepared to defend your answer:

a. A furniture salesman tells a customer that a friend of his bought a defective chair from his competitor and that the competitor disclaimed all responsibility for replacing or repairing the chair.

b. An employee gives notice of intention to quit in two weeks. The employer tells him, "Well, as far as I'm concerned you're quitting right now. Go get your pay through today and get out."

c. An employee of Firm A applies for a position with Firm B and, in an effort to get the job, he tells the employment manager of Firm B that Firm A is heavily in debt.

d. A secretary tells friends who have inquired about plans of her company that she does not know what the plans are when actually she does know because she typed the plans herself.

59B—Building Speed in Taking Dictation

Proportion Drill

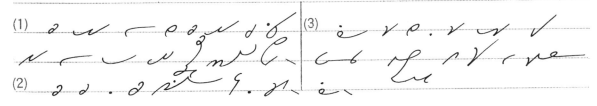

Word Spellings and Meanings

intrastate—within a state
interstate—between states

NOTE: The following material includes words presented in Lessons 55-58, as well as those given above.

72C—Acceleration Practice

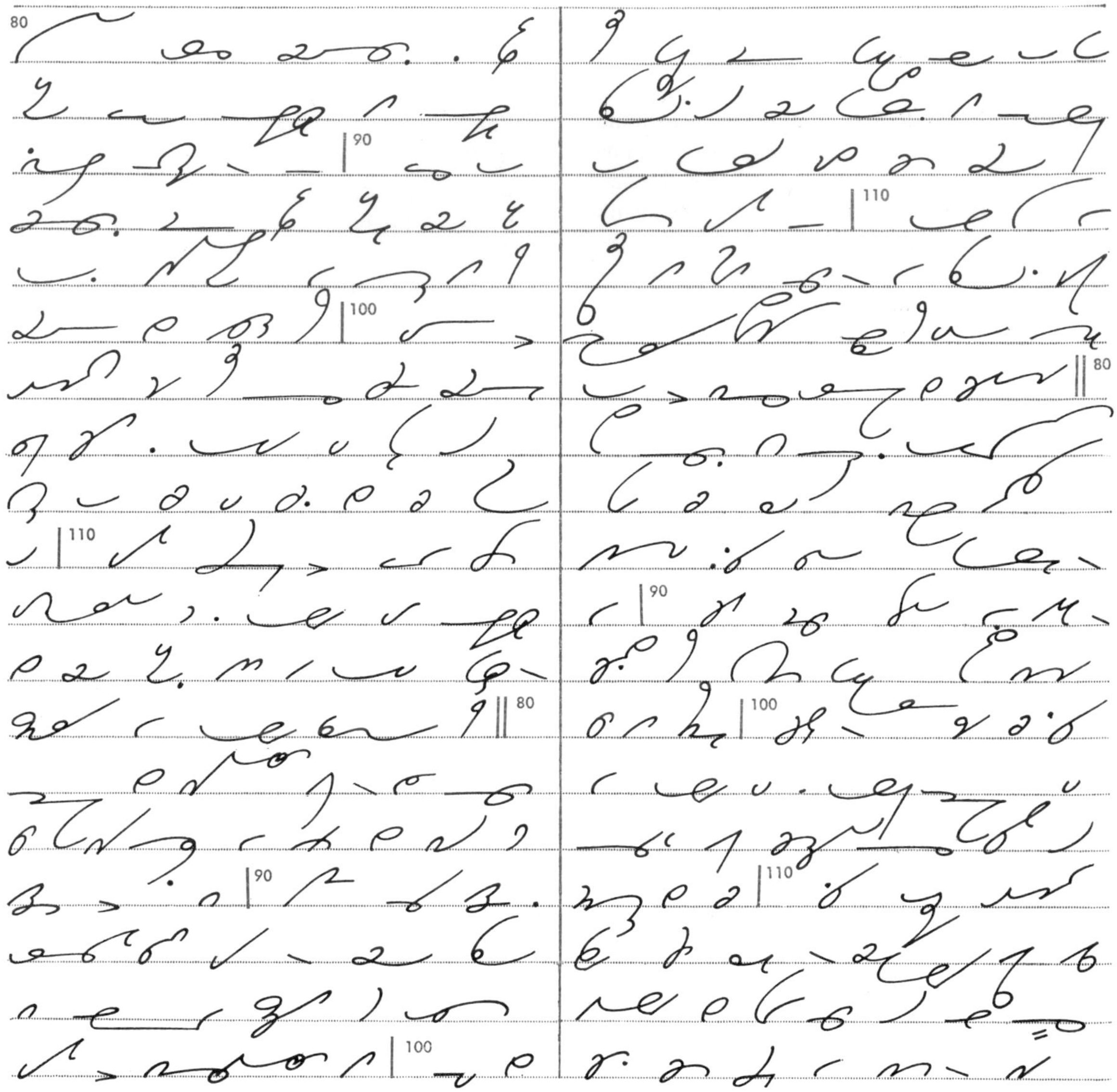

72D—Preview of New Dictation Material

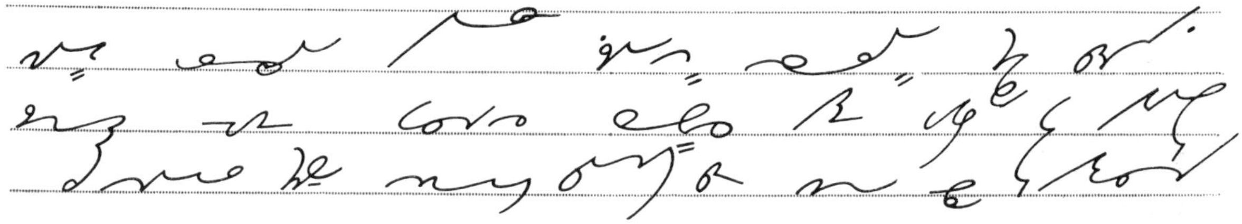

Waters, reminder, deadline, Historical, Calendar, for the past, outstanding, exclusively, no one, practically, Alaska, does not, whatsoever, publication, distribution, contrary, footwear, colorful, attractive, young, worker, next year, disregard

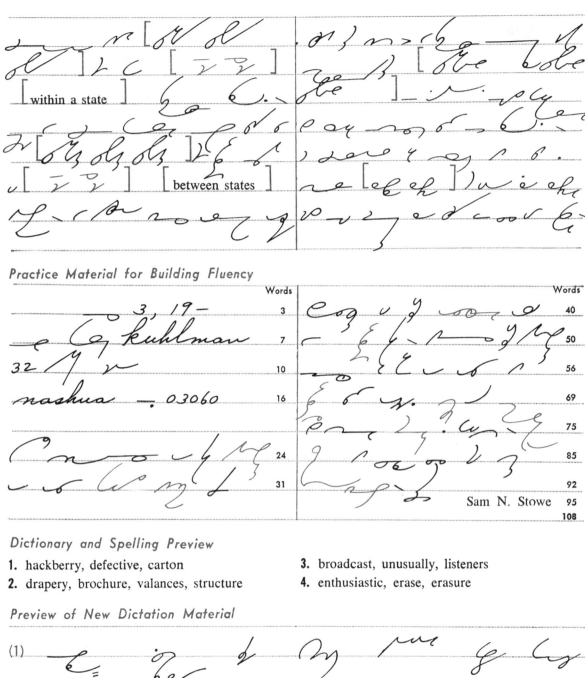

Practice Material for Building Fluency

_3, 19 —_ **3**

kuhlman **7**

_32_ **10**

nashua — _03060_ **16**

24

31

40

50

56

69

75

85

92

Sam N. Stowe **95**

108

Dictionary and Spelling Preview

1. hackberry, defective, carton
2. drapery, brochure, valances, structure
3. broadcast, unusually, listeners
4. enthusiastic, erase, erasure

Preview of New Dictation Material

(1)

Mitchell, hackberry, chest, defective, drawers, prepaid, upon receipt, replacement, carton

(2)

drapery, availability, brochure, structure, effective, not only, walls, valances, panels, minimum, settings, bulk, demonstration

72A—Review of Cities and States

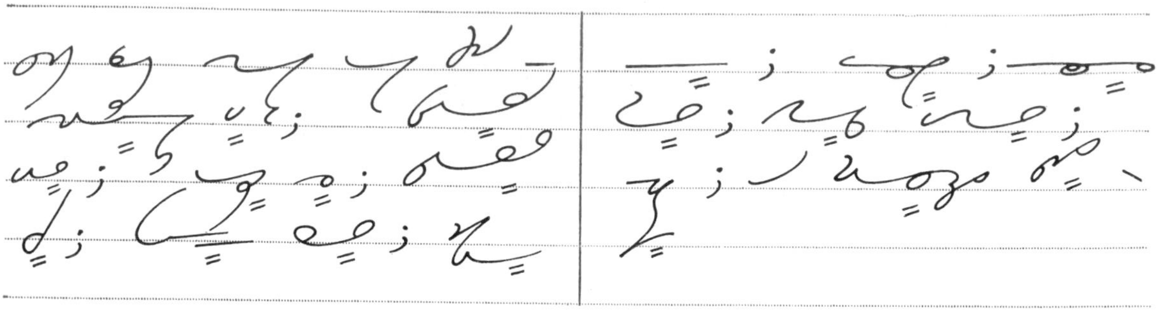

[shorthand outlines]

72B—Brief Forms and Derivatives

[shorthand outlines]

	12″	10″	8″
(1) *[shorthand]*	69	86	103
(2) *[shorthand]*	71	89	107
(3) *[shorthand]*	89	111	133
(4) *[shorthand]*	94	118	141
(5) *[shorthand]*	94	118	141

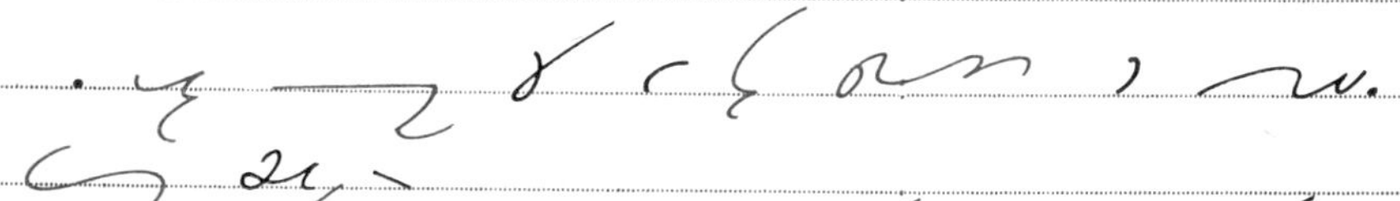

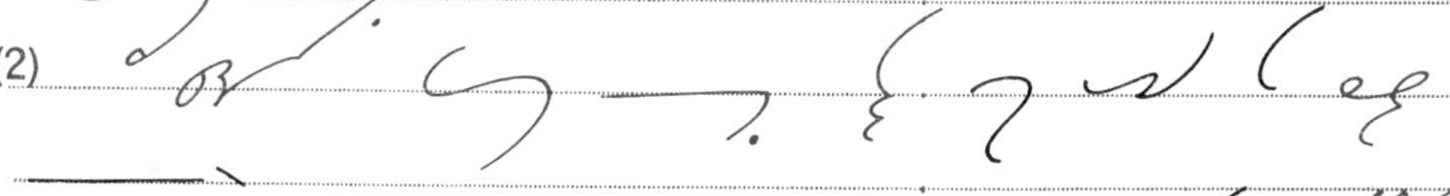

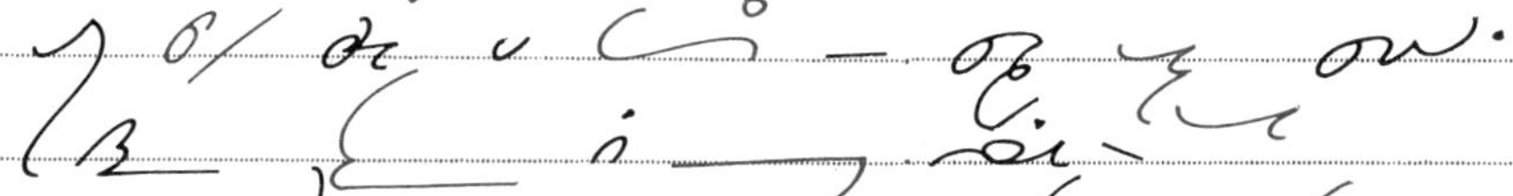

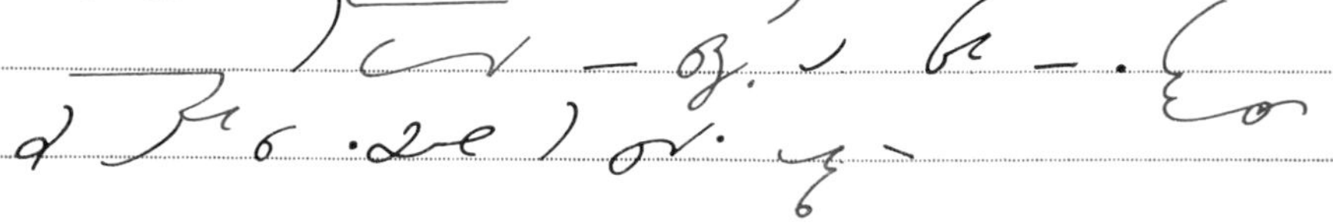

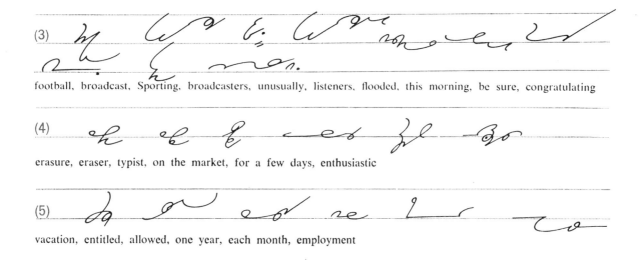

(3)

football, broadcast, Sporting, broadcasters, unusually, listeners, flooded, this morning, be sure, congratulating

(4)

erasure, eraser, typist, on the market, for a few days, enthusiastic

(5)

vacation, entitled, allowed, one year, each month, employment

Lesson 60 ⬡⬡⬡⬡⬡⬡⬡⬡⬡⬡⬡⬡⬡⬡⬡⬡⬡⬡

60A—Business Etiquette

Business ethics is concerned with what is morally right or wrong. Business etiquette, on the other hand, deals with "surface" behavior, the forms of speaking and acting prescribed in certain circumstances as proper. Business etiquette is like social etiquette in that it is based on courtesy, consideration of others, and thoughtfulness. There are some situations, however, that have no counterpart in social life.

Addressing Your Superior. Always address your superior by his or her name with the appropriate courtesy title, as *Mr.* Smith or *Mrs.* Jones. Your superior may address you by your first name, but you never call him by his first name.

Addressing a Co-Worker. When you are new in a firm, use a courtesy title in addressing any co-worker unless it is clear that everyone follows the practice of using first names or unless you have been requested by a person to use his first name. Be particularly careful not to call an older person by his first name, as it is considered a mark of respect to use a courtesy title.

Responding to a Question or Comment of Another. A response never seems as abrupt if you use the person's name in making it. For example,

"Yes, Miss Grady," sounds better than "Yes." "I don't think so, Mr. Ohms," sounds more pleasant than just "No."

Notifying Employer if Tardy or Absent from Work. If you are unavoidably tardy or absent from work, let your employer know as soon as possible what the difficulty is and when you expect to be able to be at the office ready for work.

Telling Jokes. When your employer tells a joke, you will, of course, laugh appreciatively. Remember that a sincere laugh is not necessarily a loud one. The fact that he tells a joke does not mean that you should, in turn, tell him one. Everyone enjoys a good story now and then, but do not attempt to become entertainer for the office by continually telling stories during working hours. You may become known as the "office clown" or "office comic," and such a name doesn't help you get promoted to positions of responsibility.

Interrupting a Conversation or Work. If it is necessary for you to interrupt a conversation in which others are engaged or to interrupt someone who is working, preface your remarks with "Excuse me, please," and wait to be acknowledged before continuing to talk. If you must interrupt a

71C—Acceleration Practice

The shorthand outlines below are marked for 3 minutes of acceleration practice, with the speed ranging from 80 to 110 words a minute within each minute.

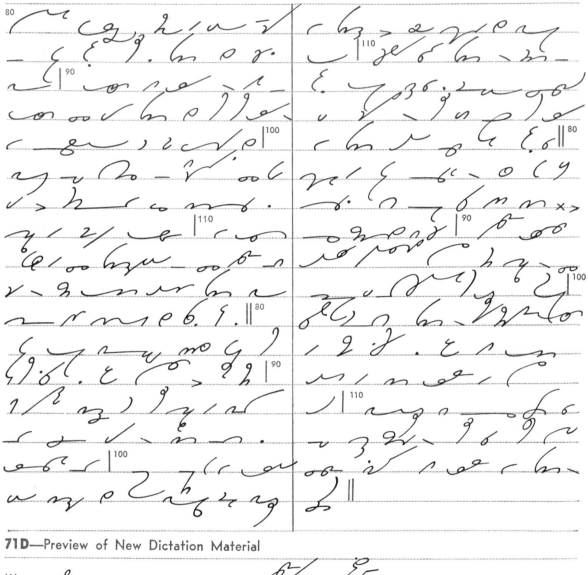

71D—Preview of New Dictation Material

(1)

toy, gift, you will note, downward, has been done, reflects, competitive, houseware, profitable, season, expanded, consequent, substantial, savings, situation, currently, continue

(2)

application, for your convenience, renewal, penny, license, coming year, calendar

conference in which your employer is involved, you may find it best to write a note stating your question or problem and lay it unobtrusively in front of him. He can glance at the note and jot down an answer or give it to you in a few words, thus minimizing the distraction to the conference.

Saying "Good Morning" and "Good Night." It is considered proper to speak to those with whom you work when you arrive for work in the morning or leave in the evening. The greetings should be made quietly and need not be followed by any further comments. If someone is engrossed in his work, do not interrupt him with a greeting. If there are several people in the office, a general "Good morning," with a glance around the room is sufficient; you need not greet everyone individually. A pleasant smile enhances the greeting.

Questions for Discussion

1. What is the difference between business ethics and business etiquette?

2. How should you address your superior? a co-worker?

3. Why should you let your employer know if you are going to be absent or tardy?

4. What are some points to remember about telling jokes?

Office Practice Problems

1. Discuss what you would do in the following situation: The taxi in which you are riding to work has a flat tire and you realize that you are going to be at least half an hour late to work.

2. You wish to reply negatively to someone's suggestion. How many different ways can you think of to respond without saying just "No"?

3. You wish to reply in the affirmative to someone's remark. How many ways can you think of to respond without saying just "Yes"?

60B—Building Speed in Taking Dictation

Repetitive Phrase Builder

Word Spellings and Meanings

principle—basis, fundamental truth, rule of action
principal—highest in rank, leader, capital sum, head of a school, main

NOTE: The following material includes words presented in Lessons 56-59, as well as those given above.

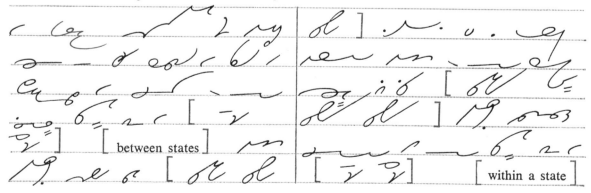

Unit 12 · Lesson 60

174

Unit **15**

Building Speed in Taking Dictation

Lesson 71

71A—Review of Cities and States

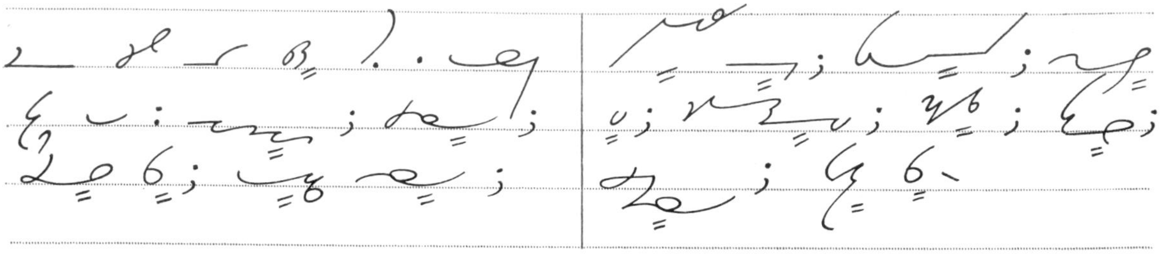

71B—Brief Forms and Derivatives

Directions. Five brief forms and some of their derivatives occur in each of the sentences below. The figures at the right indicate the speed at which you are taking dictation if you write the sentence when it is dictated in 15 seconds, 12 seconds, and 10 seconds, respectively.

	15″	12″	10″
(1)	60	75	90
(2)	66	82	99
(3)	79	96	116
(4)	86	107	129
(5)	109	136	163

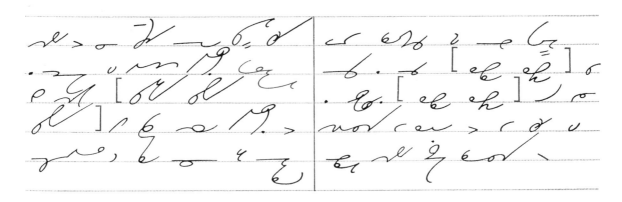

Practice Material for Building Fluency

	Words		Words
17, 19—	3		44
	7		50
	11		61
53703	16		70
			82
	23		89
	29		97
	37		99
		Jerry A. Leeds	104
			117

Dictionary and Spelling Preview

1. compelled, reluctantly, mandatory, cushions, foam
2. acknowledgment, indefinite, rescheduling
3. route, station, traffic, tourist
4. adequate, original, pencil
5. precautions, preoccupied, weight, swivel

Preview of New Dictation Material

(1)

Manor, reluctantly, compelled, slightly, prior, upholstery, necessity, cushions, standard, we regret, generally, introduced, mandatory

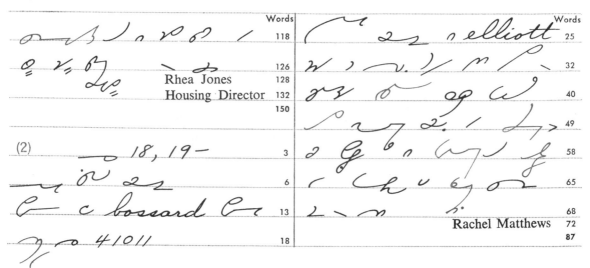

	Words		Words
	118	elliott	25
	126		32
Rhea Jones	128		40
Housing Director	132		49
	150		
(2) ___ 18, 19—	3		58
	6		65
c bossard	13		68
41011	18	Rachel Matthews	72
			87

70E—Dictionary and Spelling Preview

1. describes, in-service
2. engineering, occur
3. cosigners, endorsers, preferred

70F—Preview of New Dictation Material

(1)

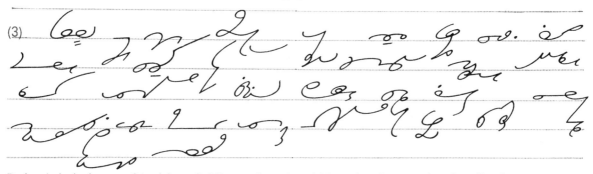

typewriting, business correspondence, shorthand, to improve, with her, employer, approval, chosen, that will be, alternated, attached, folder, Tuesdays, Thursdays

(2)

Stanley, McDaniel, promoted, Systems, Engineering, reviewed, qualifications, Arnold, Mitchell, we regret, to say, we do not have, background, meantime, we wish, employment

(3)

Brainard, invitation, confidential, availability, registered, quickly, privately, annoying, heartily, for many years, acquainted, budget, signature, cosigners, endorsers, seldom, regardless, household, appliances, acceptable, helpful, emergencies, consolidating, only one, each month, regulations, individually, preferred, identifies, absolutely, guarantee

(2) [shorthand outlines]

Seafarer, acknowledgment, in order, accurate, we do not, indefinite, liberty, rescheduling, approval, contrary

(3) [shorthand outlines]

locality, officials, route, station, chosen, point of view, emergencies, townspeople, tourist, traffic, completion

(4) [shorthand outlines]

original, adequate, to providing, tools, beautiful, pencil

(5) [shorthand outlines]

accidents, precautions, preoccupied, misjudge, cabinet, forward, opened, distance, swivel, shift

Unit **13**

Building Speed in Taking Dictation

Lesson **61** ⬡⬡⬡⬡⬡⬡⬡⬡⬡⬡⬡⬡⬡⬡⬡⬡⬡⬡

61A—Brief-Form Practice

Directions. The following paragraph has 29 brief forms and brief-form derivatives. If you can read it in 30 seconds, your reading rate will be 126 words a minute.

[shorthand outlines]

70B—Theory Review

When *t*, *d*, *n*, or *m* is followed by *-ation* or *-ition*, the circle is omitted.

The word beginning *al-* is expressed by the *o* hook.

The sound of *ul* is expressed by the *oo* hook before a forward or an upward consonant stroke.

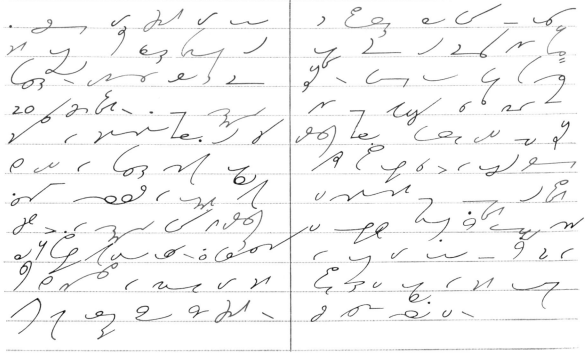

70C—Word Spellings and Meanings

NOTE: The following material includes words presented in Lesson 66.

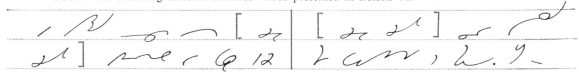

70D—Practice Material for Building Fluency

61B—Theory Review

The word beginnings *fur-*, *fore-*, and *for-* are expressed by *f* before a consonant.

Com- and *con-* are expressed by *k* before a consonant except *r* or *l*. Before *r* or *l*, they are expressed by *km* and *kn*.

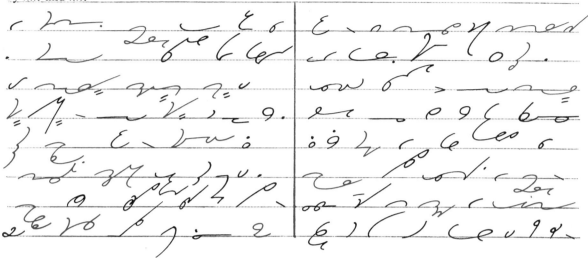

61C—Word Spellings and Meanings

all ready—everything or everybody is prepared

already—prior to some specified time, either past, present, or future (adv.)

NOTE: The following material includes words presented in Lessons 57-60, as well as those given above.

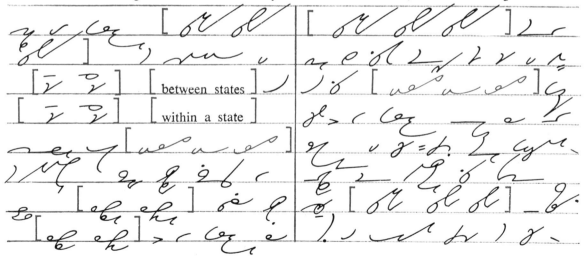

61D—Practice Material for Building Fluency

	Words		Words
1, 19—	3		22
calhoun	7		30
618 McDougal	11		38
60601	15		45

(1) 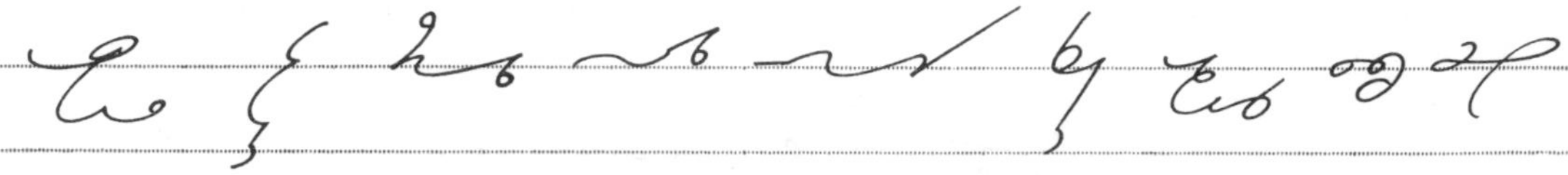 *[shorthand]*

Library, publications, if you will see, courtesy, included, charges, reciprocate, any way, we may be

(2) 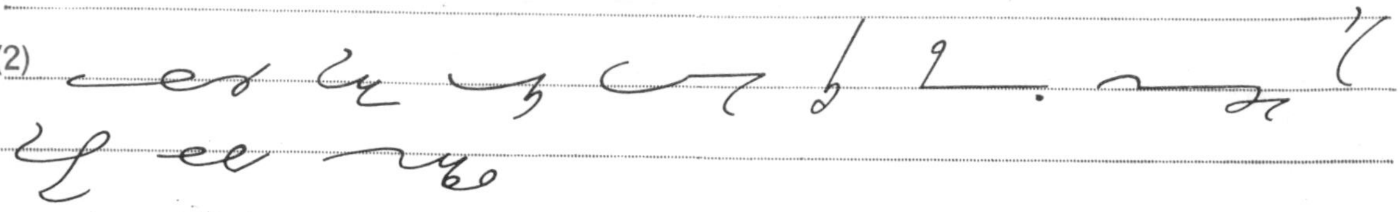 *[shorthand]*

on the market, frozen, luscious, plump, juicy, each morning, common sense, superb, flavor, nearest, grocery

(3)  *[shorthand]*

O'Reilly, we want, power, electric current, shut, substation, to be sure, that it was, this morning, perfectly, amounted

(4) 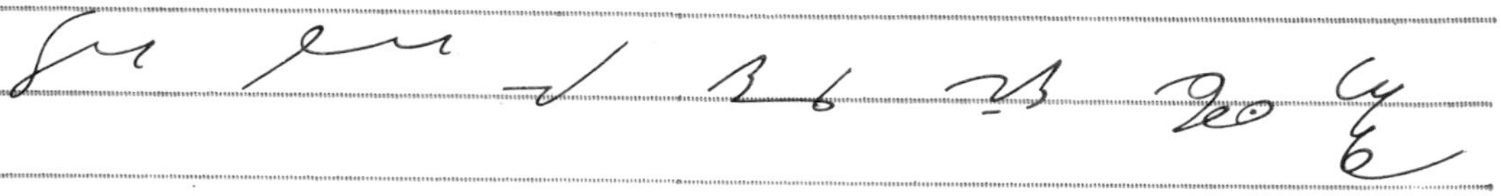 *[shorthand]*

bidders, dealers, in order, to submit, quotations, cafeteria, proposal

(5)  *[shorthand]*

inside, addressee, separate, comma, instead, official, mishandled, Post Office, appropriate, President, unusually, resulting, in such a case

Lesson **70** ⬡⬡⬡⬡⬡⬡⬡⬡⬡⬡⬡⬡⬡⬡⬡⬡⬡⬡⬡

70A—Repetitive Phrase Builder

[shorthand]

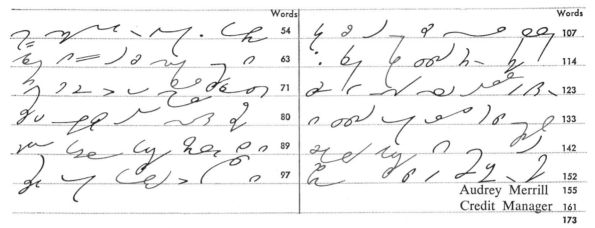

	Words
	54
	63
	71
	80
	89
	97

	Words
	107
	114
	123
	133
	142
	152
Audrey Merrill	155
Credit Manager	161
	173

61E—Dictionary and Spelling Preview

1. major, forenoon

2. colleges, universities, decided

3. floundering, functional, subsidiary, concern

4. brochure, convenience, midst

61F—Preview of New Dictation Material

(1)

Conway, for next year, contract, major, Committee, forenoon, Equipment, if that is

(2)

University, western, personalized, initials, dozens, tremendous, if you have, in this way, up to date, wholesale, packed, student, I decided

(3)

floundering, organizational, functional, strictly, adhered, consultants, thoroughly, analyzed, perfected, estimating, effective, serious, Magnolia, Terrace, subsidiary, inspired, very well, units, 200,000

(4)

Diner's, Society, brouchure, warmth, security, midst, process, membership, entry, so that, welcome, recommended

69C—Word Spellings and Meanings

NOTE: The following material includes words presented in Lessons 65 and 66.

69D—Practice Material for Building Fluency

Words		Words
4		65
8		70
11		79
15		86
26		92
34		101
45		110
51		119
58		126

Llewellyn B. Vanhorn 131

142

69E—Dictionary and Spelling Preview

1. libraries, reciprocate

2. luscious, plump, superb, grocery

3. substation

4. bidders', cafeteria

5. addressee, punctuation, mishandled

Lesson 62 ⬡⬡⬡⬡⬡⬡⬡⬡⬡⬡⬡⬡⬡⬡⬡⬡⬡⬡⬡

62A—Phrase Builder

There are 15 phrases in the following paragraph.

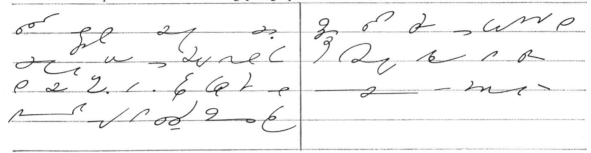

62B—Theory Review

The word ending -*gram* is expressed by a disjoined *gay*.
The word ending -*rity* is expressed by a disjoined *r*.
The word endings -*ward* and -*hood* are expressed by a disjoined *d*.

62C—Word Spellings and Meanings

core—the main or center part

corps—a body of individuals, especially a military group

NOTE: The following material includes words presented in Lessons 58-61, as well as those given above.

(3) *[shorthand outlines]*

records, we find, we haven't, aprons, we have done, dissatisfaction, existing, for your convenience, we enclose

(4) *[shorthand outlines]*

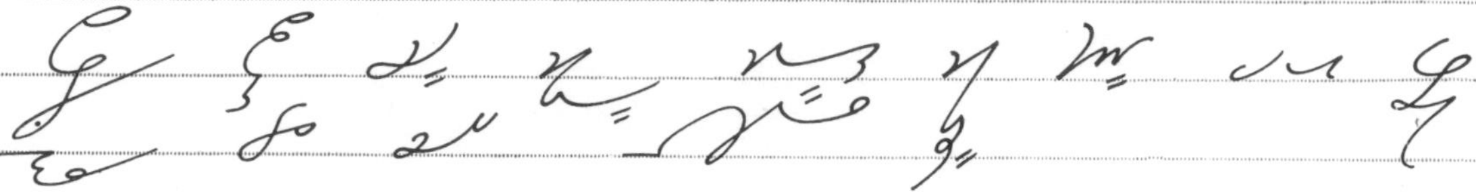

abbreviated, exceptions, Saint, St. Paul, St. Louis, St. Joseph, Fort Worth, authorities, preferable, misread, particularly, window, individually

Lesson **69** ⬡⬡⬡⬡⬡⬡⬡⬡⬡⬡⬡⬡⬡⬡⬡⬡⬡⬡⬡⬡

69A—Proportion Drill

(1) *[shorthand outlines]*

(2) *[shorthand outlines]*

(3) *[shorthand outlines]*

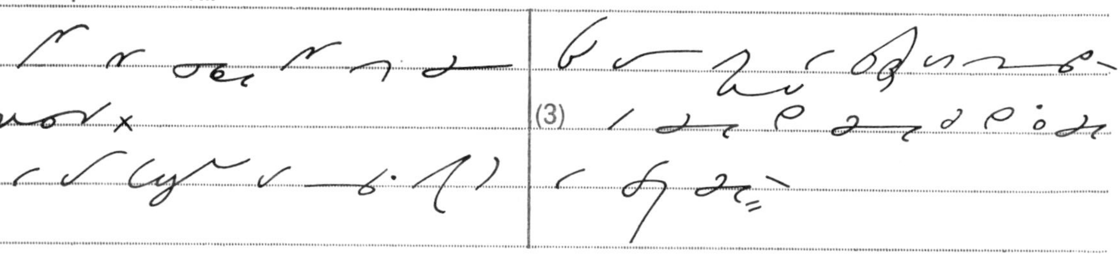

69B—Theory Review

The sound of *ng* is expressed by ⌒ ; the sound of *ngk* is expressed by ⌒ .

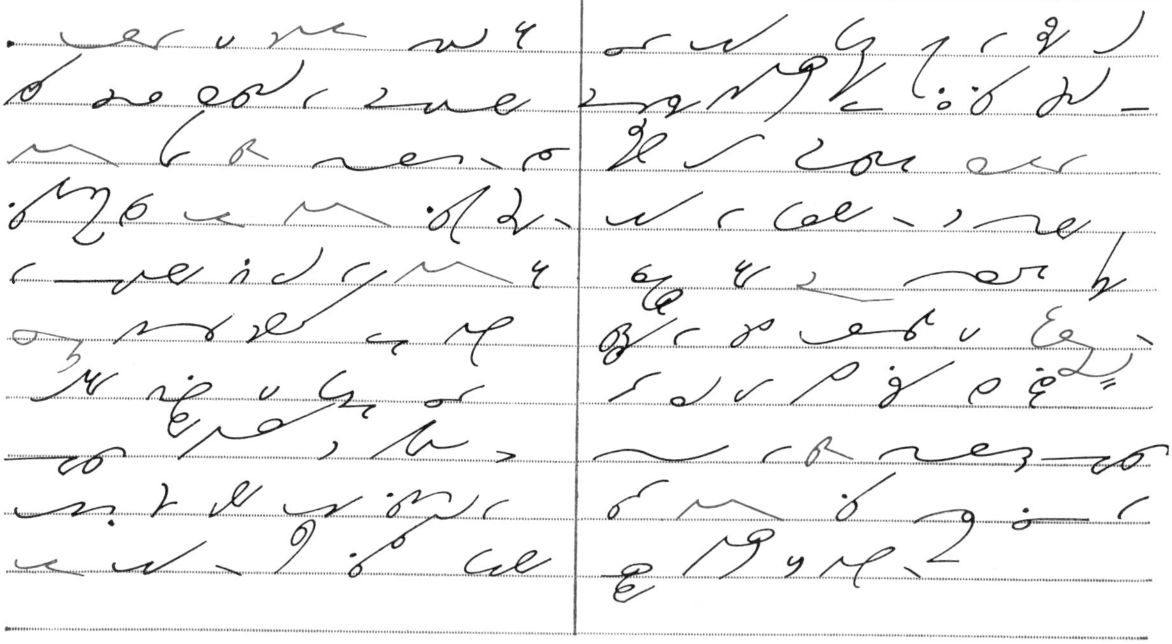

[shorthand passage]

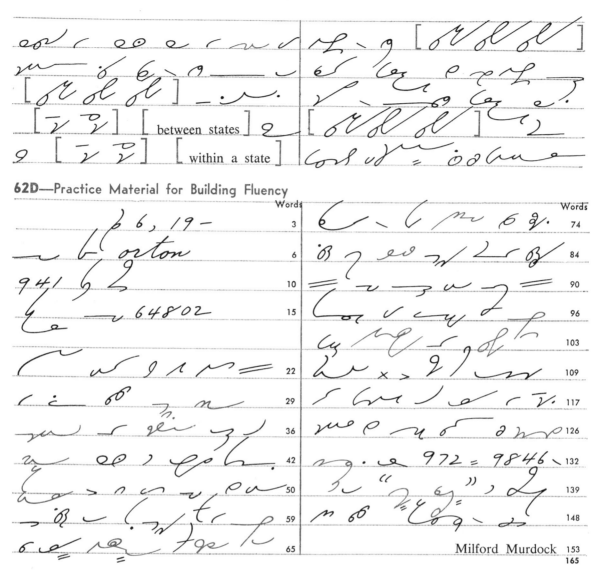

62D—Practice Material for Building Fluency

62E—Dictionary and Spelling Preview

1. neighborhood, entertainment
2. minor, omitted, similar, development
3. accommodations, restaurant, oyster, cuisine
4. eliminate, formerly, major

62F—Preview of New Dictation Material

(1)

Childhood, Dreams, viewed, human, viewer, backward, youth, congratulated, entertainment

	Words		Words
	3		71
	7		77
604	11		86
48823	17		91
	24		97
	28		103
	36	35	112
	50		120
	55	×3	132
	64	Stella Pratt	135
			148

68E—Dictionary and Spelling Preview

1. permanent, bulletins, alumni

2. athletic, stretchers, scissors, balms, liniments

3. recent, omitted, dissatisfaction

4. abbreviated, beginning

68F—Preview of New Dictation Material

(1)
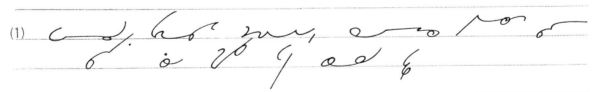

permanent, bulletins, scholarship, alumni, would like, with them, attending, higher, up to date, postage, island, possession

(2)

grateful, if you would, bid, athletic, ourselves, whatever, we feel sure, includes, items, whirlpools, stretchers, bandage, scissors, instruments, pads, braces, balms, liniments, Illinois, Wisconsin, Michigan

(2)

drawings, development, units, somewhat, obsolete, dimensions, minor, transportation, assembly, identical, finally, Village, landscaped, project, unloaded, contemplated, Denver

(3)

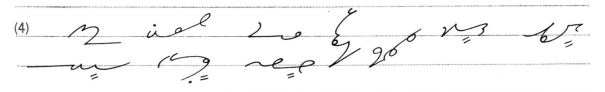

hearty, Southern, Economic, productive, accommodations, restaurant, Oyster, Memphis, Kentucky, atmosphere, unusual, tropical, cordial, New Orleans, extensive, cuisine, specializing, seafood, and see

(4)

to conform, holidays, formerly, observed, St. Louis, Independence, Memorial, Thanksgiving, Christmas, after that date

Lesson 63 ⬡⬡⬡⬡⬡⬡⬡⬡⬡⬡⬡⬡⬡⬡⬡⬡⬡⬡⬡⬡⬡

63A—Potential Rate Builder

There are 20 words in the sentence.

63B—Theory Review

The word beginnings *super-* and *supr-* are expressed by a right *s* above the line.

The word beginning *post-* is expressed by *p* above the line.

The final *r* may be dropped from words ending in *-quire*.

68A—Potential Rate Builder

There are 15 words in the sentence.

68B—Theory Review

The ending *-ment* is expressed by *m*.

The *r* is omitted in *tern, term, dern, derm, thern, therm.*

The beginnings *en-, un-,* and *in-* are expressed by *n* before a consonant; they are written in full when followed by a vowel. The beginnings *em-, im-,* are expressed by *m* before a consonant; they are written in full when followed by a vowel.

68C—Word Spellings and Meanings

NOTE: The following material includes words presented in Lessons 64-66.

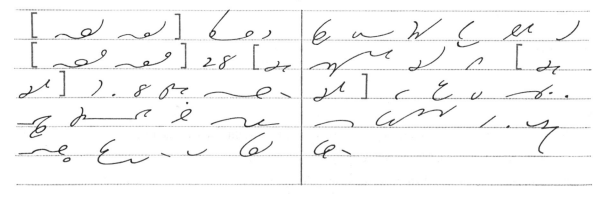

63C—Word Spellings and Meanings

moral—pertaining to character or conduct

morale—spirit or feeling of a person or persons

NOTE: The following material includes words presented in Lessons 59-62, as well as those given above.

63D—Practice Material for Building Fluency

67E—Dictionary and Spelling Preview

1. ulcers, pertinent

2. incapacitated, inquiries, mechanical

3. disappointment, readily

4. acute, impounded

5. initial, predicated, advancement

67F—Preview of New Dictation Material

(1)

Civic, employee, some of our, ulcers, that they are, why not, some of the, author's, some of them

(2)

Henderson, seriously, accident, afternoon, Indianapolis, Jeffersonville, incapacitated, undetermined, duplicating, suggest that, mechanical, we can have, to thank you for the, patronage, as soon as possible, North, inquiries

(3)

thanks, rubber, readily, disappointment, on this matter, we are writing, we hope you will receive

(4)

marked, liberty, acute, seems to be, Omaha, much more, impounded, we are making, dated

(5)

interview, financial, thereafter, performance, Florida, predicated, upon your, physical, I hope that, acceptance, assignment, advancement

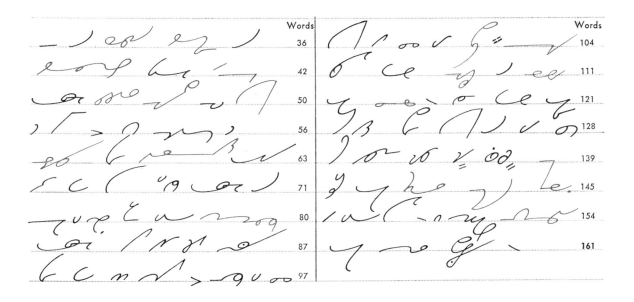

	Words		Words
	36		104
	42		111
	50		121
	56		128
	63		139
	71		145
	80		154
	87		161
	97		

63E—Dictionary and Spelling Preview

1. unusually, superior

2. enviable, achievement, transcription, earnest

3. institution, mutual, facilities, mutually

4. reorder, merchandise, exhausted

63F—Preview of New Dictation Material

(1)

unusually, Johnson City, welfare, they wanted, do you see, employer, postmaster, supervisors

(2)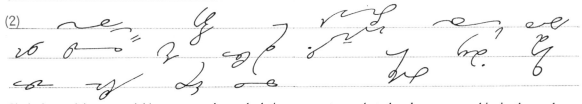

Clerical, participate, enviable, stenography, calculation, earnest, so that the, how many, this is the, only way, headquarters, registration, bookkeeping, we hope to be able, only one, notified, various, immediately

(3)

institution, we trust, mutually, banking, facilities, disposal, comments, greatly

(4)

polishers, reorder, exhausted, quickest, would like, to have you, personally, that they are, and I will

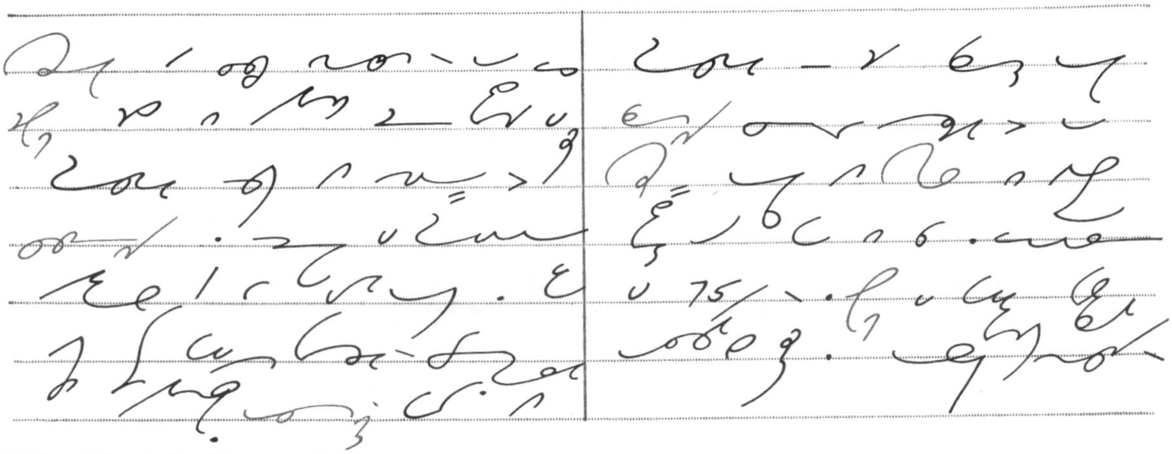

[Shorthand outlines]

67C—Word Spellings and Meanings

NOTE: The following material includes words presented in Lessons 63-66.

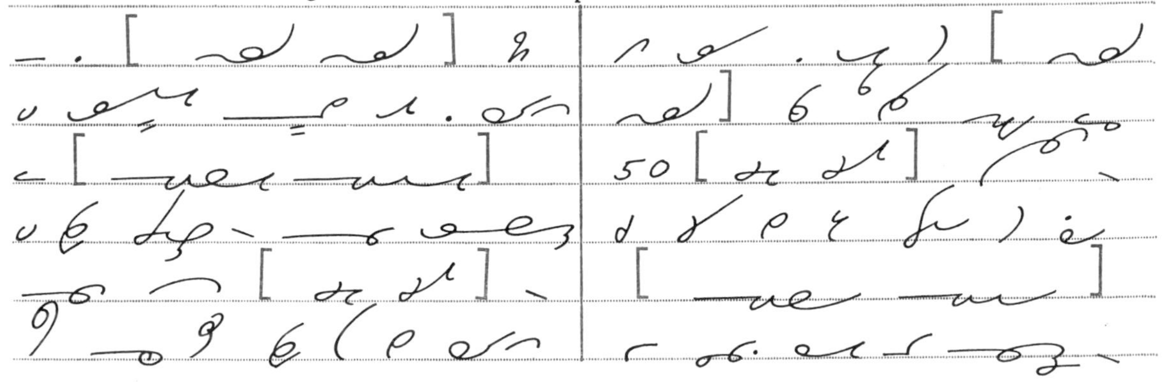

[Shorthand outlines]

67D—Practice Material for Building Fluency

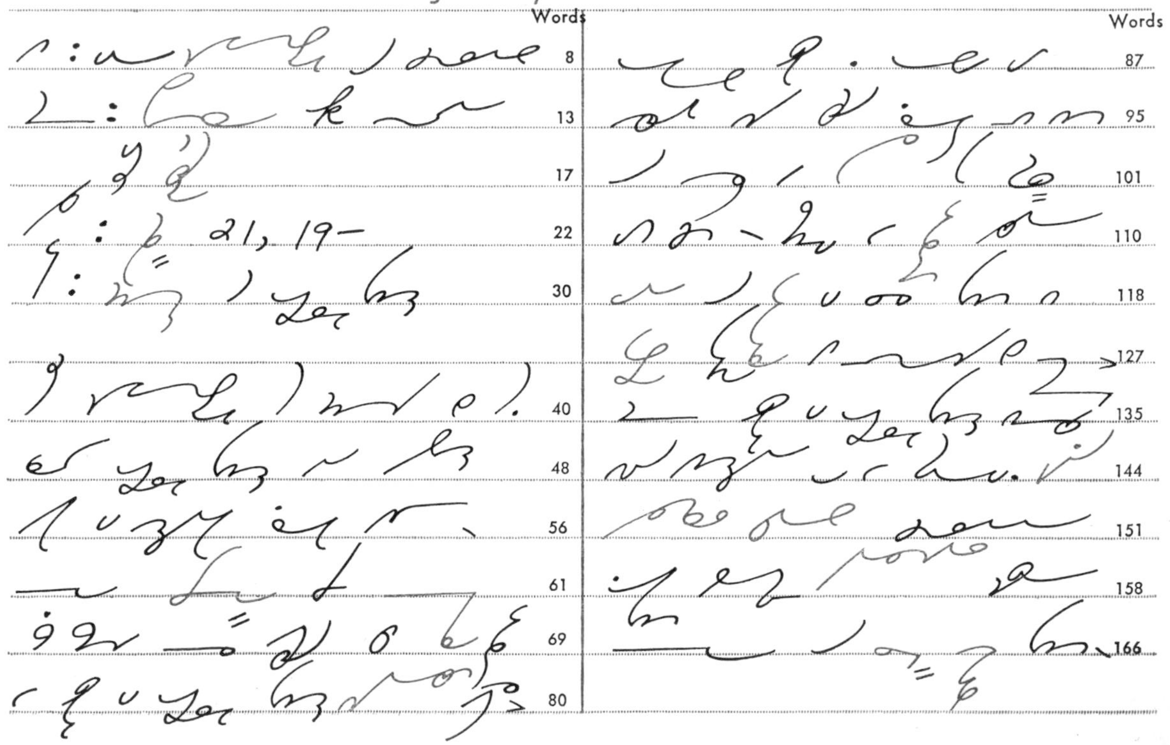

[Shorthand outlines]	Words	*[Shorthand outlines]*	Words
	8		87
	13		95
	17		101
	22		110
	30		118
	40		127
	48		135
	56		144
	61		151
	69		158
	80		166

Unit 14 · Lesson 67

192

Lesson **64** ⬡⬡⬡⬡⬡⬡⬡⬡⬡⬡⬡⬡⬡⬡⬡⬡⬡

64A—Proportion Drill

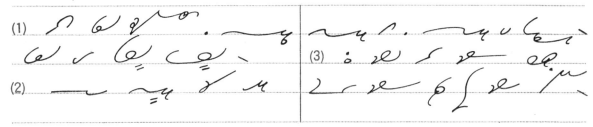

(1)

(2)

(3)

64B—Theory Review

The word ending *-ble* is expressed by *b*.

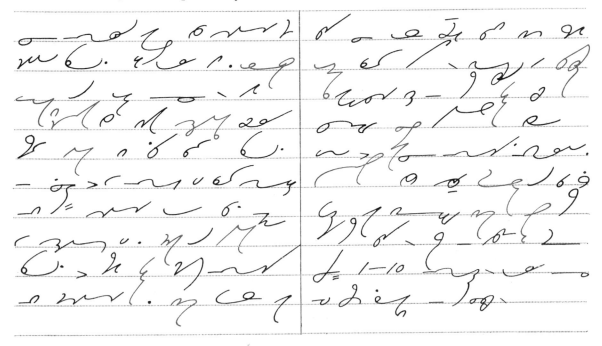

64C—Word Spellings and Meanings

past—pertaining to a former time; former

passed—moved; gone beyond; transferred from one to another

NOTE: The following material includes words presented in Lessons 60-63, as well as those listed above.

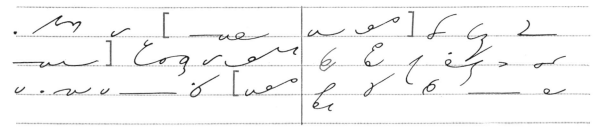

(2)  *[shorthand outlines]*

quote, Shreveport, earliest, shelving, bottom, vertical, clearance, adjustable

(3) 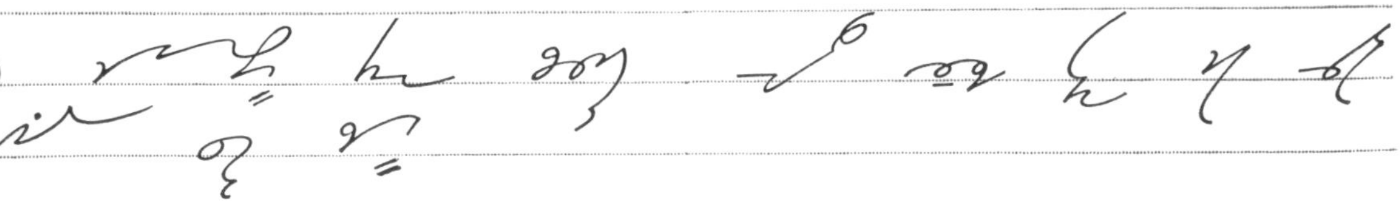 *[shorthand outlines]*

Stenographic, junior, executives, in order that the, quickest, be sure, is to be, **needs to be**, to handle, accompanies, Extension

(4) 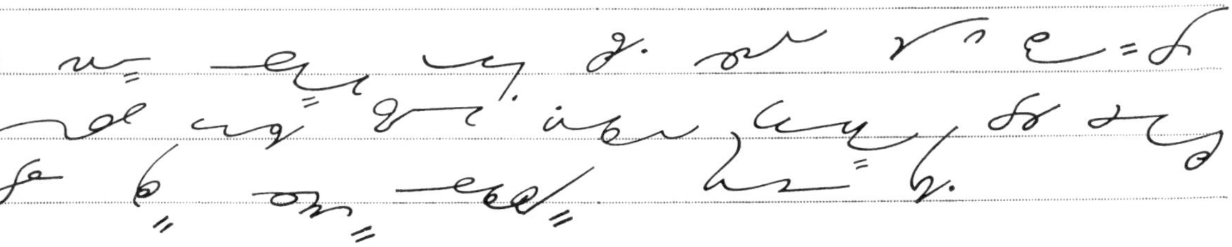 *[shorthand outlines]*

Warren, Marshall's launching, exciting, counter, stimulate, easel-back, gratis, on request, assortments, wholesaler, Promotional, packet, simplify, pattern, Bias, Nainsook, Mercerized, volume, boosting

Lesson 67 ◇⬡◇⬡◇⬡◇⬡◇⬡◇⬡◇⬡◇⬡◇⬡◇⬡◇⬡◇

67A—Phrase Builder
There are 11 phrases in the following paragraph.

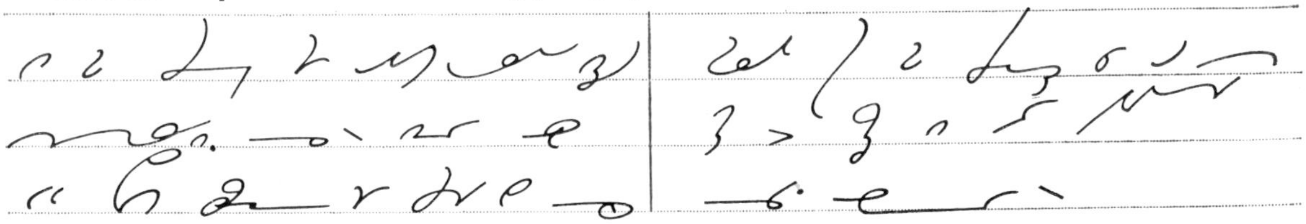

[shorthand outlines]

67B—Theory Review
The sounds of *def, dif, div,* and *dev* are expressed by ⌒.

The ending *-ulate* is expressed by a disjoined *oo* hook.

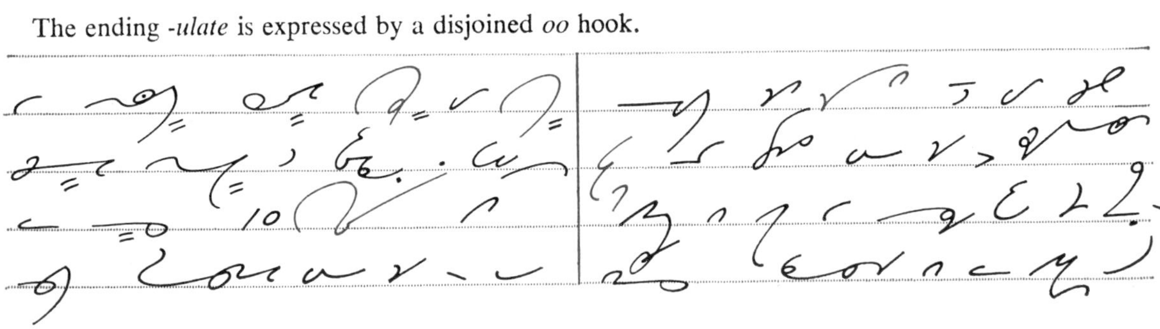

[shorthand outlines]

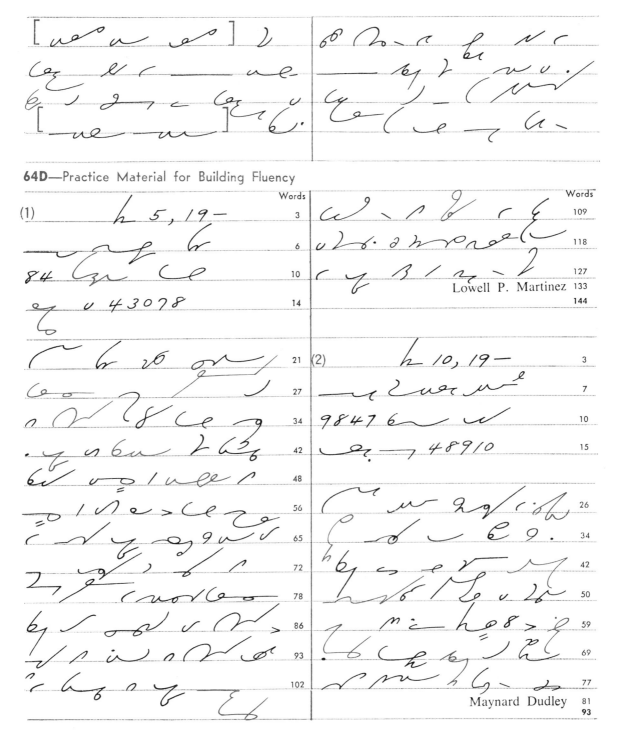

64D—Practice Material for Building Fluency

(1)

	Words
	3
	6
84	10
43078	14
	21
	27
	34
	42
	48
	56
	65
	72
	78
	86
	93
	102

	Words
	109
	118
	127
Lowell P. Martinez	133
	144

(2)

	Words
	3
	7
98476	10
48910	15
	26
	34
	42
	50
	59
	69
	77
Maynard Dudley	81
	93

64E—Dictionary and Spelling Preview

1. veneer, utilities, believe
2. coverage, Roanoke, renewal
3. postmarked
4. referred, candidates, summaries
5. thereby, confidence, truly, commitments

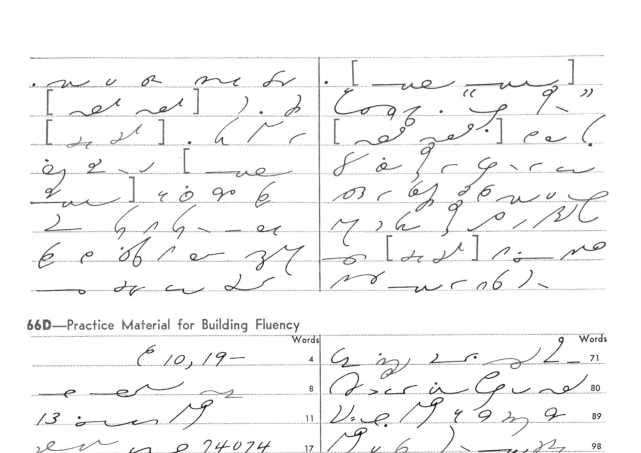

66D—Practice Material for Building Fluency

Troy Stockton

66E—Dictionary and Spelling Preview

1. university, catalog

2. clearance, adjustable

4. easel-back, gratis, specifying, mercerized, bias

66F—Preview of New Dictation Material

(1)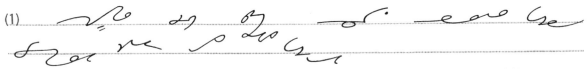

Godfrey, send us, university, maintaining, military, personnel, pamphlets, strong, and that, personalities

(1)

so many, we do not have, available, bedroom, you might be, veneer, including, utilities, any one of these, as they will, likely, inclined

(2)

Roanoke, you do not want, single, Citizen, coverage, outside, if this letter, subscription, expires, self-addressed, postage, for your convenience, remind, that it is, before your, Washington

(3)

if this is, postmarked, I will receive, before my

(4)

candidates, described, any of these, directly, summaries, indicate, graduate, you may be sure, we shall keep, touch

(5)

Roswell, extent, to become, economics, telephoned, weeks ago, truly, in a position, commitments, Edward, Wagner

Lesson **65** ⬡ ◇ ⬡ ◇ ⬡ ◇ ⬡ ◇ ⬡ ◇ ⬡ ◇ ⬡ ◇ ⬡ ◇ ⬡ ◇ ⬡ ◇ ⬡

65A—Repetitive Phrase Builder

Building Speed in Taking Dictation

Lesson **66** ⬡⬡⬡⬡⬡⬡⬡⬡⬡⬡⬡⬡⬡⬡⬡⬡⬡⬡⬡

66A—Brief-Form Practice

Directions. The following paragraph has 43 brief forms and brief-form derivatives. If you can read it in 30 seconds, you will be reading at 172 words a minute.

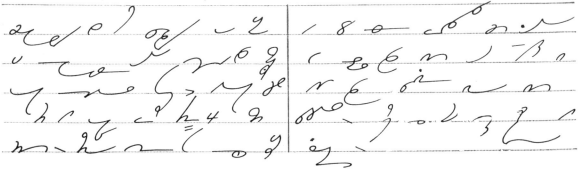

66B—Theory Review

Per- and *pur-* are expressed by *pr*. The ending *-lity* is expressed by a disjoined *l*; the ending *-lty* is also expressed by a disjoined *l*.

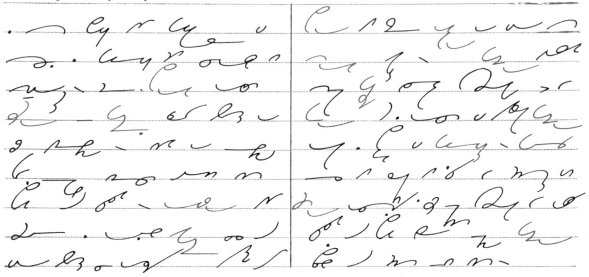

66C—Word Spellings and Meanings

sense—the meaning of the spoken or written word; to understand (v.)

cents—hundredth parts of a dollar

NOTE: The following material includes words presented in Lessons 62-65, as well as those listed above.

65B—Theory Review

The blends *nd* and *nt* are expressed by a blend of *n* and *d*.

65C—Word Spellings and Meanings

currant—a fruit
current—of the present time; general trend;
      flowing

NOTE: The following material includes words presented in Lessons 61-64, as well as those listed above.

65D—Practice Material for Building Fluency

	Words
(1)	3
	9
	11
	17
	26
	36
	46
	53

Words — *shorthand dictation, with word counts in right margin (values 63, 73, 80, 87, 92, 97, 105, 112, 123, 134, 140, 144, 158)*

Glen T. Gifford 144

Words — *shorthand dictation column (2), with word counts 3, 7, 11, 17, 24, 30, 40, 47, 55, 63, 71, 76, 80, 93*

(2)   1923 halsey   26, 19—   39187   2608   24

Everett M. Garrett

65E—Dictionary and Spelling Preview

1. overwater, underwater, fertilizer
2. often, threshold, decided, distinctive, magnifying, anniversary
3. surgical, dependent, pamphlet, preexisting

65F—Preview of New Dictation Material

(1) *shorthand outlines*

sprinkling, newly, underwater, overwater, washing, fertilizer, shrubs, bushes, soil, currant, rapidly, if we can, any way, seemingly

(2) *shorthand outlines*

it isn't, threshold, anniversary, so many things, patented, popular, arch, distinctive, magnifying, enlarges, busiest, smartest, inner, outer, nothing, yearly, easily, colorful, that there is, schoolroom

(3) *shorthand outlines*

hospital, surgical, medical, Payroll, deduction, dependent, relatives, pamphlet, comprehensive, effective, prior, waived, preexisting, assist, which has been, protection, insured, application, salary, policies